CHOICE, WELFARE, AND DEVELOPMENT

A Festschrift in Honour of
Amartya K. Sen

AMARTYA SEN

CHOICE, WELFARE, AND DEVELOPMENT

A Festchrift in Honour of
Amartya K. Sen

Edited by

K. BASU, P. PATTANAIK, AND
K. SUZUMURA

CLARENDON PRESS · OXFORD
1995

Oxford University Press, Walton Street, Oxford OX2 6DP
Oxford New York
Athens Auckland Bangkok Bombay
Calcutta Cape Town Dar es Salaam Delhi
Florence Hong Kong Istambul Karachi
Kuala Lumpur Madras Madrid Melbourne
Mexico City Nairobi Paris Singapore
Taipei Tokyo Toronto
and associated companies in Berlin Ibadan

Oxford is a trade mark of Oxford University Press

Published in the United States
by Oxford University Press Inc., New York

British Library Cataloguing in Publication Data
Data available

Library of Congress Cataloging in Publication Data
Choice, welfare, and development: a festschrift in honour of Amartya
K. Sen /edited by K. Basu, P. Pattanaik, and K. Suzumura.
p. cm.
Includes bibliographical references and index.
1. Sen, Amartya Kumar. 2. Economics—India—History—20th
century. 3. Social choice. 4. Welfare economics. 5. Economic
development. I. Basu, Kaushik. II. Pattanaik, Prasanta K.
III. Suzumura, Kōtarō, 1944– .
HB126.I43S46 1995 330.1—dc20 94–32206
ISBN 0–19–828789–5

1 3 5 7 9 10 8 6 4 2

Typeset by Pure Tech Corporation, Pondicherry, India
Printed in Great Britain
on acid-free paper by
Biddles Ltd., Guildford & King's Lynn

Contents

Notes on Contributors

KENNETH J. ARROW is Joan Kenney Professor of Economics Emeritus and Professor of Operations Research Emeritus at Stanford University. He has also taught at the University of Chicago and Harvard University. His fields of research include general equilibrium theory, the theory of social choice, and the economics of uncertainty and information. He received the John Bates Clark Medal of the American Economic Association, the Nobel Memorial Prize in Economic Science, and the John von Neumann Prize.

A. B. ATKINSON is Warden of Nuffield College, Oxford. He was President of the International Economic Association from 1989 to 1992. His publications include *The Economics of Inequality, Lectures on Public Economics* with J. E. Stiglitz, and *Poverty and Social Security*.

PRANAB BARDHAN is Professor of Economics at the University of California at Berkeley, and the editor of the *Journal of Development Economics*. He is the author of many books and articles on economic development, political economy, institutional economics, and international trade.

KAUSHIK BASU is Professor of Economics at Cornell University and the Delhi School of Economics. He was educated in Calcutta, Delhi, and London, obtaining his Ph.D. at the London School of Economics. He is a Fellow of the Econometric Society and a recipient of the Mahalanobis Memorial award. His books include *The Less Developed Economy: A Critique of Contemporary Theory and Lectures in Industrial Organization Theory*.

JEFFREY L. COLES, Professor of Finance at Arizona State University, received his Ph.D. in Economics from Stanford University. His published work includes papers on general equilibrium theory, labour economics, and dynamical systems. His current interests include welfare economics, corporate law, and organizational economics.

RAJAT DEB is an Associate Professor in the Department of Economics, Southern Methodist University. He has worked in the areas of individual and social choice and had papers published in various professional journals.

JEAN DRÈZE is Visiting Fellow at the Delhi School of Economics. He has written on a wide range of subjects in the field of development economics, including the prevention of famines, social security, cost-benefit analysis, agrarian institutions, poverty in India, and the economic consequences of war.

LOUIS GEVERS is Professor of Economics at Facultés Notre Dame de la Paix, Namur, Belgium. His main contribution to social choice theory is a clarification of the relation between utilitarianism and the leximin rule.

PETER HAMMOND has been Professor of Economics at Stanford University since 1979, and from 1989 to 1991 was on leave at the European University Institute near Florence. He was a Guggenheim Fellow in 1986–7, and held a Research Award from the Alexander von Humboldt Foundation for a visit to Germany in 1993–4. His main research interest is in economic theory, particularly welfare or public economics, broadly interpreted. He has done related work on social choice, the foundations of decision and game theory, general equilibrium theory, and optimal growth.

RAVI KANBUR is the World Bank's Resident Representative in Ghana. He has published in the leading journals in economic theory and economic development. Before joining the World Bank, he had taught at the Universities of Oxford, Cambridge, Essex, Princeton, and Warwick.

ERIC MASKIN is Professor of Economics at Harvard University. He has published on social choice theory and, more broadly, on economic theory.

ROBERT NOZICK is the Arthur Kingsley Porter Professor of Philosophy at Harvard University. He is the author of *Anarchy, State, and Utopia* (which received a national book award), *Philosophical Explanations* (which received the Ralph Waldo Emerson Award of Phi Beta Kappa), *The Examined Life*, and most recently, *The Nature of Rationality*.

SIDDIQ OSMANI is Professor of Development Economics in the University of Ulster at Jordanstown in Northern Ireland. Previously, he held research positions in the Bangladesh Institute of Development Studies in Dhaka and in the World Institute for Development Economics Research in Helsinki. He has published on a wide range of issues in development economics, with special focus on poverty, inequality, labour market, and nutrition.

PRASANTA K. PATTANAIK is Professor of Economics at the University of California, Riverside. He has worked on welfare economics and the theory of social choice, trade theory, and decision theory. He is the author of many papers and books in these areas.

KEVIN ROBERTS is Professor of Economics at the London School of Economics. He has also held positions at the Massachusetts Institute of Technology, and the universities of Oxford and Warwick. His principal research interests are the theory of welfare economics and microeconomic theory in general.

MARTIN RAVALLION is an economist in the Policy Research Department of the World Bank. He has written and advised extensively on the economics of poverty and hunger in developing countries. His publications include *Markets and Famines* and *Poverty Comparisons.*

MRINALINI SARAN is a freelance reporter, previously associated with the Hopkins-Nanjing Centre at Nanjing University. Her earlier writings are concerned with economic reform, social policy, and gender issues in China.

ROBERT M. SOLOW is Institute Professor in the Department of Economics at the Massachusetts Institute of Technology, where he has taught since 1950. His main research area has been macroeconomics, especially the aggregative theory of economic growth (*Growth Theory: An Exposition*), and also the functioning of labour markets (*The Labor Market as a Social Institution*).

KOTARO SUZUMURA is Professor of Economics at the Institute of Economic Research, Hitotsubashi University. He has taught at the LSE, Kyoto, Stanford, ANU, Pennsylvania, and UBC, and been Visiting Fellow at All Souls, Oxford and Harvard University. His publications include *Rational Choice, Collective Decisions and Social Welfare* and *Competition, Commitment, and Welfare*. He has also published extensively in the economic journals. His current research is focused on rights, welfarism, and social norms.

SERGE WIBAUT is Professor of Economics at Facultés Universitaires Saint-Louis, Brussels. He has worked mainly in the field of optimal taxation and tax reform.

Introduction

As economics advances, economists whose research straddles the expanse of the subject become fewer and fewer. Amartya Sen belongs to this rather exclusive club. Beginning with his Ph.D. thesis, completed at Cambridge University under Joan Robinson, Maurice Dobb, and Piero Sraffa, where he analysed the problem of choice of techniques for a developing country, Sen has worked and written in an astonishingly large number of areas. His book *Collective Choice and Social Welfare* (1970) is a seminal contribution to social choice theory and has motivated a large number of economists and philosophers to work in the field. Although his interest in this field goes back to his student days in Cambridge, most of Sen's work on the book was done while he was Professor at the Delhi School of Economics and during his visiting appointments at Berkeley and Harvard. In the early 1970s he moved to the London School of Economics, where he continued to work on social choice and investment planning and also began his research on famines and entitlements. His early days at the LSE saw publication of his book *On Economic Inequality* (1973), which strongly influenced many subsequent writers on the measurement of inequality, poverty, and welfare. It typifies his writing style, which is both eloquent and succinct, a rare combination indeed.

Amartya Sen has always had an active interest in philosophy and had, in fact, written on determinism while he was still a student. His research output in moral philosophy and ethics increased dramatically after he moved to All Souls College, Oxford, and then on to Harvard University. In addition to the subjects mentioned above, Sen has contributed to the economics of education, capital, and growth.

It is no exaggeration to say, however, that to know Amartya Sen only through his written word is not to know him well enough. In addition to being an outstanding writer in many branches of economics, Sen is an exceptionally stimulating teacher and expositor who can make complex ideas accessible to the least technically prepared audience. Sen grew up in the university town of Santiniketan, near Calcutta, which is known for its oral tradition. Although in the modern world the term 'oral tradition' is often viewed as a euphemism for the inability to publish, in traditional India, as indeed in several other traditional cultures, this was practised as high art. Sen clearly imbibed this art from Santiniketan. His outstanding capability as a teacher and expositor may have a lot to do with this.

All three of us have known Amartya Sen closely, having been either his student (Basu and Pattanaik) or colleague (Pattanaik and Suzumura), and have been strongly influenced by him. It is our pleasure as well as honour to be able to offer him this festschrift.

It is not possible in one volume to represent all the varied interests that mark Amartya Sen's work. We have therefore decided to restrict attention to the intersection of our research interests with his. Hence this book is focused on choice theory—individual and social—and development.

The first part of the volume consists of eight papers on choice and welfare. In the opening essay, Kenneth Arrow explores the notion of freedom which has been the subject of several recent works of Amartya Sen. He discusses the formal characteristics of a conception of freedom based on the notion of flexibility. Tony Atkinson formalizes the concept of 'capabilities' developed by Amartya Sen and then goes on to explore the link between the extent of poverty and industrial policy. The argument turns on the realistic premiss that it may be in a monopolist's interest to exclude the poorest customers from the market because trying to reach out to them would reduce revenues on existing sales. The paper is particularly apt in this volume, since it illustrates the possibility of blending developmental concerns with welfare economics. Jeffrey Coles and Peter Hammond analyse a general equilibrium model where, unlike in the traditional model of competition, individual survival is not always guaranteed. In their paper starvation is a possibility. They then establish theorems on the existence of equilibria and their optimality properties. This paper has a natural relation to the problem of entitlements discussed by Amartya Sen in the context of famines. Rajat Deb's paper is on the rationality of choice behaviour—a theme that Sen explored in several of his earlier papers and to which he has returned recently. Instead of working with the usual choice functions, Deb looks at 'choice probabilities', which is a specification of the probability of being chosen for every element in the feasible set. He isolates the necessary and sufficient conditions for rationalizing choice probabilities. Louis Gevers and Serge Wibaut consider a problem of redistribution where the tax authority knows only the probability distribution of the different types of productive abilities of the firms in their model. Eric Maskin explores a method of reducing several problems in social choice theory to the three-person, three-alternative case: he uses this technique for the Arrow impossibility theorem and the Gibbard–Satterthwaite theorem. He also proves a new result regarding transitivity under neutral and anonymous collective choice rules satisfying independence of irrelevant alternatives and the Pareto Criterion; the result has close links with Amartya Sen's work on restricted preferences and the transitivity of majority decisions. Robert Nozick's paper is on individual decision-making and deals with the symbolic value of actions. Given certain principles (e.g. 'never eat a snack between meals'), taking an action at a given point of time (e.g. eating a snack between meals *now*) can symbolize taking all other actions excluded by the principle (e.g. eating snacks between meals at various times in the future). The paper analyses different issues that arise in the context of such symbolic meaning of individual actions. Kevin Roberts presents an original theorem on dictatorship. He takes the framework where interpersonal comparisons are made by each individual. If these differ from person to person, then in fairly general situations it is shown that only one individual's opinion on these interpersonal comparisons is used.

The second part of the volume contains six papers on welfare and development. The first paper in this part, by Pranab Bardhan, deals with issues relating to local community-level co-operation in water allocation and management. In exploring these complex issues, Bardhan draws on analytical insights provided by the theoretical literature on co-operation to which Sen has made an important seminal contribution. Jean Drèze and Mrinalini Saran's paper presents a study of primary education in two villages, Palanpur in India and She Tan in China. Drèze and Saran focus on the achievements and failures in each of the two cases, and explore the link between educational achievements and economic organization. Beginning in the mid 1980s, Amartya Sen has worked on conflicts of interest *within* the family. Ravi Kanbur develops this theme by examining the relation between total household resources and intra-household inequality. Siddiq Osmani's paper presents an assessment of the literature that has developed over the years following Sen's work on famines. The household is the centre of attention in Martin Ravallion's paper. He explores the vulnerability of households to aggregate shocks, such as famines and business-cycle downturns. He brings the experience of Bangladesh and Indonesia to bear upon the analytical issues discussed in the paper. Robert Solow's paper on mass unemployment discusses some important differences between economists' approach to the issue of unemployment and the approach of sociologists and psychologists to the same problem. As he points out, though it is not quite clear how one can build an imaginative bridge between these two approaches, the need for such a bridge is obvious.

As we have indicated, practically all the papers in the volume grapple with problems that are very close to some of the central concerns of Amartya Sen. We hope that readers will find the volume intellectually stimulating and challenging.

K.B.

P.P.

K.S.

PART I
Choice and Welfare

1

A Note on Freedom and Flexibility

KENNETH J. ARROW

1. The Evaluation of Freedom

Amartya Sen has emphasized many times the limitations of the welfarist viewpoint in evaluating social alternatives. It has even reached the point that the lesson has begun to sink in. The propositions of classical welfare economics or, for that matter, of social choice theory have been naturally interpreted in purely welfare terms. But there are many dimensions not easily put into the welfarist framework. One of these is the notion of freedom of choice. As Sen notes, 'In examining the well-being aspect of a person, attention can legitimately be paid to the capability set of the person and not just to the chosen functioning vector' (Sen 1985, p. 201). (The capability set had been defined 'as the set of functioning vectors within [a person's] reach'.) He contrasts two individuals who are starving, one out of necessity, one out of choice.

The Dewey lectures just cited and Sen's Marshall Lecture (Sen 1988) discuss richly the possible meanings of freedom and the spaces of alternatives over which it is defined. However, my aim in this note is to discuss the formal characteristics of a definition of freedom, rather than its interpretation.

The intuitive issue is the following. How do we rank the opportunities available to an individual—the *opportunity sets*, in Pareto's terminology? One principle universally accepted among philosophers and ethicists (but not necessarily by psychologists) is that adding new opportunities cannot worsen the choice. In technical language, if one opportunity set is a subset of another, the latter must be at least as good (not necessarily better). What deeper ethical argument underlies this *set-inclusion principle*?

The utilitarian or hedonistic answer is straightforward. The individual can achieve a utility level by choosing an opportunity from the available set. He or she will choose the opportunity which achieves the highest level. Increasing the opportunity set will not deprive the chooser of the previously chosen element and may introduce an element which is even better. In short, the opportunity set is valued by the best available choice. This has been termed the *indirect utility approach*.

Others, who regard freedom itself as a value, would argue that giving an individual more choice is *per se* valuable. What is meant by saying that one

This study was supported by the National Science Foundation under Grant SES-920892.

opportunity set offers more freedom than another may need analysis, but on any reasonable definition set inclusion would certainly qualify.

The second viewpoint has been axiomatized, e.g. by Suppes (1987). In the more extreme forms, it leads to the proposition that freedom may be measured by the number of alternatives available in an opportunity set. This, of course, has meaning only if the number of alternatives available is finite. In the case of choice in a continuum, one would have to introduce some natural measure on the space of alternatives, and take the freedom of the opportunity set to be evaluated by this measure. I shall consider the usefulness of standard measures below.

However, there is one serious objection to a definition of freedom which does not depend in any way on preferences. Suppose one adds to the opportunity set an alternative which is clearly unacceptable, perhaps starving to death or being tortured: I think most of us would reject the view that there has been any true increase in freedom. As Anatole France remarked somewhere, 'The law in its majestic equality forbids the rich as well as the poor from sleeping on park benches.' (The updated version would be that the law, or at least custom, permits the poor as well as the rich to sleep on park benches or street corners.) Our moral intuition does not accept the idea that any increase in the scope of alternatives increases freedom in any meaningful sense. Put more strongly, the loss of a 'good' alternative is not necessarily outweighed by the addition of an arbitrarily large number of 'clearly bad' alternatives.

I am not an intuitionist in the sense of accepting intuition itself as grounds for moral judgement, but of course, intuitions are evidence of values that can and should be explicitly characterized. What I think the foregoing argument suggests is that an appropriate definition of freedom requires some reference to preferences. On the other hand, if freedom is to have any meaning apart from preference itself, the indirect utility approach cannot be maintained.

Sen (1991) has considered some of these issues in the form of alternative sets of axioms. He has explored ideas of preference-based choice related to the indirect utility approach. But I think his approach is limited by assuming that there is only one relevant preference ordering, as I will now explain.

The combination of the two lines of argument above—namely that adding 'clearly bad' alternatives does not increase freedom, and that freedom has a value beyond permitting attainment of a high utility according to some scale—suggest that, in some sense, the notion of freedom must be grounded in a multiplicity of preferences. The intuitive concept of 'clearly bad' must mean 'bad' according to a wide variety of preferences. This approach has indeed been taken by Foster (1993). He assumes that there is a relevant set of preference orderings on an underlying space of alternatives, X. Any given ordering, R, defines an ordering over opportunity sets in accordance with indirect utility approach. Then Foster defines a partial ordering over opportunity sets as the intersection of the orderings induced by R for all R in the relevant set.

I think this is basically the right approach, but I would move further in this direction. It is the right approach because it is, in general, based on a multiplicity of concepts of the good, not on just one concept. It therefore reflects the connection of freedom to the autonomy of individuals, the right of each to choose his or her goals in life and to be respected in that choice. On the other hand, it recognizes that not everything is good. There are universals of preference in the world, and opportunities that are bad by criteria that everyone accepts do not add to freedom.

But Foster's approach clearly needs to be supplemented. After all, if the concept of freedom is to have any operational meaning, it must lead to a complete ordering. I propose here another definition, which bears much the same relation to Foster's partial ordering as social utility does to Pareto preference or Bayesian statistics to admissibility of statistical procedures. This definition borrows a known though not thoroughly explored economic concept: that of *flexibility*.

Sen dismisses with little discussion the interpretation of an ordering among sets in terms of freedom as a form of flexibility, interpreted as choice when future tastes are unknown (1991, p. 21). I want to plead rather for a reconsideration of this view, since it seems to me to convey most, at least, of what we are looking for in a definition of freedom as an ordering of opportunity sets.

2. The Notion of Flexibility

The notion of flexibility in production seems to have been introduced by Albert G. Hart (1942). The idea is closely related to sequential analysis in statistical theory, introduced in a general way by Abraham Wald slightly later (1947). Hart considered an irreversible capital investment made at a point of time when future demand conditions are unknown. When the demand does become known, the firm still has to decide at what level to produce and what complementary inputs (labour, energy, and raw materials) to purchase. But the trade-offs among these short-run variables depend on the particular capital equipment chosen at the initial point of time. If the uncertainty is considerable, the firm will in general prefer a machine which permits a wide range of options at the later time, a preference for *flexibility*.

Hart envisioned an example in which there are machines which require very low variable costs for specific levels of output but for which other output levels are very costly or infeasible, while there is also a machine which can produce a wide range of outputs at roughly proportional variable costs. At any given level of output, the machine specialized for that level has lower variable costs. If the firm is reasonably certain of future output levels, it will choose a machine specialized to that level; but if it is uncertain of future demands, it will prefer a flexible machine and be willing to pay for it.

Although there was little immediate follow-up to this approach, it has become much more used recently, as in the work of Dixit and Pindyck (1994). Let us apply the concept of flexibility to consumption rather than production; there is no difference in principle. In the first period, the consumer makes a choice which determines his or her range of options in the second period. The most obvious example is the choice between savings and consumption in the first period; this determines the budget constraint in the second period. We are trying to measure the *benefit* of the first-period decision, to be compared with its cost. Hence in the first period the consumer is choosing an opportunity set for the second, and therefore has to rank the opportunity sets as part of his or her first-period decision problem.

Let A be any of the (second-period) opportunity sets among which the consumer is choosing. Let x be the second-period decision; it must be made from the set A. Let $U(x)$ be the utility of any decision made in period 2. If this function is known, then the opportunity set A permits obtaining the utility,

$$[\max U(x) \mid x \in A] = V(A)$$

say. Then the function $V(A)$ ranks the alternative possible opportunity sets A. This is the indirect utility approach.

Now suppose that the decision-maker does not know today what the utility function in period 2 will be. We can represent this uncertainty by a probability distribution over possible utility functions. To keep the notation simple, assume that the utility function in period 2 is characterized by a parameter, θ, so that the utility of second-period decision, x, is $U(x, \theta)$. The parameter, θ, is assumed to have a known probability distribution. If the opportunity set A were chosen, the achieved payoff would be

$$P(\theta, A) = [\max U(x, \theta) \mid x \in A]$$

but since θ is unknown at the time A is chosen, the value ascribed to A is the expected value of this payoff:

$$V(A) = E_\theta[\max U(x, \theta): x \, \varepsilon \, A] = E_\theta[P(\theta, A)]. \tag{1}$$

It is this function which defines an ordering on the first-period choice of opportunity sets. In the economic context, this is an ordering of sets according to their flexibility.[1]

---

[1] Following Hart and later writers, this concept of flexibility is defined completely in terms of the usual models of rational preference. I see no gain in trying to define a separately axiomatized concept of flexibility, as suggested by Koopmans (1964) and Kreps (1979).

3. Freedom as Flexibility

I propose to use the concept of flexibility with respect to a probability distribution over preferences as the definition of freedom. As already suggested, it crystallizes the idea that the underlying concept of freedom is freedom to choose preferences, the familiar philosophical idea of autonomy. Freedom as an ordering over sets I take to be derivative from the underlying principle of freedom as autonomy.

More concretely, the range of preferences and the uncertainty about them can be interpreted in several ways. One is from the point of view of the individual, at a stage where his or her preferences for the future are yet to be formed. An individual is autonomous even with respect to the self. I cannot now prescribe my future wants, nor should I feel obligated to retain past views. As Ralph Waldo Emerson put it, 'a foolish consistency is a hobgoblin of little minds'. Hence the individual will rank the opportunity sets for tomorrow to give him or her as much freedom with respect to my possible future desires.

A second interpretation is from the point of view of a governing authority or, perhaps better put, a social compact. Here, we suppose that freedom to choose must be given in an impersonal way to individuals with a wide variety of tastes. Again, the choice set for each individual (for example, the set of candidates in an election) should be chosen flexibly, as defined in the last section. This argument does presuppose the importance of the impersonality or universalizability of the government's actions in relation to its members, a point which has of course been a staple of political theory.

The second interpretation is especially strong when constitutional rather than legal questions are concerned. Here, the preferences in question are those of future as well as present individuals, and uncertainty in connection with them is an especially reasonable assertion.

4. Some Elementary Properties of Freedom as Flexibility

The function $V(A)$, defined by (1) and interpreted in Section 3, will be referred to as the *freedom evaluation function*.

It is immediately obvious from (1) that the set inclusion property holds; if A is included in B, then, for each θ,

$$\max[U(x, \theta)|x \in A] \leqslant \max[U(x, \theta)|x \in B],$$

and, therefore, from (1),

PROPERTY I. $V(A) \leqslant V(B)$ if $A \subset B$.

A second property is that only those elements which maximize $U(x, \theta)$ for some θ matter. Formally, let

$$\xi(A, \theta) = \arg \max [U(x, \theta)|x \in A],$$

and let

$$E(A) = \text{range}_\theta \, \xi(A, \theta).$$

Then, from (1),

PROPERTY II. $V(A) = V(B)$ if $E(A) = E(B)$.

Thus, adding an element to the opportunity set which is not better than all existing elements for at least one possible utility function parameter, θ, does not increase freedom.

5. Some Examples

I give four examples to indicate how the freedom valuation function, $V(A)$, can be calculated. In particular, I want to ask if the valuation can be expressed as a function of the measure of the opportunity set, as suggested by those definitions of freedom which imply that the mere size of the opportunity set is all that counts.

I will use the same two-parameter family of opportunity sets for all examples. Each set in the family is a transformation set with constant rates of transformation, with the form

$$(x/a) + (y/b) \leq 0, \qquad y \geq 0, \tag{2}$$

where (x, y) is the two-dimensional decision (choice of quantities of a pair of commodities) to be made. Instead of referring to a set A, I will refer to the pair (a, b) which defines the set whose valuation is sought. What will vary in the examples will be the utility functions.

Example 1. Here I take the utility function to be linear in the decision variables, with one parameter. Specifically, the family of utility functions is taken to be

$$U(x, y, \theta) = \theta x + (1 - \theta)y.$$

The parameter, θ, is assumed to be uniformly distributed on the unit interval $\langle 0, 1 \rangle$. For given θ, the optimal choice of (x, y) from the opportunity set (2) is $(a, 0)$ or $(0, b)$, according as

$$\theta a > (1 - \theta)b,$$

or the reverse. Thus, in the previous notation,

$$P(a, b, \theta) = \max [\theta a, (1 - \theta)b].$$

Since θ has been assumed to have a uniform distribution, integration over the interval $\langle 0, 1 \rangle$ shows that

$$V(a, b) = (a^2 + ab + b^2)/2(a + b). \qquad (3)$$

This is certainly not a function of the area of the constraint set, which is $ab/2$. For a given area, that is, a given value of ab, V is highest when $a = b$, and falls as the two parameters move apart. However, the effect is bounded. If $b = 0$, V can have a positive value; specifically,

$$V(a, 0) = a/2.$$

Hence, reducing b from some positive value to 0 (for example by prohibiting the use of commodity y) can be compensated for by a finite increase in a, the availability of commodity x.

Example 2. In the first example, there were preferred directions. For all values of θ, increases in either commodity were good. This makes it less surprising that the area is not a good indicator of freedom, since only the north-east boundary has any significance. I will now modify the distribution of the utility function parameter to permit all directions equally. Specifically, let

$$U(x, y, \theta) = (\cos\theta) x + (\sin\theta)y,$$

with θ uniformly distributed over $\langle - \pi, + \pi \rangle$. It is easy to see that

$$P(a, b, \theta) = \max(a \cos\theta, b \sin\theta, 0),$$

so that

$$P(a, b, \theta) = a \cos\theta \qquad \text{if} - \pi/2 < \theta < \tan^{-1}(a/b)$$

$$= b \sin\theta \qquad \text{if } \tan^{-1}(a/b) < \theta < \pi$$

$$= 0 \qquad \text{if} - \pi < \theta < - \pi/2.$$

Integration of P with respect to θ over the whole circle yields

$$V(a, b) = (2\pi)^{-1} [(a^2 + b^2)^{1/2} + a + b],$$

which again is certainly not a function of the area.

Again, $V(a, 0)$ is positive and increasing in a, so that, for example, prohibiting one commodity can always be compensated for.

Example 3. The use of linear utility functions means that the limitation of freedom by limiting the availability of one good is not a severe restriction, since with reasonable probability one can substitute the other commodity on not-too-unfavourable terms. It is therefore useful to consider the other extreme case—that where the goods are perfect complements. I now assume that

$$U(x, y, \theta) = \min [x/\theta), \ y/(1 - \theta)],$$

with θ uniformly distributed from 0 to 1. For given θ, the optimal choice of (x, y) requires that

$$x/w = y/(1 - w).$$

Simple calculation shows that

$$P(a, b, \theta) = ab/[\theta b + (1 - \theta)a],$$

and integration with respect to θ from 0 to 1 yields

$$V(a, b) = a, \qquad\qquad\qquad \text{if } a = b$$

$$= ab(\ln b - \ln a)/(b - a) \qquad \text{otherwise.}$$

Again, the area does not yield the same ordering of opportunity sets as the freedom valuation function.

In this case,

$$V(a, 0) = 0 \qquad \text{for all } a,$$

so that freedom can indeed be destroyed by prohibiting one commodity.

Example 4. A final example will show that it is not impossible that the flexibility approach to freedom yields the measure of the set as an indicator of freedom. Assume now a linear-logarithmic utility function,

$$U(x, y, \theta) = \theta \ln x + (1 - \theta) \ln y,$$

with again θ distributed uniformly on $\langle 0, 1 \rangle$. For given θ, the optimal choice of x, y is given by

$$x = \theta a, \qquad y = (1 - \theta)b,$$

and therefore

$$P(a, b, \theta) = - H(\theta) + \theta \ln a + (1 - \theta) \ln b,$$

where

$$H(\theta) = - [\theta \ln \theta + (1 - \theta) \ln(1 - \theta)].$$

Integration over θ yields

$$V(a, b) = \left(\frac{1}{2}\right)[\ln(ab) - 1],$$

so that the freedom valuation function and Lebesgue measure do indeed give the same ordering over opportunity sets.

6. A Remark on Constitutional Choice

One of the major themes in the literature on flexibility is the relation between information and flexibility. The discussion in Section 2 assumed that there were just two stages, one in which there is uncertainty and the second in which there is certainty, so that the information is complete. If we think of two levels of evaluating freedom, i.e. constitutional and legal, then there is uncertainty at both stages, with presumably part of the uncertainty having been removed between the time of drafting the constitution and that of enacting laws. This partial removal of uncertainty can be described as information.

It is intuitively reasonable that the greater the anticipated information, the greater the flexibility desired at the initial stage. It is rather hard, as it turns out, to define the concepts rigorously and to get definite results, so I will not go into details. Nevertheless, at least some justifications for this intuition can be found in the work of Jones and Ostroy (1984) and Kapur (1992). This suggests the following.

> REMARK. Constitutional choices should be less constrained and should give room for more legal regulation in the future, the greater is the amount of information expected to become known in the future about the preferences and needs of citizens.

References

Dixit, A. and Pindyck, R. (1994), *Investment under Uncertainty*, Princeton University Press, Princeton, NJ.

Foster, J. (1993), 'Notes on Effective Freedom', paper presented to Workshop on Economic Theories of Inequality at Stanford Institute for Theoretical Economics, sponsored by the John D. and Catherine T. MacArthur Foundation, 11–13 March 1993.

Hart, A. G. (1942), 'Risk, Uncertainty, and the Unprofitability of Compounding Probabilities', in O. Lange, F. McIntyre, and T. Yntema (eds.), *Studies in Mathematical Economics and Econometrics*, University of Chicago Press.

Jones, R. A. and Ostroy, J. M. (1984), 'Flexibility and Uncertainty', *Review of Economic Studies*, 51: 13–32.

Kapur, S. (1992), 'Flexibility and information', Economic Theory Discussion Paper no. 177, Department of Applied Economics, University of Cambridge, May 1992.

Koopmans, T. C. (1964), 'On Flexibility of Future Preference', in M. W. Shelley and G. L. Bryan (eds.), *Human Judgments and Optimality*, John Wiley, New York.

Kreps, D. M. (1979), 'A Representation Theorem for "Preference for Flexibility" ', *Econometrica*, 47: 565–78.

Sen, A. K. (1985), 'Well-being, Agency and Freedom: The Dewey Lectures 1984', *Journal of Philosophy*, 82: 169–221.

—— (1988), 'Freedom of Choice: Concept and Content', *European Economic Review*, 32: 269–94.

—— (1991), 'Welfare, Preference and Freedom', *Journal of Econometrics*, 50: 15–29.

Suppes, P. (1987), 'Maximizing Freedom of Decision: An Axiomatic Approach', in
    G. Feiwel (ed.), *Arrow and the Foundations of the Theory of Economic Policy*, New
    York University Press, 243–54.
Wald, A. (1947), *Sequential Analysis*, John Wiley, New York.

2

Capabilities, Exclusion, and the Supply of Goods

A. B. ATKINSON

1. Poverty and Capabilities

Among the many fields in which Amartya Sen has enriched our under-standing is that of the analysis of poverty. Within this field, his contribu-tions have been manifold. His article on the measurement of poverty (Sen 1976) spawned a whole literature on the design of new measures; his research on famine and hunger (Sen 1981; Drèze and Sen 1989) has been widely influential; and he has introduced the notion of 'capabilities' into the definition of poverty (Sen 1980, 1983, 1985). It is the last of these that is the starting point of the present paper.

Sen has made a forceful case that assessment of the standard of living should focus on

neither commodities, nor characteristics (in the sense of Gorman and Lancaster), nor utility, but something that may be called a person's capability. (1983, p. 160)

He illustrates this by the example of a bicycle:

It is, of course, a commodity. It has several characteristics, and let us concentrate on one particular characteristic, viz., transportation. Having a bike gives a person the ability to move about in a certain way that he may not be able to do without the bike. So the transportation *characteristic* of the bike gives the person the *capability* of moving in a certain way. That capability may give the person utility. (1983, p. 160)

Sen argues that, in the chain

Commodities → Characteristics → Capability → Utility,

it is

'the third category—that of capability to function—that comes closest to the notion of standard of living' (1983, p. 160),

and that, if this argument accepted, it provides a basis for

sorting out . . . the absolute–relative disputation in the conceptualization of poverty. At the risk of over-simplification, I would like to say that poverty is an absolute notion in the space of capabilities but very often it will take a relative form in the space of commodities or characteristics. (1983, p. 161)

Here I start from Sen's notion of poverty as an absolute standard in the space of capabilities (without necessarily accepting an absolute standard as appropriate) and examine the relation with commodity requirements and income.

As Sen has stressed, *relative* deprivation in the space of incomes can lead to *absolute* deprivation in the space of capabilities:

In a country that is generally rich, more income may be needed to buy enough commodities to achieve the *same social functioning*, such as 'appearing in public without shame'. The same applies to the capability of 'taking part in the life of the community'. (Sen, 1992 p. 115)

Where the poverty line is explicitly relative (see e.g. Townsend 1979), rising living standards in the community as a whole may lead to a raising of the poverty line in real terms. However, the precise mechanism that relates the necessary income, on the capabilities approach, to the changes in the overall distribution is not spelled out.

The aim of this paper is to develop further the link between a specified capability and the distribution of income in the society, by introducing an aspect not typically considered: the conditions under which goods are supplied.

The supply conditions enter here in two different ways. First, where a good, such as a bicycle, is necessary to perform an activity, such as travelling to work in a neighbouring town, then whether or not a specified income is sufficient to ensure this capability depends on the pricing of bicycles. If the good is supplied by a monopolist, or by monopolistically competitive suppliers, then the necessary income depends on the degree of monopoly mark-up. A profit-maximizing supplier determines this mark-up taking account of the effect on all sales. As a result, a change in the distribution of income may affect the mark-up, and hence the ability of a person with a specified money income to purchase the commodity necessary to ensure the capability to function. It is not a necessary part of the story that the good be indivisible (like a bicycle); it is sufficient that there be a strictly minimum essential quantity. Lewis and Ulph (1988) have examined the implications of there being a strictly positive quantity of certain goods required to avoid poverty, although they do not investigate the conditions under which these goods are supplied.

The effect of an increased monopoly mark-up should in theory enter the price index used to adjust the poverty line; there is however a second way in which capability to function may be affected by decisions on the supply side, and which may not be captured in a price index. This is via the range of quantities and qualities available in the shops. The standard textbook treatment of consumer decisions supposes that the quantity of a good that is bought may be infinitely varied. In reality, many goods come packaged in discrete quantities. Variations of quality are similarly important: a consumer may not be able to purchase the preferred combination of price and quality. These considerations particularly affect the poor, who may not be able to buy the qualities (e.g. cheap cuts of meat) or quantities (e.g.

small-sized packets) that they require. The achievement of a specified capacity may depend on the range of goods supplied in the market.

We have therefore to examine the *supply* side of the market, and the main point of this paper is to suggest how considerations of firm behaviour and industrial structure enter the determination of poverty. The prices and availability of goods are not fixed arbitrarily but are determined endogenously by the decisions of suppliers faced with specified market conditions. The model of monopoly supply set out in Section 2 is highly simplified, but it indicates how decisions taken by the supplier may affect the capability of the poor to function. The monopoly price may exclude some customers from the market and hence deprive them of the capacity to function. Moreover, the fact that the monopolist takes account of the full market demand means that the capabilities of the poor are influenced by living standards elsewhere in the economy. Rising average incomes may affect the decisions of the monopolist, as may increased inequality in the distribution of income.

Economic growth may lead to the introduction of new products, and the choice of goods supplied by the monopolist is the subject of Section 3. If only one quality is supplied, how is this chosen? As incomes rise, does the monopolist tend to raise product quality, and thus exclude those whose incomes do not keep up? In what situations will more than one quality be supplied? If the monopolist ceases to produce lower-quality products, then this raises the question whether it provides an opening for competition.

Section 4 examines the effect of entry into the market, either actual or potential. Does entry ensure that all customers are supplied? How is the outcome different in a perfectly contestable market? These are the kinds of question that have been asked in the recent literature on industrial organization. This literature has noted that there are circumstances in which certain customers are excluded from the market, but the implications for the living standards of these consumers have not been considered. The link has not been made with the measurement of poverty.

The interdependence of capacity to function with the conditions of supply has implications for the definition of the minimum necessary money income. It also has implications for public policy in the field of industrial economics, such as intervention to regulate monopoly profits, to facilitate entry by new suppliers, or to ensure minimum quality standards. These aspects are discussed briefly in the concluding section.

2. A Simple Monopoly Model of Exclusion and the Implications of Rising Living Standards

Behind the model of consumption adopted here is the notion that purchases of goods are an intermediate input to the production of capabilities, although, in contrast to the Gorman–Lancaster approach referred to by Sen, I follow the activity approach due to Becker (1965). Goods are an input, along with time, into the carrying out of an activity. (The household production technology is of the Leontief type, rather than treating goods as perfect substitutes in the production of characteristics.) The chain is

Commodities → Activities → Capabilities (→ Utility).

The last of these links is not considered here. We are concerned only with the capability to function and the possibility that people lack this capability and hence suffer exclusion.

To be more concrete, I concentrate on the activity of 'working' and assume that, in order to go to work in the labour market, a person requires, in addition to time, the input of a specified, indivisible commodity. The person consumes only a single unit of this commodity, which costs p. All other goods are aggregated into a numeraire. Without the capacity to travel to work, the person can only work domestically, earning a wage w, which is lower than the wage $(\lambda + 1)w$ obtainable in the labour market. The viability of work in the labour market requires that

$$\lambda w \geq p. \tag{1}$$

People differ in their values of w, which is an index of productivity, and hence in their values of how well-off they are. (There is assumed to be no other form of income.) There is a cumulative distribution function, $F(w)$, with associated density function, $f(w)$. The density is zero for all values of w below $w_{\min}$, where $w_{\min}$ is strictly positive. Of particular interest is the proportion of people 'excluded' from participation in the labour market, $F(w^*)$, where w^* is such that (1) holds with equality:

$$w^* \equiv p/\lambda. \tag{2}$$

The commodity is produced at a constant marginal cost, c, per unit. If there are no fixed costs and the industry is perfectly competitive, then the price charged is c, and all are capable of participating in the labour market where

$$w_{\min} \geq c/\lambda. \tag{3}$$

It is assumed in what follows that this condition is satisfied. Suppose however that there is a fixed cost of production, k, and that in these conditions the good is supplied by a single monopolist who sets a price p to maximize profit. Since each person buys only one unit, total sales are (using (2))

$$\begin{cases} 1 - F(p/\lambda) & \text{where } w^* \geq w_{\min} \\ 1 & \text{where } w^* < w_{\min}. \end{cases} \tag{4}$$

In the former case, the level of profit is given by

$$\Pi = (p - c)[1 - F(p/\lambda)] - k. \tag{5}$$

The derivative with respect to price is

$$\partial \Pi / \partial p = 1 - F(w^*) - (p - c) f(w^*) w^* / p. \tag{6}$$

It is evident that the monopolist will not charge a price below $\lambda w_{\min}$, since to do so would reduce revenue on existing sales without adding to total sales (since at that price all would be buying the good). It is profitable for the monopolist to raise the price above this level, and hence exclude certain people from the market, where

$$f(w_{\min})(w_{\min} - c/\lambda) < 1. \tag{7}$$

Where condition (3) holds, that is, where everyone buys the good if it is priced at marginal cost, the second term on the left-hand side (LHS) of (7) is positive, and the monopolist does not exclude customers provided the initial density is sufficiently large. However, if the initial density is sufficiently small, then there is a profit-maximizing interior solution where[1]

$$(p - c)/p = ([1 - F(w^*)]/[w^* f(w^*)]. \tag{8}$$

Whether or not the monopolist sets the price to exclude the lowest-productivity people depends on the overall distribution. This may be illustrated by two special cases. Suppose first that there is a *uniform* distribution between $w_{\min}$ and $w_{\max}$, with density

$$f(w) = 1/(w_{\max} - w_{\min}). \tag{9a}$$

Condition (7) then becomes

$$w_{\min} \geqslant \frac{1}{2} (w_{\max} + c/\lambda). \tag{10a}$$

If the productivity of the least able person is less than half that of the most able, then some customers are excluded by the monopoly pricing.[2] In this case the profit-maximizing price is given by

$$p = \frac{1}{2} (c + \lambda w_{\max}). \tag{11a}$$

In other words, it is the average of the marginal cost and the maximum that anyone is willing to pay. The value of w at which people are excluded is

---

[1] The second-order condition is satisfied where $(1 - F)f'/f^2 + 2 \geqslant 0$. A non-decreasing hazard rate ($f/(1 - F)$) is sufficient but not necessary. The second-order condition is satisfied for both of the special cases considered below.

[2] Readers familiar with the work of Shaked and Sutton (1982) will recognize my debt to their model. The assumption made about preferences is however different here, being the same as that in Tirole (1989, p. 296), although in this latter case the differences between consumers are in a taste parameter rather than in their endowment.

$$w^* = \frac{1}{2}(w_{\max} + c/\lambda).$$ (12a)

A second example is provided by the Pareto distribution, where, for w greater than or equal to $w_{\min}$,

$$1 - F(w) = (w/w_{\min})^{-\alpha},$$ (9b)

$$f(w) = \alpha(w/w_{\min})^{-\alpha-1}/w_{\min},$$

where α is greater than 1. Condition (7) then becomes

$$\alpha[1 - c/(\lambda w_{\min})] < 1.$$ (10b)

If the marginal cost is, say, three-quarters of the willingness to pay of the least able, this is satisfied where α is less than 4. In this case, the profit-maximizing price involves a mark-up,

$$(p - c)/p = 1/\alpha.$$ (11b)

With α equal to 4, the price is $\frac{4}{3}$ times the marginal cost. The value of w at which people are excluded is

$$w^* = \alpha/(\alpha - 1)(c/\lambda).$$ (12b)

2.1. Rising Living Standards and Inequality

What is the effect, in this simple model, of a general rise in living standards? Suppose that there is an equiproportional rise in w for everyone, increasing the purchasing power of wages in terms of the numeraire commodity. The cost of production, c, is unchanged. At any given p a larger proportion of the population can afford the product. However, does the monopolist react by raising the price?

The answer depends on the form of the distribution, as is demonstrated by the two special examples. With a Pareto distribution, the price is a constant multiple of the marginal cost and hence is unchanged. The income necessary to avoid exclusion is unchanged as living standards rise. On the other hand, with the uniform distribution the necessary income rises, as may be seen from (12a), where $w_{\max}$ increases. At the same time, the increase is less than proportional, and the proportion of the population excluded falls, as may be seen from the fact that, in the case of the uniform distribution,

$$F(w^*) = 1 - \frac{1}{2}(w_{\max} - c/\lambda)/(w_{\max} - w_{\min}).$$ (13)

If a rise in the average income is accompanied by widening inequality, then the outcome may be different. Suppose that, in the case of the uniform distribution, there is a rise in $w_{\max}$, holding $w_{\min}$ constant, so that the distribution becomes more thinly spread. From (13) it may be seen that the proportion excluded from the market rises towards $\frac{1}{2}$. Where the exclusion of customers was not previously profitable, it may become so, as may be seen from (7), since $f(w_{min})$ is reduced and the second term on the left-hand side is unchanged.

In the case of the Pareto distribution, a fall in α has the effect of reducing the density at w_{min} and of increasing the density at the upper tail. Again, it becomes more likely that people with low values of w are excluded. A fall in α from 4 to 3 has the effect of increasing the monopoly mark-up over marginal cost from $33\frac{1}{3}$ to 50 per cent.

These results show how the implications of a specified level of productivity, w, depend on the distribution elsewhere in society. A person in one society may have the capacity to take part in the labour market, but in another may be excluded because the existence of people with higher productivities leads the monopoly supplier to price the good out of reach. Depending on the form of the distribution, rising living standards may increase the income necessary to ensure the specified capacity, and this is accentuated by rising inequality.

3. Choice of Quality and the Range of Goods

Economic growth may not only raise average incomes; it may also bring new products. The range of goods that could contribute to the activity of 'working' may be extended. A person may be able to choose between a bicycle and a higher-quality alternative, such as a motorcycle, as a means of getting to work. The higher-quality alternative may allow the person to achieve a higher wage, because he or she can work longer hours, put in greater effort, or travel further afield, for example. The availability of this choice does however depend on the range of goods supplied.

First, the simple model of Section 2 is extended to allow the monopolist a choice over the quality, λ, of the good supplied, where λ varies between λ_{min} and λ_{max}, with associated (constant) marginal cost $c(\lambda)$ and fixed cost $k(\lambda)$. It is assumed initially that the monopolist supplies only one quality. Suppose that, at the lowest quality, the profit-maximizing price is such as to exclude part of the population. Does the availability of superior qualities lead the proportion excluded to rise or fall?

The effect on the choice of quality by the monopolist may be seen by differentiating profit (equation (5)) with respect to λ, and making use of condition (8) for the choice of price (at the lowest quality we have an interior solution):

$$\partial\Pi/\partial\lambda = [1 - F(w^*)](w^* - \partial c/\partial\lambda) - \partial k/\partial\lambda. \tag{14}$$

Whether or not this is positive depends on how the costs of production change as we move to goods of higher quality. Similarly from the condition (8), for the profit-maximizing choice of price,

$$[1 - F(w^*)] - (w^* - c/\lambda)f(w^*) = 0 \qquad (6')$$

(where the second-order conditions require the left-hand side to be a declining function of (w^*), we can deduce that whether or not w^* increases with λ depends on how c/λ changes: if c/λ rises, then w^* rises.

Various situations may be imagined with regard to the variation of costs with quality. Shaked and Sutton (1983) note that quality improvements may involve largely research and development (R and D) costs, in which case the marginal production costs may rise only slowly with increases in quality. Suppose that the effective cost per quality unit, c/λ, falls with λ, so that $\partial c/\partial \lambda$ is less than c/λ. Since by assumption the initial value of c/λ is no greater than w_{min}, and hence no greater than the initial w^*, it follows that the monopolist prefers to increase quality unless there is too large an increase in fixed cost.[3] If this holds over the whole range of possible λ, then the monopolist chooses the highest-quality λ_{max}. The production of a superior product does not however exclude poorer consumers, since the reduced cost per unit of quality (c/λ) is passed on, at least in part, to consumers and, from (6'), w^* falls. The greater effectiveness of motorcycles more than outweighs the higher price.

A different situation is that where there are diminishing returns to quality production, in that the effective cost c/λ rises with λ, and $\partial c/\partial l$ is greater than c/λ. The fact that w^* is then initially above c/λ, by assumption, is not sufficient to ensure that the first term in (14) is positive. It is therefore possible that the monopolist remains content with the lowest quality. On the other hand, it is also possible that an increase in quality is profitable, provided that fixed costs do not increase too much. If the fixed costs were to be independent of λ, then the profit-maximizing choice of quality is indicated by point B in Fig. 1, where the quality choice is that which would be made by the marginal purchaser paying the marginal cost. In this case, the quality response of the supplier has the effect of increasing w^*, and hence of excluding a larger proportion of the population. It is of course possible that an increase in quality is profitable at all λ in the feasible range (in Fig. 1 this would mean that λ_{max} is to the left of B), and that the monopolist again produces λ_{max}, even though c/λ rises with λ.

To the extent, therefore, that economic progress leads to the invention of higher-quality products, this may reduce or increase the proportion of the population excluded from purchase of a good that is necessary for them to function.

---

[3] There is clearly a difference between fixed costs that are once-for-all, like initial R and D, and those that arise each production period; k refers to the latter.

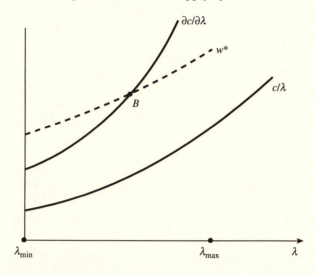

Fig. 1 Monopolist choice of single quality supplied where c/λ is rising and fixed costs are independent of

3.1 Supply of Two Qualities

Suppose that the effective cost c/λ rises with λ, and that the monopolist chooses to supply quality λ_{max}, at a price p_{max}, where this excludes a strictly positive fraction of the population. Is it then possible that he will find it profitable to produce, *in addition*, a product of lower quality, λ, where this is strictly less than λ_{max}? If the price of the inferior product, p, is less than p_{max}, then it may be bought by some of those not able to afford the superior product. In other words, is the exclusion of part of the population the result of the assumption to date that the monopolist produces only a single quality?

The choice by the consumer between the two qualities is illustrated in Fig. 2 for the case where the price per unit of quality is greater for the superior good ($p_{max}/\lambda_{max} > p/\lambda$). The person with w in excess of

$$w^{**} = (p_{max} - p)/(\lambda_{max} - \lambda) \qquad (15)$$

chooses the superior quality; the person with a wage between w^* and w^{**} chooses the inferior quality; the person with a wage below w^* is excluded. How these division lines correspond to those when only one quality is supplied depends on the profit-maximizing decisions of the monopolist. The choice of price for the lower-quality product has to balance the size of its sales against the loss from customers who are attracted away from the superior product. A reduction in p *increases* w^{**}, as well as reducing w^*.

The profit received in the case of two products is

$$\Pi = (p_{max} - c_{max})[1 - F(w^{**})] + (p - c)[F(w^{**}) - F(w^*)] - k - k_{max}, \qquad (16)$$

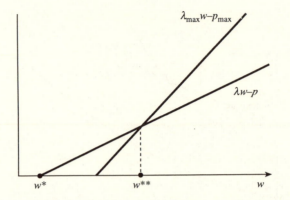

Fig. 2 Consumer's choice between two products with qualities λ and λ_{max}

where c_{max} and k_{max} are the constant marginal and fixed costs of producing the superior product, and c and k are those of the inferior product. The monopolist's choice may be seen more clearly if we define

$$\rho = p_{max} - p \quad \text{and} \quad \gamma = c_{max} - c$$

and rewrite profits as

$$\Pi = (p - c)[1 - F(w^*)] + (\rho - \gamma)[1 - F(w^{**})] - k - k_{max}, \qquad (16')$$

where we may note that

$$w^{**} - \rho/(\lambda_{max} - \lambda). \qquad (15')$$

Since the effect of variation in p is now confined to the first term in (16'), it may be seen that the choice of price for the inferior product is independent of the existence of the superior product. (The maximization conditions are identical to those in Section 2.) The 'excess' price of the superior good is also determined in the same way, with ρ replacing p, γ replacing c, $(\lambda_{max} - \lambda)$ replacing λ, and w^{**} replacing w^*. For this solution to apply, we require that

$$w_{min} < w^* < w^{**} < w_{max}. \qquad (17)$$

From this it may appear that, with the particular assumptions of the model, the availability of a superior product does not affect the probability of exclusion. However, the condition for profit maximization requires that the profit when supplying two products should exceed that when supplying only the superior product (which by assumption is greater than that when supplying only the inferior product). The fixed cost, k, of producing the inferior good represents an indivisibility. The effect may be seen in the case where the distribution is uniform. Where only the superior product is produced, the price set is

$$p_{max} = \frac{1}{2}(\lambda_{max} w_{max} + c_{max}),$$ (18)

which means that the marginal customer has wage

$$w^*_{max} = \frac{1}{2}(w_{max} + c_{max}/\lambda_{max})$$ (18′)

and the profit is given by

$$\Pi_1 = \left(\frac{1}{4} h\right)(\lambda_{max} w_{max} - c_{max})(w_{max} - c_{max}/\lambda_{max}) - k_{max},$$ (19)

where $h = w_{max} - w_{min}$. If both are produced, and some customers continue to be excluded,

$$p = \frac{1}{2}(\lambda w_{max} + c)$$ (20)

$$w^* = \frac{1}{2}(w_{max} + c/\lambda)$$ (20′)

$$p_{max} = \frac{1}{2}(\lambda_{max} w_{max} + c_{max})$$ (21)

$$w^{**} = \frac{1}{2}[w_{max} + (c_{max} - c)/(\lambda_{max} - \lambda)].$$ (21′)

The profit is given by[4]

$$\Pi_2 = \left(\frac{1}{4} h\right)(\lambda_{max} w_{max} - c_{max})[w_{max} - (c_{max} - c)/(\lambda_{max} - \lambda)]$$

$$+ \left(\frac{1}{4} h\right)(\lambda w_{max} - c)[(c_{max} - c)/(\lambda_{max} - \lambda) - c/\lambda] - k - k_{max}.$$ (22)

For Π_2 to exceed Π_1, we require that (after rearrangement)

$$k < \left(\frac{1}{4} h\right)[(c_{max} - c)/(\lambda_{max} - \lambda) - c/\lambda]^2/[1/\lambda - 1/\lambda_{max}].$$ (23)

Where the products are sufficiently close in terms of cost per unit effectiveness, or if the fixed cost is sufficiently large, then the production of the lower-quality good is not profitable to the monopolist. In this situation exclusion is not the result of an arbitrary assumption about the number of qualities supplied, but can be traced to the profit-maximizing decision of the monopolist.

4. Potential Entry into the Market

The failure of the monopolist to supply all the market may be expected to attract entrants into the industry, a possibility that has not yet been taken

---

[4] It may be checked that the assumption, made at the start of this subsection, that c/λ rises with λ ensures that w^{**} is larger than w^*. It is assumed that the degree of income inequality is such that the outer inequalities in (17) are satisfied.

into account. It has been assumed that, 'if potential entrants know that a duopoly yields negative profits, an established firm can quietly enjoy a monopoly profit without worrying about the threat of entry' (Tirole, 1989, p. 307). Where there is a single quality of the good, this is the case where potential competition is in price strategies (Bertrand competition) and where the fixed cost is irreversible. Bertrand competition drives the price down to marginal cost, and overall profit is negative for all firms. On the other hand, this argument does not carry over to the case where there is more than one type of product, since the goods are not perfect substitutes.

Suppose that a monopolist produces the superior product, λ_{max}, but does not find it profitable also to produce the inferior product, λ. A potential entrant can produce the inferior product, and sell it at a lower price, without fear that profit will necessarily be driven to zero. None the less, where the incumbent is free to adjust price, he may be expected to react to entry by reducing his price. In the case of a uniform distribution, the profit-maximizing response of the erstwhile monopolist is to charge a price

$$p_{max} = \frac{1}{2} [\lambda_{max} w_{max} + c_{max} - (\lambda w_{max} - p)]. \tag{24}$$

The term in parentheses is positive when the rival product is preferred to non-purchase by at least some consumers, and hence the price charged is less than that in the absence of the rival (compare with (18)). The entrant sets price to maximize

$$\Pi_E = (p - c)[F(w^{**}) - F(w^*)] - k. \tag{25}$$

The first-order condition for an interior solution in the case of a uniform distribution is to set

$$p = \frac{1}{2} (\lambda p_{max}/\lambda_{max} + c), \tag{26}$$

which is less than the price that would have been charged by the monopolist if he had produced the good (equation (20)). The new entrant may indeed set a price such that all consumers can purchase the good ($p = \lambda w_{min}$).

Entry may then ensure that the range of goods is widened, and that the income necessary to purchase the good is reduced. Exclusion may be eliminated by competition. At the same time, there is no guarantee that the resulting profit is sufficient to cover the fixed cost. The maximized Π_E may be negative. It is indeed possible that the monopolist's response to entry may be to reduce the price of the superior product to such a level that it is bought by all consumers, leaving a zero market share for the supplier of the inferior product. Such a threat of price-cutting may deter entry, in which case the product remains outside the reach of poorer consumers.

Moreover, if there are more than two possible qualities of the good, the potential entrant has to take account of other possible rivals. Suppose that entry takes place sequentially. A rival to the monopolist has to take account of the fact that others may follow him into the market and hence reduce the profitability of entry. Where quality (but not price) decisions are irreversible, the entrant may decide to choose a quality closer to that of the monopolist—and thus further from that affordable by the poor—so as to avoid being upstaged by a subsequent entrant. Potential entry may be double-edged in its effect, and policy intervention to stimulate competition may be counter-productive (as has been shown by Bernheim 1984).

There is however the possibility that potential competition may play a more powerful role than has been allowed so far. Baumol *et al.* (1988) have argued that, if all firms have equal access to technology, then frictionless reversible entry forces competitive-like behaviour on the monopolist. In such a 'perfectly contestable market', a monopoly firm can earn only 'zero economic profit' (p. 6). Earlier, Demsetz (1968) suggested that monopoly profit would be eliminated if potential entrants could bid to supply the whole market, an idea that he attributes to Chadwick (1859). In such a situation, it does not follow that the whole market would be served. If, with a single quality, a price of λw_{min} does not generate a sufficient excess over marginal cost to cover the fixed cost, and condition (7) holds, then zero profit involves charging a higher price, and hence excluding certain customers. At the same time, the comparative statics are different. An increase in average incomes has the effect of increasing the profit earned at any price and hence allowing the price to be reduced. The level of productivity necessary for the person to purchase the good, and hence to be capable of functioning in the labour market, in this case falls with rising living standards in the society as a whole.

As has been amply demonstrated in the recent literature, the conclusions drawn from models of imperfect competition may depend sensitively on the assumptions made. Whether markets are perfectly contestable, or whether there is room for monopoly profit, is governed by the conditions of the specific market. The purpose of the model examined in the main part of this paper has been to illustrate possibilities. Whether or not they apply in reality depends on how the notion of capabilities is put into empirical practice.

5. Conclusions

This paper has brought together the notion of poverty, in terms of an incapacity to function arising from the inability to purchase goods essential to that functioning, and the treatment of price and quality decisions in the industrial organization literature, which has shown how these decisions may lead to certain consumers being excluded from the market. If, following Sen, we define poverty as the lack of an absolute capability, and if this requires a specified input of a particular good, then the extent of poverty may depend on the supply side of the economy.

By modelling the supply side, it is possible to draw conclusions about how the degree of exclusion may change with rising living standards in the society as a whole and with increased inequality. In the context of a simple model of monopoly price and quality decisions, it has been shown how the level of endowment at which people can participate in a specified activity depends on the overall distribution. The invention of higher-quality products may, if the effective cost per quality unit falls, have the effect of reducing the number excluded; on the other hand, where the effective cost rises, the reverse may be true. It is also possible that the superior product displaces that previously available, putting the activity out of the reach of a larger proportion.

Models of this type, or different models such as those of contestable markets, may be used to examine the impact of policy intervention, such as that to regulate monopoly or encourage competition, where considerations of poverty rarely enter. The Department of Industry is not usually seen as relevant to the concerns of social security. Yet policy measures that affect the range of goods offered on the market may adversely affect low-income households. Firms may find it unprofitable to supply poor households unless, for example, they are required to do so as part of the regulatory process. Minimum quality standards may put goods out of the reach of certain consumers. The design of industrial policy has to take account of this—often overlooked—dimension.

The bringing together of the two literatures should not be taken as suggesting that industrial structure is the main determinant of poverty. The model set out in this paper leaves out many other important considerations. At the same time, it serves to underline the fact that poverty cannot be considered independently of the working of the economy—a theme that runs through many of Amartya Sen's contributions to this subject.

References

Baumol, W. J., Panzar, J. C., and Willig, R. D. (1988), *Contestable Markets and the Theory of Industry Structure*, rev. ed., Harcourt Brace Jovanovich, San Diego.

Becker, G. S. (1965), 'A Theory of the Allocation of Time', *Economic Journal*, 75: 493–517.

Bernheim, B. D. (1984), 'Strategic Deterrence of Sequential Entry into an Industry', *Rand Journal of Economics*, 15: 1–11.

Chadwick, E. (1859), 'Results of Different Principles of Legislation and Administration in Europe; of Competition for the Field, as Compared with the Competition within the Field of Service', *Journal of the Royal Statistical Society*, 22: 381–420.

Demsetz, H. (1968), 'Why Regulate Utilities?' *Journal of Law and Economics*, 11: 55–65.

Drèze, J. P. and Sen, A. K. (1989), *Hunger and Public Action*, Clarendon Press, Oxford.

Lewis, G. W. and Ulph, D. T. (1988), 'Poverty, Inequality and Welfare', *Economic Journal*, 98 (conference issue): 117–31.

Sen, A. K. (1976), 'Poverty: An Ordinal Approach to Measurement', *Econometrica*, 44: 219–31.

—— (1980), 'Equality of What?' in S. McMurrin (ed.), *Tanner Lectures on Human Values*, i, Cambridge University Press; reprinted in Sen (1982).

—— (1981), *Poverty and Famines: An Essay on Entitlement and Deprivation*, Clarendon Press, Oxford.

—— (1982), *Choice, Welfare and Measurement*, Basil Blackwell, Oxford.

—— (1983), 'Poor, Relatively Speaking', *Oxford Economic Papers*, 35: 153–69; reprinted in Sen (1984).

—— (1984), *Resources, Values and Development*, Harvard University Press, Cambridge, Mass.

—— (1985), *Commodities and Capabilities*, North-Holland, Amsterdam.

—— (1992), *Inequality Re-examined*, Harvard University Press, Cambridge, Mass.

Shaked, A. and Sutton, J. (1982), 'Relaxing Price Competition through Product Differentiation', *Review of Economic Studies*, 49: 3–13.

—— —— (1983), 'Natural Oligopolies', *Econometrica*, 51: 1469–83.

Tirole, J. (1989), *The Theory of Industrial Organization*, MIT Press, Cambridge, Mass.

Townsend, P. (1979), *Poverty in the United Kingdom*, Allen Lane, London.

3

Walrasian Equilibrium without Survival: Existence, Efficiency, and Remedial Policy

JEFFREY L. COLES and PETER J. HAMMOND

It is unquestionably true, that in no country of the globe have the government, the distribution of property, and the habits of the people, been such as to call forth, in the most effective manner, the resources of the soil. Consequently, if the most advantageous possible change in all these respects could be supposed at once to take place, it is certain that the demand for labour, and the encouragement to production, might be such as for a short time, in some countries, and for rather a longer time in others, to lessen the operation of the checks to population which have been described.

Malthus (1830, pp. 247–8 of Flew (1970))

A society in which some people roll in luxury while others live in acute misery can still be Pareto optimal if the agony of the deprived cannot be reduced without cutting into the ecstasy of the affluent.

Sen (1990)

It would appear that, on the level of individual nations and of inter-national relations, *the free market* is the most efficient instrument for utilizing resources and effectively responding to needs. But this is true only for those needs which are 'solvent', insofar as they are endowed with purchasing power, and for those resources which are 'marketable', insofar as they are capable of obtaining a satisfactory price. But there are many human needs which find no place on the market. It is a strict duty of justice and truth not to allow fundamental human needs to remain unsatisfied, and not to allow those burdened by such needs to perish. It is also necessary to help these needy people to acquire expertise, to enter the circle of exchange, and to develop their skills in

This work was originally supported by National Science Foundation Grant SES-85-20666 to Hammond at the Institute for Mathematical Studies in the Social Sciences, Stanford University. Coles wishes to thank the University of Utah Research Committee for financial support. An early draft was presented to the Fifth World Congress of the Econometric Society in Boston, August 1985. Earlier versions of the paper also appeared in 1986 as IMSSS Economics Technical Report no. 483, and in 1991 as European University Institute Working Paper ECO no. 91/50. The main new idea for this last revision arose during a visit by Coles to the European University Institute, financed in part through its research budget. In addition, we wish to thank William Novshek and T. N. Srinivasan for helpful conversations, and David Kiefer and Leslie Reinhorn for helpful comments. Also, Hammond is grateful to Paul Hare and to Partha Dasgupta for arousing and maintaining his interest in the topic over many years. Our debt to Amartya Sen is evident.

order to make the best use of their capacities and resources. Even prior
to the logic of a fair exchange of goods and the forms of justice
appropriate to it, there exists *something which is due to man because he
is man*, by reason of his lofty dignity. Inseparable from that required
'something' is the possibility to survive and, at the same time, to make
an active contribution to the common good of humanity.

Pope John Paul II's Encyclical Letter
Centesimus Annus (1991), section 34

1. Introduction

Students of economics are routinely taught the efficiency of free markets. Mathematical economists, following Arrow (1951), Debreu (1954,
1959), Arrow and Debreu (1954), McKenzie (1954, 1959, 1961), and others,
have provided rigorous foundations to these teachings by proving the
existence of Walrasian or 'competitive' equilibrium, as well as the two
fundamental efficiency theorems of welfare economics which relate Pareto-
efficient allocations to Walrasian equilibria. As Sen (1977, 1981*a*, 1981*b*) has
pointed out, however, the standard theorems deal with the issue of survival by assuming that all agents can always survive without trade. This we
call the 'survival assumption'. Since trading opportunities cannot then
detract from what is possible without trade, all agents can survive with
trade too. Thus, according to the standard theory, in any Walrasian
equilibrium there is universal survival. Yet the survival assumption is clearly
counter to the facts of life and death in almost all the worlds' economies, whatever their stage of development or their economic system. Only
a very few peasant societies are truly self-sufficient. Even in those that are,
few individual consumers are likely to be able to survive for long on their
own.

  In fact it is all too evident that, even in wealthy countries, some people
do die for want of adequate nourishment, for lack of simple and cheap
life-saving drugs, or because they cannot afford to keep warm during bitter
winter weather. So the world does not fit this standard model of Walrasian
equilibrium. It is of some importance, however, to know whether this is due
to the equally evident failure of economies to conform to the Walrasian
market model because of monopolies, externalities, taxes, or other 'market
failures', or, alternatively, whether it is the survival assumption itself that
needs to be questioned. For if the personal tragedies of starvation or disease
are the result of market failures and/or government intervention in markets,
that creates a justification for *laissez-faire* economic policies (including the
promotion of competition and remedies for the most serious external
diseconomies). On the other hand, if such personal tragedies are in part the
result of market forces when the people are unable to survive without, for

instance, being able to trade their labour power or skills, then *laissez-faire* becomes much less acceptable.

For this reason, it seems important to know whether the survival assumption really does play a crucial role in the standard Walrasian theory of competitive markets. This requires a theory of how competitive markets can work in the absence of the survival assumption. One of our aims, therefore, will be to see what it takes to assure survival—either free markets on their own, or else some redistributive policies such as welfare programme or land reform.

Among past writers, Malthus (1798, 1830) certainly described features of economies in which the growth of population was limited only by drastic scarcity. He also realized that the distribution of wealth was an important influence on the numbers of survivors from one generation to the next. Earlier, Turgot, as government representative for the Limousin region of central France, had recorded his impression that the 1770 famine owed much more to lack of purchasing power than to grain shortages (see Rothschild 1992). Other references to discussions of starvation by classical economists can be found in Sen (1986). Yet, as far as the modern literature on Walrasian economics is concerned, we have found that only the papers by Bergstrom (1971), Moore (1975), and McKenzie (1981) really consider the implications of abandoning the standard survival assumption, and even they do so only to discuss conditions that suffice to ensure the existence of a Walrasian equilibrium in which all survive. We are not aware of anybody who has yet considered formal general models of Walrasian equilibrium in which some individuals do not survive. Koopmans (1957, p. 62), however, did at least pose the question, noting that 'there is considerable challenge to further research on the survival problem', and going on to suggest, more-over, that 'One "hard-boiled" alternative would be to assume instantaneous elimination by starvation of those whose resources prove insufficient for survival, and to look for conditions ensuring existence of an "equilibrium" involving survival of some consumers.' This is the key idea that appears not to have been followed up at all thoroughly or systematically as yet, and which will be explored in this paper.

One reason for economists' failure to tackle this problem may be the general belief that standard general equilibrium theory somehow breaks down or does not apply when survival of all agents is not guaranteed. Indeed, in an otherwise illuminating presentation of some examples of entitlement failure, Desai (1989, p. 430) first points out that 'If there is no market failure, then relative price movements should lead to optimal outcomes', which is quite correct if we interpret 'optimal' to mean just 'Pareto-efficient'. He then goes on, however, to state and even emphasize that, 'while an equilibrium exists, relative prices fail to play an allocative role'. It is true that he does not discuss Pareto efficiency directly. Yet these sentences suggest to us a belief that entitlement failures, while not preventing the existence of (competitive) equilibrium, nevertheless do cause the price mechanism to break down in a way that leads to (Pareto-) suboptimal or inefficient outcomes. Now, unless entitlement failures are themselves regarded as a form of market failure, this would clearly contradict the most robust result in general equilibrium theory—namely, the first efficiency theorem of welfare economics, stating that, whenever Walrasian equilibrium allocations exist, they must be Pareto-efficient. Yet we shall show that entitlement failures do nothing to create any Pareto inefficiencies, and so cannot possibly be market failures in any normal sense. Another purpose of this paper, therefore, is to correct the apparently common misconception that, because some individuals are starving to death, the usual results of general equilibrium theory somehow do not apply.

So we will reconsider the theory of Walrasian economic equilibrium without imposing the usual survival assumption. Indeed, we will consider when and in what sense equilibrium allocations can occur without the survival of all individuals. The more technical later sections show that the standard theorems concerning existence and Pareto efficiency of Walrasian equilibrium are still valid, with some modifications. The most major of these arises from the simple observation that the number of surviving people is a discrete variable, so that there are inherent non-convexities; whereas standard Walrasian theory assumes convexity. Yet the proportion of survivors in a large population is, to a very good approximation, a continuous variable. Thus, we choose to work with a continuum of agents in the way that Aumann (1964, 1966) pioneered. And we shall also prove a version of the core equivalence theorem for such continuum economies.

For existence proofs in particular, it will also be necessary in general to assume that the distribution of 'needs'—of what individuals need in order to be on the margin of survival—is dispersed or, technically, is a non-atomic measure. Then mean demand per individual will be continuous and so existence will be assured under the other usual assumptions.

The formal part of the paper begins in Section 2 with an extended discussion of a particular example. This incorporates a Leontief technology for using land and labour in order to produce a single consumption good. Labour is supplied inelastically by those who survive. Conditions on exogenous parameter values which permit survival are derived. It is shown how the proportion of survivors is determined under a *laissez-faire* Walrasian equilibrium when these conditions are not met and when inequality causes some people to starve. Remedial policy is also considered. We show that either lump-sum or land redistribution, or a poll subsidy financed by income taxes, can ensure survival whenever it is physically feasible. Food subsidies, however, are no help at all even in increasing the proportion of survivors.

The example of Section 2 illustrates how it is possible to model the survival issue by adding survival as a good in its own right and then specifying each agent's consumption set as the union of a 'survival' set with a disjoint 'non-survival' set. Section 3 considers a general continuum economy in which each agent's consumption set C is such a union, which is non-convex, of course. Accordingly, we use methods for dealing with such non-convex consumption sets such as those developed by, among others, Hildenbrand (1968, 1969), Mas-Colell (1977), Yamazaki (1978, 1981), Coles (1986), and Funaki and Kaneko (1986). Thus, Section 3 shows that most of the standard theorems of general equilibrium analysis—notably, existence of equilibrium, the two fundamental efficiency theorems of welfare economics, and core equivalence—do still hold.

Finally, Section 4 contains conclusions and discusses some important reservations.

2. An Example

2.1. Description of the Economy

The economy is assumed to consist of a large number (in fact, a continuum) of small farmers who each produce the same crop using identical technologies. Farmers also have identical tastes and consumption sets; only their endowments of land differ.

Each farmer has preferences defined over the three-dimensional consumption set

$$C := \{(-t, -h, c)| t \geq 0, 0 \leq h \leq l, c \geq \underline{c} \}. \tag{1}$$

Here t denotes the (exogenous) amount of land which the farmer has available to supply or use in production, c denotes consumption of the crop, h denotes labour supply, and $\underline{c}$, l are two positive constants representing the minimum subsistence food consumption and the maximum possible supply of labour, respectively.

The constant-returns-to-scale Leontief technology to which each farmer has access requires λ units of labour and τ units of land in order to produce each unit of the crop. The cumulative distribution function of land endowments is $F(t)$ which is defined for all $t \geq 0$. The mean holding of land is denoted by $\bar{t}$, and the proportion of farmers who own no land by $f_0 := F(0)$. Assume that $\bar{t} > \tau\underline{c}$ and $l > \lambda\underline{c}$, so there is more land and each person has more labour than the minimum needed to produce subsistence for everyone.

It will be assumed that farmers care only for consumption. Perhaps leisure is a luxury good that poor farmers cannot afford. Contingent upon survival $(c \geq \underline{c})$, each farmer prefers allocations with more consumption to those with less, and supplies the maximum amount of labour $(h = l)$ in order to have as much food as possible, whether it is produced directly or purchased out of wage income.

There are assumed to be perfectly competitive markets for output (corn), labour, and land, with corresponding prices denoted by p, w, and r respectively. As usual, Walrasian equilibrium requires utility maximization, profit maximization, and market clearing. It is clear from the usual no-pure-profit condition that, in any Walrasian equilibrium with positive production, the price system must satisfy $p = w\lambda + r\tau$. Thus, $p \geq w\lambda \geq 0$ and $p = \lambda w$ when $r = 0$. For later reference, we note that the rental–price ratio $r/p \in [0, 1/\tau]$ is determined by the equation

$$r/p = [1 - (w/p)\lambda]/\tau \tag{2}$$

for each wage–price ratio w/p in the closed interval of possible values $[0, 1/\lambda]$.

Because production takes place under constant returns to scale, it is also true that in Walrasian equilibrium each farmer is completely indifferent to the allocation of his land and labour between different farming enterprises, including any that he himself may own. Each farmer is also indifferent to how much land and labour he hires from other farmers (cf. Newbery 1977).

2.2. Equilibrium with Survival

Consumption demand by a farmer who has t units of land must satisfy the budget equation $pc = wl + rt$. Equilibrium with positive wages therefore requires that mean consumption per head $\bar{c}$ must satisfy $p\bar{c} = wl + r\bar{t}$ and also $l = \lambda\bar{c}$, $\bar{t} \geq \tau\bar{c}$.

When $\bar{t} > \tau l/\lambda$, there is more land than can possibly be cultivated even if the farmers use all the available labour, so land must be a free good in any equilibrium. This implies that $r = 0$ and $p = \lambda w$. The distribution of land holdings is then irrelevant. There is in fact an obvious equilibrium in which every farmer consumes $\bar{c} = l/\lambda > \underline{c}$ and supplies l units of labour.

When $\bar{t} = \tau l/\lambda$ there is just enough labour to farm all the land, and then any wage–price ratio w/p in the interval $[\underline{c}/l, 1/\lambda]$ is a potential equilibrium. By (2) it follows that r/p lies in the interval $[0, (l - \lambda\underline{c})/\tau l]$. One has $\bar{c} = l/\lambda = \bar{t}/\tau$ and also $p\bar{c} = wl + r\bar{t} \geq wl \geq p\underline{c}$. Thus, all markets clear and all agents survive, supplying l units of labour. Of course, this case is non-generic and so we shall not have much to say about it in the rest of the paper.

2.3. Non-survival

Another, and for us a much more interesting, possibility occurs when there is surplus labour and the per capita land endowment is therefore small, with $\bar{t} < \tau l/\lambda$. Then, if there are some farmers who own no land, no Walrasian equilibrium exists in the usual sense, with everybody surviving. This is because the only possible equilibrium wage is zero, which does not permit the landless to afford subsistence consumption.

To avoid this non-existence problem, we now modify our concept of equilibrium by allowing that some agents may not survive. To do so, let us add to the commodity space a fourth dimension with an indicator variable $i \in \{-1, 0\}$ representing either survival, if $i = 0$, or non-survival, if $i = -1$. The number -1 can be thought of as signifying that the agent has to give up his life in order to achieve any feasible plan of net consumption within his budget constraint. Then we replace C in (1) above by the new four-dimensional *survival set*:

$$S := \{(-t, -h, c, i) \mid t \geq 0, 0 \leq h \leq l, c \geq \underline{c}, i = 0\}. \tag{3}$$

But we also append to the set S another, *non- survival*, set defined as

$$N := \{(-t, -h, c, i) \mid t \geq 0, h = 0, c \geq 0, i = -1\}. \tag{4}$$

Note that if $c \geq \underline{c}$, then the individual can choose either survival or non-survival. Of course, we expect survival to be chosen whenever it is feasible. The consumption set then becomes the union $C = S \cup N$ of the extended survival set S in (3) above with this additional non-survival set N. This is depicted in Fig. 1, which shows the projection of the two sets S and N onto the three-dimensional set of points $(-h, c, i)$ for which land supply t is treated as an exogenous constant. Note that, apart from the indivisible good 'survival', the consumption set is convex and allows free disposal.

Allocations in which the farmer supplies no labour ($h = 0$) but consumes less than the subsistence level ($0 \leq c < \underline{c}$) are now assumed to be feasible provided that the farmer does not survive. Note how it is assumed that a non-surviving farmer's labour dies with him, as he is too weak or malnourished to be able to add his labour to the pool of surplus labour. Thus his consumption is limited to the proceeds from selling any land endowment. Of course, if a farmer's land endowment is large enough relative to

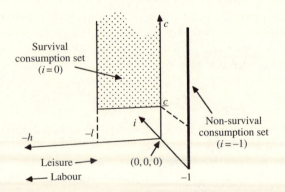

Fig. 1

existing prices, he may attain subsistence consumption and sell his labour endowment at the going wage, thereby attaining survival in S.

Assume that survival of any sort is preferred to non-survival. Also, whereas Green (1976, pp. 32 and 36), for instance, postulates that there is no preference ordering over points at which the consumer does not survive, we assume that the preference ordering does extend to points of N. Indeed, we assume that, whether the farmer survives or not, more food is always preferred to less food.

Consider now the difficult case where some farmers are landless and also $\bar{t} < \tau l/\lambda$, so that there would be surplus labour if all farmers were to survive. Then there is no equilibrium in which every farmer can attain the survival portion of the consumption set. Incorporate into the model the augmented consumption set $C = S \cup N$ defined above. Also, allow the possibility of compensated equilibrium (in the sense of Arrow and Hahn, 1971), in which farmers at a minimum expenditure point in the survival section S of the consumption set C may be arbitrarily restricted to an allocation in the non-survival portion N of the consumption set that costs the same. In compensated equilibrium utility is maximized by all agents except some of those at the minimum expenditure level needed to attain the survival portion of the consumption set. These agents on the margin of survival minimize expenditure subject to reaching a given indifference curve, but they may or may not maximize utility. Indeed, those whose utility is not maximized may not even survive, and moreover, the survivors among those on the margin are arbitrarily chosen according to the requirements of market equilibrium. It should be noted that Dasgupta and Ray (1986–7) use a similar concept of equilibrium in their efficiency wage explanation of involuntary unemployment. Also, observe how admitting compensated equilibrium in this way resolves the existence problem by closing the graph of the aggregate excess demand correspondence. Then a continuum of agents will guarantee that mean excess demand is convex-valued (see Section 3).

An important feature of this kind of equilibrium is that agents who have some land but do not survive are still allowed to trade in order to maximize their consumption of food. Unlike labour, land does not perish with its owner. Rather, non-survivors sell all their land for its rental value r and use the proceeds to consume what they can afford before they succumb. We are not sure that this faithfully represents Koopmans's (1957, p. 62) 'instant elimination' of non-survivors. But it seems more realistic than imposing zero consumption on all non-survivors. It is, moreover, a crucial feature permitting existence and efficiency of equilibrium. For if agents who did not survive were unable to consume, the set C^N defined in (4) would consist only of the half-line through the origin with $t \geqslant 0$. Then agents' preferences would be locally satiated, since all points of this half-line are equally abhorrent.

Given that there is now no equilibrium with all farmers surviving, we consider three cases.

CASE A. $l\tau(1 - f_0) \leqslant \lambda\bar{t} < l\tau$, and all those with any land survive.

In this case there will turn out to be a compensated equilibrium at a subsistence real wage of $w/p - \underline{c}/l$, which is just enough to enable the survival of a landless person who works l hours. The excess labour is removed by starvation. Each landless farmer is a marginal survivor in this compensated Walrasian equilibrium. By (2), the rental–price ratio is therefore given by $r/p = (l - \lambda\underline{c})/l\tau$. A proportion $f_n \leqslant f_0$ of the population will be unable to survive, however, because they remain involuntarily unemployed; for these, $c = 0$ and $h = 0$. All who starve are landless. Yet, among the landless farmers, a proportion $f_0 - f_n$ of the total population do manage to survive at the least-cost point of the survival portion S of their consumption set; for these, $c = \underline{c}$ and $h = l$. Of course, all farmers with positive land endowment survive; for these one has $h = l$ and $c = \underline{c} + (l - \lambda\underline{c})t/\tau l$. Note how clearing of all markets requires that

$$\bar{h} = (1 - f_n)l = \lambda\bar{t}/\tau \quad \text{and} \quad \bar{c} = (1 - f_n)\underline{c} + (l - \lambda\underline{c})\bar{t}/\tau l = \bar{t}/\tau. \tag{5}$$

Both these equations are satisfied when the proportion of survivors is $1 - f_n$, where $f_n := 1 - (\lambda\bar{t}/l\tau)$. So the allocation that we have described must be a compensated equilibrium. There is no uncompensated equilibrium.

Note finally that $0 < f_n \leqslant f_0$ precisely when the inequalities defining this case are both satisfied.

CASE B. $l\tau[1 - F(\tau\underline{c})] < \lambda\bar{t} < l\tau(1 - f_0)$ for some $t < \tau\underline{c}$ and not all farmers with land survive.

Here there will be a compensated equilibrium with the minimum amount of land needed for survival being given by some number s in the range $0 < s < \tau\underline{c}$. Since $p\underline{c} = wl + rs$ and, in addition, (2) must still be true, the corresponding equilibrium wage–price and rental–price ratios must be

$$\frac{w}{p} = \frac{\tau\underline{c} - s}{\tau l - \lambda s} \quad \text{and} \quad \frac{r}{p} = \frac{l - \lambda\underline{c}}{\tau l - \lambda s}. \tag{6}$$

Farmers whose land holdings t exceed the critical value s survive with $h = l$ and $c = (wl + rt)/p > \underline{c}$. But those with $t < s$ could not afford to consume $\underline{c}$ even if they could somehow supply l units of labour; they are therefore unable either to survive or to work, and so find themselves with $h = 0$ and $c = rt/p < rs/p < \underline{c}$.

Finally, according to the requirements of market clearing, some of the farmers with land endowment exactly equal to s survive, while others do not. Indeed, the proportion q of non-survivors in the total population is determined so that the labour market-clearing condition $\lambda\bar{c} = l(1 - q)$ is satisfied. Actually, since the land market must clear as well, one must also have $\bar{t} = \tau\bar{c}$ and so $\lambda\bar{t}/\tau = l(1 - q)$. This determines a unique value of q which, in the case being considered, must lie in the interval $f_0 < q < F(\tau\underline{c})$. The corresponding value of s must then be given by

$$s = \inf \{t \,|\, 1 - F(t) \leqslant \lambda\bar{t}/l\tau\} = \sup \{t \,|\, 1 - F(t) > \lambda\bar{t}/l\tau\}. \qquad (7)$$

This is the unique value of s which ensures that $F(t) > q$ whenever $t > s$ and that $F(t) < q$ whenever $t < s$. If there is a negligible set of farmers whose land endowment equals s exactly, then $t = s$ will solve the equation $F(t) = q$. In this latter case the compensated equilibrium found here becomes a Walrasian equilibrium, since only agents in a negligible set are failing to maximize their preferences. Generally, however, there is only a compensated equilibrium, in which some farmers whose landholding is s survive, while others do not.

CASE C. $\lambda\bar{t} \leqslant l\tau[1 - F(t)]$ for all $t < \tau\underline{c}$ and only the self-sufficient survive.

In this final case there is so much labour and so little land that the only possible Walrasian equilibrium prices satisfy $w/p = 0$ and $r/p = 1/\tau$. At these prices all agents with $t < \tau\underline{c}$ do not survive, since they can only afford to have $h = 0$, and must sell all their land in order to consume at $c = t/\tau < \underline{c}$. But every farmer who has $t \geqslant \tau\underline{c}$, and so has enough land to produce subsistence consumption using his own labour, does survive by choosing $h = l$ and $c = t/\tau \geqslant \underline{c}$. Even though the wage is zero, the threat of starvation motivates the self-sufficient farmers to work. Consumption then satisfies $\bar{c} = \bar{t}/\tau$, while labour supply is given by $\lim_{t \to \tau\underline{c}^-} l\,[1 - F(t)] \geqslant \lambda\bar{c}$. So markets clear with labour as a free good, and there is a Walrasian equilibrium at prices $w/p = 0$ and $r/p = 1/r$.

2.4. Remedial Policy

Despite the potential for non-survival when $\bar{t} < \tau l/\lambda$, note that a programme of land redistribution can always be used to ensure that everybody survives, because of the assumption that $\bar{t} > \tau\underline{c}$ and $l > \lambda\underline{c}$. For if land is redistributed so that all farmers have access to the same amount $\bar{t}$, then each farmer is obviously able to attain survival through production using only his own land and labour.

Moreover, a balanced-budget tax-transfer system can achieve the same effect. To see this, suppose that all rental income from land is taxed at the flat rate θ, with the resulting tax revenues being redistributed equally to all agents by means of a poll subsidy or uniform lump-sum transfer m. Real transfers of $m/p = \underline{c}$ and a tax rate of $\theta = \tau\underline{c}/\bar{t} < 1$ will then give rise to an equilibrium with an excess supply of labour (since $l > \lambda\bar{t}/\tau$) and so with prices given by $w/p = 0$ and $r/p = 1/\tau$. Each farmer's budget constraint takes the form $c \leqslant \underline{c} + [(1/\tau) - (\underline{c}/\bar{t})]t$. Because of our assumption that $\bar{t} > \tau\underline{c}$, the right-hand side of this constraint exceeds $\underline{c}$ and so every farmer can certainly afford to survive even though there is no wage income. The government's budget balances with $m = \theta r \bar{t}$.

Such a tax-transfer scheme is also equivalent to a system under which the government uses the proceeds from a rental income tax at rate $\theta = \tau \underline{c} / \bar{t}$ in order to purchase $\underline{c}$ units of food per head on the open market and then distribute this amount equally to all farmers. This system is not a food subsidy, of course, but distribution in kind. Notice that wage income is always zero in each of these equilibria, so there is no scope for redistribution financed by a tax on wage income.

In contrast, any system of food subsidies, financed by a tax on landlords or on labour income or on any combination of the two, completely fails to reduce the extent of starvation or even to alter the allocation in any way. Let (p^e, w^e, r^e) denote the (compensated) equilibrium prices in the absence of any taxes or subsidies. In addition, let γ be the *ad valorem* rate of subsidy on food purchases and let ω and ρ denote the *ad valorem* rates of tax on wage income and on land rents respectively. The budget constraint for a farmer with landholding t then becomes

$$p(1 - \gamma)c \leqslant w(1 - \omega)l + r(1 - \rho)t. \tag{8}$$

We will show that, when such taxes and subsidies are introduced and the government balances its budget, there is a new equilibrium in which producer prices (p, w, r) adjust so that prices to consumers are still given by

$$p^e = p(1 - \gamma); \qquad w^e = w(1 - \omega); \qquad r^e = r(1 - \rho), \tag{9}$$

exactly as before. Then, since consumer prices are entirely unchanged, so is the demand side of the economy and the entire equilibrium allocation of consumption, work, land, and survival opportunities to all consumers.

Indeed, to show that there is a new equilibrium as described, it suffices to check that, when faced with the new producer prices (p, w, r), producers are still maximizing profits at the same zero level when they choose the same output–land and labour–land ratios $\bar{c}/\bar{t}$ and $\bar{h}/\bar{t}$ as in the original equilibrium. Since both consumers and the government are balancing their budgets in any new equilibrium, one must have $p^e \bar{c} = w^e \bar{h} + r^e \bar{t}$, or

$$p(1 - \gamma)\bar{c} = w(1 - \omega)\bar{h} + r(1 - \rho)\bar{t}, \tag{10}$$

and also

$$p\gamma\bar{c} = w\omega\bar{h} + r\rho\bar{t}. \tag{11}$$

But then, adding (10) and (11) gives

$$p\bar{c} = w\bar{h} + r\bar{t} = w\lambda\bar{c} + r\tau\bar{c} = (w\lambda) + r\tau)\bar{c}, \tag{12}$$

where the second equality holds because clearing of the labour and land markets implies that $\bar{h} = \lambda \bar{c}$ and $\bar{t} = \tau \bar{c}$. Since $\bar{c}$ must be positive in the original equilibrium, the no-pure-profit condition $p = w\lambda + r\tau$ is a direct implication of (12). (The fact that the no-pure-profit condition is satisfied by both the new producer prices and consumer prices is reminiscent of the result presented by Diamond and Mirrlees, 1976.) So is the optimality of the output–land and labour–land ratios $\bar{c}/\bar{t}$ and $\bar{l}/\bar{t}$.

This means that there is indeed an equilibrium with taxes in which neither consumer prices nor quantities change. In particular, the food subsidy does nothing at all to lower the price of food faced by consumers or to help the starving. Instead, the subsidy is entirely passed on to the producers and then is all taxed away in order to finance the food subsidies. Of course, this result depends crucially on the fixed coefficients production technology. Otherwise taxes and land and labour would affect the equilibrium labour–land ratio.

3. General Equilibrium Analysis

3.1. Agents' Feasible Sets

Sen (1977, 1981*a*, *b*) chose to use an 'exchange entitlements' approach to analyse the question of whether individuals could afford to survive. This certainly has a powerful intuitive appeal. Yet, as Srinivasan (1983) has observed, it is not strictly necessary; and essentially the same idea can also be captured, at least for the results presented below, by the usual kind of budget set within a finite-dimensional commodity space $\mathfrak{R}^G$. The issue of whether an individual survives depends on whether this budget set intersects the set of net trade vectors which that individual needs in order to survive. If it does, then the individual will be able to survive by a judicious choice of consumption and production plans. But if the intersection is empty, then the economic system condemns the agent to starve.

So we consider an economy in which all agents are both consumers and workers who may or may not own land and other primary resources. The typical agent has a survival consumption set C^S, together with a non-survival consumption set C^N. Each vector $c \in C^S \cup C^N$ is a net consumption vector which may have negative components corresponding to the kinds of labour the agent supplies. The two sets C^S and C^N are both assumed to be closed convex subsets of $\mathfrak{R}^G$ that allow free disposal. The consumption set then becomes the union $C^S \cup C^N$ of two convex sets.

Fig. 2 shows the consumption set of Fig. 1 after it has been projected onto the space $\mathfrak{R}^2$ of consumption–leisure pairs. As Fig. 2 indicates, the two sets C^S and C^N may intersect. Then, if $c \in C^S \cap C^N$, the agent has the choice between surviving and not. Of course, it is presumed that the agent always chooses survival in this case. It is only when $c \in C^N \backslash C^S$ that survival

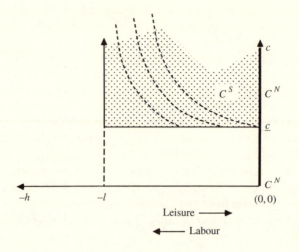

Fig. 2

becomes impossible and the agent starves. It is also presumed that $0 \in C^S \cup C^N$, so that no trade is always feasible at least for an agent who does not survive. Usually, of course, $0 \in C^N \backslash C^S$, because few agents are entirely self-sufficient.

It now seems natural to have preferences for the consumer defined over the set $C^S \cup C^N$, and to assume that any point in C^S is preferred to any point in C^N, though within C^N more food is always preferred to less. This approach, however, leads to certain difficulties which are illustrated in Fig. 2, where possible indifference curves are displayed. Notice that $(-t, 0, \underline{c})$ is strictly preferred to $(-t, -l, \underline{c})$. Yet the lower contour set of points, which are weakly worse than $(-t, -l, \underline{c})$, is not closed, since it includes points of the form $(-t, 0, \underline{c} - \varepsilon)$ for all small positive ε, but not the limit point $(-t, 0, \underline{c})$.[1] Thus, not only is the consumption set non-convex, but also preferences are typically discontinuous at $(-t, 0, \underline{c})$.

To avoid such discontinuities, we shall make use of the simple trick set out in Section 2.3. This involves treating survival as an extra good in its own right, labelled as good 0. So we add to the commodity space $\mathcal{R}^G$ an extra dimension with an indicator variable $i \in \{-1, 0\}$ representing either survival, if $i = 0$, or non-survival, if $i = -1$. The extra good can be thought of as life itself, which has to be given up if the individual does not consume enough to survive. The price of this extra good will always be zero. The two values -1 and 0 have been chosen so that: (i) preferences can still be monotone in the extended space $\mathcal{R}^{G+1}$, with life preferred to death; (ii) the

[1] In fact, earlier versions of this paper used precisely this formulation, and used particular ad hoc methods in order to overcome the difficulties created by the resulting discontinuities. In this context, note that Zaman (1986) considers a rather different kind of discontinuity in preferences.

aggregate excess demand for good 0 could never be positive, thus allowing equilibrium to occur with a non-negative demand even for good 0, whose price is always zero anyway.

This leads us to define the *consumption set* as the union

$$C := (\{0\} \times C^S) \cup (\{-1\} \times C^N) \subset \{-1, 0\} \times \mathcal{R}^G \tag{13}$$

of the two disjoint extended convex sets $\widetilde{C^S} := \{0\} \times C^S$ and $\widetilde{C^N} := \{-1\} \times C^N$. Note that C is not convex, and even incorporates survival as an indivisible good.

As in the example of Section 2, assume that production is undertaken by many small and individually owned production units. Following Rader (1964), assume that each agent has access to a convex production possibility set $Y \subset \mathcal{R}^{G+1}$. It is assumed here that Y includes 0 and allows free disposal of all goods except 0, and that $y \in Y$ implies $y_0 = 0$ because only labour and not life itself can be used as an input to the production process. Finally, Y is assumed to be bounded above because any individual agent can control only bounded quantities of inputs and these produce bounded outputs.

To survive, the agent requires a net trade vector in the *survival set*:

$$X^S := \widetilde{C^S} - Y = \{x \in \mathcal{R}^{G+1} | \exists c \in \widetilde{C^S}; \exists y \in Y : x = c - y\}. \tag{14}$$

The corresponding *non-survival set* $X^N := \widetilde{C^N} - Y$ is also feasible for the agent. Notice that both X^S and X^N are convex because $\widetilde{C^S}$, $\widetilde{C^N}$, and Y are all convex. Also, because of (13), the agent's set of feasible net trades is

$$X = X^S \cup X^N = (\widetilde{C^S} - Y) \cup (\widetilde{C^N} - Y) = (\widetilde{C^S} \cup \widetilde{C^N}) - Y \tag{15}$$

$$= (\{0\} \times C^S) \cup (\{-1\}) \times C^N) - Y \subset \{-1, 0\} \times \mathcal{R}^G.$$

To summarize, we have so far made the following assumption.

ASSUMPTION A1. Each agent has a feasible set of net trades taking the form $X = C - Y$, where the consumption set $C \subset \{-1, 0\} \times \mathcal{R}^G$ satisfies (13), with $C^S, C^N \subset \mathcal{R}^G$ and the production set $Y \subset \{0\} \times \mathcal{R}^G$ satisfying the conditions that: (i) both sets C^S and C^N are closed, convex, bounded below, and allow free disposal of all physical commodities $g \in G$; (ii) $0 \in C^S \cup C^N$; (iii) Y is convex, bounded above, and allows free disposal of all goods except 0; (iv) $0 \in Y$.

These assumptions on the two sets C and Y have implications for the set X which are summarized in the following lemma.

LEMMA. X is a closed subset of the commodity space $\{-1, 0\} \times \mathcal{R}^G$ such that: (i) $0 \in X$; (ii) X allows free disposal of all goods except 0; (iii) X is bounded below by a vector x; (iv) X is the union of two disjoint convex sets $X^S \subset \{0\} \times \mathcal{R}^G$ and $X^N \subset \{-1\} \times \mathcal{R}^G$, as specified in (15) above.

Proof. Since all the other properties claimed in the lemma are obvious, we prove only that X is closed.

Indeed, suppose that $x^v \in X$ where $x^v = c^v - y^v$ with $(c^v, y^v) \in C \times Y$ for $v = 1, 2, \ldots$, and suppose that $x^v \to x^*$ as $v \to \infty$. Then, since C has a lower bound $\underline{c}$ and Y has an upper bound $\bar{y}$, it follows that

$$\underline{c} \geqq c^v = x^v + y^v \leqq x^v + \bar{y} \to x^* + \bar{y}$$

and

$$\bar{y} \geqq y^v = c^v - x^v \geqq \underline{c} - x^v \to \underline{c} - x^*$$

as $v \to \infty$.[2] Hence the sequence of pairs $(c^v, y^v) \in C \times Y$ must be bounded, and so has a convergent subsequence with a limit (c^*, y^*) which, because the two sets C and Y are both closed, must be a member of $C \times Y$. But now $c^v - y^v = x^v \to x^*$ as $v \to \infty$, which is possible only if $x^* = c^* - y^* \in C - Y = X$. ∎

In future, a typical vector $z \in \{-1, 0\} \times \mathcal{R}^G$ will be written in the partitioned form $z = (z_0, z^G)$, where $z_0 \in \{-1, 0\}$ and $z^G \in \mathcal{R}^G$.

3.2. Agents' Preferences

Each agent is also assumed to have a (complete and transitive) preference ordering R on the consumption set C, and to be unconcerned about production except in so far as it affects consumption and labour supply, etc. It is assumed that these preferences are:

1. *monotone* in the sense that $c' \geqq c$ implies $c' \, R \, c$ and also that $b \gg b'$ implies $(i, b) \, P \, (i, b')$ whenever $b, b' \in \mathcal{R}^G$ and $i \in \{-1, 0\}$ (where P denotes the strict preference relation corresponding to R);
2. *continuous* in the sense that the upper and lower contour sets $\{c \in C \mid c \, R \, c'\}$ and $\{c \in C \mid c' \, R \, c\}$ are both closed for every $c' \in C$.

Of course, it is assumed that consumers prefer survival, so that $(i, b) \, P \, (i', b')$ whenever $b, b' \in \mathcal{R}^G$, $i = 0$ and $i' = -1$. In this sense, life is lexicographically prior to physical commodities in each consumer's preference ordering. We summarize as follows.

ASSUMPTION A2. There is a continuous and monotone preference ordering R defined on the consumption set C with the property that $(0, b) \, P \, (-1, b')$ whenever $b \in C^S$ and $b' \in C^N$.

---

[2] We use the following notation for vector inequalities: (1) $a \geqq b$ indicates that $a_k \geqq b_k$ for every component k; (2) $a > b$ indicates that (1) is true but also $a \neq b$; (3) $a \gg b$ indicates that $a_k > b_k$ for every component k.

The agent's preferences R for consumption can be converted into preferences for net trades. For given any fixed net trade vector $x \in X$, define

$$\gamma(x) := \{c \in C \mid \exists \hat{y} \in Y : c = x + \hat{y} \quad \text{and} \quad \forall y \in Y : c\,R(x+y)\} \quad (16)$$

as the agent's set of optimal consumption vectors. Because Y is closed and bounded above, whereas C is closed and bounded below, and because the upper contour sets of the preference ordering R are all closed, the set $\gamma(x)$ is indeed non-empty for every $x \in X$. Moreover, if c and c' both belong to $\gamma(x)$ for any $x \in X$, then c and c' must be indifferent. So there is a well defined preference ordering $\succsim$ on X such that

$$x \succsim x' \Leftrightarrow [\forall c \in \gamma(x); \forall c' \in \gamma(x') : c\,R\,c']. \quad (17)$$

Of course, to be an ordering, $\succsim$ must be not only complete—as it obviously is, because R is complete—but also transitive. However, transitivity of $\succsim$ follows readily from transitivity of R.

Notice that, when the agent chooses $\hat{x}$ to maximize the preference ordering $\succsim$ over X subject to a budget constraint of the form $px \leq m$, this implies that $c = \gamma(\hat{x})$ maximizes R over C subject to the constraint $pc \leq m + p\hat{y}$, where $\hat{y}$ is any net output vector that maximizes (net) profits py subject to $y \in Y$. So preference maximization by the agent implies profit maximization.

An immediate implication of our assumptions regarding R is that the preference ordering $\succsim$ constructed above and the corresponding strict preference relation $>$ must satisfy the following lemma.

LEMMA. There is a (complete and transitive) preference ordering $\succsim$ on the feasible set X which is monotone and satisfies the following conditions:
  (i) For every $x' \in X$, the upper contour set $\{x \in X \mid x \succsim x'\}$ is closed.
  (ii) $x > x'$ whenever $x \in X^S$ and $x' \in X^N$.

Note how it is *not* claimed that the lower contour set $\{x \in X \mid x' \succsim x\}$ is closed for all $x' \in X$. Indeed, this is generally not true.

The typical agent is therefore characterized by the non-convex but closed consumption set C, the closed production set Y, and the continuous preference ordering R on C. Thus, the space Θ of agents' characteristics will consist of triples (C, Y, R) satisfying Assumptions A1 and A2, and this will be given the closed convergence topology for continuous preferences that is described in Hildenbrand (1974, p. 96). Note that, because the corresponding preference ordering $\succsim$ for net trade vectors is not continuous in general, the closed convergence topology cannot be applied to the space consisting only of pairs $(X, \succsim)$. Write $\mathcal{B}(\Theta)$ for the family of Borel measurable sets in Θ with its topology of closed convergence.

3.3. A Continuum Economy

Following Aumann (1964, 1966) and Hildenbrand (1974), assume that there is a non-atomic measure space of agents $(A, \mathcal{A}, \alpha)$. Then a *continuum economy* is a mapping $E : A \to \Theta$ which is measurable with respect to the two σ-algebras $\mathcal{A}$ and $\mathcal{B}(\Theta)$—i.e. $E^{-1}(H) \in \mathcal{A}$ for every measurable set $H \in \mathcal{B}(\Theta)$. For every $a \in \mathcal{A}$, write the feasible set and preferences for net trades associated with a's characteristic $E(a)$ as $(X_a, \succsim_a)$. Because each such characteristic must satisfy Assumption A1, in particular there exists a lower bound $\underline{x}_a$ to X_a. We make the following assumption.

ASSUMPTION A3. The vector function $\underline{x} : A \to \mathcal{R}^{G+1}$ is measurable and the integral $\int \underline{x}$ over A is finite.

An *allocation* of net trade vectors in the economy E is a measurable mapping $f : A \to \mathcal{R}^{G+1}$ such that $f(a) \in X_a$ a.e. and $\int f \leq 0$.

Define the modified price simplex

$$\Delta := \{ p \in \mathcal{R}^{G+1} \mid p_0 = 0; \ p_g \geq 0 \, (g = 1, 2, \dots, G); \text{ and } \sum_{g=1}^{G} p_g = 1 \} \quad (18)$$

with relative interior

$$\Delta^0 := \{ p \in \mathcal{R}^{G+1} \mid p_0 = 0; \ p_g > 0 \, (g = 1, 2, \dots, G); \text{ and } \sum_{g=1}^{G} p_g = 1 \}. \quad (19)$$

As explained above, the price of life is taken to be zero—the right to live cannot be bought or sold, even though some agents may not be able to afford the commodities they need in order to ensure their own survival.

For each agent $a \in A$ and price vector $p \in \Delta$, define:

1. the *budget set* $B_a(p) := \{ x \in X_a \mid px \leq 0 \}$;
2. the *demand set* $\xi_a(p) := \{ x \in B_a(p) \mid x' >_a x \Rightarrow px' > 0 \}$;
3. the *compensated demand set* (Arrow and Hahn 1971):

$$\xi_a^C(p) := \{ x \in B_a(p) \mid x' \succsim_a x \Rightarrow px' \geq 0 \},$$

   which Hildenbrand (1968) had earlier called the 'expenditure-minimizing' set;
4. the *weak demand set* (Khan and Yamazaki 1981):

$$\xi_a^W(p) := \{ x \in B_a(p) \mid x' >_a x \Rightarrow px' \geq 0 \}.$$

Note that $\xi_a(p) \cup \xi_a^C(p) \subset \xi_a^W(p)$ always, trivially. Because of locally non-satiated preferences, it is easy to see that $\xi_a(p) \subset \xi_a^C(p) = \xi_a^W(p)$ for all $p > 0$. In addition, because $0 \in X_a$, $B_a(p) \neq \emptyset$ always. Because X_a is bounded below, $B_a(p)$ is compact whenever $p \in \Delta^0$. Because the upper contour sets of $\succsim$ are closed, it follows that $\emptyset \neq \xi_a(p)$ whenever $p \in \Delta^0$.

A *Walrasian equilibrium* (f, p) is an allocation f of net trade vectors, together with a price vector $p \in \Delta$ satisfying $f(a) \in \xi_a(p)$ a.e. in A and

$\int pf = 0$. Because $p > 0$ and $\int f \leqq 0$ for an allocation, it follows from this definition that, for all $g \in \{0\} \cup G$, one has both $\int f_g \leqq 0$ and also $p_g = 0$ whenever $\int f_g < 0$—the usual 'rule of free goods'.

To show that a Walrasian equilibrium exists, it will be convenient to prove first the existence of a *compensated equilibrium* (f, p) consisting of an allocation f and a price vector $p \in \Delta$ such that $f(a) \in \xi_a^C(p)$ a.e. in A and $\int pf = 0$ (Arrow and Hahn 1971). As with Walrasian equilibrium, the rule of free goods must be satisfied.

An allocation f is *Pareto-efficient* if there is no other (feasible) allocation f' such that $f'(a) >_a f(a)$ a.e. in A. An allocation f is in the *core* if there is no measurable *blocking coalition* K with an alternative allocation $f': K \to \mathscr{R}^{G+1}$ such that

$$\text{(i)} \ f'(a) >_a f(a) \text{ a.e. in } K; \quad \text{(ii)} \ \int_K f' \leqq 0; \quad \text{(iii)} \ \alpha(K) > 0. \tag{20}$$

The following two results are standard because Assumptions A1 and A2 together guarantee that consumers have locally non-satiated preferences.

FIRST EFFICIENCY THEOREM. If (f, p) is a Walrasian equilibrium, then the allocation f is Pareto-efficient.

FIRST CORE THEOREM. If (f, p) is a Walrasian equilibrium, then f is in the core.

Because of the Walrasian equilibria without survival which were exhibited in Section 2, these trivial results already establish that Pareto efficiency by no means guarantees survival of all agents. Nor can non-survivors necessarily block an allocation in order to bring about their own survival.

It is much less trivial to prove the other three promised results:

1. existence of a Walrasian equilibrium;
2. the second efficiency theorem: any Pareto efficient allocation is Walrasian after suitable lump-sum taxes and transfers have been made;
3. core equivalence: not only is every Walrasian allocation in the core, as in (2), but also, every core allocation is Walrasian for some price vector.

Indeed, Sections 3.9 and 3.10 below introduce extra assumptions in order to ensure that a compensated equilibrium is actually a Walrasian equilibrium. Moreover, because of our insistence that $p_0 = 0$—that life should be a free good—not even standard proofs for economies with indivisible goods can be applied without a few minor changes.

3.4 Continuity of Compensated Demand

A proof of existence of compensated equilibrium in somewhat different economies with non-convex consumption sets has been provided by Khan and Yamazaki (1981, Proof of Prop. 2, pp. 223–4). However they actually prove existence of 'weakly competitive allocations', which are not the same because they do not assume local non-satiation of preferences. Also, they do not normalize agents' endowments to zero as we would do in a pure exchange economy. Their proof in turn relies heavily on the work of Hildenbrand (1974) as amplified by Debreu (1982).

A key part of the existence proof relies on the continuity result below, which is of some general interest that goes beyond the specific model being considered here. The lemma concerns the continuity properties of the typical agent's profit function $\pi(Y, p)$, and of the net output, compensated consumption demand, and compensated net trade demand correspondences $\eta(Y, p)$, and $\zeta(C, R, p, m)$, and $\xi(C, Y, R, p)$, respectively. These are defined for every consumption set C, production set Y, and preference ordering R that satisfies Assumptions A1 and A2 above, as well as for every price vector $p \in \Delta^0$ and income level m, as follows:

$$\left.\begin{array}{l} \pi(Y, p) := \max \\[4pt] \eta(Y, p) := \arg\max \end{array}\right\} \{py \mid y \in Y\}; \tag{21}$$

$$\zeta(C, R, p, m) := \{c \in C \mid pc \leqslant m \quad \text{and} \quad [c' \in C, c' R c \Rightarrow pc' \geqslant m]\};$$

$$\xi(C, Y, R, p) := \zeta(C, R, p, \pi(Y, p)) - \eta(Y, p). \tag{22}$$

Note how each agent does choose $y \in \eta(Y, p)$, and so faces the budget constraint $pc \leqslant \pi(Y, p)$, because there are no direct preferences over production.

LEMMA. Under Assumptions A1 and A2, the profit function $\pi(Y, p)$ is continuous when the space $\Theta \times \Delta$ is given its product topology, and the three correspondences $\eta(Y, p)$, $\zeta(C, R, p, m)$, and $\xi(C, Y, R, p)$ all have closed graphs relative to the appropriate spaces $\Theta \times \Delta \times \mathcal{R}^{G+1}$ or $\Theta \times \Delta \times \mathcal{R} \times \mathcal{R}^{G+1}$ when each is given its appropriate product topology, and when Θ is given its topology of closed convergence.

Proof. (i) *Continuity of profit and of supply.* Let $(Y^\nu, p^\nu, y^\nu)(\nu = 1, 2,...)$ be any infinite sequence of points in the graph of $\eta(Y, p)$ which converges to $(\bar{Y}, \bar{p}, \bar{y})$ as $\nu \to \infty$. Then $\pi(Y^\nu, p^\nu) = p^\nu y^\nu \to \bar{p}\bar{y}$. Also, because $y^\nu \in Y^\nu \to \bar{Y}$ in the closed convergence topology, so $\bar{y} \in \bar{Y}$.

Now, for any $y = (y_0, y^G) \in \bar{Y}$, consider any other $\underline{y} = (\underline{y}_0, \underline{y}^G) \in \mathcal{R}^{G+1}$ such that $\underline{y}_0 = y_0 = 0$ and $\underline{y}^G \ll y^G$. Because $Y^\nu \to \bar{Y}$ as $\nu \to \infty$, for each large enough ν there must exist $\bar{y}^\nu = (\bar{y}_0^\nu, \bar{y}^{\nu G}) \in Y^\nu$ such that $\bar{y}_0^\nu = y_0 = 0$ and $\tilde{y}^{\nu G} \gg \underline{y}^G$. Since each $p^\nu > 0$, it follows from profit maximization that

$$p^\nu y^\nu = \pi(Y^\nu, p^\nu) \geqslant p^\nu \tilde{y}^\nu \geqslant p^\nu \underline{y} \to \bar{p}\underline{y}$$

as $\nu \to \infty$. Since $p^\nu y^\nu \to \bar{p}\bar{y}$ as $\nu \to \infty$, it follows that $\bar{p}\bar{y} \geqslant \bar{p}\underline{y}$ whenever $\underline{y}_0 = y_0 = 0$ and $\underline{y}^G \ll y^G$. Therefore $\bar{p}\bar{y} \geqslant \bar{p}y$. Since this is true for all

$y \in \bar{Y}$, and since $\bar{y} \in \bar{Y}$, it must be true that: (*a*) $\bar{y} \in \eta(\bar{Y}, \bar{p})$; (*b*) $\pi(\bar{Y}, \bar{p}) = \bar{p}\bar{y}$. From (*a*) it follows directly that $\eta(Y, p)$ has a closed graph. From (*b*), on the other hand, since $p^{\nu} y^{\nu} \to \bar{p}\bar{y}$ as $\nu \to \infty$, it follows that $\pi(Y^{\nu}, p^{\nu}) \to \pi(\bar{Y}, \bar{p})$. So $\pi(Y, p)$ is a continuous function.

(ii) *Continuity of compensated consumption demand.* Let $(C^{\nu}, R^{\nu}, p^{\nu}, m^{\nu}, c^{\nu})(\nu = 1, 2, \ldots)$ be any infinite sequence of points in the graph of $\zeta(C, R, p, m)$ which converges to $(\bar{C}, \bar{R}, \bar{p}, \bar{m}, \bar{c})$ as $\nu \to \infty$. Then $p^{\nu} c^{\nu} \leqslant m^{\nu}$ and $c^{\nu} \in C^{\nu}$ for $\nu = 1, 2, \ldots$, so that in the limit as $\nu \to \infty$ one has $\bar{p}\bar{c} \leqslant \bar{m}$ and also $\bar{c} \in \bar{C}$.

Suppose that $c \in \bar{C}$ with $c P \bar{c}$. Because preferences are continuous and monotone in all goods except 0, and because Assumption A1 is satisfied, there exists $z = (z_0, z^G) \in \mathcal{R}^{G+1}$ with $z_0 = \bar{c}_0$ and $z^G \gg \bar{c}^G$ such that $c P z$. Also, for all large enough ν one must have $z_0 = c_0^{\nu}$ and $z^G \gg c^{\nu G}$, implying that $z \in C^{\nu}$ with $z P^{\nu} c^{\nu}$.

Now let $w = (w_0, w^G) \in \mathcal{R}^{G+1}$ satisfy $w_0 = c_0$ and $w^G \gg c^G$. Then, since $c \in \bar{C}$ while $C^{\nu} \to \bar{C}$ as $\nu \to \infty$, free disposal implies that $w \in C^{\nu}$ for all large enough ν. Also, monotone preferences imply that $w P c$. Because we have already shown that $c P z$, transitive preferences imply that $w P z$. Thus (z, w) does not lie in the graph of the relation R, and so there must be an infinite sequence of values of ν for which (z, w) does not lie in the graph of R^{ν} either. But then, since $w, z \in C^{\nu}$ for all large enough ν, there must be infinitely many values of ν for which $w P^{\nu} z$ and so $w P^{\nu} z P^{\nu} c^{\nu}$. By transitivity of P^{ν}, it follows that $w P^{\nu} c^{\nu}$ for all these values of ν. Since $c^{\nu} \in \zeta(C^{\nu}, R^{\nu}, p^{\nu}, m^{\nu})$ for $\nu = 1, 2, \ldots$, this implies that $p^{\nu} w \geqslant p^{\nu} c^{\nu} = m^{\nu}$ for infinitely many ν. But $p^{\nu} \to \bar{p}$ and $m^{\nu} \to \bar{m}$ as $\nu \to \infty$, so $\bar{p} w \geqslant \bar{m}$. Since this is true whenever $w_0 = c_0$ and $w^G \gg c^G$, it follows that $\bar{p} c \geqslant \bar{m}$.

So we have proved that $c P \bar{c}$ implies $\bar{p} c \geqslant \bar{m}$. Because preferences are monotone and so locally non-satiated, it follows that $c R \bar{c}$ implies $\bar{p} c \geqslant \bar{m}$. This confirms that $\bar{c} \in \zeta(\bar{C}, \bar{R}, \bar{p}, \bar{m})$, as required for the compensated demand correspondence $\zeta(C, R, p, m)$ to have a closed graph.

(iii) *Continuity of compensated net trade demand.* Finally, let $(C^{\nu}, Y^{\nu}, R^{\nu}, p^{\nu}, x^{\nu})(\nu = 1, 2, \ldots)$ be any infinite sequence of points in the graph of $\zeta(C, Y, R, p)$ which converges to $(\bar{C}, \bar{Y}, \bar{R}, \bar{p}, \bar{x})$ as $\nu \to \infty$. By definition of ξ, there exist sequences $c^{\nu} \in \zeta(C^{\nu}, R^{\nu}, p^{\nu}, \pi(Y^{\nu}, p^{\nu}))$ and $y^{\nu} \in \eta(Y^{\nu}, p^{\nu}) \subset Y^{\nu}$ such that $x^{\nu} = c^{\nu} - y^{\nu}(\nu = 1, 2, \ldots)$.

Now, as $\nu \to \infty$, so $Y^{\nu} \to \bar{Y}$ and $C^{\nu} \to \bar{C}$ in the topology of closed convergence. But $\bar{Y}$ is bounded above, while $\bar{C}$ is bounded below, so the two sequences $y^{\nu} \in Y^{\nu}$ and $c^{\nu} \in C^{\nu}$ must be bounded above and below, respectively. Yet then y^{ν} is also bounded below, because $y^{\nu} = c^{\nu} - x^{\nu}$ and $x^{\nu} \to \bar{x}$ as $\nu \to \infty$. Therefore y^{ν} is actually bounded both above and below, and so must have a convergent subsequence with a limit point $\bar{y} \in \bar{Y}$. But then, since $x^{\nu} \to \bar{x}$ as $\nu \to \infty$, the corresponding subsequence of c^{ν} must also have a limit point $\bar{c} \in \bar{C}$ given by $\bar{c} := \bar{x} + \bar{y}$.

Because of the continuity properties of $\pi(Y, p)$, $\eta(Y, p)$, and $\zeta(C, R, p, m)$ which have just been proved in parts (i) and (ii) above, it now follows that $\bar{y} \in \eta(\bar{Y}, \bar{p})$, that $\pi(\bar{Y}, \bar{p}) = \bar{p}\bar{y}$, and also that $\bar{c} \in \zeta(\bar{C}, \bar{R}, \bar{p}, \pi(\bar{Y}, \bar{p}))$. Therefore

$$\bar{x} = \bar{c} - \bar{y} \in \zeta(\bar{C}, \bar{R}, \bar{p}, \pi(\bar{Y}, \bar{p})) - \eta(\bar{Y}, \bar{p}) = \xi(\bar{C}, \bar{Y}, \bar{R}, \bar{p}),$$

thus confirming that $\xi(C, Y, R, p)$ does have a closed graph. ∎

3.5   Existence of Compensated Equilibrium

THEOREM.   Under Assumptions A1–A3 there exists a compensated equilibrium.

Proof. From the continuity result of Section 3.4, it follows that the correspondence $\hat{\xi} : A \to \mathcal{R}^G$ defined by $\hat{\xi}(a) := \xi(E(a), p)$ has a measurable graph because, by hypothesis, E is a measurable function, and because ξ has a closed and so a measurable graph (Hildenbrand 1974, p. 59, prop. 1(b)). Moreover, for each positive integer $k \geqslant G$ the budget correspondence $B_a(p)$ is integrably bounded on the restricted domain $A \times \Delta_k$, where

$$\Delta_k := \{p \in \Delta \mid \forall g \in G : p_g \geqslant 1/k\}. \tag{23}$$

So the mean compensated demand correspondence $\beta_k : \Delta_k \twoheadrightarrow \mathcal{R}^{G+1}$ defined by $\beta_k(p) := \int_A \xi_a^C(p)\, d\alpha$ has all the relevant properties of Khan and Yamazaki's (1981, p. 223) mapping $F_k(p)$—in particular, it has non-empty, compact, and convex values, a closed graph, and the range $\beta_k(\Delta_k)$ is also compact. As a result, for each $k = G, G+1, G+2,\ldots$, the correspondence $\psi_k : \Delta_k \times \beta_k(\Delta_k) \twoheadrightarrow \Delta_k \times \beta_k(\Delta_k)$, that is defined throughout its domain by

$$\psi_k(p, z) := \arg_{\tilde{p}} \max \{\tilde{p}z \mid \tilde{p} \in \Delta_k\} \times \beta_k(p),$$

has a fixed point $(p_k, z_k) \in \psi_k(p_k, z_k)$. So there exist infinite sequences of price vectors $p_k \in \Delta_k$, quantity vectors $z_k \in \mathcal{R}^{G+1}$, and integrably bounded measurable mappings $f_k : A \to \mathcal{R}^{G+1}(k = G, G+1, G+2,\ldots)$ such that: (i) $f_k(a) \in \xi_a^C(p_k)$ a.e. in A; (ii) $z_k = \int f_k$; (iii) $pz_k \leqslant 0 \; \forall \; p \in \Delta_k$. But then $z_k \geqq \int \underline{x}$. Also, because $(1/G)(1, 1,\ldots, 1) \in \Delta_k$, (iii) above implies that $\Sigma_{g \in G} z_{kg} \leqslant 0$ for all $k \geqslant G$. So the sequence of fixed points (p_k, z_k) always lies in the compact set $\Delta \times Z$, where

$$Z := \{z \in \mathcal{R}^{G+1} \mid z \geqq \int \underline{x} \quad \text{and} \quad \Sigma_{g \in G} z_g \leqslant 0\}.$$

Hence there must exist some subsequence of $(p_k, z_k)(k = G, G+1, G+2,\ldots)$ which converges to a limit point $(p^*, z^* \in \Delta \times Z$. Moreover, Fatou's Lemma in many dimensions (see e.g. Hildenbrand 1974, p. 69) can now be applied to show that there exists a subsequence $k(m)(m = 1, 2,\ldots)$

of $k = G, G + 1, G + 2, \ldots$, together with some $p \in \Delta$ and some measurable function $f : A \to \mathscr{R}^{G+1}$, such that: (iv) $\int f \leqq z*$; and also, as $m \to \infty$, (v) $p_{k(m)} \to p^*$; (vi) $\int f_{k(m)} = z_{k(m)} z^*$; (vii) $f_{k(m)}(a) \to f(a)$ a.e. in A.

Now, for any positive integers m and r such that $k(m) \geq r$, (iii) implies that $p \int f_{k(m)} \leq 0$ for all $p \in \Delta_r \subset \Delta_{k(m)}$. Because of (vi), taking the limit as $m \to \infty$ gives $pz^* \leq 0$ for all $p \in \Delta_r$. Since this is true for any positive integer r, one has $pz^* \leq 0$ for all $p \in \Delta^0 = \cup_{r=1}^\infty \Delta_r$. But $p_0 = 0$, and so $p^G z^{*G} \leq 0$ for all $p^G \geqslant 0$ satisfying $\Sigma_{g \in G} p_g = 1$. Hence $z^{*G} \leqq 0$. Moreover, since nobody can ever have a positive demand for good 0 and so $z_0^* \leq 0$, it follows that $z^* \leqq 0$—and so, by (iv) above, that $\int f \leqq 0$.

Finally, since (i) implies that $f_{k(m)}(a) \in \xi_a^C(p_{k(m)})$ a.e. in A, and since (v) and (vii) above are both true, the closed-graph property of the compensated demand correspondence implies that $f(a) \in \xi_a^C(p^*)$ a.e. in A. So (f, p^*) together form a compensated equilibrium. ∎

3.6 Core Allocations are Compensated Equilibria

THEOREM. *Under Assumptions A1 and A2 above, any core allocation is a compensated equilibrium.*

Proof. Let $f : A \to \mathscr{R}^{G+1}$ be any (measurable) allocation in the core. Now define the four correspondences

$$\phi^N(a) := \{b \in \mathscr{R}^G \mid (-1, b) \in X_a \quad \text{and} \quad (-1, b) >_a f(a)\}$$

$$\phi^S(a) := \{b \in \mathscr{R}^G \mid (0, b) \in X_a \quad \text{and} \quad (0, b) >_a f(a)\}$$

$$\phi(a) := \phi^N(a) \cup \phi^S(a) \tag{24}$$

$$= \{x^G \in \mathscr{R}^G \mid \exists\, x_0 \in \{-1, 0\} : (x_0, x^G) \in X_a \quad \text{and} \quad (x_0, x^G) >_a f(a)\}$$

$$\psi(a) := \phi(a) \cup \{0\}$$

on the common domain A, and for the common range space $\mathscr{R}^G$. Arguing as in Hildenbrand (1974, pp. 133–5), it follows that the two correspondences $\phi^N(a)$ and $\phi^S(a)$ both have measurable graphs in $A \times \mathscr{R}^G$. So therefore does the correspondence ψ, since its graph is the union of the measurable graphs of the correspondences $\phi^N(a)$ and $\phi^S(a)$ with the measurable set $A \times \{0\}$. Also, $\int \psi d\alpha$ is a convex subset of $\mathscr{R}^G$ including 0.

Suppose it were true that $z \in \int \psi d\alpha$ for some $z \in \mathscr{R}^G$ such that $z \ll 0$. Then there must be a measurable set $K \subset A$ for which $z \in \int_K \phi(a) d\alpha$, and so K must be a blocking coalition. Hence, if f is indeed in the core, the two convex sets $\int \psi d\alpha$ and $\{z \in \mathscr{R}^G \mid z \ll 0\}$ must be non-empty and disjoint. So they can be separated by a hyperplane $p^G z = 0$ through the origin with $p^G > 0$ and $\Sigma_{g \in G} p_g + 1$. Thus, $p^G z \geqslant 0$ whenever $z \in \int \psi d\alpha$. Let $p := (0, p^G) \in \Delta$ be the corresponding $G + 1$-dimensional price vector in which life is given a price of zero. Then, a.e. in A, it must be true that

$x >_a f(a)$ implies $px \geq 0$. In particular, a.e. in A, $px \geq 0$ whenever $x^G \geq f^G(a)$. Then, because $f^G(a)$ is the limit of an infinite sequence $(x^{\vee G})$ of points satisfying $x^{\vee G} \gg f^G(a)$, it follows that, a.e. in A, $p f(a) \geq 0$. Yet $p > 0$ and so, since feasibility implies that $\int f \leq 0$, it must be true that $\int pf \leq 0$. Now the last two sentences will contradict each other unless $\int p f = 0$, and in fact $p f(a) = 0$ a.e. in A. Therefore (f, p) is a compensated equilibrium. ∎

3.7 Pareto-Efficient Allocations are Compensated Competitive

THEOREM. Under Assumptions A1 and A2 above, any Pareto-efficient allocation $f : A \to \mathscr{R}^{G+1}$ is a compensated equilibrium at some price vector $p \in \Delta$ when each consumer $a \in A$ receives the net lump-sum transfer $p f(a)$.

Proof. The separation argument used in Section 3.6 above can be easily be adapted as follows. Indeed, $\int \phi d\alpha$ and $\{z \in \mathscr{R}^G \mid z \ll 0\}$ are non-empty convex sets which must be disjoint if f is a Pareto-efficient allocation. Now we can follow the argument of Hildenbrand (1974, p. 232) in order to show the existence of a normalized price vector $p^G > 0$ such that $p^G \int f^G = 0$, and also, a.e. in A, $x^G \in \phi(a)$ implies $p^G x^G \geq p^G f^G(a)$. But then, if we let $p := (0, p^G) \in \Delta$, it follows that $p \int f = 0$; and also, a.e. in A, $x >_a f(a)$ implies $px \geq pf(a)$. ∎

3.8 The Cheaper Point Lemma

LEMMA. Suppose that (C, Y, R) satisfy Assumptions A1 and A2 above, while $(X, \succsim)$ are derived as in Sections 3.1 and 3.2. Suppose that $\hat{x} \in X$ is such that, for all $x \in X$, one has $px \geq p\hat{x}$, whenever $x \succsim \hat{x}$. Then:
  (a) If $\hat{x} \in X^S$ and there also exists $x^* \in X^S$ for which $px^* < p\hat{x}$, then for all $x \in X$ one has $px > p\hat{x}$ whenever $x > \hat{x}$.
  (b) If $\hat{x} \in X^N$ and there also exists $x^* \in X^N$ for which $px^* < p\hat{x}$, then for all $x \in X^N$ one has $px > p\hat{x}$ whenever $x > \hat{x}$.

Proof. Under the hypothesis of the lemma, there must exist $\hat{c} \in C$ and $\hat{y} \in Y$ such that $\hat{x} = \hat{c} - \hat{y}$ while $cR\hat{c} \Rightarrow px \geq p\hat{c}$ and $y \in Y \Rightarrow py \leq p\hat{y}$. Now:

  Case (a): $\hat{c} \in \tilde{C}^S$. In this case there must also exist $c^* \in \tilde{C}^S$ and $y^* \in Y$ for which $x^* = c^* - y^*$ and $px^* < p\hat{x}$. Then $py^* \leq p\hat{y}$ and so $pc^* = px^* + py^* < p\hat{x} + p\hat{y} = p\hat{c}$. By a standard argument for the convex consumption set C^S and the continuous preference ordering R, it now follows that, whenever $c \in \tilde{C}^S$ with $cP\hat{c}$, then $pc > p\hat{c}$. Hence, if $x \in X$ with $x > \hat{x}$, so that there exist $c \in \tilde{C}^S$ and $y \in Y$ for which $x = c - y$ and $cP\hat{c}$, then $p\hat{y} \geq py$ and so

$$px + py = pc > p\hat{c} = p\hat{x} + p\hat{y} \geq p\hat{x} + py.$$

Therefore $px > p\hat{x}$, as required for the lemma to be true.

Case (b): $\hat{c} \in \tilde{C}^N$. As in the proof of Case (a) above, here there must exist $c^* \in \tilde{C}^N$ such that $pc^* < p\hat{c}$. Once again, by a standard argument applied to the convex consumption set $\tilde{C}^N$ and the continuous preference ordering R, it follows that, whenever $c \in \tilde{C}^N$ with $cP\hat{c}$, then $pc > p\hat{c}$. Hence, if $x \in X^N$ with $x > \hat{x}$, so that there exist $c \in \tilde{C}^N$ and $y \in Y$ for which $x = c - y$ and $cP\hat{c}$, then $px > p\hat{x}$ as in case (a). ∎

3.9. Conditions for Compensated Equilibria to be Walrasian

First we make the following assumption.

> ASSUMPTION A4. 0 is in the interior of the projection of the set $\int_A X_a \alpha(da)$ onto the subspace $\mathcal{R}^G$.

Effectively, A4 requires that some trade is possible in every direction of the physical commodity space $\mathcal{R}^G$, thereby ruling out the 'exceptional case' presented by Arrow (1951).

The irreducibility assumption due to McKenzie (1959, 1961, 1981, 1987) has been adapted by Hildenbrand (1972; 1974, p. 143, prob. 8) for a continuum economy. We next generalize Hildenbrand's version of this assumption somewhat, along the lines discussed in Hammond (1993). There too rather more motivation is provided, along with a further weakening. Here we assume the following.

> ASSUMPTION A5. For every allocation f and every measurable partition of A into two sets A_1 and A_2 of positive measure, there exist measurable functions $t : A \to \mathcal{R}^{G+1}$, $y : A_2 \to \mathcal{R}^{G+1}$, and a set $A^* \subset A_1$ whose measure is positive, such that: (i) $\int_A t d\alpha + \int_{A_2} y d\alpha \leq 0$; (ii) $y(a) \in X_a$ a.e. in A_2; (iii) $t(a) \succsim_a f(a)$ a.e. in A; (iv) $t(a) \succ_a f(a)$ a.e. in A^*.

Thus, A5 requires that there exist balanced net trades $t(a)(a \in A)$ and $y(a)(a \in A_2)$ which, if there were duplicates of the agents $a \in A_2$ who could be required to provide the net supply vectors $- y(a)$, would make possible a Pareto improvement with every agent $a \in A$ having the new net trade vector t(a), and with a non-null set A^* of agents $a \in A_1$ becoming strictly better off.

For the usual reasons, A4 and A5, when combined with the earlier Assumptions A1 and A2, will together ensure that, at any compensated equilibrium price vector $p \in \Delta$, almost all agents a can afford a net trade vector $x \in X_a$ with positive value $px > 0$. However, there may still be a non-negligible set of agents on the margin of survival who create a discontinuity in mean demand and prevent the existence of a Walrasian equilibrium. For every price vector $p \in \Delta$ and every income level m, it is agents in the set

$$A(p, m) := \{a \in A \mid \exists\, x \in X_a^S : px = m \quad \text{and} \quad \forall x' \in X_a^S \{: px' \geq m\} \quad (25)$$

who are on the margin of survival when faced with the budget constraint $px \leq m$. If $a \in A(p, m)$, then in fact m can be regarded as a's minimum subsistence expenditure, because it must be equal to $\min_x \{px \mid x \in X_a^S\}$.

The following assumption is more than sufficient for our purposes.

ASSUMPTION A6*. For every $p > 0$ and $m \in \mathcal{R}$, one has $\alpha(A(p, m)) = 0$.

This is a 'dispersed needs' version of Yamazaki's (1981) 'dispersed endowments' assumption. It states that there can be no atoms in the distribution of subsistence expenditures at any given price vector $p > 0$. An obvious implication of A6* is the following much weaker assumption.

ASSUMPTION A6. For every $p > 0$, one has $\alpha(A(p, 0)) = 0$.

The three extra Assumptions A4–A6 will combine with A1 and A2 to ensure that any compensated equilibrium is Walrasian. Indeed, given the compensated equilibrium (f, p), define the two sets of agents

$$A' := \{a \in A \mid \exists\, x \in X_a : px < 0\}; \qquad \overline{A} := A(p, 0). \quad (26)$$

The set $\overline{A}$ consists of those agents whose budget constraint $px \leq 0$ leaves them on the margin of survival. By a standard argument, Assumption A4 implies that A' has positive measure; otherwise it would be true that $p \int x_a d\alpha \geq 0$ whenever $x_a \in X_a$ for a.e. $a \in A$. Now we make use of the following two lemmas.

LEMMA A. Let (f, p) be a compensated equilibrium in an economy satisfying Assumptions A1, A2, and A4–A6, and let a be any agent in the set $A' \setminus \overline{A}$. Then $x >_a f(a)$ implies $px > 0$, and so $f(a) \in \xi_a(p)$.

Proof. There are two different cases to consider.

Case S: $f(a) \in X_a^S$. Then $\tilde{x} = f(a)$ is a member of X_a^S satisfying $p\tilde{x} = 0$. Since $a \notin \overline{A}$, there must exist $x^* \in X_a^S$ such that $px^* < 0$. But $x >_a f(a)$ is only possible in this case if $x \in X_a^S$.

Case N: $f(a) \in X_a^N$. In this case $x \in X_a^S$ implies that $x >_a f(a)$ and so $px \geq 0$. Since $a \notin \overline{A}$, there can be no $x \in X_a^S$ for which $px = 0$. Hence $x \in X_a^S$ implies $px > 0$. So we need only consider the case when $x \in X_a^N$. Yet by hypothesis $a \in A'$ and so there exists $x^* \in X_a$ such that $px^* < 0$. Of course, this cheaper point must satisfy $x^* \in X_a^N$ because we have already seen that $x^* \in X_a^S$ would imply that $px^* > 0$.

Now note that because preferences are monotone and (f, p) is a compensated equilibrium, $p f(a) = 0$ a.e. in A. Let $x \in X_a$ be any feasible net trade vector satisfying $x >_a f(a)$. In either case S or N, the Cheaper Point Lemma of Section 3.8 can then be applied to show that $px > p f(a) = 0$. ■

LEMMA B. Under Assumptions A1, A2, and A4–A6, any compensated equilibrium (f, p) is a Walrasian equilibrium.

Proof. Suppose that (f, p) is a compensated equilibrium for which Assumptions A1, A2, A4, and A5 are all satisfied. Let $A_2 := A \backslash A'$ and $A_1 := A'$. By Assumption A4, it must be true that $\alpha(A_1) > 0$.

Suppose also that $\alpha(A_2) > 0$. Then Assumption A5 implies that there exist mappings $t : A \to \mathcal{R}^{G+1}$, $y : A_2 \to \mathcal{R}^{G+1}$, and a set $A^* \subset A_1$ such that: (i) $\alpha(A^*) > 0$; (ii) $\int_A t \, d\alpha + \int_{A_2} y \, d\alpha \leq 0$; (iii) $y(a) \in X_a$ a.e. in $A_2 = A \backslash A'$; (iv) $t(a) \gtrsim_a f(a)$ a.e. in A; and (v) $t(a) >_a f(a)$ a.e. in A^*. Then, since $p > 0$ it follows from (ii), (iii), and the definitions of A_2, A' that

$$\int_A p t \, d\alpha \leq - \int_{A_2} p y \, d\alpha \leq 0.$$

But (iv) implies that $pt(a) \geq p f(a) = 0$ a.e. in A, and so the above inequality can be true only if $pt(a) = 0$ a.e. in A. Now, together with the above lemma, (v) clearly implies that $A^* \subset A \backslash (A' \backslash \bar{A})$. Yet $A^* \subset A_1 = A'$, and so

$$A^* \subset A' \cap [A \backslash (A' \backslash \bar{A})] = A' \cap [A' \backslash (A' \backslash \bar{A})] = A' \cap \bar{A} \subset \bar{A}.$$

Since $\alpha(A^*) > 0$ by (i) above, this implies that $\alpha(\bar{A}) > 0$. This contradicts Assumption A6, however.

So all three assumptions (A4–A6) can be satisfied only if $\alpha(A_2) = \alpha(A \backslash A') = 0$. Because $\alpha(\bar{A}) = 0$, this clearly implies that the set $A \backslash (A' \backslash \bar{A})$ must also have zero measure. Hence (f, p) must in fact be a Walrasian equilibrium, because of Lemma A above. ■

Combined with our earlier results in Sections 3.5 and 3.6, we now have the following theorems.

EXISTENCE THEOREM. Under Assumptions A1–A6, there exists a Walrasian equilibrium.

CORE EQUIVALENCE THEOREM. Under Assumptions A1–A6, the core coincides with the set of Walrasian equilibrium allocations.

3.10. Second Efficiency Theorem

Here we give sufficient conditions for a particular Pareto-efficient allocation to be competitive, in the sense that there exists a price vector $p > 0$ such that $p \int f \, d\alpha = 0$ and, a.e. in A, $x >_a f(a)$ implies $px > p f(a)$. Then f could be decentralized by facing each agent $a \in A$ with the budget constraint $px \leq p f(a)$, each agent receiving a net lump-sum transfer equal to $p f(a)$.

We have already shown in Section 3.7 that a Pareto-efficient allocation is compensated competitive at some price vector $p > 0$ with $p_0 = 0$. To show that it is competitive at p, it suffices to make modified versions of Assumptions A4 and A5 above.

First, for the fixed allocation f, define the sets of survivors and of non-survivors as

$$A^S := \{a \in A \mid f(a) \in X_a^S\} \quad \text{and} \quad A^N := \{a \in A \mid f(a) \in X_a^N\}, \quad (27)$$

respectively. Then the modified version of Assumption A4 which we shall use here is as follows.

ASSUMPTION A4′. 0 belongs to the interior of the projection of the set $\int_{A^S} X_a^S \mathrm{d}\alpha + \int_{A^N} X_a \mathrm{d}\alpha$ onto the subspace $\mathcal{R}^G$.

And the modified version of Assumption A5 is the following 'non-oligarchy' condition.

ASSUMPTION A5′. For the particular allocation f and for every measurable partition of A into two sets A_1 and A_2 of positive measure, there exists a measurable function $t : A \to \mathcal{R}^{G+1}$ with $t_0(a) = 0$ (all $a \in A$) and a measurable set $A^* \subset A_1$ of positive measure, such that: (i) $\int_A t \mathrm{d}\alpha \leqq 0$; (ii) $t(a) \in X_a$ a.e. in A_2; (iii) $t(a) \in X_a^S$ a.e. in $A_2 \cap A^S$; (iv) $t(a) \gtrsim_a f(a)$ a.e. in A_1; (v) $t(a) >_a f(a)$ a.e. in A^*.

The above condition requires that there be no 'oligarchy'—i.e. no proper subset A_1 of agents who are so well off with the allocation f that collectively they could not possibly ever be made any better off even if they were given access to all the resources that the other agents in the complementary set A_2 could supply. Except for part (iii), it has been taken directly from Hammond (1993). Here part (iii) has been added because, as will be seen, it guarantees that almost no agent is on the boundary of X_a^S. For the survivors in A_2, it restricts the complementary coalition to use only those resources that can be taken without driving them below subsistence.

SECOND EFFICIENCY THEOREM. Let f be any Pareto-efficient allocation satisfying Assumptions A4′ and A5′ in an economy E satisfying Assumptions A1, A2, and A3. Then there exists a price vector $p > 0$ at which f is competitive;—i.e., a.e. in A, $x >_a f(a)$ implies $px > p f(a)$.

Proof. Define

$$\tilde{A}^S := \{a \in A^S \mid \exists\, x \in X_a^S \colon px < p f(a)\};$$
$$\tilde{A}^N := \{a \in A^N \mid \exists\, x \in X_a \colon px < p f(a)\}; \quad (28)$$
$$A' := \tilde{A}^S \cup \tilde{A}^N$$

Then, by the standard argument which we recapitulated previously, $\alpha(A') > 0$ because of Assumption A4′ and because $\int p f = 0$. Also, the

Cheaper Point Lemma of Section 3.8 shows that, a.e. in A', $x >_a f(a)$ implies $px > p f(a)$. So it suffices to show that $\alpha(A \backslash A') = 0$. To this end, note how $\alpha(A \backslash A') > 0$ would allow Assumption A5′ to be applied with $A_1 = A'$ and $A_2 = A \backslash A'$. A standard argument would then establish a contradiction, so in fact $\alpha(A \backslash A') = 0$. Hence the allocation f must indeed be competitive at prices p. ■

3.11. A Sufficient Condition for Universal Survival

Finally, we find a sufficient condition like Moore's (1975) and McKenzie's (1981, 1987) for the existence of a Walrasian equilibrium in which all agents survive. We modify the old conditions (A4 and A5) so that they become the following assumptions.

ASSUMPTION A4^S. 0 belongs to the interior of the projection of the set $\int X_a^S d\alpha$ onto the subspace $\mathcal{R}^G$.

ASSUMPTION A5^S. For every allocation f and every measurable partition of A into two sets A_1 and A_2 of positive measure, there exist measurable functions $t : A \to \mathcal{R}^{G+1}$ with $t_0(a) = 0$ (all $a \in A$), $y : A_2 \to \mathcal{R}^{G+1}$ with $y_0(a) = 0$ (all $a \in A_2$), and a measurable set $A^* \subset A_1$ of positive measure, such that: (i) $\int_A t\,d\alpha + \int_{A_2} y\,d\alpha \leqq 0$; (ii) $y(a) \in X_a^S$ a.e. in A_2; (iii) $t(a) \gtrsim_a f(a)$ a.e. in A; (iv) $t(a) >_a f(a)$ a.e. in A^*.

Now we come to the Survival Theorem.

SURVIVAL THEOREM. Let E be an economy satisfying Assumptions A1–A3, A4^S, and A5^S. Then there exists a Walrasian equilibrium, and, in any Walrasian equilibrium, almost all agents survive. The same is true of the core allocations, and the core coincides with the set of Walrasian equilibrium allocations.

Proof. Suppose that (f, p) is a compensated Walrasian equilibrium. Let

$$\overline{A}^S := \{a \in A \mid \exists\ x \in X_a^S : px < 0\}. \tag{29}$$

Then Assumption A4^S evidently implies that $\alpha(\overline{A}^S) > 0$. By a standard argument, one has $f(a) \in \xi_a(p)$ a.e. in $\overline{A}^S$. The 'survival' irreducibility assumption (A5^S) then establishes that $\alpha(A \backslash \overline{A}^S) = 0$, by another standard argument. So (f, p) must be a Walrasian equilibrium in which almost all agents in $\overline{A}^S$, and so almost all agents in A, do survive. ■

4. Conclusions and Reservations

Section 2 considered an example showing how to extend the usual Walrasian model of a competitive market economy in order to deal seriously with the issue of survival, which standard general equilibrium theory is quite unable to discuss. That example was also able to offer considerable support for the Malthusian insight that more equality in the distribution of land would help more people to survive. As Woodham-Smith has written of the Irish Famine:

All this wretchedness and misery could, almost without exception, be traced to a single source—the system under which land had come to be owned and occupied in Ireland, a system produced by centuries of successive conquests, rebellions, confiscations and punitive legislation. (Woodham-Smith 1962, p. 20)

Also, in that example a system of food subsidies financed by a tax on land, on labour, or on both was not even able to reduce starvation, much less guarantee complete survival. In another model not presented here, where labour supply is elastic, we were able to show essentially the same results, and also to conclude that redistribution permits more people to survive than a welfare programme financed by a (distortionary) income tax.

Section 3 then presented a general model of a continuum economy with individual production. With relatively minor modifications, the standard results of general equilibrium theory were shown to apply even when one takes into account the possibility that not all agents survive. The modifications were needed to deal with the inherent non-convexities in each individual's consumption set as one passes between survival and death. Existence of Walrasian equilibrium was proved without any survival assumption when there is a continuum of individuals whose needs for subsistence net trade vectors are dispersed. A Walrasian equilibrium, however, may require that some individuals do not survive. Even when it does, as happens in some of the cases presented in Section 2, such an equilibrium is still Pareto-efficient; to allow more individuals to survive, for instance, would require sacrifices from some of those who are fortunate enough to be able to survive anyway in equilibrium. And any Pareto-efficient allocation, even one without complete survival, is a Walrasian equilibrium for a suitable system of lump-sum transfers. Thus, all the classical existence and efficiency theorems apply. Core equivalence holds as well. Non-survivors lack the resources they need to block a Walrasian equilibrium and ensure their own survival. Finally, the paper presented sufficient conditions analogous to McKenzie's (1981) for survival of the whole population.

So the tragedy of starvation can arise in economies characterized by perfect competition. Then starvation is not a result of market failure. Like the involuntary unemployment that arises in Dasgupta and Ray (1986–7), it is not the result either of unnecessary institutional rigidities in the labour market. Instead, it is an entirely natural phenomenon of a neoclassical economy with surplus labour. Only after excess labour has been removed through starvation can general equilibrium arise. As Joan Robinson (1946, pp. 189) wrote, 'The hidden hand will always do its work, but it may work by strangulation.' Or, as Benjamin Jowett (formerly master of Balliol College, Oxford) was once moved to remark (according to *The White Plague*, by Frank Herbert), 'I have always felt a certain horror of political economists, since I heard one of them say that he feared the famine of 1848 would not kill more than a million people, and that would be scarcely enough to do much good.' Even then, (compensated) Walrasian equilibrium with starvation is Pareto-efficient. To allow more individuals to survive requires sacrifices from some of those who survive anyway.

The fact that both Walrasian equilibrium and Pareto efficiency do not require all to survive should really be no great surprise. If the analysis seems heartless in the face of human misery, that is a true reflection of the price mechanism in a *laissez-faire* economy which general equilibrium theory is intended to model. It also illustrates the ethical inadequacy of the Pareto criterion unless it is supplemented by further value judgements concerning the distribution of income or at least the alleviation of extreme poverty. For starvation may well be Pareto-efficient, just as maximizing the preference ordering of a dictator is. Nor do the starving have the economic power to 'block' a competitive market allocation in which they starve—they can only hope for non-market remedies, some of which were discussed in Section 2.

We have heard the view expressed that, if people really care enough about such poverty, then private charities will arise to assist the destitute. Yet such charity is effectively a public good, subject to the well-known free-rider problem, as has been discussed by Mirrlees (1973), Arrow (1981), and many others. It can also be argued that charity exploits unduly those who have a charitable disposition. While the coercion of a tax-financed welfare programme may not necessarily be the best resolution of this particular free-rider problem, more suitable alternatives have yet to be found, and the starving can hardly afford to wait for one.

This is clearly a problem for which a political economist should be able to give useful advice. Blind adherence to *laissez-faire* economic policy and neglect of distributional issues lead to starvation (cf. Rashid 1980). As Sen wrote, 'In the past, economic policies regarding food have often been ineffective, or worse, precisely because of concentrating on misleading variables, e.g. total food output, physical transport capacity. Unhappily, these mistakes are still made . . .' (1984, p. 31). Similar ideas are also discussed, of course, in Sen (1983), in Drèze and Sen (1989), and elsewhere. In our model, the right kind of government intervention, if it is possible, modifies Walrasian equilibrium to ensure complete survival. If market forces cannot be brought under control, complete survival may be impossible (cf. Hammond 1987). We hope to have helped in making more economists understand how there are almost no limits to the cruel injustices that are possible in even a 'perfect' market economy, and to encourage them to allow more 'imperfections' or 'distortions' into a market system if those are what even limited distributive justice requires.

The major limitation of our work is that we have considered only static Walrasian equilibria. Yet issues of survival are essentially dynamic. Death from malnutrition is gradual, and anyway is often indirect because it increases susceptibility to diseases which then appear to strike at random. The margin of survival, in the dynamic sense, is not so much a discrete boundary. Famine especially is inherently dynamic, as crops fail, food prices rise rapidly, and populations of whole villages leave their land in a desperate search for something to eat. A realistic dynamic model would be much more complicated, but it is our belief that it would not greatly modify or add to what the simple static model has to teach us concerning the existence and efficiency of Walrasian equilibrium without survival.

One other important question, however, certainly cannot be discussed in our static model. This is the Malthusian issue: if more of the population is enabled to survive today, does this only serve to render intolerable the increased pressure of population tomorrow? We have nothing here to add to this old and much discussed question, except for the common and hopeful observation that going beyond survival and into moderate prosperity appears to limit fertility. We believe, then, that Malthusian arguments do not provide us with any justifiable excuse for not trying to help more of the poorest in the world to survive, going beyond *laissez-faire* to do so wherever necessary.

References

Arrow, K. J. (1951), 'An Extension of the Basic Theorems of Classical Welfare Economics', in J. Neyman (ed.), *Proceedings of the Second Berkeley Symposium on Mathematical Statistics and Probability*, University of California Press, Berkeley, pp. 507–32.

—— (1981), 'Optimal and Voluntary Income Distribution', in S. Rosefielde (ed.), *Economic Welfare and the Economics of Soviet Socialism: Essays in Honor of Abram Bergson*, Cambridge University Press, pp. 267–88.

—— and Debreu, G. (1954), 'Existence of an Equilibrium for a Competitive Economy', *Econometrica*, 22: 265–90.

—— and Hahn, F. H. (1971), *General Competitive Analysis*, Holden Day, San Francisco.

Aumann, R. J. (1964), 'Markets with a Continuum of Traders', *Econometrica*, 32: 39–50.

—— (1966), 'Existence of Competitive Equilibria in Markets with a Continuum of Traders', *Econometrica*, 36: 1–17.

Bergstrom, T. C., (1971), 'On the Existence and Optimality of Competitive Equilibrium for a Slave Economy', *Review of Economic Studies*, 38: 23–36.

Coles, J. (1986), 'Nonconvexity in General Equilibrium Labor Markets', *Journal of Labor Economics*, 4: 415–37.

Dasgupta, P. S. and Ray, D. (1986–7), 'Inequality as a Determinant of Malnutrition and Unemployment: Theory' and '——: Policy', *Economic Journal*, 96: 1011–34 and 97: 177–88.

Debreu, G. (1954), 'Valuation Equilibrium and Pareto Optimum', *Proceedings of the National Academy of Sciences of the USA*, 40: 588–92.

—— (1959), *Theory of Value*, John Wiley, New York.

—— (1982), 'Existence of Competitive Equilibria', in K. J. Arrow and M. D. Intriligator (eds.), *Handbook of Mathematical Economics*, ii, North-Holland, Amsterdam, pp. 697–743.

Desai, M. (1989), 'Rice and Fish: Asymmetric Preferences and Entitlement Failures in Food Growing Economies with Non-Food Producers', *European Journal of Political Economy*, 5: 429–40.

Diamond, P. A. and Mirrlees, J. A. (1976), 'Private Constant Returns and Public Shadow Prices', *Review of Economic Studies*, 43: 41–7.

Drèze, J. P. and Sen, A. K. (1989), *Hunger and Public Action*, Clarendon Press, Oxford.

Flew, A. (ed.) (1970), *Malthus: An Essay on the Principle of Population*, Penguin Books, Harmondsworth, Middx.

Funaki, Y. and Kaneko, M. (1986), 'Economies with Labor Indivisibilities: I, Optimal Tax Schedules'; 'II, Competitive Equilibrium under Tax Schedules', *Economic Studies Quarterly*, 37: 11–29 and 199–222.

Green, H. A. J. (1976), *Consumer Theory*, rev. edn., Macmillan, London.

Hammond, P. J. (1987), 'Markets as Constraints: Multilateral Incentive Compatibility in Continuum Economies', *Review of Economic Studies*, 54: 399–412.

—— (1993), 'Irreducibility, Resource Relatedness and Survival in Equilibrium with Individual Non-convexities', in R. Becker, M. Boldrin, R. Jones, and W. Thompson (eds.), *General Equilibrium, Trade and Growth*, ii, *The Legacy of Lionel W. McKenzie* Academic Press, New York.

Hildenbrand, W. (1968), 'The Core of an Economy with a Measure Space of Economic Agents', *Review of Economic Studies*, 35: 443–52.

—— (1969), 'Pareto Optimality for a Measure Space of Economic Agents', *International Economic Review*, 10: 363–72.

—— (1972), 'Metric Measure Spaces of Economic Agents', in L. Le Cam, J. Neyman, and E. L. Scott (eds.), *Proceedings of the Sixth Berkeley Symposium on Mathematical Statistics and Probability*, University of California Press, Berkeley, pp. 81–95.

—— (1974), *Core and Equilibria of a Large Economy*, Princeton University Press, Princeton, NJ.

Khan, M. A. and Yamazaki, A. (1981), 'On the Cores of Economies with Indivisible Commodities and a Continuum of Traders', *Journal of Economic Theory*, 24: 218–25.

Koopmans, T. C. (1957), *Three Essays on the State of Economic Science*, McGraw-Hill, New York.

Malthus, T. R. (1798), *An Essay on the Principle of Population*, in Flew (1970).

—— (1830), *A Summary View of the Principle of Population*, in Flew (1970).

Mas-Colell, A. (1977), 'Indivisible Commodities and General Equilibrium Theory', *Journal of Economic Theory*, 16: 443–56.

McKenzie, L. W. (1954), 'On Equilibrium in Graham's Model of World Trade and Other Competitive Systems', *Econometrica*, 22: 147–61.

—— (1959), 'On the Existence of General Equilibrium for a Competitive Market', *Econometrica*, 27: 56–71.

—— (1961), 'On the Existence of General Equilibrium: Some Corrections', *Econometrica*, 29: 247–8.

—— (1981), 'The Classical Theorem on Existence of Competitive Equilibrium', *Econometrica*, 49: 819–41.

—— (1987), 'General Equilibrium', in *The New Palgrave: A Dictionary of Economics*, Macmillan, London.

Mirrlees, J. A. (1973), 'The Economics of Voluntary Contributions', paper presented to the European Meeting of the Econometric Society, Oslo.

Moore, J. C. (1975), 'The Existence of "Compensated Equilibrium" and the Structure of the Pareto Efficiency Frontier', *International Economic Review*, 16: 267–300.

Newbery, D. M. G. (1977), 'Risk Sharing, Sharecropping and Uncertain Labour Markets', *Review of Economic Studies*, 44: 585–94.

Rader, T. (1964), 'Edgeworth Exchange and General Economic Equilibrium', *Yale Economic Essays*, 4: 133–80.

Rashid, S. (1980), 'The Policy of Laissez-Faire during Scarcities', *Economic Journal*, 90: 493–503.

Robinson, J. (1946), 'The Pure Theory of International Trade', in Robinson (1966).

—— (1966), *Collected Economic Papers*, i, Basil Blackwell, Oxford.

Rothschild, E. (1992), 'Commerce and the State: Turgot, Condorcet and Smith', *Economic Journal*, 102: 1197–1210.

Sen, A. K. (1977), 'Starvation and Exchange Entitlements: A General Approach and Its Application to the Great Bengal Famine', *Cambridge Journal of Economics*, 1: 33–59.

—— (1981a), *Poverty and Famines: An Essay on Entitlement and Deprivation*, Clarendon Press, Oxford.

—— (1981b), 'Ingredients of Famine Analysis: Availability and Entitlements', *Quarterly Journal of Economics*, 95: 433–64.

—— (1983), 'Development: Which Way Now?' *Economic Journal*, 93: 745–62.

—— (1984), *Resources, Values and Development*, Basil Blackwell, Oxford, and Harvard University Press, Cambridge, Mass.

—— (1986), 'Food, Economics and Entitlements', *Lloyds Bank Review*, no. 160: 1–20.

—— (1990), 'Welfare and Social Choice', preprint, Harvard University.

Srinivasan, T. N. (1983), review of Sen (1981a), *American Journal of Agricultural Economics*, 65: 200–1.

Woodham-Smith, C. (1962), *The Great Hunger: Ireland 1845–1849*, Harper and Row, New York.

Yamazaki, A. (1978), 'An Equilibrium Existence Theorem without Convexity Assumptions', *Econometrica*, 46: 541–55.

—— (1981), 'Diversified Consumption Characteristics and Conditionally Dispersed Endowment Distribution: Regularizing Effect and Existence of Equilibria', *Econometrica*, 49: 639–54.

Zaman, A. (1986), 'Microfoundations for the Basic Needs Approach to Development: The Lexicographic Utility Function', *Pakistan Journal of Applied Economics*, 5: 1–11.

4

Rationalizing Choice Probabilities using the Random Utility Model: A Necessary and Sufficient Condition

RAJAT DEB

1. Introduction

For choice to be rationalized as maximizing behaviour based on a preference ordering, the choice function needs to be consistent.[1] The 'resolution' of this so-called integrability problem (Richter 1966) is plagued by the fact that in practice choice is often inconsistent. In the case of choice by an individual agent, psychologists have found that, when asked to choose from the same set, on different occasions the agent will often make different choices (see e.g. Suppes, *et al.* 1990). In the case of group choice, inconsistency can arise because of the well-known problem associated with the 'voting paradox'. Faced with inconsistent choices, one may either give up traditional notions of rational behaviour by allowing for intransitive and even cyclic preferences,[2] or model the inconsistency as *random* utility-maximizing behaviour.

The Random Utility Maximization Model (RUM) dates back to Thurstone (1927*a*, *b*). Unlike traditional (deterministic) utility maximization, which tells us what is picked from the available set, random utility maximization gives us the *probability* of any alternative being picked. Thus, for budget sets B and elements x of B, the RUM generates choice probabilities $p(x, B)$ of x being picked from B. One could, on the other hand, start with an arbitrary function $p(x, B)$ specifying choice probabilities, viewing these numbers as parameters of some underlying multinomial distribution, and ask whether these choice probabilities could be generated by some RUM. This, clearly, is the analogue of the integrability problem of traditional utility theory.

The work on the integrability problem for the RUM has focused on two cases: the Complete Domain Model of Choice Probabilities (CMCP) and the Pairwise Model of Choice Probabilities (PMCP). In the CMCP, the set B may be any set belonging to the set of all non-empty subsets of the set of

I am indebted to Professor Mark Machina for drawing my attention to the problem addressed in this paper.

[1] For a necessary and sufficient condition, see Richter (1966).
[2] See e.g. Deb (1977).

alternatives. In this case, the solution (a necessary and sufficient condition for integrability) has been provided by Falmagne (1978) (see also Cohen 1980 and Barbera and Pattanaik 1986). In the case of the PMCP, the set B may be any set belonging to the set of all possible pairs of alternatives. In this case, Marschak (1960) and Block and Marschak (1960) provide a necessary and sufficient condition for integrability *for models with three alternatives or less*. Furthermore, Marschak (1960) conjectures that this condition is necessary and sufficient for any arbitrary number of alternatives. This conjecture has been disproved by Cohen and Falmagne (1978), who provide additional necessary conditions. A necessary and sufficient condition for integrability in this case and the completely general model, the model where the set of Bs is arbitrary, has been analysed in the integrability literature for RUMs by McFadden and Richter (1990). The purpose of this paper is to examine an alternative approach suggested by McFadden and Richter (1990) (a verifiable necessary and sufficient condition) for the integrablity problem for PMCPs and to explain how their solution extends to cover the general model.

In Section 2 the PMCPs are analysed. It is shown that any such model may be associated with a linear programming problem. For a PMCP and a linear programming problem associated with it, it is proved that the choice probabilities are explainable in terms of a RUM if and only if the associated linear programming problem has a solution at the sum vector (i.e. at $e = (1, 1, 1, ..., 1)$). In Section 3 this approach is used to analyse Marschak's conjecture, thus bringing out the relationship between our results and the existing analysis of PMCPs in the literature. In Section 4 it is shown that this approach need not be restricted to the pairwise case and that it readily extends to general models of choice probabilities.

2. The Pairwise Model of Choice Probabilities

Let X be a finite non-empty set of alternatives. A Pairwise Model of Choice Probabilities (PMCP) is a function p from X^2 to $[0,1]$ such that, for all $x_1, x_2 \in X$: $p(x_1, x_2) + p(x_2, x_1) = 1$. The pairwise choice probabilities, $p(\cdot \cdot \cdot)$, may be thought of as underlying parameters of a sequence of Bernoulli trials (see Suppes *et al.* 1990).

Thurstone (1927a, b) modelled the generation of a PMCP as an outcome of the process of random utility maximization. He viewed alternatives as jointly distributed random variables, with the probability of x_1 being chosen from the pair (x_1, x_2) being given by the probability of x_1 being greater than x_2. Alternatively, the agent can be viewed as having alternative moods or personalities, each represented by a ranking on X. The agent could then be viewed as having a probability distribution on the rankings. The probability of x_1 being picked from (x_1, x_2) would then be given by the sum of the probabilities of rankings in which x_1 ranks above x_2. This model can also be given a social choice interpretation by interpreting the rankings as individuals and the probability distribution as a social aggregation procedure (Barbera and Sonnenschein 1978; Heiner and Pattanaik 1983; McLennan 1980). These two random utility models—the 'random alternative' model and the 'random ordering' model—can in fact be shown to be equivalent (Block and Marschak 1960; also see Suppes *et al.* 1990, p. 432). Using the second of these two equivalent models of random utility maximization, we will analyse the integrability problem for PMCPs.

DEFINITION 1. Let Γ be the set of all linear orderings[3] on X. A PMCP, p, can be *rationalized* using a RUM, q, iff

(i) q is a function from Γ to [0,1] such that $\Sigma_{R \in \Gamma} \, q(R) = 1$;
(ii) for all $x_1, x_2 \in X$: $p(x_1, x_2) = \Sigma_{R \in \Gamma(x_1, x_2)} q(R)$, where $\Gamma(x_1, x_2) = \{R \mid R \in \Gamma$ and $x_1 R x_2\}$.

Example 1. Let $X = (x_1, x_2, x_3)$ and let $p(x_1, x_2) = 0.7$, $p(x_2, x_1) = 0.3$, $p(x_2, x_3) = 0.6$, $p(x_3, x_2) = 0.4$, $p(x_3, x_1) = 0.6$ and $p(x_1, x_3) = 0.4$. Then a probability distribution which attaches 0.4 to the linear ordering $x_1 R x_2 R x_3$, 0.2 to $x_2 R x_3 R x_1$, 0.3 to $x_3 R x_1 R x_2$, and 0.1 to $x_3 R x_2 R x_1$ rationalizes p. For instance, $p(x_3, x_1) = 0.2 + 0.3 + 0.1 = 0.6$, $p(x_1, x_2) = 0.4 + 0.3 = 0.7$, and so on.

Central to our analysis of rationalizability is a concept of a test matrix: a matrix that can be used to test whether or not any PMCP, p, is rationalizable. To understand how a test matrix may be constructed, consider the following example.

Example 2. Let $X = (x_1, x_2, x_3)$ and $\bar{R}$ be a linear ordering on X^2 given by $(x_1, x_2) \, \bar{R}(x_2, x_3) \, \bar{R}(x_3, x_1) \, \bar{R}(x_3, x_2) \, \bar{R}(x_2, x_1) \, \bar{R}(x_1, x_3)$. Consider the six columns $R(1)$–$R(6)$ below to represent the six possible linear orderings on X (with the top element being ranked highest and the bottom one lowest):

$R(1)$	$R(2)$	$R(3)$	$R(4)$	$R(5)$	$R(6)$
x_1	x_2	x_3	x_3	x_2	x_1
x_2	x_3	x_1	x_2	x_1	x_1
x_3	x_1	x_2	x_1	x_3	x_2

Then consider the Boolean matrix A_3, given by

$$
A_3 = \begin{bmatrix}
1 & 0 & 1 & 0 & 0 & 1 \\
1 & 1 & 0 & 0 & 1 & 0 \\
0 & 1 & 1 & 1 & 0 & 0 \\
0 & 0 & 1 & 1 & 0 & 1 \\
0 & 1 & 0 & 1 & 1 & 0 \\
1 & 0 & 0 & 0 & 1 & 1
\end{bmatrix}.
$$

[3] A linear ordering is a transitive, reflexive, connected, and antisymmetric binary relation on X.

Each column represents an ordering and each row an ordered pair of alternatives. The rows are ranked according to $\bar{R}$ and the columns by the i in $R(i)$, $i = 1, 2, \ldots, 6$. Thus, the ones in the first column represent $x_1 R(1) x_2$, $x_2 R(1) x_3$, and $x_1 R(1) x_3$ the zeros the fact that $x_3 R(1) x_1$, $x_3 R(1) x_2$, and $x_2 R(1) x_1$ and are false. Let $q = 0.4$, $(0.2, 0.3, 0.1, 0, 0)$. Notice that $A_3 q = (0.7, 0.6, 0.6, 0.4, 0.3, 0.4) = [p(x_1, x_2), p(x_2, x_3), p(x_3, x_1), p(x_3, x_2), p(x_2, x_1), p(x_1, x_3)]$, where p is specified as in Example 1. In general, any point q in the six-dimensional unit simplex may be uniquely identified with a probability distribution on $R(1)$, $R(2), \ldots$, $R(6)$, the ith component being the probability of $R(i)$. Under this interpretation, $A_3 q$ would gives us 'pairwise' probabilities, with the jth component of the vector $A_3 q$ giving us the probability of the jth pair under the ordering $\bar{R}$. Thus, if $A_3 q = P_{\bar{R}}$, then the p associated with $p_{\bar{R}}$ would be rationalizable by a RUM. Let $\tilde{A}_3$ be A_3 augmented by adding a row of ones. For any prespecified PMCP p, if $\tilde{A}_3 q = \tilde{p}_{\bar{R}}$ for some $q \geq 0$ and $\tilde{p}_{\bar{R}} = (p_{\bar{R}}, 1)$, then, clearly, q does lie on the unit six simplex and the p associated with the $p_{\bar{R}}$ is rationalizable. Conversely, if p is rationalizable, $A_3 q = p_{\bar{R}}$ for some q on the unit six simplex (where $p_{\bar{R}}$ is the six-dimensional vector associated with p), and hence $\tilde{A}_3 q = \tilde{p}_{\bar{R}}$ for some non-negative q where $\tilde{p}_{\bar{R}} = (p_{\bar{R}}, 1)$. We will call A_3 a test matrix and $\tilde{A}_3$ an augmented test matrix for this model.

Let X^2 have m elements, let Γ (the set of linear orderings on X) have n elements, and let $\bar{R}$ be an arbitrary fixed linear ordering of X^2. Furthermore, let each PMCP, p, be identified with $p_{\bar{R}}$, the $m \times 1$ vector whose ith component is given by $p(x_1, x_2)$ iff (x_1, x_2) occupies the ith position under $\bar{R}$.

Using this notation, we have the following definition.

> DEFINITION 2. An $m \times n$ Boolean matrix A is said to be a *test matrix* whenever A is such that, for every PMCP p, p is rationalizable iff $\tilde{A} q = \tilde{p}_{\bar{R}}$ has a *non-negative* solution q, where $\tilde{A}$ is a $(m + 1) \times n$ matrix given by $\tilde{A} = \begin{bmatrix} A_T \\ e_n \end{bmatrix}$ and $e_n^T = (1, 1, \ldots, 1)$ is the n-dimensional (row) sum vector and $\tilde{p}_{\bar{R}}$ is the $(m + 1)$-dimensional column vector $\begin{bmatrix} p_{\bar{R}} \\ 1 \end{bmatrix}$. We will refer to $\tilde{A}$ as the *augmented test matrix*.

The method for obtaining a test matrix described in Example 2 is quite general.

> PROPOSITION 1. Given an ordered set $(R(1), R(2), \ldots, R(n))$ of the possible linear orderings on X and $\bar{R}$ the linear ordering on X^2, $|X^2| = m$, the $m \times n$ Boolean matrix with the entry in the ith row and jth column given by
>
> $a_{ij} = 1$ if for the ith ordered pair (x, y) under $\bar{R}$, we have $x R(j) y$
> $\quad\quad = 0$ otherwise is a test matrix.

DEFINITION 3. Let p be a PMCP and $\tilde{A}^T$ the transpose of the augmented test matrix $\tilde{A}$. A *linear programming problem associated with p* (LP(p)) is given by

$$\min_{v \in V} \tilde{p}_{\bar{R}}^T v \quad \text{where } V = \{v/v \in \mathbb{R}_+^{m+1} \quad \text{and} \quad \tilde{A}^T v \geqslant \tilde{A}^T e_{m+1}\}$$

and $\mathbb{R}_+^{m+1}$ and $e_{m+1} = (1, 1, ..., 1)$ represent the non-negative orthant of $(m + 1)$-dimensional real space and the $(m + 1)$-dimensional (column) sum vector, respectively.

THEOREM 1. The PMCP p is rationalizable iff LP(p) has a solution at $v = e_{m+1}$.

Remark 1. Theorem 1 provides a simple and usable characterization for the rationalizability of PMCPs using the RUM. Given p, standard linear programming algorithms can be used to check whether or not p is rationalizable.

The proof of this theorem follows easily as a consequence of the following well-known result (see e.g. Dorfman *et al.* 1958).

FARKAS'S Lemma. Let $\tilde{A}$ be a $(m + 1) \times n$ matrix and $\tilde{p}_{\bar{R}} \in \mathbb{R}^{m+1}$. Then, $\tilde{A} q = \tilde{p}_{\bar{R}}$ has a non-negative solution q iff there does not exist an s satisfying $\tilde{A}^T s \geqslant 0$ and $\tilde{p}_{\bar{R}}^T s < 0$.

Proof of Theorem 1. First we will show that, if the LP(p) in Definition 3 reaches a constrained minimum at $v = e_{m+1}$, then p is rationalizable.

If the LP(p) has a minimum at $v = e_{m+1}$, since at e_{m+1} the non-negativity constraints are *all* slack, it follows that $\min_{v \in \bar{V}} \tilde{p}_{\bar{R}}^T v$, with $\bar{V} = \{v \mid v \in \mathbb{R}^{m+1}$ and $\tilde{A}^T v \geqslant \tilde{A}^T e_{m+1})$, also attains a minimum at $v = e_{m+1}$. In other words, for all v satisfying $\tilde{A}^T v \geqslant \tilde{A}^T e_{m+1}$, we have $\tilde{p}_{\bar{R}}^T v \geqslant \tilde{p}_{\bar{R}}^T e_{m+1}$. Thus, $\tilde{A}^T(v - e_{m+1}) \geqslant 0$ implies that $\tilde{p}_{\bar{R}}^T(v - e_{m+1}) \geqslant 0$. Letting $s = v - e_{m+1}$ and applying Farkas's Lemma, there exists a non-negative q such that $\tilde{A} q = \tilde{p}_{\bar{R}}$. Since, $\tilde{A}$ is an augmented test matrix, it follows (from Definition 2) that p is rationalizable.

To complete the proof, we will argue that if p is rationalizable then LP(p) has a solution at $v = e_{m+1}$.

If p is rationalizable, then (by Definition 2) there exists q such that $\tilde{A} q = \tilde{p}_{\bar{R}}$ for some non-negative q. By Frakas's Lemma, $\tilde{A}^T s \geqslant 0$ and $\tilde{p}_{\bar{R}}^T s < 0$ has no solution s. In other words, for all s satisfying $\tilde{A}^T s \geqslant 0$, we have $\tilde{p}_{\bar{R}}^T s \geqslant 0$. Hence, $\tilde{A}^T(v - e_{m+1}) \geqslant 0$ implies $\tilde{p}_{\bar{R}}^T(v - e_{m+1}) \geqslant 0$. Thus, the problem $\min_{v \in \bar{V}} \tilde{p}_{\bar{R}}^T v$ where $\bar{V} = \{v \mid v \in \mathbb{R}_+^{m+1}$ and $\tilde{A}^T v \geqslant \tilde{A}^T e_{m+1}\}$ reaches a minimum at $v = e_{m+1}$. This implies, in particular, that $\min_{v \in V} \tilde{p}_{\bar{R}}^T$ where $V = \{v \mid v \in \mathbb{R}_+^{m+1}$ and $\tilde{A}^T v \geqslant \tilde{A}^T e_{m+1}\}$ reaches a minimum at $v = e_{m+1}$. ∎

3. Farkas's Lemma and Marschak's Conjecture

One of results that the integrability literature on PMCPs has been concerned with is a theorem by Marschak (1960) providing necessary and sufficient conditions for the rationalizability of PMCPs when X has three or fewer alternatives. Marschak had conjectured—a conjecture disproved by Cohen and Falmagne (1978)—that the necessary and sufficient condition for three alternatives was also necessary and sufficient for larger sets. The approach adopted in Section 2 above provides interesting insights into this result. Using Farkas's Lemma, we shall now examine the intuitive basis for Marschak's theorem. We can 'explain' why his conjecture fails and provide a reason why the literature dealing with Marschak's conjecture has come up with further necessary conditions which have failed to be sufficient.

THEOREM 2. (Marschak 1960; Block and Marschak 1960). Let X have three elements. A PMCP, p, is rationalizable iff, for all $x_1, x_2, x_3 \in X$,

$$1 \le p(x_1, x_2) + p(x_2, x_3) + p(x_3, x_1) \le 2.$$

Consider the seven equations given by $\tilde{A}q = \tilde{p}_{\bar{R}}$ where $\tilde{A} = \tilde{A}_3$ is derived from A_3 in Example 2. Since, for all $x, y \in X$, $p(x, y) + p(y, x) = 1$, if the first three equations in $\tilde{A}q = \tilde{p}_{\bar{R}}$ are satisfied, then the next three will also automatically hold. Hence, using the first three and the seventh equation from $\tilde{A}q = \tilde{p}_{\bar{R}}$ and applying Farkas's Lemma to this subsystem, we have that p is rationalizable iff the system of equations (i)–(vii), given by

(i) $p(x_1, x_2) s_1 + p(x_2, x_3) s_2 + p(x_3, x_1) s_3 + s_4 < 0$

(ii) $s_1 + s_2 + s_4 \ge 0$ (v) $s_3 + s_4 \ge 0$

(iii) $s_1 + s_3 + s_4 \ge 0$ (vi) $s_2 + s_4 \ge 0$

(iv) $s_2 + s_3 + s_4 \ge 0$ (vii) $s_1 + s_4 \ge 0$,

has no solution $(\bar{s}_1, \bar{s}_2, \bar{s}_3, \bar{s}_4)$.

We will call vectors (s_1, s_2, s_3, s_4) such that $s_1 = s_2 = s_3$ 'almost symmetric'. For any almost symmetric s, the system (i)–(vii) reduces to

$$\lambda s_1 + s_4 < 0 \qquad\qquad\qquad\qquad\qquad (a)$$

$$2s_1 + s_4 \ge 0 \qquad\qquad\qquad\qquad\qquad (b)$$

$$s_1 + s_4 \ge 0, \qquad\qquad\qquad\qquad\qquad (c)$$

where $\lambda = p(x_1, x_2) + p(x_2, x_3) + p(x_3, x_1)$. For any solution $(\bar{s}_1, \bar{s}_4)$ to (a), (b), and (c), since $\lambda \ge 0$, $\bar{s}_4 = 0$ is impossible.

CASE 1. If $\bar{s}_4 > 0$, then (b) implies (c). Using (b) and (a), $\lambda \bar{s}_1 < 2\bar{s}_1$; since $\bar{s}_1 < 0$, we get $\lambda > 2$. Conversely, if $\lambda > 2$, $\bar{s}_1 = -(\bar{s}_4/2)$ for any $\bar{s}_4 > 0$ is a solution to (a), (b), and (c).

CASE 2. If $\bar{s}_4 < 0$, using an argument similar to Case 1, a solution to (a), (b), and (c) exists if and only if $\lambda < 1$.

Thus, $1 \leq \lambda \leq 2$ becomes a necessary and sufficient condition for an almost symmetric solution *not* to exist for (i)–(vii). Since it is possible to establish that, *when X has three alternatives*, (i)–(vii) has a solution, this implies that (i)–(vii) has an almost symmetric solution (see the Appendix), $1 \leq \lambda \leq 2$ is, by Farkas's Lemma, a necessary and sufficient condition for rationalizability in the three alternative cases.

To understand the failure of Marschak's conjecture for 'larger' sets, consider the case where X has four alternatives. Following a procedure analogous to the case of three alternatives, it is possible to arrive at a set of inequalities for $s = (s_1, s_2, s_3, s_4, s_5, s_6, s_7)$ such that p is rationalizable iff these inequalities *fail* to have a solution. As before, 'almost' symmetry (i.e. $s_1 = s_2 = s_3 = s_4 = s_5 = s_6$), together with arguments analogous to the case of three alternatives, gives the condition $2 \leq p(x_1, x_2) + p(x_2, x_3) + p(x_3, x_1) + p(x_4, x_1) + p(x_3, x_4) + p(x_2, x_4) \leq 4$ as being necessary and sufficient *for an almost symmetric solution not to exist*. It is quite easy to come up with examples where, even though Marschak's condition on triples is satisfied, (the right-hand side of) this inequality is violated.[4] Since an almost symmetric solution is a solution, this implies that Marschak's conjecture cannot be true.

Notice, however, that conditions based on 'sums' of $p(x_i, x_j)$ can only provide necessary and sufficient conditions for *almost symmetric* solutions to exist. However, since in general the existence of a solution need not imply the existence of an almost symmetric solution (i.e. the analogue of the result in the Appendix may not hold), inequalities such as these provide only necessary (and not necessary and sufficient) conditions for rationalizability in the more-than-three-alternatives case.

4. Extensions and Generalizations

So far, to facilitate exposition and to compare my results with existing results in the literature, I have confined myself to the special case of the Thurstonian pairwise model. In this section I comment on two straightforward generalizations of the above analysis.

The first extension is to the general model of choice probabilities mentioned in the Introduction. Given the set of alternatives X, let Λ be an *arbitrary* non-empty set of non-empty subsets of X. A general model of choice probabilities is a function $p : X \times \Lambda \rightarrow [0, 1]$ such that, for all $B \in \Lambda$, $\sum_{x \in B} p(x, B) = 1$. When Λ is the set of all pairs this model becomes equivalent

---

[4] For instance, let $p(x_1, x_2) = p(x_2, x_3) = p(x_3, x_1) = p(x_2, x_4) = \frac{2}{3}$; $p(x_2, x_1) = p(x_3, x_2) = p(x_1, x_3) = \frac{1}{3}$; $p(x_4, x_1) = p(x_1, x_4) = \frac{1}{2}$; $p(x_3, x_4) = 1$ and $p(x_4, x_3) = 0$.

to a PMCP. When Λ consists of all non-empty subsets of X, we get the Complete Domain Model of Choice Probabilities (see e.g. Falmagne 1978).

The second extension generalizes the above model further by following Barbera and Pattanaik (1986) and relaxing the probabilistic equivalent of the 'univalence' assumption in deterministic choice theory. For all $B \in \Lambda$ and any non-empty subset $\bar{B}$ of B, the probabilistic choice model p would specify a number $p(\bar{B}, B)$ in [0,1] such that $\Sigma_{B \in \chi(B)} p(\bar{B}, B) = 1$ where $\chi(B)$ is the set of all non-empty subsets of B. In the special case when $p(\bar{B}, B) = 0$ for all B that are not singletons, one would get a model equivalent to the general model discussed in the last paragraph. This second extension is particularly important for economic models, since most standard (deterministic) revealed preference models allow for multivalent choice functions (i.e. for several alternatives to be simultaneously selected). We will call the model accommodating both extensions the Extended Model of Choice Probabilities (EMCP).

To consider the problem of rationalizing multivalent choice functions, it is clearly necessary to allow for indifference in the preference ordering. Hence, to rationalize EMCPs we can no longer confine ourselves to RUMs based on *linear* orderings.

Let $\tilde{\Gamma}$ be the set of all possible orderings on X; then an EMCP, p, is said to be rationalized by a RUM, $\tilde{q}$, iff

(i) $\tilde{q} : \tilde{\Gamma} \to [0, 1]$ such that $\Sigma_{R \in \tilde{\Gamma}} \tilde{q}(R) = 1$;

(ii) for all $B \in \Lambda$ and all non-empty subsets $\bar{B}$ of B, $p(\bar{B}, B) = \Sigma_{R \in \tilde{\Gamma}(\bar{B}, B)} \tilde{q}(R)$ where $\tilde{\Gamma}(\bar{B}, B)$ is the set of orderings which, when restricted to B, has $\bar{B}$ as the best elements.

As in Section 2, given an arbitrary linear ordering $\bar{R}$ on the set $\{(\bar{B}, B) \mid B \in \Lambda \text{ and } \varnothing \neq \bar{B} \subseteq B\}$ with m elements, if there are n elements $R(1), R(2), ..., R(n)$ in Γ, it is possible to define a $m \times n$ test matrix A whose ijth element a_{ij} is given by

$$a_{ij} = 1 \text{ if for the } i\text{th ranking element } (\bar{B}, B) \text{ of } \bar{R}, \bar{R}(j) \in \tilde{\Gamma}(\bar{B}, B)$$
$$= 0 \text{ otherwise.}$$

Keeping the definition of augmented test matrix and associated linear programming problems unchanged,[5] one can restate Theorem 1 by simply replacing PMCP with EMCP. Its proof as stated remains valid.

5. Conclusion

In this paper, a necessary and sufficient condition, suggested by McFadden and Richter (1990), has been used to analyse models of choice probabilities

---

[5] Except for replacing 'PMCP' with 'EMCP'.

and to check whether these models are rationalizable by a random utility function. Given a model of choice probabilities, I have argued that it is possible to construct a test matrix which can be used to associate it with a linear programming problem. The linear programming problem is such that the choice model is rationalizable iff the associated programming problem has a solution at the sum vector. Not only is the characterization simple and applicable to even the most general models of probabilistic choice, it is also easily verifiable using standard linear programming algorithms.

Appendix

LEMMA A1. *If a set of inequalities* (i)–(vii) *given by*

(i) $p(x_1, x_2) s_1 + p(x_2, x_3) s_2 + p(x_3, x_1) s_3 + s_4 < 0$

(ii) $s_1 + s_2 + s_4 \geq 0$ (v) $s_3 + s_4 \geq 0$

(iii) $s_1 + s_3 + s_4 \geq 0$ (vi) $s_2 + s_4 \geq 0$

(iv) $s_2 + s_3 + s_4 \geq 0$ (vii) $s_1 + s_4 \geq 0$

has a solution $(\bar{s}_1, \bar{s}_2, \bar{s}_3, \bar{s}_4)$, *then it has a solution* $(\bar{\bar{s}}_1, \bar{\bar{s}}_2, \bar{\bar{s}}_3, \bar{\bar{s}}_4)$ *with* $\bar{\bar{s}}_1 = \bar{\bar{s}}_2 = \bar{\bar{s}}_3$.

Proof. Since $p(x_i, x_j) \geq 0$, for $i, j = 1, 2, 3$, $i \neq j$, it is immediate, from (i), (v), (vi), and (vii), that $\bar{s}_4 = 0$ is impossible. Hence, we need consider two cases: $\bar{s}_4 < 0$ and $\bar{s}_4 > 0$.

Case 1. If $\bar{s}_4 < 0$, define $\bar{\bar{s}}_i = \min_{j \in \{1, 2, 3\}} \bar{s}_j$ for $i = 1, 2, 3$. For $(\bar{\bar{s}}_1, \bar{\bar{s}}_2, \bar{\bar{s}}_3, \bar{\bar{s}}_4)$ with $\bar{\bar{s}}_4 = \bar{s}_4$ defined as above, we have (v)–(vii) being satisfied and hence (ii)–(iv) being satisfied. Moreover, by the choice of $\bar{\bar{s}}_i$, $i = 1, 2, 3$ as minimum of $\bar{s}_j$, $j = 1, 2, 3$, (i) is satisfied by $(\bar{\bar{s}}_1, \bar{\bar{s}}_2, \bar{\bar{s}}_3, \bar{\bar{s}}_4)$.

Case 2. If $\bar{s}_4 > 0$, consider the problem

$$\min_{s_1, s_2, s_3} p(x_1, x_2) s_1 + p(x_2, x_3) s_2 + p(x_2, x_3) s_3,$$

subject to (ii)–(vii) with $s_4 = \bar{s}_4$. Since the constraint set is closed and bounded from below, a solution (s_1^*, s_2^*, s_3^*) to the problem will exist. Moreover, it is clear that $(s_1^*, s_2^*, s_3^*, \bar{s}_4)$ will be a solution to (i)–(vii) with $s_i^* \leq 0$ for $i = 1, 2, 3$.[6] Furthermore, two of the three inequalities (ii)–(iv) must be binding at $(s_1^*, s_2^*, s_3^*, \bar{s}_4)$.[7]

Without loss of generality, let (ii) and (iii) be binding. This implies $s_2^* = s_3^*$.

If $s_2^* = s_3^* = 0$, (vii) and (i) will contradict each other. Thus, $s_2^* = s_3^* < 0$. By (ii), this implies that (vii) holds with a strict inequality. Hence there exists

---

[6] Without loss of generality, say $s_1^* > 0$. Then $(0, s_2^*, s_3^*)$ satisfies (ii)–(vii) and $p(x_1, x_2)(0) + p(x_2, x_3) s_2^* + p(x_3, x_1) s_3^* < p(x_1, x_2) s_1^* + p(x_2, x_3) s_2^* + p(x_3, x_1) s_3^*$. This contradicts the choice of s_1^*.

[7] Say (ii) and (iii) are slack; then it would be possible to find $\tilde{s}_1$ such that $\tilde{s}_1 < s_1^*$, and at $(\tilde{s}_1, s_2^*, s_3^*, \bar{s}_4)$ (ii)–(vii) are satisfied. This would contradict the minimality of $(\bar{s}_1, s_2^*, s_3^*, \bar{s}_4)$.

$\delta > 0$ such that $(s_1^* - \delta, s_2^* + \delta, s_3^* + \delta, \bar{s}_4)$ satisfies (ii)–(vii). By the choice of (s_1^*, s_2^*, s_3^*) as a solution to the constrained minimization problem, we have $p(x_1, x_2)(-\delta) + p(x_2, x_3)\delta + p(x_3, x_1)\delta \geqslant 0$. Hence

$$p(x_2, x_3) + p(x_3, x_1) \geqslant p(x_1, x_2)\ldots \tag{A1}$$

Either (iv) holds with a strict inequality or, using (ii), $s_1^* = s_2^* = s_3^*$ and $(s_1^*, s_2^*, s_3^*, \bar{s}_4)$ is an almost symmetric solution of (i)–(vii). If (iv) holds with a strict inequality, then there exists a $\delta > 0$ such that $(s_1^* + \delta, s_2^* - \delta, s_3^* - \delta, \bar{s}_4)$ satisfies (ii)–(vii). Arguing as before by the choice of (s_1^*, s_2^*, s_3^*), we get $p(x_1, x_2) \geqslant p(x_2, x_3) + p(x_3, x_1)$. Thus, using (A1), $p(x_1, x_2) = p(x_2, x_3) + p(x_3, x_1)$. Using this equality, it is easy to verify[8] that $s_i^{**} = (s_1^* + s_2^*)/2$, $i = 1, 2, 3$, together with $s_4^{**} = \bar{s}_4$, gives us an almost symmetric solution $(s_1^{**}, s_2^{**}, s_3^{**}, s_4^{**})$ of (i)–(vii).

References

Barbera, S. and Pattanaik, P. K. (1986), 'Falmagne and the Rationalizability of Stochastic Choices in Terms of Randomized Orderings', *Econometrica*, 54: 707–15.
—— and Sonnenschein, H. (1978), 'Preference Aggregation with Randomized Social Orderings', *Journal of Economic Theory*, 18: 244–54.
Block, H. D. and Marschak, J. (1960), 'Random Orderings and Stochastic Theories of Responses', in I. Olkin, S. Ghyre, W. Hoeffding, W. Madow, and H. Mann (eds.), *Contributions to Probability and Statistics*, Stanford University Press, Stanford, Calif.
Cohen, M. (1980), 'Random Utility Systems: The Infinite Case', *Journal of Mathematical Psychology*, 22: 1–23.
—— and Falmagne, J.-C. (1978), 'Random Scale Representation of Binary Choice Probabilities: A Counterexample to a Conjecture of Marschak', *Mathematical Studies in Perception and Cognition*, 3 (New York University).
Deb, R. (1977), 'On Schwartz's Rule', *Journal of Economic Theory*, 16: 103–10.
Dorfman, R., Samuelson, P. and Solow, R. (1958), *Linear Programming and Economic Analysis*, McGraw-Hill, New York.

[8] Clearly, $(s_1^{**}, s_2^{**}, s_3^{**}, s_4^{**})$ satisfies (ii)–(vii). Moreover,

$$p(x_1, x_2)\left(\frac{s_1^* + s_2^*}{2}\right) + p(x_2, x_3)\left(\frac{s_1^* + s_2^*}{2}\right) + p(x_3, x_1)\left(\frac{s_1^* + s_2^*}{2}\right) + \bar{s}_4$$

$$= p(x_1, x_2)\left(s_1^* + \frac{s_2^* - s_1^*}{2}\right) + p(x_2, x_3)\left(s_2^* - \frac{s_2^* - s_1^*}{2}\right) + p(x_3, x_1)\left(s_2^* - \frac{s_2^* - s_1^*}{2}\right) + \bar{s}_4$$

$$= p(x_1, x_2)s_1^* + p(x_1, x_2)\delta + p(x_2, x_3)s_2^* - p(x_2, x_3)\delta + p(x_3, x_1)s_2^* - p(x_3, x_1)\delta + \bar{s}_4$$

where $\delta = (s_2^* - s_1^*)/2$. Since $s_2^* - s_3^*$ and $p(x_1, x_2) = p(x_2, x_3) + P(x_3, x_1)$, the terms involving δ add up to zero and we get $p(x_1, x_2)s_1^{**} + p(x_2, x_3)s_2^{**} + p(x_3, x_1)s_3^{**} + s_4^{**} = p(x_1, x_2)s_1^* + p(x_2, x_3)s_2^* + p(x_3, x_1)s_3^* + \bar{s}_4 < 0$.

Falmagne, J.-C. (1978), 'A Representation Theorem for Finite Random Scale Systems', *Journal of Mathematical Psychology*, 18: 52–72.

Heiner, R. and Pattanaik, P. K. (1983), 'The Structure General Probabilistic Group Decision Rules', in P. K. Pattanaik and M. Salles (eds.), *Social Choice and Welfare*, North-Holland, Amsterdam.

McFadden, D. and Richter, M. K. (1990), 'Stochastic Rationality and Revealed Stochastic Preference' in J. S. Chipman, D. McFadden, and M. K. Richter (eds.) *Essays in Honor of Leonid Hurwick*, Westview Press, Boulder, Colo.

McLennan, A. (1980), 'Randomized Preference Aggregation: Additivity of Power and Strategy Proofness', *Journal of Economic Theory*, 22: 1–11.

Marschak, J. (1960), 'Binary Choice Constraints and Random Utility Indicators', in K. J. Arrow, S. Karlin, and P. Suppes (eds.), *Mathematical Methods in Social Sciences*, Stanford University Press, Stanford, Calif., first published 1959.

Richter, M. (1966), 'Revealed Preference Theory', *Econometrica*, 34: 635–45.

Suppes, P., Krantz, D. M., Luce, R. D., and Tversky, A. (1990), *Foundations of Measurement*, ii, Academic Press, San Diego, Calif.

Thurstone, L. L. (1927a), 'A Law of Comparative Judgement', *Psychological Review*, 34: 273–86.

—— (1927b). 'Psychophysical Analysis', *American Journal of Psychology*, 38: 368–89.

5
Private Information and the Shape of the Redistribution Frontier

LOUIS GEVERS and SERGE WIBAUT

1. Introduction

This paper deals with the cost of moving towards equality; it attempts to explain what accounts for the size of it. In order to introduce our problem, we shall draw heavily on Sen's (1982) Tanner lecture, which he delivered in 1979.

After noting that a general concern for morality implies a concern for equality, Sen provides a characteristically lucid discussion of what should be equalized. Every individual in society can choose among various levels of consumption and effort within a given set of opportunities. By exerting his or her choice, the decision-maker produces a given list of functionings, some or all of which generate, in turn, his or her utility or welfare level. From the point of view of an ethical observer, certain basic functionings seem especially relevant: Sen quotes, among others, moving about, getting properly fed, participating in the social life of the community. He moves away from a time-honoured tradition, following which economists had been evaluating policy choices by means of their eventual consequences for individual welfare. Those of them concerned with equality had been comparing welfare levels or welfare gains among individuals. In *A Theory of Justice*, Rawls (1971) criticizes this approach and stresses the importance of what he calls primary goods, be they income, wealth, or the social basis of one's self-respect. Sen builds on Rawls and emphasizes that the ability to achieve basic functionings with a given combination of effort and goods depends heavily on personal characteristics. He argues persuasively that one should be concerned with equality not so much in terms of goods or welfare or actual functionings, but rather in terms of capabilities to achieve basic functionings.

Even though the practical task of checking whether basic capabilities are achieved seems relatively easier than making interpersonal comparisons of welfare levels or gains, the informational problem of the ethical observer may become acute in either case if some relevant actions or personal characteristics remain hidden. Redistributing goods from the more able to the less able may prove unfeasible if the former finds it advantageous to choose the latter's earning posture. In this extreme situation, the equality debate seems pointless. Under happier circumstances, enhancing someone's basic capabilities involves reducing someone else's level of functionings. This is the trade-off we would like to clarify. Our territory has been chartered by many authors; we shall content ourselves with mentioning Mirrlees (1971), Hammond (1979), Guesnerie (1980), Stiglitz (1987), and Blackorby and Donaldson (1988).

The model we have chosen to study is so rudimentary that Sen's careful distinction between equality concerns loses its biting power. In other words, our model seems relevant not only for his approach, but also for the previous ones. We imagine a tax authority dealing with m artisans and knowing only the probability distribution of their K different types of productive abilities. There is only one input, the market of which is controlled by the tax authority and which is bought outside at constant unit cost. All artisans need this input, and they are externally alike. The tax authority knows the production function of each type and assumes that each one wishes to maximize its net profit, i.e. its total output minus what it has to pay in exchange for input. Net profit is different from value added whenever the unit price of input does not equal one. If the tax authority could recognize types *ex ante*, equality could be achieved by means of lump-sum transfers without reducing total valued added: undominated net profit distributions make up a flat hypersurface. Banning this, and assuming that it has to rely on equilibrium based on dominant strategies, the tax authority is in the same position as a monopolist issuing a set of K contracts among which customers can choose freely.

In the sections that follow, our main task is to study the set of undominated net profit distributions under private information and to explain the shape of this second-best set by means of the underlying production or value added functions. We conclude this introduction by sampling some results.

We start with the observation that uniform taxation for the benefit of the tax authority does not reduce total value added as long as every type's net profit is non-negative, whereas transferring income from type j towards type i must imply a reduction of total value added if i has the same buying strategy as i in competitive equilibrium. In contrast, total value added can be transferred to type i at no social cost if every type chooses a competitive equilibrium buying strategy and if type i's strategy is so markedly different from the others that a hypothetical adoption by i of every other type's technology in succession would imply a negative total profit in each case.

If the tax authority chooses to go beyond the non-negativity limits of uniform taxation and to act as an incompletely informed discriminating monopoly that maximizes its profit, the fraction of total value added that may get lost as a consequence can approach $(K - 1)/K$ and it can never exceed this number. This result is of interest in the field of industrial organization.

Second-best transfers among types can be impossible or infinitely costly. This would of course be the case between two types that would in fact be the same. If $K = 2$, transfers from type 1 to type 2 prove also impossible if type 2's value added function can be obtained by rescaling type 1's value added function and the scaling factor is larger than the fraction of type 1 producers. In contrast, if the scaling factor vanishes, i.e. if type 2 is wholly unproductive, we are back in the first-best world.

In order to gauge locally the cost of transferring income from type 1 to type 2, we compute the marginal effect on average income of the change of type 1's income. As we show, this amounts to the ratio of type 2's marginal value added to type 1's evaluated at type 2's input level. A low positive ratio reflects a marked difference between types: it is synonymous with a low marginal transfer cost.

In our final section we deal with an alternative case, in which the tax authority controls the market for output. Although the results are the same in nature, they prove to be more complicated. Moreover, the set of undominated net profit distributions under private information may look very different in either case.

2. Basic Assumptions of the Model

We consider a tax authority concerned only with redistribution and facing $m + 1$ agents. Each of these agents owns an individual firm. There are m manufacturing firms producing the same output by transforming the same input. Both goods are private in nature. Externalities are ruled out. Output is directly sold on the world market at a constant unit price. The remaining firm, called firm 0 or the trading agent, buys the good used as input at a constant world price and sells it to the m manufacturing firms. By assumption, it enjoys a monopoly position on the home market for input. As it turns out, the trading agent is a mere puppet of the tax authority, and one can merge them at will.

World prices for both input and output are assumed fixed throughout our analysis. We shall choose our units for both goods so that their world price is one, and assume that every firm-owner's consumption is equal to the amount of profit he gets after tax. We assume this amount to be non-negative. We are interested in the set of undominated allocations of after-tax profit among our $m + 1$ agents, under various assumptions concerning the state of information of the tax authority.

Throughout the paper, we maintain the assumption that there exists for each firm at least one input level that maximizes its profit under perfect competition. Total profit is assumed strictly positive in competitive equilibrium, and in every firm a positive output requires a strictly positive amount of input, of which there is no initial inventory. Lying idle is also assumed feasible; hence competitive profit levels are non-negative. Whenever returns to scale are constant, profit cannot be positive in competitive equilibrium. In particular, the trading firm must have zero profit under this regime, as the selling price of the input must be the same as the buying price. Every manufacturing firm shares the characteristics we have described, but it may have a production set of its own. We shall assume that there are altogether K types of production sets, denoted by index k running from 1 to K. Type k's production function, defined on the non-negative half-line, is denoted F_k and its input level is denoted y_k. If the input market is competitive, type k's profit may by assumption reach a unique maximum value R_k^* for a set Y_k^* of optimal buying policies. In other words,

$$\forall\, y_k^* \in Y_k^*, \quad \forall\, y_k \geq 0, \quad R_k^* =: F_k(y_k^*) - y_k^* \geq F_k(y_k) - y_k. \quad (1)$$

Readers will have noticed that in competitive equilibrium private profit is synonymous with value added when input can be bought at world prices. The following abbreviations will prove useful:

$$V_k(y_k) =: F_k(y_k) - y_k$$

$$Y^* =: \Pi_k Y_k^*$$

It is a simple matter to apply the two fundamental theorems of welfare economics to our setup. If there are m_k firms of type k, it is easy to see that the set of undominated net profit vectors consists of all vectors of $\mathcal{R}_+^{m+1}$ exhausting total maximal profit or value added, viz. $\Sigma_k m_k R_k^*$. This is of course based on the omniscient planner assumption. If there exists an equally omniscient tax authority, the second fundamental theorem of welfare economics tells us that personalized profit taxes and subsidies can be used to dissociate net from gross profits so as to achieve any undominated vector of non-negative individual net profits. These Pareto-efficient allocations will serve as a background for our study.

We want to do away with the omniscient tax authority. Instead, we assume that the tax authority can distinguish the trading firm from the m others but cannot tell apart the K manufacturing types. The tax authority only knows the F_k and their frequency distribution. Our goal is to describe the Pareto set contraction as omniscience is lost. In our economy, there would seem to be little reason for treating differently the members of any given type. Hence we shall consider only $(K + 1)$-tuples of final profit levels. In the first-best (full-information) situation, the appropriate Pareto set $\mathcal{P}_1$ can be defined as follows:

$$\mathcal{P}_1 =: \left\{ R \in \mathcal{R}_+^{K+1}, \quad R_0 + \Sigma_k m_k R_k = \Sigma_k m_k R_k^* \right\}.$$

When we deal with asymmetric (or private) information we observe that, as a rule, new constraints further limit what can be achieved by the tax authority, and it is no longer possible to disentangle efficiency from distribution considerations.

3. Incentive Constraints

The tax authority is assumed to control the input market and to know only the F_k and their frequency distribution. Moreover, the tax authority believes that each agent knows his type, but it has no information about what beliefs an agent may entertain with respect to other agents. Had it such an information, it could, under appropriate circumstances, set up a game inducing the agents to reveal the types of the others (Piketty 1993). Furthermore, we assume that manufacturing firms cannot resell whatever input they have bought. We also assume that the tax authority cannot control or inspect output levels; otherwise omniscience would reappear. In Section 6 below we study the opposite polar situation, where only the market for output is under direct control.

Under our assumptions, the natural policy for the tax authority is to issue a set of proposed contracts and to take advantage of the fact that each type may be safely assumed to choose its favourite contract or, more precisely, to adopt a dominant strategy. It would of course be even more advantageous for the tax authority to make sure that no type has the possibility of picking another type's contract. This amounts to perfect discrimination and it is consistent with first-best Pareto efficiency. Yet it would rely on information that the tax authority does not possess by assumption. It is precisely the freedom of choice that has to be left to the manufacturing firms that is responsible for the Pareto losses we shall probe in the sequel. If the market for input is directly controlled, a contract consists of a pair of numbers: an input level y_i, and a total amount to be paid in exchange, denoted t_i. Type i selects $((y_i, t_i))$ if it is at least as good as any other contract and yields a non-negative profit level:

$$R_i =: F_i(y_i) - t_i = \max_k \{F_i(y_k) - t_k\} \tag{2}$$

$$R_i \geq 0. \tag{3}$$

It should be clear that the tax authority cannot gain anything by offering more than K distinct contracts. We shall adopt in the sequel the usual notational convention implicit in equation (2): viz., contract i is the one preferred by type i. This equation is known in the literature under at least three names: information constraint, incentive constraint, and self-selection constraint. Constraint (3) is aptly called a participation constraint. It reflects the technical opportunity to remain idle. The term 'individual rationality constraint' is also used but is somewhat ambiguous.

Turning to the trading firm, the tax authority will offer it a single contract, which balances off all the contracts struck with the manufacturing firms. In particular, the tax authority may be interested in maximizing the trading firm's profit, in which case our study is not different from an exercise in exerting the power of an incompletely informed discriminating monopoly. The trading firm's receipts amount to $\Sigma_k m_k t_k$; it has to deliver an input amount $\Sigma_k m_k y_k$. Hence, in view of the left-hand side of (2), noting that $t_k = F_k(y_k) - R_k$, we can write successively

$$R_0 = \Sigma_k m_k t_k - \Sigma_k m_k y_k = \left[\Sigma_k m_k F_k(y_k) - \Sigma_k m_k R_k \right] - \Sigma_k m_k y_k$$

$$= \Sigma_k m_k V_k(y_k) - \Sigma_k m_k R_k \geq 0. \tag{4}$$

Going back again to (2), we observe that the definition on the left-hand side may also be used to do away with t_i and t_k in every inequality implied by the right-hand side. In particular, with respect to type j, (2) implies that

$$R_i \geq F_i(y_j) - t_j = F_i(y_j) - [F_j(y_j) - R_j].$$

Since (2) applies to every type, we eventually obtain for every pair i,j the following set of constraints:

$$F_i(y_i) - F_j(y_i) \geq R_i - R_j \geq F_i(y_j) - F_j(y_j) \tag{5}$$

or, equivalently,

$$V_i(y_i) - V_j(y_i) \geq R_i - R_j \geq V_i(y_j) - V_j(y_j). \tag{6}$$

This tells us that the excess of profit of type i over type j is bounded above by the advantage that i enjoys over j in terms of value added by using its technology or marketing outlets instead of j's, while keeping its input level constant. Moreover, it is bounded below by an analogous advantage evaluated with j's input level. We notice at once that R_i is bounded above by a set of inequalities that depend exclusively on y_i. This property will be used many times in the sequel.

We shall spend much time analysing the contraction of the Pareto set implied by the set of constraints (5). We shall proceed by first studying that part of the constrained or second-best Pareto set which is in fact identical to a subset of the original first-best set $\mathcal{P}_1$, and then really making an inroad in the second-best jungle as we study that part which lies in the interior of $\mathcal{P}_1$.

4. Extent to which First- and Second-Best Agree

It is helpful at this stage to introduce some notation. For any given input vector $y \in \mathcal{R}_+^K$, we shall define $R(y) \subseteq \mathcal{R}_+^{K+1}$ as the set of final profit allocations that can be sustained by y, while satisfying the relevant incentive constraints

$$R(y) =: \{R \in \mathcal{R}_+^{K+1}, \qquad R_0 + \Sigma_k m_k R_k = \Sigma_k m_k V_k(y_k),$$
$$\forall \, i, j, \; V_i(y_i) - V_j(y_i) \geq R_i - R_j \geq V_i(y_j) - V_j(y_j)\}.$$

Next, we define $\mathcal{P}_2$, the second-best Pareto set, as the set of undominated profit vectors of the union of all $R(y)$ when y roams over $\mathcal{R}_+^K$. Our immediate task is to study what final allocations can be achieved with competitive profit-maximizing input levels $y^* \in Y^*$. We remark first that, by definition, every $R(y^*)$ must be a subset of the original first-best Pareto set. Hence it must also be a subset of $\mathcal{P}_2$. Moreover, if $y \notin Y^*$, that is if total value added is less than maximum, then $R(y)$ does not intersect $\mathcal{P}_1$. Thus, $\mathcal{P}_1 \cap \mathcal{P}_2$ is equivalent to the union of all R (y^*), as y^* takes up successively every possible value in Y^*.

Formally, we have the following proposition.

PROPOSITION 1. $\mathcal{P}_1 \cap \mathcal{P}_2 = \cup_{y^* \in Y^*} R(y^*)$.

The next question to be raised is how large a subset $R(y^*)$ is. In any case, $R(y^*)$ contains one element consistent with every value of the R_0 entry, where $R_0 \leq m \min_k(R_k^*)$. This is the vector $(R_0, R_1^* - R_0/m \ldots, R_K^* - R_0/m$. We call this set the first-best base line. Redistribution in favour of the trading firm is thus socially costless to a certain extent; indeed, by assumption, it can be told apart by the tax authority.

PROPOSITION 2. For every $y^* \in Y^*$,

$$R(y^*) \supseteq \left\{ R \in \mathcal{R}_+^{K+1}, \quad \forall \, k, \; R_k = R_k^* - \frac{R_0}{m} \right\}.$$

Proof. The proof is very easy. We reconsider (6) and subtract $R_i^* - R_j^* + R_0/m - R_0/m$ from each side. After suitable grouping and cancellations, we get, for $y = y^* \in Y^*$,

$$[V_i(y_i^*) - R_i^*] - [V_j(y_i^*) - R_j^*)] \geq R_i - \left(R_i^* - \frac{R_0}{m}\right) - \left[R_j - \left(R_j^* - \frac{R_0}{m}\right)\right]$$
$$\geq [V_i(y_j^*) - R_i^*] - [V_j(y_j^*) - R_j^*]$$

and

$$R_j^* - V_j(y_i^*) \geq \left[R_i - \left(R_i^* - \frac{R_0}{m}\right)\right] - \left[R_j^* - \left(R_j^* - \frac{R_0}{m}\right)\right] \geq V_i(y_j^*) - R_i^*. \qquad (7)$$

We notice that the left-hand side is always non-negative, whereas the right-hand side is always non-positive, so that the first-best base line always agrees with the self-selection constraints. ∎

The left-hand side of (7) also shows that the relative advantage of type i over type j with respect to the first-best base line depends essentially on how close y_i^* is to Y_j^* the set of arguments maximizing V_j. In particular, if $y_i^* \in Y_j^*$,

$R_j^* = V_j(_i^*)$ and type i is not in position to obtain any relative advantage over type j.

Let us formalize this remark and study some impacts of symmetry.

PROPOSITION 3. For every $y^* \in Y^*$, if $\exists\ i,j$ such that $y_i^* \in Y_j^*$, then $R(y^*)$ is such that

$$R_j - \left(R_j^* - \frac{R_0}{m} \right) \geqslant R_i - \left(R_i^* - \frac{R_0}{m} \right).$$

Moreover, if $\exists\ i, j$ such that $Y_i^* = Y_j^*$, then, $\forall\ y^* \in Y^*$, $R(y^*)$ is such that

$$R_j - \left(R_j^* - \frac{R_0}{m} \right) = R_i - \left(R_i^* - \frac{R_0}{m} \right).$$

Finally, if $Y_i^* = Y_j^*$ for every i, j, then, $\forall\ y^* \in Y^*$, $R(y^*) = \mathcal{P}_1 \cap \mathcal{P}_2$.

The last equality proceeds from Proposition 1 and the observation that $R(y^*)$ and the first-best base line are equivalent for every $y^* \in Y^*$, given our assumptions. The interpretation is not difficult: first-best redistribution between manufacturing types is impossible if they are too much alike as far as their competitive demands for input are concerned, when the price of both input and output is unity.

We shall next address the complementary question: under what conditions can one be sure that income redistribution does not imply any deadweight loss? In general, if there exist i and j such that $Y_i^* \neq Y_j^*$, there is hope of obtaining some redistribution between these types without efficiency loss. If $K = 2$ this hope can be fully confirmed, as we shall show readily. If $K = 2$, the definition of $R(y)$ can be made more transparent. Indeed, the left-hand side of (4), our conservation equation, now spells out as

$$R_0 + m_1 R_1 + m_2 R_2 = m_1 V_1(y_1) + m_2 V_2(y_2). \tag{8}$$

Besides, type i's profit is bounded above by a single incentive constraint that depends only on y_i. For this reason, we shall call it type i's incentive constraint, although it actually pertains to the equilibrium behaviour of the other type. We rewrite (6) as

$$m_2 V_1(y_1) - m_2 V_2(y_1) \geqslant m_2 R_1 - m_2 R_2 \geqslant m_2 V_1(y_2) - m_2 V_2(y_2).$$

Combining this set of inequalities with (8), we get

$$m V_1(y_1) + m_2 [V_2(y_2) - V_2(y_1)] \geqslant R_0 + m R_1 \geqslant m_1 V_1(y_1) + m_2 V_1(y_2). \tag{9}$$

Symmetrically, we obtain

$$m V_2(y_2) + m_1 [V_1(y_1) - V_1(y_2)] \geqslant R_0 + m R_2 + m_2 V_2(y_2) + m_1 V_2(y_1) \tag{10}$$

In view of (8), one of these two pairs of inequalities is redundant. It is also easy to check that reaching the upper bound on one line implies that the lower bound must be binding on the other line.

Now if $y_1^* \in Y_1^*$ and $y_2^* \in Y_2^*$, we have $V_1(y_1^*) = R_1^*$ and $V_2(y_2^*) = R_2^*$. By substituting these values in (10), we get, after division by m and some rearrangements,

$$\frac{m_1}{m} [R_1^* - V_1(y_2^*)] \geq \frac{R_0}{m} + (R_2 - R_2^*) \geq \frac{m_1}{m} [V_2(y_1^*) - R_2^*]. \tag{11}$$

The reader is invited to compare these inequalities with (7). As we already stressed, type 2's income is bounded above not only by the left-hand side of (11), but also by type 1's participation constraint. In view of (8), we can write successively

$$0 \leq m_1 R_1 = -m_2 R_2 - R_0 + m_1 V_1(y_1) + m_2 V_2(y_2)$$

$$m_2 R_2 \leq -R_0 + m_1 V_1(y_1) + m_2 V_2(y_2)$$

$$R_2 - R_2^* + \frac{R_0}{m} \leq -R_2^* + \frac{R_0}{m} - \frac{R_0}{m_2} + \frac{m_1}{m_2} V_1(y_1) + V_2(y_2)$$

$$R_2 - \left(R_2^* - \frac{R_0}{m}\right) \leq [V_2(y_2) - R_2^*] + \frac{m_1}{m_2} \left[V_1(y_1) - \frac{R_0}{m}\right]. \tag{12}$$

We are now ready to put together the explicit constraints (11) and (12) binding type 2's advantage; we choose $y^* \in Y^*$, so that $V_2(y_2^*) = R_2^*$ and $V_1(y_1^*) = R_1^*$.

PROPOSITION 4. Let $K = 2$; $\forall\, y^* \in Y^*$, $\forall\, R_0 \geq 0$,

$$\frac{R_0}{m} \leq \min\{R_1^*, R_2^*\}, \quad R \in R(^*)$$

if

$$0 < R_2 - \left(R_2^* - \frac{R_0}{m}\right) \leq \min\left\{\frac{m_1}{m}[R_1^* - V_1(y_2^*)], \frac{m_1}{m_2}\left(R_1^* - \frac{R_0}{m}\right)\right\}.$$

Thus given $y^* \in Y^*$, type 2's advantage over and above the first-best base line is the smaller of two numbers, one of which reflects directly type 1's participation constraint, while the other is a fraction of the hypothetical loss of value added that would be incurred if type 1 were to adopt type 2's optimal input level. We can confirm that first-best redistribution in favour of type 2 is feasible if Y_2^* does not coincide with Y_1^* and $R_1^* > 0$. Type 2's gain is largest if $y_2^* \in Y_2^*$ is chosen so as to minimize $V_1(y_2^*)$. If V_1 is concave we want V_2 to be unlike V_1, or more precisely, we want y_2^* to lie far away from Y_1^*.

We would now like to know under what circumstances the incentive constraints can never be binding, owing to the fact that they are less strict than the participation constraints. We start with $K = 2$. In Proposition 4, we let

$$\frac{m_1}{m_2}\left(R_1^* - \frac{R_0}{m}\right) < \frac{m_1}{m}[R_1^* - V_1(y_2^*)].$$

After rearrangement, this inequality becomes $m_1 R_1^* + m_2 V_1(y_2^*) \le R_0$. In particular, if $y_2^* \in Y_1^*$, we get $m R_1^* \le R_0$, and there is no scope for advantaging type 2 as was to be expected from Proposition 3. Looking at the other extreme pole, we seek conditions under which $\mathcal{P}_2$ does not imply any efficiency loss whenever $R_2 > R_2^*$. For this purpose, we let $R_0 = 0$ in the last inequality and we rearrange it to obtain

$$m_1 R_1^* \le - m_2 V_1(y_2^*). \tag{13}$$

Inequality (13) depends only on V_2 through the set of its maximizers Y_2^*. Thus, either all V_2 functions that have some particular $y_2^* \in Y_2^*$ in common meet (13), or they all fail to meet it. In particular, the size of R_2^* is irrelevant. On the other hand, the probability of meeting (13) increases as we move from a V_2 with a narrow set of maximizers to another one with a more comprehensive set. If V_2 happens to be constant over the real half-line, then the likelihood of socially costless redistribution in favour of type 2 is as high as possible, provided $R_1^* > 0$.

We can of course perform the same analysis after permuting types, and derive a condition analogous to (13). We can now state the fifth proposition.

PROPOSITION 5. When $K = 2$, $\mathcal{P}_1 = \mathcal{P}_2$ iff $\exists \, y^* \in Y^*$ such that

$$m_1 R_1^* \le - m_2 V_1(y_2^*)$$

and

$$m_2 R_2^* \le -m_1 V_2(y_1^*).$$

This double inequality tells us how different V_1 and V_2 have to be from each other; it says that, for some given $y^* \in Y^*$, any uniformization of technology would imply an unproductive manufacturing sector. For non-pathological V functions this requires a positive setup cost for at least one type.

We illustrate Proposition 5 on Fig. 1. Input (resp. output) is measured along the horizontal (resp. vertical) axis. We assume $R_1^* = R_2^*$. We choose

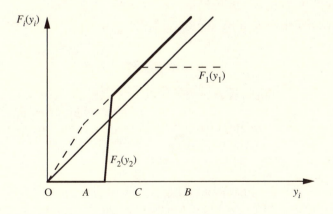

Fig. 1

$y_1^* = OA$ and $y_2^* = OB$, and verify the two conditions of Proposition 5 if we assume $m_1 = m_2$.

Unfortunately, Proposition 5 does not generalize without adaptation to $K = 3$. Suppose indeed we add a third manufacturing type to our example, such that $F_3(y_3) = \max \{F_1(y_3), F_2(y_3)\}$, and that we select $y_3^* = OC$, keeping everything else unchanged. By construction, $y_1^* \in Y_3^*$, $y_2^* \in Y_3^*$, $y_3^* \in (Y_1^* \cap Y_2^*)$ so that, in view of the first · part of Proposition 3, $R_1 - R_1^* = R_3 - R_3^* = R_2 - R_2^*$. In other words, for this particular choice of y_3^* there cannot be any redistribution between type 1 and type 2 without efficiency loss.

However, adapting Proposition 5 for $K \geqslant 3$ proves easy. We select $y^* \in Y^*$, and we note first that the participation constraints of the other types prevent any given type i from claiming more than total value added. Thus,

$$m_i(R_i - R_i^*) \leqslant \Sigma_{k \neq i} m_k R_k^*.$$

Secondly, we rearrange the left-hand side of (6) and multiply through by m_i to obtain, for every $j \neq i$,

$$m_i(R_i - R_i^*) \leqslant m_i[R_j - V_j(y_i^*)]. \tag{14}$$

As $R_j \geqslant 0$, this inequality always holds if

$$m_i(R_i - R_i^*) \leqslant - m_i[R_j - V_j(y_i^*)].$$

In conclusion, all the self-selection constraints depending on y_i^*, that is the constraints of the form (14), are superfluous if

$$\sum_{k \neq i} m_k R_k^* \leqslant - m_i V_j(y_1^*) \qquad \text{for every } j \neq i.$$

It is easy to check that this set of conditions is necessary as well as sufficient.

We can now state the following proposition.

PROPOSITION 6. For any finite K, $\mathcal{P}_1 = \mathcal{P}_2 \; \exists \; y^* \in Y^*$ such that $\forall \; i$, $\forall \; j \neq i$,

$$\Sigma_{k \neq i} \, m_k R_k^* + m_i V_j(y_i^*) \leqslant 0.$$

Again the interpretation is easy: given an input allocation y^*, we select any type i and check whether the manufacturing sector remains productive as type i exchanges technology with every other type j in succession. If the answer is negative for every j, then total profit can be split evenly between manufacturers of type i at no social cost. If this condition holds for every i, then $\mathcal{P}_1 = \mathcal{P}_2$.

From the example illustrated on Fig. 2, it should be clear that Proposition 6 is not empty. In this example $K = 3$, $m_1 = m_2 = m_3$, and $R_1^* = R_2^* = R_3^*$.

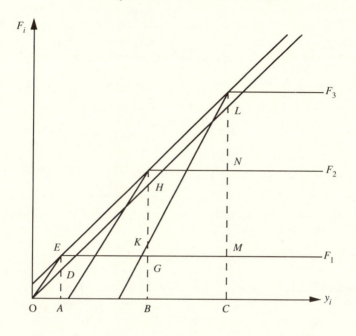

Fig. 2

Production functions are piecewise linear with larger and larger setup costs. We let $y_1^* = OA$, $y_2^* = OB$, $y_3^* = OC$. It is easy to check that the inequalities of Proposition 6 hold. First we want min $\{-V_2(y_1^*), -V_2(y_3^*)\} \geq 2R_1^*$. Given R_1^*, this inequality holds if we make sure that y_1^* is large enough and also that type 2 and type 3 have a large enough setup cost. On Fig. 2, $R_1^* = ED$ and $-V_2(y_1^*) = -V_2(y_3^*) = AD$. Similarly, $-V_1(y_2^*) = HG$, $-V_3(y_2^*) = HK - V_1(y_3^*) = LM$, and $-V_2(y_3^*) = LN$, and all these numbers exceed $2R_1^*$.

In order to develop an example for $K > 3$ with R_1^* unchanged, we want the relevant $-V_j(y^*) \geq (K - 1)R_1^*$, and this can be constructed by pushing every type's capacity to the right.

5. Clearing Trails in the Jungle

Having studied the extent to which the second-best agrees with the first-best, we shall now deal with less favourable circumstances. For simplicity, we stick to the model with $K = 2$. We are interested in redistributing from type 1 to type 2. If there does not exist any y^* for which (13) holds, then it becomes necessary to explore what can be achieved by picking y values for which total value added is not maximal.

For this purpose, we have to go back to our general inequalities, combining the incentive constraints (6) with the conservation equation (7); turning to (10) and letting R_2 reach its upper bound, we have

$$R_0 + mR_2 = mV_2(y_2) + m_1 V_1(y_1) - m_1 V_1(y_2), \tag{15}$$

so that R_1 reaches its lower bound in (9). Thus, we also have

$$R_0 + mR_1 = m_1 V_1(y_1) + m_2 V_1(y_2). \tag{16}$$

From (15) and (16), it is clear that both types have a common interest in choosing $V_1(y_1) = R_1^*$. Let us record this observation, as follows.

PROPOSITION 7. *If $K = 2$, second-best redistribution between types always requires that the type that is paying for the transfer be technically efficient, i.e. that $y_i \in Y_i^*$ if*

$$R_i < R_i^* - \frac{R_0}{m}.$$

Geometrically, this property is self-evident (see Fig. 3). Let us pick $y^* \in Y^*$ that is best from type 2's viewpoint. For any given R_0 value, $R(y^*)$ defines a negatively sloped line segment in the R_1, R_2 non-negative quadrant (segment ee' on Fig. 3), with extremities marked by the intersections of the conservation equation with the incentive constraints (segments

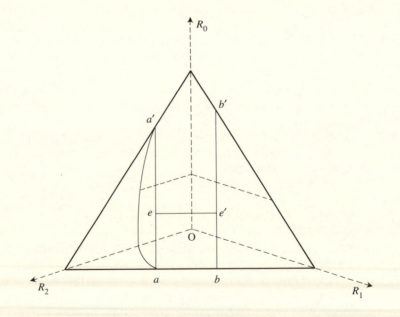

Fig. 3

aa' and bb'), unless any one or both participation constraints are effective. To increase R_2, we go to the appropriate extremity and we tamper with efficiency by modifying the relevant constraint, which depends only on y_2. By doing this, we push aside type 2's incentive constraint, in a direction favourable to R_2; but at the same time we reduce total value added. Thus, R_2 may increase or decrease, depending on the relative intensity of the two effects.

Let us illustrate this discussion analytically by resuming the study of equations (15) and (16). Substituting R_1^* for $V_1(y_2)$, dividing through by m, and rearranging, we get

$$R_2 - \left(R_2^* - \frac{R_0}{m}\right) = \frac{m_1}{m}\,[R_1^* - V_1(y_2)] - [R_2^* - V_2(y_2)] \tag{17}$$

$$R_1 - \left(R_1^* - \frac{R_0}{m}\right) = \frac{m_2}{m}\,[V_1(y_2) - R_1^*]. \tag{18}$$

According to (17), type 2's advantage with respect to the first-best base line can be viewed as a difference between a revenue curve and a cost curve. The latter $(R_2^* - V_2(y_2))$ reflects the loss of total value added that an agent of type 2 can inflict on the economy when choosing y_2. If F_2 is concave, the curve is convex; the loss decreases until Y_2^* is reached; for $y_2 \in Y_2^*$ the loss vanishes, and, further on, it goes on increasing.

The revenue curve $(m_1/m)\,[R_1^* - V_1(y_2)]$ is also convex and U-shaped if F_1 is concave; a typical example is illustrated in Fig. 4. It describes a pure transfer from type 1 to type 2. Indeed, the gain of an agent of type 1 amounts to $(m_2/m)\,[V_1(y_2) - R_1^*]$, so that the grand total, summed over all m manufacturing agents, is identically zero for all $y_2 \geqslant 0$. Owing to the convexity of the revenue curve, the maximization of R_2 with respect to y_2 cannot rely on purely local arguments.

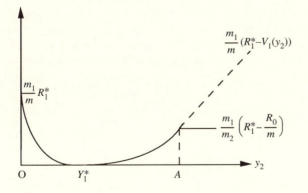

Fig. 4

At this stage, we are ready for a complete description of the problem, which includes type 1's participation constraint as it is reflected in (12).

PROPOSITION   8. Let $K = 2$; $\forall\ R \in \mathcal{P}_2\backslash(\mathcal{P}_1 \cap \mathcal{P}_2)$ such   that $R_2 > R_2^* - R_0/m$, $\forall\ y$ such that $R \in R(y)$, R and y must satisfy

$$R_2 - \left(R_2^* - \frac{R_0}{m}\right) = \min\left\{\frac{m_1}{m}\ (R_1^* - V_1(y_2)),\ \frac{m_1}{m_2}\left(R_1^* - \frac{R_0}{m}\right)\right\}$$

$$- [R_2^* - V_2(y_2)]. \tag{19}$$

As we consider in succession the various parts of the revenue curve, we recognize that, for $V_1(0) = R_0 = 0$, its intercept $(m_1/m) R_1^*$ is smaller than $(m_1/m_2) R_1^*$, so that inequality (12) is not binding and equation (17) applies until (12) binds. If R_0 is concave, (12) becomes relevant from then on. This situation is depicted in Fig. 4. However, if R_0 is large enough and F_1 is concave, we may have three parts in succession: viz. (12), (17), and (12), in that order.

Propositions 4 and 8 complement each other: they describe, rather fully, transfer opportunities in favour of type 2. Some unexpected results may emerge. For instance, suppose that type 2 is wholly unproductive, with F_2 concave, $F_2(0)$, and $F_2(y_2) < 0$ if $y_2 > 0$. In this case, $\mathcal{P}_2$ may be discontinuous and maximizing R_2 may imply a y_2 value so large that $R_1 = 0$. Thus, a little sin against productive efficiency may be of no help, whereas a less timid policy, implying a larger loss of total value added, may be defensible by a second-best argument.

To throw further light on second-best transfer opportunities, we shall assume that V_1 and V_2 are differentiable and denote v_1 and v_2 their respective derivatives. A significant measure of the cost of an additional transfer is provided by the marginal change in average income per extra unit of income forgone by each type 1 agent. Along the first-best surface, this ratio vanishes. As we want to evaluate it along a second-best contour line, we compute the partials of (17) and (18): $\partial R_2/\partial y_2 = v_2(y_2) - m_1/m v_1(y_2$ and $\partial R_1/\partial y_2 = (m_2/m)\ v_1(y_2)$; if $\partial R_2/\partial y_2 = 0$, i.e. if $v_2(y_2)/v_1(y_2) = m_1/m$, we have have a critical point that does not necessarily coincide with a maximum R_2 value. Our local transfer cost measure is given by

$$\frac{\frac{m_1}{m}\ dR_1 + \frac{m_2}{m}\ dR_2}{dR_1} = \frac{\frac{m_1}{m}\frac{m_2}{m}\ v_1 + \left(\frac{m_2}{m}\ v_2 - \frac{m_2}{m}\frac{m_1}{m}\ v_1\right)}{\frac{m_2}{m}\ v_1}.$$

After simplifying and dividing by m_2/m, we obtain a more transparent expression.

PROPOSITION 9. Suppose R_0 is given, $R_1^* - (R_0/m) > R_1 > 0$, and $y_2 \notin Y_2^*$, $y_2 > 0$. Assume V_1 and V_2 are differentiable. Then, if R_2 is maximum, $v_2(y_2)/v_1(y_2) = m_1/m$. Moreover, the marginal change in average income per extra unit of income forgone by every type 1 agent is given by

$$\frac{\dfrac{m_1}{m} \, dR_1 + \dfrac{m_2}{m} \, dR_2}{dR_1} = \frac{v_2(y_2)}{v_1(y_2)}. \tag{20}$$

Not surprisingly, our measure has value m_1/m if $dR_2/dR_1 = 0$, and $v_2/v_1 > m_1/m$ would be inconsistent with v_2, as it would imply $dR_2/dR_1 > 0$. Furthermore, we remark that the cost expression may take any value smaller than m_1/m along the second-best contour line as $v_2(y_2)/v_1(y_2)$ is not necessarily positive. This ratio may be interpreted as indicating how closely V_2 resembles V_1 in an appropriate sense; indeed, v_2/v_1 is a marginal rate of substitution for the value added functions of the two types, computed at the hypothetically common input level y_2. Having v_2/v_1 close to zero means that the type gaining from the transfer is marginally less productive than the type that is paying for it, assuming that the latter would receive the same amount of input, whatever the actual input level $y_1^* \in Y_1^*$.

Proposition 9 provides further insights in cases where $\mathcal{P}_2$ has piecewise linear contour curves; it aids in the understanding of the relation between $\mathcal{P}_2$ and its parent functions V_1 and V_2.

PROPOSITION 10. Suppose $K = 2$ and, for some non-degenerate interval I of y_2 values, V_1 and V_2 are such that (17) and (18) yield a linear contour segment in the positive quadrant of the R_1, R_2 plane for some R_0; then there exist two numbers a, b such that either $V_2 = a + b V_1$ or $V_1 = a + b V_2$ over I. This condition is also sufficient.

If $V_2 = a + b V_1$, the image of I is such that $\Delta R_2/\Delta R_1 = (b - m_1/m)/(m_2/m)$. It is thus independent of the shape of V_1 over I.

The proof of the necessity part can be found in the Appendix.

Proof of the sufficiency part. Substituting $(a + b) V_1$ for V_2 in (17), we get

$$R_2 - \left(R_2^* - \frac{R_0}{m} \right) = a + b V_1(y_2) - R_2^* - \frac{m_1}{m} [V_1(y_2) - R_1^*]$$

$$= \left(b - \frac{m_1}{m} \right) [V_1(y_2) - R_1^*] + a + b R_1^* - R_2^*.$$

Next we multiply (18) through by m/m_2 and substitute in the last expression:

$$R_2 - \left(R_2^* - \left(R_2^* - \frac{R_0}{m} \right) \right) = \frac{b - m_1/m}{m_2/m} \left[R_1 - \left(R_1^* - \frac{R_0}{m} \right) \right] + a + b R_1^* - R_2^*. \tag{21}$$

Thus, the linear contour segment has slope $\Delta R_2/\Delta R_1 = (b - m_1/m)/(m_2/m)$. Here b is the relevant indicator of how close type 2 is to type 1. If $b = 0$ the slope is as favourable as along the first-best surface, but as b gets closer and closer to m_1/m, redistribution from type 1 to type 2 proceeds on less and less favourable terms, and it becomes unfeasible if type 2 is too close to type 1 i.e. if $b \geq m_1/m$.

6. Social Cost of Monopoly

In this section, we study contract policies designed to increase the trading agent's profit R_0 above its competitive value. First of all, we shall compare the marginal transfer cost from type 1 to type 2 with the marginal cost of transfer towards the trading agent when the burden is uniformly borne by every manufacturing type. Consider the strictly second-best surface as it is described for instance by (17) and (18). If no participation constraint is binding, we can write $dR_0/m = -dR_1 = -dR_2$ without tampering with the right-hand side, so that total income is not affected.

The same result holds *a fortiori* over that part of $\mathcal{P}_2$ which is included in $\mathcal{P}_1$.

PROPOSITION 11. If $R_1 > 0$ and $R_2 > 0$, a small uniform transfer increment from the manufacturing types to the trading agent does not decrease total income.

One single fact accounts for this observation: this transfer policy is not hindered by the state of incomplete information we have been assuming.

Suppose we start from the first-best base line and we want to increase R_0/m over and above min $\{R_1^*, R_2^*\}$ which we take to be R_2^*; in other words, we hit the participation constraint of type 2, assumed to be the less productive among our two types in competitive equilibrium. Suppose we proceed along the edge of $\mathcal{P}_2$. Once we get beyond $\mathcal{P}_1 \cap \mathcal{P}_2$, the situation may be described by (17) and (18), where we set $R_2 = 0$. We can now look for the y_2 value that is most profitable for the trading agent.

Our findings are summarized in the following proposition.

PROPOSITION 12. Suppose $R_2 = 0$, $R_1^* - R_0/m > R_1 > 0$, and $y_2 \notin Y_2^*$, $y_2 > 0$. Assume V_1 and V_2 are differentiable. Then, if R_0 reaches a local maximum for y_2, $v_2(y_2)/v_1(y_2) = m_1/m$. Moreover, the marginal change in average income per extra unit of income forgone by every type 1 agent is given by

$$\frac{\dfrac{m_1}{m} dR_1 + \dfrac{dR_0}{m}}{dR_1} = \frac{v_2(y_2)}{v_1(y_2)} \frac{\dfrac{m_2}{m}}{1 - \dfrac{v_2(y_2)}{v_1(y_2)}}. \tag{22}$$

Proof. The proof of this proposition proceeds directly from the inspection of equation (17) and the first assertion of Proposition 9. The remainder of the proof is based on the differentiation of (17) and (18): it is left as an exercise for the interested reader.

It is worth while to compare Proposition 12 with Proposition 9, and to bear in mind the comments following the latter. If we are in $\mathcal{P}_2$, y must be such that $m_1/m \geqslant v_2/v_1$. Hence $1 - (v_2/v_1)$ is positive, and it must equal at least m_2/m. The privileged position of the trading agent which is established in Proposition 11 when $R_2 > 0$ is thus confirmed if $R_2 = 0$ and $v_2/v_1 > 0$. ∎

Of course, we would like to have a more global view of the monopolist's profit maximization as well as of transfer costs. To clarify the matter, we go back to Proposition 10 and we extend interval I to the whole of $\mathcal{R}_+$, generating the simplest family of examples one can think of. As we maintain as an assumption $V_k(0) = 0$ for every type, we let $V_2(y_2) = bV_1(y_2)$ for every $y_2 \geqslant 0$. As a consequence, we let $a = 0$ and $bR_1^* = R_2^*$ in (21), and the latter describes global redistribution possibilities towards type 2. If we choose b such that $1/b \geqslant m_2/m$, we can invoke a symmetry argument and there are no redistribution or transfer possibilities towards type 1.

Thus, if $m/m_2 \geqslant b \geqslant m_1/m$, $\mathcal{P}_2$ consists only of the first-best base line. For $m_1/m > b > 0$, $\mathcal{P}_2$ is the subset of $\mathcal{R}_+^3$ described by (21). After rearrangement, this equation becomes

$$R_0 = \frac{m_1 - mb}{1 - b} (R_1^* - R_1) + \frac{m_2}{1 - b} (R_2^* - R_2), \tag{23}$$

or, alternatively,

$$m_1(R_1 - R_1^*) = \frac{m_1 m_2}{m_1 - mb} (R_2^* - R_2) - \frac{m_1(1 - b)}{m_1 - mb} R_0. \tag{24}$$

$\mathcal{P}_2$ turns out to be a negatively sloped quadrangle having only one edge in common with $\mathcal{P}_1$, viz. the first-best base line.

If $b = 0$, the first-best base line degenerates: it contains the single point $(0, R_1^*, 0)$. $\mathcal{P}_2$ is a triangle described by (23), which coincides with $\mathcal{P}_1$.

This family of examples allows us to describe easily what a profit-maximizing monopoly must do if given the same information about manufacturing types as the fiscal authority we have been dealing with previously. If $m/m_2 \geqslant b \geqslant m_1/m$, $R_0/m = \min\{R_1^*, R_2^*\}$, $R_1 = R_1^* - R_0/m$, $R_2 = R_2^* - R_0/m$, and this profit allocation is in $\mathcal{P}_1$. At the other extreme pole, if $b = 0$, $R_0 = mR_1^*$, $R_1 = R_2 = 0$ and this is also included in $\mathcal{P}_1$. Efficiency losses occur for intermediate values of b, i.e. for $m_1/m > 0$. In monopoly equilibrium, one obtains.

$$R_0 = \frac{m_1 - mb}{1 - b} R_1^* + \frac{m_2}{1 - b} R_2^*,$$

together with $R_1 = R_2 = 0$.

A more global view of transfer costs should provide us with a better picture of the monopoly profit maximization. In order to achieve this, we use competitive profit levels as a benchmark, and, after transferring all income to one type of agent, we compute the ratio of total loss to total gain. We call this ratio the average transfer cost. With the family of examples described by (23) and (24), average transfer costs are easy to compute. We have respectively, for $R_0 = R_1 = 0$,

$$\frac{m_1 R_1^*}{m_2 (R_2 - R_2^*)} = \frac{m_1}{m_1 - mb}$$

and for $R_1 = R_2 = 0$,

$$\frac{m_1 R_1^* + m_2 R_2^*}{R_0} = \frac{m_1 R_1^* + m_2 b R_2^*}{(m_1 - mb) R_1^* + m_2 b R_2^*} (1 - b)$$

$$= \frac{(m_1 + m_2 b)(1 - b)}{m_1 (1 - b)}$$

$$= 1 + \frac{m_2}{m_1} b.$$

We notice that the average transfer cost in favour of type 2 increases without bound as b approaches m_1/m. On the other hand, the average transfer cost in favour of the trading agent approaches $1 + (m_2/m)$ as b gets close to m_1/m. Obviously, for $K = 2$, the average transfer cost in favour of the trading agent never exceeds 2. We conclude this section with a generalization of this remark.

PROPOSITION 13. The average transfer cost implied by the trading agent's profit maximization never exceeds the number of manufacturing types. It can be arbitrarily close to this bound. The fraction of total value added captured by the profit maximizing trading agent is at least equal to $1/K$. It can be arbitrarily close to this bound.

Proof. The second part of Proposition 13 is proved by constructing a family of examples, which is done in the Appendix. The first part is easy to prove. Indeed, in the presence of K manufacturing types the monopolist can always at least capture the entire value added of whichever type he selects, by using a single 'take it or leave it' contract proposal that treats the chosen type as if there were no other type. As a result, $R_0 \geq m_k R_k^*$, for every k. Hence the average transfer cost is bounded as follows:

$$\frac{\Sigma_k m_k R_k^*}{R_0} \leq \frac{\Sigma_k m_k R_k^*}{\max_k \{m_k R_k^*\}} \leq K. \quad \blacksquare$$

Proposition 3 allows us to compute the fraction of total value added V^* that could get lost by monopoly profit maximization: as V^*/R_0 gets arbitrarily close to $K(V^* - R_0)/V^*$ gets arbitrarily close to $1 - 1/K$.

7. Control of the Output Market

We wish now to study the case in which the tax authority controls the output market. As we shall see, the results obtained in the following are not totally symmetrical to the case in which the fiscal authority controls the market for inputs. In this section we shall stress mainly the points of divergence between the two approaches.

We denote by x_i agent i's level of output and by $C_i(x_i)$ the cost function associated with this level. A contract consists now of a pair (x_i, s_i) where s_i denotes the total amount received in exchange of x_i. Self-selection and participation constraints are written as

$$R_i =: s_i - C_i(x_i) = \max_k \{s_k - C_i(x_k)\}.$$

Value added is given by

$$V_i(x_i) =: x_i - C_i(x_i),$$

and we also note X_k^* the set of k's optimal output policies.

In this setup the trading firm's profit becomes

$$R_0 = \Sigma_k m_k x_k - \Sigma_k m_k s_k$$

$$= \Sigma_k m_k V_k(x_k) - \Sigma_k m_k R_k \geq 0. \tag{25}$$

Corresponding to the self-selection constraints for any i, j summarized by (5) and (6), we now write

$$C_i(x_j) - C_j(x_j) \geq R_j - R_i \geq C_i(x_i) - C_j(x_i) \tag{26}$$

or

$$V_i(x_j) - V_j(x_j) \geq R_j - R_i \geq V_i(x_i) - V_j(x_i). \tag{27}$$

For any output vector $x \in \mathcal{R}_+^{K+1}$, we can define a set $R(x) \subseteq \mathcal{R}_+^{K+1}$ of profit allocations sustained by x and which satisfy the incentive constraints. As in the previous section, we are interested in the relation between the first-best and second-best sets. In this respect it is not difficult to show that there exist (output-) equivalents to Propositions 1 and 7: this analysis is entirely symmetrical to what has been carried out previously and will therefore not be reproduced here.

However, one point deserves our full attention. We have seen above (and limiting ourselves here to the case $K = 2$) that first-best redistribution towards type 1 is impossible if every competitive demand of type 1 turns out to be a competitive demand of type 2, i.e. if $y_1^* \in Y_2^*$. The same holds in the output case (i.e., no redistribution is possible if $x_1^* \in X_2^*$), but this property does not imply that, if redistribution is impossible when, say, controlling inputs, it will also be impossible when controlling the market for output.

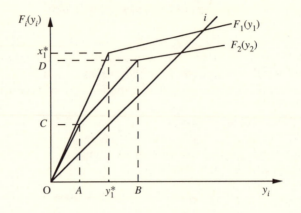

Fig. 5

More formally, $y_1^* \in Y_2^*$ does not imply $x_1^* \in X_2^*$. An example of this is depicted in Fig. 5. In this figure, the optimal input set for agent 2 is the interval AB and therefore $X_2^* = CD$. On the other hand, the optimal input amount for 1 is $y_1^* \in AB$ but $x_1^* \notin X_2^*$.

Our first contrast therefore shows up whenever first-best redistribution is possible using inputs, whereas it may not be so when controlling outputs. The second contrast appears once we turn to the study of second-best redistribution. With $K = 2$, the incentive constraint is

$$V_2(x_1) - V_1(x_1) \geqslant R_1 - R_2 \geqslant V_2(x_2) - V_1(x_2). \tag{28}$$

Multiplying this double inequality by m_2 and adding the conservation equation yields

$$m_1 V_1(x_1) + m_2 V_2(x_2) - m_2 [V_1(x_1) - V_2(x_1)] \geqslant R_0 + mR_1$$

$$\geqslant m_1 V_1(x_1) + m_2 V_2(x_2) - m_2 [V_1(x_2) - V_2(x_2)]. \tag{29}$$

Symmetrically, one obtains

$$m_1 V_1(x_1) + m_2 V_2(x_2) - m_1 [V_2(x_2) - V_1(x_2)] \geqslant R_0 + mR_2$$

$$\geqslant m_1 V_1(x_1) + m_2 V_2(x_2) - m_1 [V_2(x_1) - V_1(x_1)]. \tag{30}$$

If we are interested in transferring resources from type 1 to 2, we let R_2 reach its upper bound in (30) and R_1 its lower bound in (29) in order to obtain

$$R_2 - \left(R_2^* - \frac{R_0}{m}\right) = \frac{m_1 V_1(x_1) + m_2 V_2(x_2)}{m} - \frac{m_1}{m} [V_2(x_2) - V_1(x_2)] - R_2^* \tag{31}$$

$$R_1 - \left(R_1^* - \frac{R_0}{m}\right) = \frac{m_1 V_1(x_1) + m_2 V_2(x_2)}{m} - \frac{m_2}{m} [V_1(x_2) - V_2(x_2)] - R_1^*. \tag{32}$$

It appears that the output levels x_1 and x_2) must be such that profits for both types show a discrepancy with respect to average value added. Some fraction of this discrepancy is equal to (plus or minus) the lower bound of $R_1 - R_2$ that is compatible with the incentive constraint (28).

From (31) and (32), we observe that both types have an interest in setting $V_1(x_1) = R_1^*$ (i.e. requiring the paying type to be efficient). This result is consonant with that obtained in Section 2 (see (17) and (18)). However, the analogy stops here. Indeed, equation (31) can be rewritten as

$$R_2 + \frac{R_0}{m} = \frac{m_1}{m} [V_1(x_2) + V_1(x_1)] + \frac{m_2 - m_1}{m} V_2(x_2),$$

which implies that, if $m_2 > m_1$ and if F_1, F_2 are concave, this expression is concave in x_2. Its maximization will therefore yield an optimal value lying in between the optimal values of V_1 and V_2, i.e. between X_1^* and X_2^*.[1] This conclusion is definitely at odds with our remark in Section 2 regarding the general impossibility to guarantee that R_2 will be concave in y_2.

In Section 2, we assumed the piecewise linearity of the contour curve of $\mathscr{P}_2$ in order to cast some light on our second-best results. In Proposition 10, we were able to show that a necessary and sufficient condition for this linearity to obtain is that $V_2(y_2) = a + b V_1(y_2)$. Not surprisingly, the same kind of results holds here if $V_2(x_2) = a + b V_1(x_2)$.

PROPOSITION 14. Suppose $K = 2$ and, for some non-degenerate interval I of x_2 values, V_1 and V_2 are such that (31) and (32) yield a linear contour segment in the positive quadrant of the R_1, R_2 plane for some R_0. Then there exist two numbers a, b such that either $V_2 = a + b V_1$ or $V_1 = a + b V_2$ over I. This condition is also sufficient.

If $V_2 = a + b V_1$, the image of I is such that $\Delta R_2/\Delta R_1 = [b(m_2 - m_1) + m_1]/(2b - 1) m_2$.

One should keep in mind, however, that the existence of a linear relationship between value added expressed in terms of output does not imply that the same kind of relation holds if value added is expressed in terms of inputs (unless the production functions are linear). This naturally implies that the linearity of the second-best contour curve that underlies Proposition 14 is generally inconsistent with the linearity of the contour curve studied in Proposition 10.

With respect to the latter, however, one should notice that the slope of the second-best contour curve is now different. If $b = 1$ the two types are very similar, which means that $\Delta R_2/\Delta R_1 = 1$ and that no redistribution can

---

[1] If C_1 and C_2 are differentiable at x_2, the sufficient first-order condition for a global maximum of R_2 (or, alternatively, for a local maximum of R_0) is $v_1(x_2)/v_2(x_2) = - m_2/m < 0$. This should be compared with the analogous condition for a critical point in Propositions 10 and 12.

take place. If $b = 0$, then $\Delta R_2/\Delta R_1 = m_1/m_2$ and redistribution can take place as on first-best terms. The crucial point is surely $b = 0.5$, since, together with the relative size of m_1 and m_2, it will decide whether or not $\Delta R_2/\Delta R_1$ is positive. Besides, in the neighbourhood of this point, the absolute value of the slope of the contour curve could be infinitely high.

Although the transfer cost formulae of Propositions 9 and 12 are no longer valid, the content of Propositions 11 and 13 need not be changed in the case where the output market is controlled by the tax authority.

Appendix

Proof of the necessary part of Proposition 10

Assume that (17) and (18) yield a linear contour segment in the R_1, R_2 plane for a given R_0. Let us denote α and β the parameters of this linear relation; i.e.

$$R_2 - \left(R_2^* - \frac{R_0}{m} \right) = \alpha + \beta \left[R_1 - \left(R_1^* - \frac{R_0}{m} \right) \right].$$

Substituting both sides by their definition given in (17) and (18) yields

$$\frac{m_1}{m} [R_1^* - V_1(y_2)] - [R_2^* - V_2(y_2)] = \alpha + \beta \frac{m_2}{m} [V_1(y_2) - R_1^*]$$

or

$$V_2(y_2) = \left[\alpha + R_2^* - \frac{R_1^*}{m} (\beta m_2 + m_1) \right] + \frac{(\beta m_2 + m_1)}{m} V_1(y_2). \quad \blacksquare$$

Proof of Proposition 13

We consider a one-parameter family of manufacturing sectors consisting each of K types. Our parameter is denoted g, $g > 1$. Each firm of type h is either inactive with zero value added, or has an activity level equal to one.

All firms buy their input from the same constant-average-cost monopolist. Under our assumptions, there is no difference between an ordinary monopolist and an incompletely informed discriminating monopolist. A type 1 firm has a value added $V_1 = 1$ and the other types are exponentially less productive; thus, by assumption, $V_h = g^{1-h}$, $h \geq 1$.

We want the cumulative distribution of frequencies to be exponentially increasing in a reciprocal way, i.e. $\Sigma_{k=1}^{h} m_k = g^{h-1}$. It is an easy exercise to verify that this an implication of the following distribution: $m_1 = 1$ and $m_k = g^{k-2}(g-1)$, $k \geq 2$.

If the monopolist sets his absolute mark-up at a level V_h, his profit is $V_h \Sigma_{k=1}^{h} m_k = 1$, by construction. Thus, the set of optimal mark-up policies for the monopolist is given by $\{V_h, h = 1, ..., K\}$, so that the average transfer cost implied by mark-up V_1 is given by

$$\frac{\Sigma_{h=1}^{K} V_h m_h}{m_1 V_1} = \Sigma_h V_h m_h$$

$$= 1 + \Sigma_{h \geqslant 2}(g - 1)\, g^{h-2} g^{1-h} = 1 + \Sigma_{h \geqslant 2}(g - 1)/g$$

$$= 1 + (K - 1)(g - 1)/g = K - \frac{K-1}{g}.$$

As g may be chosen arbitrarily large, we conclude that average transfer cost towards a monopolist may be arbitrarily close to the number of types of customers. ∎

References

Blackorby, C. and Donaldson, D. (1988), 'Cash versus Kind: Self-Selection, and Efficient Transfers', *American Economic Review*, 78: 691–700.

Guesnerie, R. (1980), *Modèles de l'économie publique*, Editions du CNRS, Paris.

Hammond, P. J. (1979), 'Straightforward Individual Incentive Compatibility in Large Economies', *Review of Economic Studies*, 46: 263–82.

Mirrlees, J. (1971), 'An Exploration in the Theory of Optimum Income Taxation', *Review of Economic Studies*, 38: 175–208.

Piketty, Th. (1993), 'Implementation of First-Best Allocations via Generalized Tax Schedules', mimeo, Delta.

Rawls, J. (1971), *A Theory of Justice*, Harvard University Press, Cambridge, Mass.

Sen, A. K. (1982), 'Equality of What?' in A. K., Sen, *Choice, Welfare and Measurement*, Basil Blackwell, Oxford, ch. 16.

Stiglitz, J. E. (1987), 'Pareto Efficient and Optimal Taxation and the New Welfare Economics', in A. J. Auerbach and M. Feldstein (eds.), *Handbook of Public Economics*, ii, North-Holland, Amsterdam, ch. 15.

6

Majority Rule, Social Welfare Functions, and Game Forms

ERIC S. MASKIN

1. Introduction

In his classic article, 'A Possibility Theorem on Majority Decisions' (Sen 1966), Amartya Sen showed that, in seeking domains of preferences on which the method of majority rule is transitive, one can, in effect, reduce the search to the case of three alternatives and three individuals. More specifically, he identified a condition—*value restriction*[1]—that is defined for triples of alternatives, and demonstrated that, provided the number of individuals is odd, majority rule is transitive regardless of how individuals' preferences are drawn from the domain $\mathcal{R}$, if and only if $\mathcal{R}$ satisfies value restriction for each triple (hence the reduction to three alternatives). Moreover, value restriction is the necessary and sufficient condition *regardless* of the number of individuals, and so we have transitivity with n individuals (n odd) for domain $\mathcal{R}$ if and only if we have transitivity with three individuals for domain $\mathcal{R}$ (hence the reduction to three individuals).

Reducing a social choice problem to the case of three alternatives and three individuals is, I believe, quite a powerful and general technique. In this paper I apply Sen's technique to establish simple proofs of two other well-known results from social choice theory: the Gibbard–Satterthwaite theorem on the impossibility of strategy-proof game forms, and the Arrow impossibility theorem for social welfare functions.

I then go on to establish a new result for a majority rule. Just as Sen showed that value restriction is a necessary condition on a domain of preferences for majority rule to be transitive, so one can establish that the same is true of *any* anonymous and neutral collective choice rule (CCR) that

It is a great pleasure to dedicate this paper to Amartya Sen. Not only was his article on majority rule the direct inspiration for the methods I use here, but, more generally, his work has long exerted a profound influence on my thinking. Indeed, my fascination with his beautiful monograph *Collective Choice and Social Welfare* (Sen 1970) was the principal reason I first tried my hand at social choice theory many years ago.

Research support from the NSF is gratefully acknowledged. I should like to thank D. Campbell, K. Suzumura, and S. Tadelis for helpful comments.

[1] The domain $\mathcal{R}$ satifies *value restriction* for the triple $\{a, b, c\}$ if, for some $x \in \{a, b, c\}$, (i) for all $R \in \mathcal{R}$, x is not strictly preferred to both of the other alternatives; or (ii) for all $R \in \mathcal{R}$, x is not strictly between the other two alternatives; or (iii) for all $R \in \mathcal{R}$, the other two alternatives are not both strictly preferred to x.

satisfies independence of irrelevant alternatives and the Pareto property. Hence, if F is some such CCR and is transitive on domain $\mathcal{R}$, then majority rule is transitive on $\mathcal{R}$ as well (as long as the number of individuals is odd). Moreover, unless F is itself majority rule, there exists a domain of preferences $\mathcal{R}'$ on which F is not transitive but majority rule is. Thus, among CCR's satisfying the above properties, majority rule is the one (and the *only* one) that is transitive on the widest class of domains of preferences. This conclusion gives us another characterization of majority rule to complement the one provided by May (1952).

2. The Gibbard–Satterthwaite Theorem

Let A be a non-empty set (possibly infinite) of social alternatives. Let $N = \{1, \ldots, n\}$ be the set of players. Given abstract strategy spaces S_1, $S_2, \ldots, S_n$, an n-person *game-form* g for A is a mapping $g: S_1 \times \cdots \times S_n \to A$, where the mapping is *onto* A. Let $\mathcal{R}_A$ be the class of all orderings of the elements of A. For $R_i \in \mathcal{R}_A$ and $i \in N$, the strategy $\bar{s}_i \in S_i$ is said to be *dominant* for player i with preference ordering R_i if, for all $s_i \in S_i$, and $s_{-1} \in \underset{j \neq i}{\times} S_j$,[2]

$$g(\bar{s}_i, s_{-i}) \, R_i \, g(s_i, s_{-i}).$$

Given a subclass $\mathcal{R} \subseteq \mathcal{R}_A$, g is said to be *strategy-proof* on $\mathcal{R}$ if, for all $i \in N$ and all $R_i \in \mathcal{R}$, player i with ordering R_i has a dominant strategy. Player $i \in N$ is a *dictator* for g if, for all $a \in A$, there exists $s_i^a \in S_i$ such that, for all $s_{-i} \in \underset{j \neq i}{\times} S_j$

$$g(s_i^a, s_{-i}) = a.$$

If some player is a dictator for g, g is *dictatorial*. The basic result on strategy-proof game forms is as follows.

> THEOREM (Gibbard–Satterthwaite). Suppose that $\#(A) \geqslant 3$ and $n \geqslant 2$.[3] Then, if an n-person game-form for A is strategy-proof on $\mathcal{R}_A$, it is dictatorial.

Gibbard (1973) proved this theorem by showing that the existence of a strategy-proof game-form (SPGF) on $\mathcal{R}_A$ implies the existence of a social

---

[2] The notation $g(\bar{s}_i, s_{-i})$ is equivalent to $g(s_1, \ldots, s_{i-1}, \bar{s}_i, s_{i+1}, \ldots, s_n)$. For a coalition $C(\subseteq \{1, \ldots, n\})$, the notation $g(\bar{s}_C, s_{-C})$ is equivalent to $g(s_1^*, \ldots, s_n^*)$ where

$$s_i^* = \begin{cases} \bar{s}_i, & i \in C \\ s_1, & i \notin C \end{cases}$$

[3] $\#(A)$ denotes the cardinality of A.

welfare function (SWF) satisfying Arrow's conditions (see Section 3). Arrow's theorem states that such a SWF must be dictatorial, and it is a simple matter to translate the dictatorship of a SWF to that of the game-form. Satterthwaite (1975), and Schmeidler and Sonnenschein (1975), proved the result without appealing to the Arrow theorem, but they required rather lengthier arguments.

I offer quite a short proof. In the spirit of 'reductionism', we shall consider the theorem to be proved if we can establish that the existence of a non-dictatorial n-person SPGF on $\mathcal{R}_A$ implies the existence of a three-person non-dictatorial SPGF on $\mathcal{R}_B$ where $B \subseteq A$ and $\#(B) = 3$. Showing that there is no non-dictatorial SPGF in the three-person, three-alternative case can then readily be shown by purely mechanical calculation.

Proof. Consider an n-player non-dictatorial game-form $\dot{g} : S_1 \times \cdots \times S_n \to A$ that is strategy-proof on $\mathcal{R}_A$. We first claim that there exists a three-player non-dictatorial game-form that is strategy-proof on $\mathcal{R}_A$. If $n = 2$, we can extend g to three players by adding a dummy player who has no influence on the outcome. This extended game-form is clearly non-dictatorial and strategy-proof. If $n > 3$, then there exists a two-player coalition that is not decisive for g (a coalition is decisive if, for all $a \in A$, the coalition has a strategy vector that results in a regardless of the strategies of the complementary coalition), since, if C is decisive, $N \backslash C$ is not decisive. Assume without loss of generality that $\{n - 1, n\}$ constitutes a non-decisive coalition. Define the $(n - 1)$-player game-form g^{**}: $S_1^{**} \times \cdots \times S_{n-1}^{**} \to A$ so that, for $i = 1, \ldots, n - 2$, and $S_i^{**} = S_i$, and $S_{n-1}^{**} = S_{n-1} \times S_n$, and for all $(s_1, \ldots, s_{n-2}, s'_{n-1}) \in S_1^{**} \times \cdots \times S_{n-1}^{**}$,

$$g^{**}(s_1, \ldots, s_{n-2}, s'_{n-1}) = g(s_1, \ldots, s_{n-2}, s_{n-1}, s_n),$$

where $s'_{n-1} = (s_{n-1}, s_n)$. (Notice that g^{**} is obtained from g by 'collapsing' players $n - 1$ and n into a single player $n - 1$). The game-form g^{**} is non-dictatorial because g is non-dictatorial and $\{n - 1, n\}$ is non-decisive. Notice that, for $i = 1, \ldots, n - 2$ and $R_i \in \mathcal{R}_A$, if $\bar{s}_i$ is a dominant strategy for player i with ordering R_i in g, it remains a dominant strategy in g^{**}. Moreover, if, for $R \in \mathcal{R}_A$, $\bar{s}_{n-1}$ and $\bar{s}_n$ are dominant strategies for players $n - 1$ and n with the same ordering R in g, then the strategy $\bar{s}'_{n-1} = (\bar{s}_{n-1}, \bar{s}_n)$ is dominant for player $n - 1$ with ordering R in g^{**}. Hence g^{**} is strategy-proof, and so we have shown that the existence of an n-player game-form that is non-dictatorial and strategy-proof implies the existence of an $(n - 1)$-player game-form with the same properties. Thus our first claim is established.

Henceforth assume that $n = 3$. Because g is non-dictatorial, we can choose a three-element subset $B = \{a, b, c\} \subseteq A$ such that, for all $i = 1, 2, 3$, there exists $x \in B$ that player i cannot force. (Player i can *force* x in game-form g if there exists s_i^x such that, for all $s_{-i} \in \underset{j \neq i}{\times} S_j$, $g(s_i^x, s_{-i}) = x$.) Let

$\mathcal{R}_A^B$ consist of all orderings in A that rank the alternatives of B strictly above all other alternatives. For each $i = 1, 2, 3$, let $S_i^B = \{s_i \in S_i \mid \exists\ R \in \mathcal{R}_A^B$ such that s_i is a dominant strategy for player i with preference ordering R.

Consider the restriction g^B of g to $S_1^B \times S_2^B \times S_3^B$. We claim that the range of g^B is B. Suppose that there exist strategies $(s_1, s_2, s_3) \in S_1^B \times S_2^B \times S_3^B$ such that $g^B(s_1, s_2, S_3) \notin B$. By construction, each s_i is dominant for player i with some ordering $R_i \in \mathcal{R}_A^B$. Now because g is onto A, there exist strategies (s_1', s_2', s_3') such that $g(s_1', s_2', s_3') \in B$. Because s_1 is dominant for player 1, and player 1 prefers any element in B to anything in $A \backslash B$, $g(s_1, s_2', s_3') \in B$. Similarly, $g(s_1, s_2, s_3'), g(s_1, s_2, s_3) \in B$, a contradiction. Hence the range of g^B must be contained in B. But a similar argument shows that if, for $i = 1, 2, 3$ s_i is dominant for R_i and R_i ranks a above all other alternatives, then $g(s_1, s_2, s_3) = a$. Hence the range of g^B equals B.

Now, g^B is clearly strategy-proof on $\mathcal{R}_B$ because it is strategy-proof on $\mathcal{R}_A^B$. If it is also non-dictatorial, we are done. Hence, assume that some player, say player 1, is a dictator for g^B. But, by choice of B, there exists some alternative in B, say a, that player 1 cannot force in g. Thus, if $s_1^a \in S_1^B$ is a dominant strategy for player 1 with an ordering that ranks a above all other alternatives, there exist $d \in A \backslash B$ and $(s_2^d, s_3^d) \in S_2 \times S_3$ such that $g(s_1^a, s_2^d, s_3^d) = d$. Let $B' = \{a, b, d\}$, and define $g^{B'}$ by analogy with g^B. Player 1 is not a dictator for $g^{B'}$ since, from the above argument, he cannot force a. But players 2 and 3 are not dictators either, since, from our hypotheses about player 1 in g^B, $g^B(s_1^*, s_2^*, s_3^*) = g^{B'}(s_1^*, s_2^*, s_3^*) = a$ whenever (i) s_1^* is a dominant strategy for an ordering that ranks a above all other alternatives, and (ii) s_2^* and s_3^* are dominant strategies for orderings that rank a and b above all other alternatives. Thus, $g^{B'}$ is a 3×3 non-dictatorial, strategy-proof game-form, as required. ∎

3. The Arrow Impossibility Theorem

Let A and $\mathcal{R}_A$ be as in Section 2 except that A is now restricted to be finite. For $\mathcal{R} \subseteq \mathcal{R}_A$, an n-person social welfare function (SWF) on $\mathcal{R}$ is a mapping

$$f: \mathcal{R}^n \to \mathcal{R}_A.$$

Following Arrow (1951), we define the following properties of SWFs.

PARETO PROPERTY. The SWF f satisfies the Pareto property if, for all $a, b \in A$ and all $(R_1, ..., R_n) \in \mathcal{R}^n$, aPb provided that ap_ib for all $i = 1, ..., n$ (where aPb means 'a is strictly socially preferred to b, given $f(R_1, ..., R_n)$', and P_i is the strict ordering for individual i corresponding to R_i).

INDEPENDENT OF IRRELEVANT ALTERNATIVES (IIA). The SWF f satisfies IIA if, for all a, $b \in A$ and all $(R_1, ..., R_n)$ and $(R'_1, ..., R'_n) \in \mathcal{R}^n$, we have aRb iff $aR'b$ (where R and R' are the social orderings corresponding to $(R_1, ..., R_n)$ and $(R'_1, ..., R'_n)$, respectively), provided that, for all $i \in N$, aR_ib iff aR'_ib.

An individual $i \in N$ is a *dictator* on B for f if, for all a, $b \in B$ and all $(R_1, ..., R'_n) \in \mathcal{R}^n$, aP_ib implies aPb.

NON-DICTATORSHIP. The SWF f satisfies non-dictatorship if there is no dictator on A for f.

We shall call a SWF f on $\mathcal{R}$ satisfying the Pareto property, IIA, and non-dictatorship an *Arrow social welfare function* (ASWF).

ARROW IMPOSSIBILITY THEOREM. If $n \geqslant 2$ and $\#(A) \geqslant 3$, there exists no *n*-person ASWF on $\mathcal{R}_A$.

Proof. Once again, we shall be satisfied to reduce the question of existence to the three-person, three-alternative case. (See Suzumura (1988) for an alternative proof that reduces the problem to the three-person case.) We first show that, if f is an *n*-person ASWF on $\mathcal{R}$, then there exists a three-person ASWF on $\mathcal{R}^*$, where $\mathcal{R}^*$ consists of the strict orderings of A. If $n = 2$, then we can add a 'dummy' person (who has no effect on the social ordering) and trivially extend f to the three-person case. Assume, therefore, that $n \geqslant 4$. Then there exists a two-person subset of players that is not *decisive* (a subset $M \subseteq N$ is decisive if, for all a, $b \in A$ aPb wherever aP_ib for all $i \in M$). Without loss of generality, suppose that the subset $\{n - 1, n\}$ is not decisive. Define $f^*: \mathcal{R}_A^{n-1} \to \mathcal{R}_A$ such that, for all $(R_1, ..., R_{n-1}) \in \mathcal{R}_A^{n-1}$,

$$f^*(R_1, ..., R_{n-1}) = f(R_1, ..., R_{n-1}, R_{n-1}).$$

That is, we are 'collapsing' individuals $n - 1$ and n in f into a single individual to obtain f^*. Clearly, f^* satisfies the Pareto property and IIA. Because $\{n - 1, n\}$ is not decisive for f, individual $n - 1$ is not a dictator for f^*. If nobody else is a dictator either, we are done. Suppose, therefore, that some other individual, say individual 1, *is* a dictator for f^*. Now, individual 1 is *not* a dictator for f. Thus for some a, $b \in A$ and some profile $(\hat{R}_1, ..., \hat{R}_n) \in (\mathcal{R}_A^*)^n$ $a\hat{P}_1b$ but a is not preferred to b socially under $f(\hat{R}_1, ..., \hat{R}_n)$. Since 1 *is* a dictator for f^*, $\hat{R}_{n-1}$ and $\hat{R}_n$ cannot rank a and b the same way (if $\hat{R}_{n-1}$ and $\hat{R}_n$ rank a and b the same way, then f^* determines the social ordering of a and b). Thus there exists some other individual, say $n - 2$, such that $\hat{R}_{n-2}$ ranks a and b the same as either $\hat{R}_{n-1}$ or $\hat{R}_n$. For simplicity, assume the former (i.e., $\hat{R}_{n-2}$ and $\hat{R}_{n-1}$ rank a and b the same way). Define $f^{**}: (\mathcal{R}_A^*)^{n-1} \to \mathcal{R}_A$ so that, for all $(R_1, ..., R_{n-1}) \in (\mathcal{R}_A^*)^{n-1}$,

$$f^{**}(R_1, ..., R_{n-1}) = f(R_1, ..., R_{n-2}, R_{n-2}, R_{n-1}).$$

That is, we are 'collapsing' individuals $n - 2$ and $n - 1$ in f into a single individual, $n - 2$, to obtain f^{**}. Now individual 1 cannot be a dictator for f^{**} (from IIA and our argument about $\hat{R}_1, ..., \hat{R}_n$)). Moreover, nobody else can be a dictator for f^{**} either, because if 1 prefers a to b and everyone else prefers b to a, the fact that 1 is a dictator for f^* implies that a is socially preferred to b under f^* and hence f^{**}. Thus f^{**} is an ASWF, and so we may assume that $n = 3$.

Choose $a \in A$, and for any $R \in \mathcal{R}_A$ let R^a be the restriction of R to $A \backslash a$. Define the three-person SWF f^a to be the restriction of f to $R_{A \backslash a}$. Because f satisifies IIA, f^a is well defined. Clearly, f^a satisfies the Pareto property and IIA. Thus, if f^a satisfies non-dictatorship, we have succeeded in reducing the cardinality of A by 1. Assume, therefore, that some individual—say individual 1—is a dictator for f^a on $A \backslash a$. Because 1 is not a dictator for f, however, there exists $b \in A \backslash a$ such that 1 is not a dictator on (a, b) for f. Choose $c \in A \backslash \{a, b\}$. Consider f^c (defined by analogy with f^a). Individual 1 is not a dictator for f^c because 1 is not a dictator on $\{a, b\}$. Moreover, no other individual is a dictator for f^c because, for any $d \in A \backslash \{a, b, c\}$, 1 is a dictator on $\{b,d\}$ (since by assumption he is a dictator for f^a on A\a). Therefore f^c is an ASWF on $\mathcal{R}_{A \backslash c}$. Proceeding iteratively, we may infer the existence of a three-person ASWF on $\mathcal{R}_B$, where B is a three-alternative subset of A.   ∎

4. Majority Rule

An *n*-person *collective choice rule* (CCR) is a function that maps profiles of preferences $(R_1, ..., R_n)$ drawn from $\mathcal{R}_A$ to a complete binary relation on A. This relation represents social preferences, but is not necessarily transitive. A CCR is *anonymous* if it is invariant with respect to permutations of the individuals' labels $\{1, ..., n\}$; it is *neutral* if it is invariant with respect to permutations of the alternatives' labels $\{a, b, ...\}$. The most familiar CCR is the *method of majority rule* (MMR): if R^M is the majority rule social relation corresponding to the profile $((R_1, ..., R_n)$, then, for all a and b, aR^Mb if and only if $\#\{i \,|\, aP_ib\} \geqslant \#\{i \,|\, bP_ia\}$.

May (1952) characterized MMR by establishing that it is the unique CCR defined on $\mathcal{R}_A$ (see Campbell (1982) and (1988) for extensions to the case of restricted domains; see Bordes (1976) and Campbell (1980) for alternative characterizations) satisfying anonymity, neutrality, the Pareto property (see Section 3), and *positive responsiveness*. (If there is a shift in someone's preference ordering in favour of alternative a relative to b, and a was previously no worse than b socially, then a must now be strictly socially preferred to b; note that positive responsiveness implies IIA.) I shall provide an alternative characterization. We know from Arrow's theorem (Section 3) that there exists no anonymous SWF satisfying IIA and the Pareto property on the unrestricted domain of preferences $\Re_A$. Thus, for example, MMR is intransitive for the celebrated Condorcet profile, that is, it is not a social welfare function for the unrestricted domain. But we may ask for which *restricted* domains of preferences $\Re$ a given CCR constitutes a SWF, i.e. on which domains it is transitive. This is precisely the question that Sen (1966) answered for MMR: (provided that the number of individuals is odd) MMR is a SWF on domain $\Re$ if and only if $\Re$ satisfies value restriction (see fn. 1). I will show that, among CCRs satisfying anonymity, neutrality, the Pareto property, and IIA, MMR is transitive on the widest class of domains of preferences (and is the unique such CCR).

> THEOREM. Let F be an *n*-person (*n* odd) CCR satisfying anonymity, neutrality, the Pareto property, and IIA. Suppose that $\Re$ is a domain of strict preferences on which F is transitive, i.e. a social welfare function. Then MMR is also an SWF on $\Re$. Moreover, unless F is itself MMR, there exists some domain $\Re'$ on which MMR is a SWF but F is not.

Proof. Consider a domain $\Re$ on which a CCR F satisfying the hypotheses of the theorem is a SWF for some *n* odd. We claim that $\Re$ satisfies value restriction (VR), and so will conclude, from Sen (1966), that MMR is a SWF on this domain too.

If $\Re$ fails to satisfy VR, then for some triple of alternatives $\{a, b, c\}$ there exists a triple of 'cyclic' preferences $R(abc)$, $R(bca)$, $R(cab) \in \Re$ such that $aP(abc)\,bp(abc)\,c$, $bP(bca)\,cP(bca)\,a$, and $cP(cab)\,aP(cab)\,b$. To see this, note that if VR fails then, for some $\{a, b, c\}$, there exists $R \in \Re$ such that R ranks *a* highest (among $\{a, b, c\}$). Because the labels '*b*' and '*c*' are arbitrary, we might as well suppose that $R = R(abc)$ Now, similarly, there exist R', $R'' \in \Re$ such that R' ranks *b* highest and R'' ranks *c* highest (again, among $\{a, b, c\}$). Now, either R, R', and R'' together form a triple of cyclic preferences (there are two such cycles), or else two of the three orderings belong to the same cycle and the third belongs to the other cycle. In the former case our assertion is established. Thus, we might as well assume that $R' = R(bca)$ and $R'' = R(cba)$. Because VR fails, there exists $r \in \Re$ that ranks *a* strictly between *b* and *c*. Therefore, we might as well suppose that $\hat{R} = R(bac)$. (If $\hat{R} = R(cab)$, then R, R' and $\hat{R}$ belong to the same cycle.) Similarly, the failure of VR implies that there exists $\hat{\hat{R}} \in \Re$ that ranks *b* strictly below *a* and *c*. As noted above, we might as well assume that $\hat{\hat{R}} \neq R(cab)$. But then $\hat{\hat{R}} = R(acb)$, and so the cycle $R(acb)$, $R(bac)$, $R(cba)$ belongs to $\Re$, as asserted. Henceforth, therefore, assume that $R(abc)$, $R(bca)$, $R(cab) \in \Re$.

Consider a profile $(R_1, \ldots, R_n)$ in which $aP_1 b$ and $bP_i a$ for all $i \neq 1$. Let R^F be the corresponding social ordering under F. There are three possible cases: (i) $bP^F a$, (ii) $aI^F b$ society is indifferent between *a* and *b*, and (iii) $aP^F b$. We will consider each of these in turn. Suppose first that $aP^F b$. From IIA, anonymity, and neutrality, we infer from $bP^F a$ that, for any alternatives

x and y and any profile in which all individuals but one prefer x to y, x is socially preferred to y. Consider the profile $(\hat{R}_1, ..., \hat{R}_n)$ such that $\hat{R}_1 = R(abc)$, $\hat{R}_2 = R(bca)$, and $\hat{R}_3 = \cdots = \hat{R}_n = R(cab)$. Let $\hat{R}^F$ be the corresponding social ordering. Now, everybody but individual 2 prefers a to b. Hence, from anonymity and IIA, we have $a\hat{P}^Fb$. Similarly, everybody but individual 1 prefers c to a. Therefore, from neutrality, $c\hat{P}^Fa$. We infer, from transitivity, that $c\hat{P}^Fb$. Notice, moreover, that all individuals but 1 and 2 prefer c to b. IIA, anonymity, and neutrality therefore imply that, whenever all but two individuals prefer alternative x to y, x is socially preferred to y.

Consider the profile $(\hat{R}_1, ..., \hat{R}_n)$ such that $\hat{R}_1 = R(abc)$, $\hat{R}_2 = \hat{R}_3 = R(bca)$ and $\hat{R}_4 = ... = \hat{R}_n = R(cab)$. Arguing as above, we conclude that $c\hat{p}^Fb$, where $\hat{R}^F$ is the social ordering corresponding to the profile. Continuing in the same way, we conclude that, for any $m < n$, any alternatives x and y, and any profile in which all but m individuals prefer x to y, x is socially preferred to y. But this is contradictory, because if all but m individuals prefer x to y, then all but $n - m$ individuals prefer y to x, and so socially y should be preferred to x. Thus, case (i), where bP^Fa, is impossible.

We can derive the same contradiction in case (iii), where aP^Fb. Suppose, therefore, that aI^Fb. Arguing as above, we can show that, for all $m < n$, if all but m individuals prefer a to b, then society is indifferent between a and b. Now, consider the profile $\bar{R}_1, ..., \bar{R}_n$), in which $\bar{R}_1 = \cdots = \bar{R}_{n-1} = R(abc)$ and $\bar{R}_n = R(bca)$. From the above conclusion, we have $a\bar{I}^Fb$ and $a\bar{I}^Fc$, and so, from transitivity, $b\bar{I}^Fc$. But everyone in this profile prefers b to c, a contradiction of the Pareto property.

We conclude that $\mathfrak{R}$ must satisfy VR after all. Hence, from Sen (1966), MMR is a SWF on $\mathfrak{R}$.

We next turn to the second assertion of the theorem. Suppose that F is an anonymous and neutral n-person CCR that satisfies IIA and the Pareto principle. Suppose, moreover, that $F \neq$ MMR. Hence there exist a profile $(R_1, ..., R_n)$ and alternatives a and b such that $n - m$ individuals (where $n - m > m$) prefer a to b and yet a is not socially preferred to b. Let $A = \{a, b, c\}$ and $\mathfrak{R}' = \{R(cab), R(bca), R(cba)\}$. Notice that $\mathfrak{R}'$ satisfies VR (a is never on top), and so MMR is transitive on $\mathfrak{R}'$. Consider the profile $\hat{R}_1, ..., \hat{R}_n)$ in which $\hat{R}_1 = \cdots = \hat{R}_m = R(cab)$, $\hat{R}_{m+1} = \cdots = \hat{R}_{2m} = R(bca)$, and $\hat{R}_{2m+1} = \cdots = \hat{R}_n = R(cba)$. Notice that $n - m$ individuals prefer b to a, and so, from the above assumption about F, $a\hat{R}^Fb$, where $\hat{R}^F$ is the social ordering corresponding to the profile. Similarly $b\hat{R}^Fc$, and so, from transitivity, $a\hat{R}^Fc$. But everyone in the profile prefers c to a, and so, from the Pareto property, $c\hat{P}^Fa$, a contradiction. We conclude that F is not transitive on $\mathfrak{R}'$. ∎

To illustrate this theorem, consider the *Pareto extension rule* (PER), which, after majority rule, is probably the best known CCR satisfying the theorem's hypotheses. PER is the rule defined so that, for all $(R_1, ..., R_n)$ and all $a, b \in A$, aR^pb (where R^p is the social preference relation corresponding to $(R_1, \ldots R_n)$) if and only if b does not strictly Pareto-dominate a. It can readily be shown that PER is transitive on domain $\mathcal{R}$ consisting of strict orderings if and only if $\mathcal{R}$ satisfies *quasi-agreement* (QA): for all $B = \{a, b, c\} \subseteq A$, there exists $x \in B$ such that either (i) for all $R \in \mathcal{R}$, x is ranked higher than the other two alternatives in B; or (ii) for all $R \in \mathcal{R}$, x is ranked in between the other two alternatives in B; or (iii) for all $R \in \mathcal{R}$, x is ranked below the other two alternatives in A. But QA is clearly strictly stronger than VR. In particular, for the six strict orderings of the alternatives $\{a, b, c\}$, VR requires the deletion of no more than two (one ordering from each triple of cyclic preferences). Thus, for example, $\{R(abc), R(bca), R(acb), R(cba)\}$ constitutes a domain satisfying VR (a is never in between). In contrast, QA requires the deletion of at least four orderings. For example, $\{R(abc), R(acb)\}$ constitutes a maximal domain satisfying QA; the addition of any of the four other orderings would lead to a violation.

To conclude, I shall examine the roles of the neutrality and anonymity assumptions in the above theorem, since they are not required in Arrow's treatment of social welfare functions. If we are willing to dispense with neutrality, then it becomes possible to define SWFs on domains strictly bigger than those satisfying value restriction. For example, let $A = \{a, b, c\}$, and define the CCR F^* so that, for all profiles $(R_1, \ldots, R_n)$ and all $x, y \in \{a, b, c\}$ xP^*y if and only if $xP(abc)y$ unless yP_ix for all i, in which case yP^*x. It is not hard to see that F^* is transitive on the domain consisting of all strict orderings but $R(cab)$, i.e. on a domain including one more ordering than any value-restricted domain.

If we drop anonymity, it is easy to construct a CCR other than MMR that satisfies all other hypotheses of the theorem as well as non-dictatorship and, moreover, is transitive on any value-restricted domain. For example, for $n > 3$, consider the CCR that determines social preferences according to majority rule applied to individuals 1, 2, and 3 alone, so that the remaining individuals are 'dummies' having no affect on the social ranking. Such a CCR is clearly transitive whenever the same is true of ordinary majority rule, and thus it demonstrates that the theorem is false if we simply substitute non-dictatorship for anonymity. I conjecture, however, that the theorem can be restored if we replace anonymity with the *conjunction* of non-dictatorship and a 'no dummy' assumption (so that every individual has some influence on the social ranking). This conjecture, however, must be left to future work.

References

Arrow, K. (1951), *Social Choice and Individual Values*, John Wiley, New York.

Bordes, G. (1976), 'Consistency, Rationality and Collective Choice', *Review of Economic Studies*, 43: 447–57.

Campbell, D. (1980), 'Algorithms for Social Choice Functions', *Review of Economic Studies*, 47: 617–27.

—— (1982), 'On the Derivation of Majority Rule', *Theory and Decision*, 14: 133–40.

—— (1988), 'A Characterization of Simple Majority Rule for Restricted Domains', *Economics Letters*, 28: 307–10.

Gibbard, A. (1973), 'Manipulation of Voting Schemes: A General Result', *Econometrica*, 41: 587–601.

May, K. (1952), 'A Set of Independent, Necessary, and Sufficient Conditions for Simple Majority Decision', *Econometrica*, 20: 680–4.

Satterthwaite, M. (1975), 'Strategy-Proofness and Arrow's Conditions: Existence and Correspondence Theorems for Voting Procedures and Social Welfare Functions', *Journal of Economic Theory*, 10: 187–217.

Schmeidler, D. and Sonnenschein, H. (1975), 'The Possibility of a Nonmanipulable Social Choice Function', mimeo, Northwestern University.

Sen, A. (1966), 'A Possibility Theorem on Majority Decisions', *Econometrica*, 34: 491–9.

—— (1970), *Collective Choice and Social Welfare*, Holden Day, San Francisco.

Suzumura, K. (1988), 'Reduction of Social Choice Problems: A Simple Proof of Arrow's General Possibility Theorem', *Hitotsubashi Journal of Economics*, no. 2, 219–21.

7

Symbolic Utility

ROBERT NOZICK

The symbolic meaning of actions enters legitimately into choice among acts. A theory of rational decision should take explicit account of symbolic meaning, rather than subsuming (and losing sight of) it within a more encompassing category. We can begin by considering how principles help to get us past temptations, hurdles, distractions, and diversions; for symbolic meaning plays a role in this.

1. Principles and the Overcoming of Temptation

The psychologist George Ainslie has presented a theory of why we behave impulsively in what we know to be against our long-term interests, and of what devices we use to cope with the temptations of such behaviour (Ainslie 1975, 1986). Curves, describing the time-preferenced discounting of future rewards, need not be straight lines or exponential; they may be hyperbolic.[1] Ainslie noticed that two such highly bowed curves (as the hyperbolic) can cross, and he traced out the implications of this fact. (See Fig. 1: the utility of a reward is measured on the y-axis; its utility for a person at a given time is measured by the height of its curve at that time. The curve slopes downward to the left because a future reward has a lesser value earlier.)

Suppose there are two projects for action leading to two different rewards, where receiving the earlier possible reward (the smaller of the two), will thwart receiving the later larger one. A person proceeds, staying with the project having the highest utility at that time. In the time interval A the more distant reward has the greater utility; in the time interval B, though, the nearer reward has the greater utility. Since the larger reward can be actually collected only at the end of the time interval C, the person must get through that middle time period B without turning to the smaller reward. This presents a problem, because during that middle time interval the prospect of receiving that smaller reward *soon* has greater utility than the prospect of receiving the greater reward later.

This essay is extracted from a larger work, 'Decisions of Principle, Principles of Decision', which appeared in the *Tanner Lectures on Human Values*, xiv (University of Utah Press, Salt Lake City, 1992), which lecture in turn is part of a still larger work, *The Nature of Rationality*, (Princeton University Press, 1993).

[1] This last shape is a consequence of the 'matching law' equations: see Herrnstein (1961).

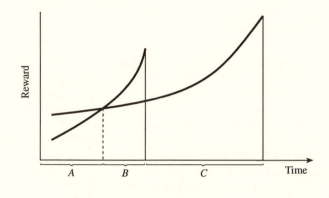

Fig. 1

Why assume that the person *should* try to get past that intermediate time period? Why shouldn't the smaller but more immediate reward be taken?[2] What makes the two time periods *A* and *C*, wherein the larger reward looms largest, the appropriate ones for deciding which choice is appropriate? During them the person will prefer acting to gain the larger reward, whereas during time period *B* he will prefer acting to gain the smaller one—that is, the one that is smaller when he gains it than the other one would be when it was gained. Where are *we* standing when we say that avoiding the temptation is the better alternative, and why is that standpoint more appropriate than the person's standpoint within the time interval *B*?

The time interval *B* is not the appropriate benchmark for deciding what the person ought to do because *B* is not a representative sample of his view of the matter; the time intervals *A* and *C* sum to a longer interval. Moreover, when we add his judgements *after* the moment the rewards are to be realized, and graph which rewards seem largest to him *then*, we find that soon after consuming the smaller reward he wishes he had not done this, but after consuming the larger reward (at the end of the time interval *C*) he continues to prefer having chosen that larger reward to having chosen the smaller one. I suggest that, often, what makes resisting the temptation and taking the larger reward the preferred option is that this is the person's preference for a majority of the time; it is his stable preference, whereas the other is his preference at a non-representative moment.[3] (Leaving aside the

---

[2] I thank Amartya Sen for raising this question.

[3] There also is the phenomenon of *regret*, a lowering of current utility that arises when looking back upon currently undesired past action. Having a tendency towards regret might help one to get over the temptation during *B*, since during *B* one can anticipate the lowered utility level during *C* and afterwards too if one takes the smaller closer reward now. But will this anticipation feed back sufficiently into the overall utilities during *B* to affect the choice made then?

issue of after-the-fact preferences, we can ask whether the Ainslie situation of crossed curves could be constructed if the time interval *B* lasted for longer than the intervals *A* and *C*? And would it be clear *in that case* that the temptation should be resisted?)

I do not, therefore, claim that the temptation should *always* be resisted, but only when the desire for the larger reward (including the preference after the fact) is the person's preference for the larger amount of time. The criterion I propose here is meant to be defeasible, although not conclusive. It does have the virtue of staying close to a person's preferences, although the criterion is not wedded to a particular local preference. (Contrast this with stepping outside and saying that it simply *is* in the person's interests to resist the temptation, or that the relevant criterion is—and resisting temptation serves—the maximization of utility over a lifetime.[4])

Ainslie describes various devices for getting oneself past that intermediate period of temptation. These include taking an action during interval *A* that makes it impossible to pursue the smaller reward during *B* (e.g. Odysseus' tying himself to the mast); taking an action during interval *A* (e.g. making a bet with another person) that adds a penalty if you take the smaller reward, thereby altering *its* utility during interval *B*; taking steps during *A* to avoid noticing or dwelling upon the virtues of the smaller reward during *B*; and, more to our current point, formulating a general principle of personal behaviour.

A general principle of behaviour groups actions; it classifies a particular act with others—for example 'never eat snacks between meals'; 'never smoke another cigarette'. (I do not, for present purposes, make any distinction between principles and rules.)

We might try to represent the effect of this principled grouping of actions within utility theory and decision theory as follows. By classifying actions as of type *T*, and by treating them similarly, a principle links the utilities of these *T*-actions (or the utilities of their outcomes). It would be too strong to say that, because of the principle, all *T*-actions must have the same utility; there may be some types and principles that one particular *T*-action falls under while another *T*-action does not, so their utilities may diverge. What a principle sets up is a *correlation* between the utilities of the various actions falling under it. Stating this at the level of preference, when acts of type *T* are ranked with other actions in a preference ordering, there will be a correlation between the rank orders of the *T*-acts. However, if this correlation were the only effect that adopting or accepting principles had on the utilities of the actions falling under them, then principles would not be of help in getting us past temptations.

The mark of a principle ('never eat snacks between meals'; 'never smoke another cigarette') is that it ties the decision about whether to take an

---

[4] For a critical discussion of the single goal of maximizing the total utility over a lifetime, see Nozick (1989, pp. 100–2).

immediate particular action (eating *this* snack, smoking *this* cigarette) to the whole class of actions of which the principle makes it a part. This act now stands for the whole class. By adopting the principle, it is as if you have made the following true: if you take this one particular action in the class, you will take them all. Now the stakes are higher, for the utility of this act of snacking is tied to the disutility of all those acts of snacking in the future, and this addition may help you to get through the period *B* of temptation, for it alters the utility for you of this particular snack. It comes to stand for all the snacks, and at this early point the current utility of being thin or healthy later far outweighs the current utility of those distant pleasures of eating; the current disutility of poor health or a poor figure becomes a feature of the currently contemplated act of snacking.[5]

But why assume that the person will formulate his principle during the time period *A* rather than during the time period *B*? Why won't he take the snack this time and formulate a principle of always snacking or, more generally, a principle of always giving in to immediate temptation? However, formulating and accepting such a principle (alongside the action of taking the snack now) will not itself bring immediate reward or maximize reward over time. It does reduce delay in reward, but during time period *B*, facing one particular temptation, do I want *always* to reduce delay in any and every reward? No; for, although I am in that *B*-period with respect to one particular reward, with regard to many other (pairs of) rewards I am in the *A*-period (or the *C*-period). With regard to these other, more distant, pairs of lesser and greater rewards, I do not now want always to take the more immediate one, even though I do wish now to take one *particular* reward (which I am in the *B*-period of). It is because temptations are spread out over time that, at any *one* time, we are in more *A* (or *C*) periods than *B*-periods. Hence we would not accept a principle always to succumb to temptation.[6]

By adopting a principle, we make one action stand for many others and thereby we change the utility or disutility of this particular action. But *how*

---

[5] In its focus upon the whole group of actions of a certain kind in the personal realm, this may remind some readers of rule utilitarianism in the public realm. However, our question is how the acceptance of a general principle affects the choice of a particular action that, in the absence of the principle, would not have maximal utility. The comparable question would be how someone with act-utilitarian desires who (somehow) decides upon a rule-utilitarian principle can manage to put it into effect in particular choice situations.

[6] The proponent of succumbing to temptation may reply, 'You are saying that we don't always *want* to succumb to temptation. But you say a principle is the device to get us past what may be our current desire. So perhaps we need a principle to get us past the desire not always to succumb to temptation.' Leaving aside the skirting of paradox, a principle is (most easily) adopted during a time period *t* when a contrary desire is stronger than the temptation. (The temptation will reach full strength later than *t*.) And there will not be a time period when the desire *always* to succumb is not weaker than a contrary desire. (Or, if such a temporary time period did arise, any principle adopted then would soon be overturned on the basis of a later desire that wasn't just momentary.)

are we able to do this? Violating the principle once does not necessitate that we will always violate it; having this snack does not necessitate that we shall become continual snackers. If it was not true, before we adopted the principle, that doing the act once would involve doing it always, how does adopting the principle forge that connection, so that now the penalty for violating the principle this time becomes violating it always?

We have no reason to think that the next occasion will be any different from this one. If each occasion is the same, and if we do it this time, won't we do it on all such occasions? Unless we can distinguish this occasion from the later ones, and also have reasons for believing that *later* this distinction will carry weight with us so that we won't indulge by formulating another distinction, which again we won't adhere to still later, then taking the action this time will lead us to expect that we shall repeat it. (To formulate a distinction that permits this one act yet excludes future repetitions is to formulate yet another principle, and we must have more reason to think we shall adhere to that one than to this, or the reformulating will give no credibility to our abstention in the future.) Performing the act this one time, in *this* situation, means we shall continue to do it in the future. Isn't this enough to alter the utility of doing it this one time, thereby attaching to this particular act now the disutility of all its future repetitions?

We expect that if we do it this one time we will also do it repeatedly in the future, but does our performing it this once actually *affect* the future? Does it *make* it more likely that we shall repeat the action? Or does it simply affect our *estimate* of how likely that repetition is? There are two situations to consider. When no principle had previously been adopted that excludes the action, performing the action now may have a minor effect on the probability of repetition in accordance with the psychologist's 'law of effect': positive reinforcement of an action raises its probability of occurrence in the future. And the estimate of the probability of repetition may be raised somewhat if this action is added to a number of similar ones in the past. When a principle has been adopted previously, acting in violation of the principle will raise our estimate, and the individual's own estimate too, of how likely the person is to repeat this particular act in future. Also, it makes it more likely that the act will be repeated. The principle has broken down; one bar to the action has been removed. Moreover, realizing this may produce discouragement and make it less likely that the person will exert effort in the future to avoid the action. (Notice that an action that affects *his estimate* of the probability of similar future actions may then produce discouragement in him and thereby may affect the actual probability of repetition.) Formulating a principle that would constitute an additional bar to any of the actions it excludes is a way of actually tying the effects of all to the effects of any previous one. The more one has invested in a principle, the more effort one has previously put behind adhering to it, the greater the cost in violating it now. (For how likely is it that you will continue to adhere to another one if you couldn't manage to stick to this one despite so much effort?) Moreover, adhering to the principle this time is also a type of action that is subject to the law of effect; its being positively reinforced makes it more probable that adherence to the principle will occur in the future.

I have spoken of how your violating a particular principle concerning a type of action affects the probability of your adhering to that principle in the future, and of your succeeding in formulating and adhering to another principle concerning that type of action in the future. But the effects of violating a principle may be more general still, for the probability or credibility of your successfully utilizing *any* principles at all in *any* arena (when faced with a temptation as strong as the one that caused you to succumb this time) may be affected. To be sure, you may try to demarcate and limit the damage to this *one area*, but this presents the same problem— one level up—as limiting the damage *within* this area to just *this one* violative action. Deontological principles may have the greatest weight when their violation directly threatens *any* and all principled action in the future: if I violate *this* principle (in this circumstance), how can I believe I will succeed in adhering to any principle ever again? Someone might try, in an excess of Kantian zeal, to increase the potential effect of spreading disaster by formulating a (meta-)principle never to violate any principle. But, while making any violation stand for all might lessen the probability of any given violation, the actual consequences of the slightest violation would get dangerously magnified.

Since adopting a principle is itself an action that affects the probability linkages among other actions, some care is appropriate in choosing which principles to adopt. One must consider not only the possible benefits of adherence, but also the probability of its violation and what the future effects of that would be. It might be better to adopt a less good principle (when followed) but one easier to adhere to, especially since that principle may not always be available as a credible fall-back principle if one fails to adhere to the more stringent one. No doubt, a theory of the optimal choice of principles could be formulated, taking such considerations into account.

I have said that a principle speaks for all the actions in a group, and makes one action stand for all. To perform its functions, it must speak for *all* the actions of a certain kind. We do not have principles that say: *most* P's should be Q's; or, 15 per cent of P's have to be Q's. Sometimes, though, all we need is to do something most or some of the time, e.g. skipping desserts most evenings, paying most of our bills each month. The way we achieve this, through principles, is nevertheless to formulate one that speaks of 'all', 'each', or 'every', yet is coextensive with the mix we desire. *Each* month pay most of your bills; *every* week skip desserts most evenings. A teacher (not myself) whose principle it is not to give very many A's, grades *every* class on a curve; thereby, each week, or month, or class, comes to stand for all. Thus, we can explain why principles concern all the members of a class, not just some. (A norm could concern itself with $n\%$, where n is not 0 or 100; but a principle cannot.) A principle has certain functions, and to perform these functions one instance must stand for or symbolize all. The observed 'all'-character of principles thus provides support for our view of the function of principles, the ways in which principles perform these functions.[7]

2. Sunk Costs

One method Ainslie mentions for getting past the tempting time interval B is by committing oneself during the earlier interval A to seeking the larger reward during C. One mode of such commitment is, during A, to invest many resources in the future pursuit of that larger reward. If I think it would be good for me to see many plays or attend many concerts this year, and I know that frequently when the evening of the performance arrives I will not feel like rousing myself to go out, then I can buy tickets to many of these events in advance, even though I know that tickets still will be available at the box office on the evening of the performance. Since I will not want to waste the tickets I have bought, i.e. to waste the money already spent on these tickets, I will attend more performances than I would if I left the decisions about attendance to each evening. True, I may not use *all* these tickets—lethargy may triumph on some evenings—yet I will attend more frequently than if no tickets had been purchased in advance. Knowing all this, I purchase the tickets in advance in order to drive myself to attend.

Economists present a doctrine that all decisions should be future-oriented, paying attention only to the consequences of various alternative actions. The costs of investing resources in these courses of action have already been incurred, and while these resources may affect the consequences of the various actions now open to me—already possessing the ticket, I can attend the performance, with no additional payment—and hence may be taken into account the mere fact that costs have already been incurred to further a certain project should not carry any weight at all as a person makes a decision. These 'sunk costs' are a thing of the past; what matters now is only the future stream of benefits. Thus, sitting at home this evening, if I would now prefer staying at home to going out and attending a performance (for no monetary payment), then the evening at home has higher utility for me than attending the performance, and therefore I should stay at home; it should make no difference that I have already spent money on the ticket for

---

[7] An alternative explanation of this phenomenon wherein principles incorporate 'all' might propose that principles codify reasons and that reasons are universal (though defeasible); hence principles are too. But why is it that reasons are not 'for the most part' but instead are 'universal but defeasible', even though the percentages may be the same?

the performance—so runs the economists' doctrine that sunk costs should be ignored.[8]

This may be a correct rule for the maximization of monetary profits, but it is not an appropriate general principle of decision, for familiar reasons. We do *not* treat our past commitments to others as of no account, except in so far as they affect our future returns, e.g. when breaking a commitment may affect another's trust in us and hence our ability to achieve other future benefits; and we do *not* treat the past effort we have devoted to ongoing projects of work or of life as of no account, except in so far as this makes their continuance more likely to bring benefits than other freshly started projects would. Such projects help define our sense of ourselves and of our life.[9]

The problem of temptation indicates yet another defect in the doctrine of ignoring sunk costs as a general principle of decision. The fact that we do not ignore sunk costs provides one way to get past the temptation of choosing the smaller but more immediate reward during the *B* time interval. Earlier, during the time interval *A*, when we can clearly see the benefits of the larger but more distant reward, we can sink resources and effort into achieving that reward, knowing that, when the time *B* of temptation comes, the fact that we do *not* want (and will not want) to waste those resources will count for us as a reason against choosing the smaller reward, adding to its disutility. If I know I will be tempted some evening in the future by the smaller immediate reward of comfort—e.g. not having to go out into the rain—yet I also know that now and afterwards too I will be happy to have attended all those performances, then I can buy the tickets in advance to spur myself to forgo staying home when that evening arrives.

Everyone sees succumbing to the smaller reward during the time interval *B* as a problem, an irrationality, or an undesirable short-sightedness. The person himself sees it that way—beforehand and later, if not at the time—and we too see it thus as we think about it. The economist sees another type of behaviour, the honouring of sunk costs, as irrational and undesirable. But now we see that this latter behaviour, if anticipated, can be used to limit and check the first type of undesirable behaviour, viz. succumbing to the smaller but nearer reward. We can knowingly utilize our tendency to take sunk costs seriously as a means of increasing our *future* rewards. If this tendency is irrational, it can be rationally utilized to check and overcome another irrationality. If someone offered us a pill that would henceforth make us people who *never* honoured sunk costs, we would be ill-advised to accept it; for this would deprive us of one valuable tool for

---

[8] People frequently do not adhere to the doctrine of ignoring sunk costs, as indicated by their decisions when presented with hypothetical choices. On this, see Arkes and Blumer (1985). Arkes and Blumer see the people who deviate from the doctrine in the ticket-example as being irrational.

[9] See Bernard Williams's essay in Smart and Williams (1973); see also Williams (1976).

getting past temptations of the (future) moment. (Mightn't such a tendency to honour sunk costs, which is or can be adaptive, even have been selected for in the evolutionary process?)

Earlier, I mentioned that the greater the investment in a principle designed to get one past the temptations of the moment, and the more effort one has previously put behind adhering to it, the greater will be the cost in violating it now. It is unlikely that you will manage to stick to another principle if you cannot stick to this one despite so much previous effort. Realizing this gives you much reason to hold on to this one—it's the one life-raft in sight—and therefore gives great weight to not violating it in the face of this particular temptation. Groupings of action that we have succeeded in following in order to avoid immediate temptations thereby gain a further tenacity.

Notice that this too involves a sunk-cost phenomenon. My reasoning behind sticking to *this* principle, and its associated grouping, involved saying that, if I could not stick to it despite so much previous effort, how could I hope to stick to another? It is only if I *am* someone who honours sunk costs that I will be able to make this argument; only such a person would have a reason to adhere now to his current principle for bypassing temptation, rather than succumbing this one time and then formulating a different principle, which too will succumb to temptation when the time comes, perhaps at the very first test. It is sunk costs that makes *this* principle the place to take a stand. (Do not argue that these are considerations about the future consequences of the two different courses of action—sticking to the present policy *v.* succumbing to the temptation and then formulating a new policy—and hence that the person who does not honour sunk costs can go through the same line of reasoning; it is only because of the known tendency to honour sunk costs that one course of action will have significantly different consequences from the other—otherwise, why is it less likely that I will adhere to the new principle after violating the old one, than that I will continue to adhere to the old principle if I don't violate it now?)

I have described some functions performed by honouring sunk costs, but the economist might reply that honouring sunk costs is not desirable at all in an otherwise perfectly rational person; only someone with some *other* irrationality should indulge in it. However, this is not so evident, even leaving aside commitments made to other persons, and past investment in our projects of work and life. For it might be interpersonally useful, as a way of discouraging their making threats or carrying them out,[10] to have a means of convincing others that we shall stick to projects or aims even in the face of threats that seem to make this adherence work to our future disadvantage.

---

[10] See Schelling (1966); see also Schelling's discussion of 'the rationality of irrationality'.

This might be useful even if there is no other tendency to irrational behaviour, and if the others you are trying to convince have none either.[11] However, the theme of countering or fencing in one irrationality with another is one worth marking. Might some other things that we think irrational—perhaps weakness of will, self-deception, or fallacies of reasoning—consciously be put to use to thwart or limit still other irrationalities or undesirable happenings? (And might the total package of such counter balancing irrational tendencies even work together better than the *total* package of—when separately considered—rational tendencies?)

3. Symbolic Utility

I have said that, given the principle, performing the particular short-sighted action once in this situation *means* we shall continue to do it in the future. This act *stands for* all the others that the principle also excludes; this one *symbolizes* the rest. Is this fact of *meaning, standing for*, and *symbolizing*— constituted by the intertwining of the two strands of connection between acting now and repeating the act in the future which have already been discussed—the way doing it now affects your estimate of the probability of doing it again, and the way doing it now alters the very probability of your doing it in the future? Or is symbolizing a further fact not exhausted by these two strands, that itself affects the utility of alternative actions and outcomes? Symbolizing, I believe, is a further important strand, one that an adequate decision theory must treat explicitly.

Freudian theory explains the occurrence or persistence of neurotic actions or symptoms in terms of symbolic meaning. Producing evident bad consequences and appearing to be irrational, these actions and symptoms have an unobvious symbolic significance; they symbolize something else, call it M. Yet the mere fact of having such symbolic meaning cannot explain the occurrence or persistence of an action or symptom. We have to add that what they symbolize, that is, M, itself has some utility or value for the person (or, in the case of avoidance, some disutility or negative value) and, moreover that this utility of the M that is symbolized is imputed back to the action or symptom, thereby giving *it* greater utility than it appeared to have. Only thus can it explain why it was chosen or manifested. Freudian theory holds not only that actions and outcomes can symbolize still further events for a person, but that they can draw upon themselves the emotional meaning (and utility values) of these other events. Having a symbolic

---

[11] It might also be a useful trait, especially for the young, to be optimistic about the chances of success of possible projects—otherwise, no new and daring things would be tried—yet also to tend to stick to ongoing projects in which significant investment has been made; for otherwise at the first serious difficulty one might turn to another untried project which one is still (overly) optimistic about.

meaning, the actions are treated as having the utility of what they symbolize; a neurotic symptom is adhered to with a tenacity appropriate to what it stands for. (I am not aware of a clear statement in the Freudian literature of this equation, or of the weaker claim that *some* of the utility of what is symbolized is imputed back to the symbol, despite some such version being presupposed, I believe, in some Freudian explanations.) Disproportionate emotional responses to an actual event or occasion may indicate their standing for other events or occasions to which the emotions are more suited. Once an action or outcome comes to symbolize others, its presence may get taken as evidence for the others or as causes of them; but this is a result of the symbolizing, and not its original fabric (although this evidential or causal role may then reinforce the strength of the symbolic connection).

For the symbolic action to be performed, *it* must somehow come to have a higher utility than the other actions available to the agent.[12] I have suggested that it happens in this way: the action (or one of its outcomes) symbolizes a certain situation, and the utility of this symbolized situation is imputed back, through the symbolic connection, to the action itself. Notice that the standard decision theory also believes in an imputation back of utility, along a (probabilistic) causal connection. By virtue of producing a particular situation with certainty, an action comes to have, or to have imputed to it, the utility of that situation; by virtue of probabilistically producing certain situations, an action comes to have, to have imputed to it, the utilities of those situations in the form of an expected utility. What the current view adds is that utility can flow back, can be imputed back, not only along causal connections but also along symbolic ones.

One mark that it is an action's symbolic connection to an outcome that plays a central role in the decision to do it, rather than the apparently causal connection (I am thinking of cases where the agent does not think the action is itself intrinsically desirable or valuable) is the persistence of the action in the face of strong evidence that it does not have the presumed causal consequence, and perhaps even the refusal to look at or countenance such evidence or consider other evidence about harmful consequences of the action or policy. (One might claim that certain anti-drug enforcement measures *symbolize* reducing the amount of drug use, and that minimum wage laws *symbolize* helping the poor.) A reformer who wishes to avoid such harmful consequences may find it necessary to propose another policy (without such consequences) which equally effectively symbolizes acting towards or reaching the goal; simply halting the current action would deprive people of its symbolic utility, something they are unwilling to permit.

---

[12] A maximizing decision theory would assume this. There are other forms of normative decision theory, such as Herbert Simon's 'satisficing' theory, but this too would require the action that is done to end up with, or have imputed to it, a utility above the (shifting) level of aspiration.

Of course, *according* a particular symbolic meaning to an action A has causal consequences of its own, as it affects which actions we perform; so a purely consequentialist theory can say something about that. It can speak of whether giving such symbolic meaning (or, later, refraining from extinguishing that symbolic meaning) is itself a causally optimal action. However, this will be different from a purely consequentialist theory of the action A itself, and it does not imply that we must assess the according or tolerating of symbolic meaning solely by its causal consequences.

Since symbolic actions often are *expressive* actions, another view would be the following. The symbolic connection of an action to a situation enables the action to be expressive of some attitude, belief, value, emotion, or whatever. Expressiveness, not utility, is what flows back. What flows back along the symbolic connection to the action is: (the possibility of) expressing some particular attitude, belief, value, emotion, etc. Expressing this then has high utility for the person, and so the symbolic action is performed.[13]

There may not seem to be much difference between these two ways of structuring our understanding the choice of a symbolic action. The first, wherein utility is imputed back to the action along the symbolizing connection, faces this puzzle. Presumably the symbolizing connection always holds, so that for example an action of hand-washing always symbolizes removing guilt. Since the symbolized situation, i.e. being guilt-free, presumably always has high utility, then if utility is imputed back why won't the action of hand-washing always have maximal utility, so that the person will always be doing it? (Apparently this does happen with some compulsive hand-washers, but not with all, and not with all actions undertaken because of their symbolic meaning.) The *expressiveness theory* says that the possibility of expressing some attitude towards being guilt-free is always present, as a result of the ever-present symbolic connection; but the utility of expressing this may vary from context to context, depending upon, say, how recently one has expressed it, or what one's other needs and desires are. The utility of expressing that attitude, emotion, etc., competes with other utilities. The *utility imputation theory* describes this differently. The absolute or relative utility of the symbolized situation for the person can fluctuate; the utility of being guilt-free can actually become less if the person has recently taken steps to alleviate guilt—there now (temporarily) being less to deal with; or the utility of being guilt-free can remain constant while the utility of other competing goods, such as eating, temporarily rises to become greater than the utility of removing guilt. Let us leave in abeyance the question of the proper structure for understanding symbolic expressiveness. What I want to emphasize now is the *importance* of this phenomenon.

---

[13] Not that it need always be expressiveness that flows back along the symbolic connection. Other things may, and these will give rise to new characteristics of the action which themselves have high utility for the agent. The point is that it is not utility that flows back.

When utility is imputed to an action or outcome in accordance with its symbolic meaning, that is, when the utility of an action or outcome is equated with the utility of what it symbolically means, we are apt to think this irrational. When this symbolic meaning involves repressed child-hood desires and fears, or certain current unconscious ones, this may well result in behaviour doomed to be frustrating, unsatisfying, or tormenting. Yet mightn't symbolic meanings based upon unconscious desires also add gratifying reverberations to consciously desired goods? In any case, not all symbolic meanings will be rooted in Freudian material. However, many of these others, too, will look strange to someone outside that network of meanings; recall the dire consequences some people bear in order to avoid 'losing face', the deaths they risked and sometimes met in duels to 'maintain honour' or in exploits to 'prove manhood'. Yet we should not too quickly conclude that it would be better to live without any symbolic meanings at all, or never to impute utilities in accordance with symbolic meanings.

Ethical principles codify how to behave towards others in a way that is appropriate to their value and to our fellow-feelings with them. Holding and following ethical principles, in addition to the particular purpose it serves, also has a symbolic meaning for us. Treating people (and value in general) with respect, responsiveness, and love puts us 'on the side of' that value, perhaps allies us with everything else on its side, and symbolizes our intertwining with it. (Does it symbolize this to a greater extent than the actual intertwining, or does a welcomed symbolic connection constitute an actual intertwining?) Kant felt that in acting morally we act as a member of the kingdom of ends, a free and rational legislator. The moral action doesn't *cause* us to become a member of that kingdom: it is what we would do as a member, an instance of what would be done under such circumstances, and hence it symbolizes doing it under those circumstances. The moral acts become grouped with other possible events and actions, and come to stand for and to mean them. Thereby being ethical acquires a symbolic utility commensurate with the utility these other things it stands for actually have. (This depends, then, upon these further things actually having utility for the person—a contingency Kant would be loath to rely upon.)

There are a variety of things an ethical action might symbolically mean to someone: being a rational creature who gives itself laws; being a law-making member of a kingdom of ends; being an equal source and recognizer of worth and personality; being a rational, disinterested, unselfish person; being caring; living in accordance with nature; responding to what is valuable; recognizing someone else as a creature of God. The utility of these grand things, symbolically expressed and instantiated by the action, becomes incorporated into that action's (symbolic) utility. Thus, these symbolic meanings become part of one's reason for acting ethically. Being ethical is one of our most effective ways of symbolizing (a connection to) what we value most highly. And that is something a *rational* person would not wish to forgo.[14]

A large part of the richness of our lives consists in symbolic meanings and their expression—the symbolic meanings our culture attributes to things, or the ones we ourselves bestow. It is unclear, in any case, what it would be like to live without any symbolic meanings, to have no part of the magnitude of our desires depend upon such meanings. What then would we desire? Simply material comfort, physical security, and sensual pleasure? And would no part of how much we desired these be due to the way they might symbolize maternal love and caring? Simply wealth and power? And would no part of how much we desired this be due to the way these might symbolize release from childhood dependence, or success in competition with a parent, and no part either be due to the symbolic meanings of what wealth and power might bring? Simply the innate unconditioned reinforcers that evolution has instilled and installed in us, and other things only in so far as they are effective means to these? These served to make our ancestors more effective progenitors or protectors of related genes. Should we choose this as our only purpose? And, if we valued it highly, might we not value also whatever symbolized being an effective progenitor? 'No,' someone might object, 'not if that conflicted with actually being one, and in any case one should value only actually bearing or protecting progeny and relatives, and the effective means to this that evolution has marked out, namely, the unconditioned reinforcers, and also too the means to *these*.' (Notice, though, that evolution's having instilled desires that serve to maximize inclusive fitness does not mean that it has instilled the desire to be maximally inclusively fit. Males now are not, I presume, beating at the doors of artificial insemination clinics in order to become sperm donors, even though that would serve to increase their inclusive fitness.)

But why is leading to something so much better than symbolizing it that symbolization doesn't count at all? Because 'that's the bottom line, what actually occurs; all the rest is talk'. But why is this bottom line better than all other lines? In any case, if we are symbolic creatures—and anthropology attests to the universal nature of this trait—then presumably evolution made us so, and therefore the attractive pleasures of symbolization, and symbolic satisfactions, are as solidly based as the other innate reinforcers. Perhaps a capacity for symbolization served to strengthen other desires, or to maintain them through periods of deprivation in reinforcement by their actual objects. Whatever the evolutionary explanation, though, this capacity, like

---

[14] Notice that symbolic meanings might not all be good ones, just as desires or preferences might not be either. The point is that a theory of rationality need not *exclude* symbolic meanings. However, these do not guarantee good or desirable content. For that, one would need to develop a contentful theory of which symbolic meanings, and which preferences and desires, were admissible, using that to constrain which particular meanings and desires could be fed into the more formal theory of rationality.

other cognitive capacities, is not mired in its original adaptive function; it can be employed in other valuable ways, just as mathematical capacities can be employed to explore abstract number theory and theories of infinity, although this was not the function for which they were evolutionarily selected. Once the capacity for symbolic utility exists, it may enable us, for example, to achieve in some sense—that is, symbolically—what is causally or conceptually impossible, thereby gaining utility from that, and it may also enable us to separate good features from the bad ones they are linked with, gaining only the former through something that symbolizes it alone.

This is not to deny the dangers opened by symbolic meanings and symbolic utilities. Conflicts may quickly come to involve symbolic meanings that, by escalating the importance of the issues, induce violence. Is there a general structural criterion about the kind of links that establish symbolic meanings which can distinguish the good symbolic meanings from the bad, or must we simply be vigilant in certain kinds of situation—conflict is one—to isolate and exclude particular symbolic meanings? For whatever reason, many undesirable symbolic meanings are not in equilibrium under knowledge of their causes; if we knew what gave rise to these meanings, or the role they are playing in our current actions, we would not want to act upon them.[15] Some symbolic meanings do withstand this test, though, for example the symbolic meaning of a romantic gesture to the person you love.

Symbolic meaning also is a component of particular ethical decisions. It has been argued that the symbolic meaning of efforts to save a currently threatened person—a trapped miner, for instance—or of refusing to make those efforts, affects our decision in allocating resources to current efforts to save versus accident-prevention measures. (This issue has been termed one of 'actual *v.* statistical lives'; see Fried 1970, pp. 207–18.) It has also been argued that the symbolic meaning of feeding someone, giving sustenance, enters into the discussion of the ways in which the lives of critically ill people may permissibly be terminated—e.g. turning off their artificial respirator, but not halting their food and starving them to death (see Carson 1986).

We live in a rich symbolic world, partly cultural and partly of our own individual creation, and we thereby escape or expand the limits of our situation, not simply through fantasies, but in actions. We impute to actions and events utilities co-ordinate with what they symbolize, and we strive to realize (or avoid) them as we would strive for what they stand for.[16] A broader decision theory is needed, then, to incorporate such symbolic connections and to detail the new structuring these introduce.

Among social scientists, anthropologists have paid the most attention to the symbolic meanings of actions, rituals, and cultural forms and practices,

---

[15] For a discussion of acts in equilibrium, see Nozick (1981, pp. 348–52).

[16] For a discussion of how some advertising of products utilizes this phenomenon, see Nozick (1989, pp. 121–2).

and to their importance in the ongoing life of a group (see Firth 1973; Geertz 1973). By incorporating an action's symbolic meaning, its symbolic utility, into (normative) decision theory, we might link theories of rational choice more closely to anthropology's concerns. There are two directions in which such a linkage might go. The first, the upward direction, explains social patterns and structures in terms of individual choice behaviour that incorporates symbolic utility. This, the methodological individualist and reductionist direction, is not the one I am proposing here.[17] The second, the downward direction, explains how the patterns of social meanings that anthropologists delineate have an impact within the actions and behaviour of individuals, that is, through their decisions which give some weight to symbolic utility.

How does the symbolic utility of an action (or an outcome) work? What is the nature of the symbolic connection or chain of connections? And in what way does utility, or the possibility of expressiveness, flow through this chain from the situations symbolized to the actions (or outcomes) that enact the symbolizing? Notice first that symbolic meaning goes beyond the way in which the adoption of principles makes some actions stand for others. There, an action stood for other things of the same type—other actions—or for a whole group of these; while symbolic meaning can connect an action with things other than (a group of) actions, for instance with being a certain sort of person, with the realization of a certain state of affairs.

Some useful and suggestive categories have been provided by Nelson Goodman (1968, pp. 45–95). According to Goodman, A denotes B when A refers to B; A *exemplifies* P when A refers to P and A is an instance of P—that is, is denoted by P (either literally or metaphorically); A *expresses* P when A refers to P and A has the property P figuratively or metaphorically (so that P figuratively denotes A) and, in exemplifying P, A functions as an aesthetic symbol. These relations can be chained together. A *alludes to* B when A denotes some C and that C exemplifies B, or when A exemplifies some C and that C denotes B. Even longer chains are possible,[18] some of whose links will be figurative or metaphorical. These chains, and others, can connect an action to further and larger situations or conditions, the ones it can symbolically represent or allude to or . . . , and the utility of these larger situations then provides the action itself with a *symbolic utility*

---

[17] Indeed, given the extent to which symbolic meaning is socially created, maintained, and co-ordinated, as well as limited by social factors, we might find here a limit to methodological individualist explanations—an important one, given the effects and consequences of such meanings. For a symbolic utility might be social not only in being socially shaped, and in being shared—that is, the same for many people in the society—but also viewed as shared, the sharing being intrinsic to its having that symbolic utility. It is not clear how methodologically individualist explanations might cope with the intricacies involved.

[18] Catherine Elgin, *With Reference to Reference*, Hackett Publ. Co., Indianapolis, 1983, p. 143, discusses a particular chain with 5 links.

that enters into decisions about it. These chains need not be very long; when A is in the literal extension of a term P and B is in that term's metaphorical extension, A might have B as part of its symbolic meaning. Sometimes an action may symbolically mean something by being our best instantiated realization of that thing, the best we can do. The symbolic utility of an action might be viewed as an *interpretation* of that action, a way of seeing oneself or it in a certain way—Kant interpreted being ethical as being a law-making member of a kingdom of ends. Hence the various modes of interpretive linkage, and full theories of interpretation itself, might enter into the specification of symbolic utility.

In what particular way is the symbolic utility (or expressiveness) of an action determined by the utility of that larger situation which the chain connects the action to, and by the nature of the chain itself? Do shorter chains transmit more utility/expressiveness from the larger situation to the action itself? Is utility/expressiveness lost, the more linkages there are? Do different kinds of linkages transmit differing proportions of (or possibilities of expressing) the larger situation's utility? (I am assuming that the symbolic utility of an action cannot be greater than the utility of the larger situation it is connected to by the chain, and that it can be less.) Do only some symbolic connections induce the imputation of utility back, and what determines which ones these are?

These questions all arise about situations of choice under certainty; further issues arise about choice under risk or uncertainty. Is there a probabilistic discounting along some particular chains? Do some kinds of larger situations, even when they are not certain to occur, transmit their full utility back to the action that might yield them? And, of course, the very fact that an action has particular risks or uncertainties associated with it may itself give it a particular symbolic meaning and utility, connected perhaps with being a daring and courageous person or a foolhardy one. Sometimes, though, the presence of probabilities rather than certainty may remove a symbolic meaning altogether. It is *not* the case that a one-half or a one-tenth chance of realizing a certain goal always itself has one-half or one-tenth the symbolic utility of that goal itself—it need not symbolize that goal, even partially. Here is another reason why symbolic utilities must be treated as a separate component of a theory of decision and not simply incorporated within existing (causal and evidential) decision theories. For such symbolic utilities do not obey an expected value formula. We might attempt to understand and explain *certain* of the observed deviations from an expected value formula, and from the associated axioms of decision theory, by attributing these to the presence of symbolic utilities. I have in mind here the Allais paradox, the certainty effect, certain deviations from Savage's 'Sure Thing' principle, and so on. There is a symbolic utility to us of *certainty* itself. The difference between

0.9 and 1.0 is greater than that between 0.8 and 0.9,[19] though this difference between differences disappears when each is embedded in larger, otherwise identical, probabilistic gambles—this disappearance marks the difference as symbolic.[20]

A detailed theory of symbolic utility awaits development. What we can do now is mark a place for it within the structure of a more general theory of decision.

4. Decision-Value and Prisoner's Dilemma

The traditional principle of maximizing expected utility (EU) treats the expected utility of an action A, EU(A), as the weighted sum of the utilities of its (exclusive) possible outcomes, weighted by their probabilities which sum to 1:

$$EU(A) = \text{prob}(01) \times u(01) + \text{prob}(02) \times u(02) + \ldots + \text{prob}(0n) \times u(0n),$$

$$= \Sigma_{i = 1, \ldots, n} \text{prob}(0i) \times U(0i).$$

A more adequate principle, noticing that the outcomes need not be probabilistically independent of the actions, specifies the expected utility as weighted not by the simple probabilities of the outcomes, but by the

---

[19] Double-digit inflation has the symbolic meaning of inflation out of control, so there is more concern about a rise from 9% to 10% than from 16% to 17%; if we counted in base 11, the (symbolic) line would be fixed elsewhere. In *Anarchy, State, and Utopia* (Nozick 1974), I commented on the symbolic meaning of *eliminating* a problem completely, so that there is a greater difference between reducing the number of instances of an evil from 1 to 0 than there is in reducing the number from 2 to 1. There I referred to this as a mark of an ideologue (p. 266); it is better seen as a mark of symbolic meaning.

[20] Notice that the certainty effect, when it occurs, requires utility to be measured by a slightly different procedure from the usual one. In the usual procedure, two outcomes x and z are assigned utility numbers ordered in accordance with the preference between them, and the utility of any third thing y is found in accordance with the Archimedean condition. This condition says that, when x is preferred to y and y is preferred to z, then there is a unique probability p (between 0 and 1 exclusive) such that the person is indifferent between y and an option consisting of a probability p of x and a probability $(i - p)$ of z. When the person is fully satisfying all the von Neumann–Morgenstern conditions there will be no problem, but when the certainty effect occurs, that intermediate certain option y will be assigned a misleading utility. A better procedure might be to measure utility without considering any certain outcomes, by embedding all the preceding within canonical probability mixtures, for instance, with probability $\frac{1}{2}$. The person would then be asked to find the probability p such that he is indifferent between a $\frac{1}{2}$ chance of nothing and a $\frac{1}{2}$ chance of y, and a $\frac{1}{2}$ chance of nothing and a $\frac{1}{2}$ chance of {a probability p of x and a probability $1 - p$ of z}. Thereby we control for the certainty effect. Of course, such a procedure can work only if it is not sensitive to the particular probability, in this example $\frac{1}{2}$, within the canonical probability mixture. It would have to be the case that the same results would be achieved with a wide variety of probabilities within the canonical mixture, perhaps with all but those within epsilon of 0 and 1.

conditional probabilities of the outcomes given the actions; call this the
evidentially expected utility of A, EEU(A):[21]

$$EEU(A) = \text{prob}(01/A) \times u(01) + \text{prob}(02/A) \times u(02) + \ldots + \text{prob}(0n/A) \times u(0n),$$

$$= \Sigma_{i = 1, \ldots, n} \text{prob}(0i/A) \times u(0i).$$

A different principle of decision has been proposed by some writers,
spurred by Newcomb's Problem. This problem is well known and I shall
just describe it briefly here.[22]

A being in whose power to predict your choices correctly you have great
confidence is going to predict your choice in the following situation. There
are two boxes, B1 and B2; box B1 contains $1,000 and box B2 contains
either $1,000,000 ($M) or nothing. You have a choice between two actions:
(1) taking what is in both boxes; (2) taking only what is in the second box.
Furthermore, you know, and the being knows you know, etc., that if the
being predicts you will take what is in both boxes, he will not put the $M
in the second box; if the being predicts you will take only what is in the
second box he will put the $M in the second box. First the being makes his
prediction; then he puts the $M in the second box (or not, according to his
prediction); then you make your choice.

The problem is not only to decide what to do, but also to understand
precisely what is wrong with one of the two powerful arguments, which
conflict. The first argument is this: if you take what is in both boxes, the
being almost certainly will have predicted this and will not have put the $M
in the second box, and so you will almost certainly get only $1,000; whereas
if you take only what is in the second box, the being almost certainly will
have predicted that and will have put the $M into the second box and so
you will almost certainly get $M. Therefore, you should take only what is
in the second box. The second argument is this: the being already has made
his prediction and has already either put the $M into the second box, or has
not. The $M is either already sitting in the second box, or it is not, and
which situation obtains is already fixed and determined. If the being has
already put the $M in the second box, then if you take what is in both boxes
you will get $M + $1,000, whereas if you take only what is in the second

[21] On the maximization of conditionally expected utility, though not the term 'evidential
utility', see my 1963 Princeton University doctoral dissertation, *The Normative Theory of
Individual Choice* (since published: see Nozick 1990). 'The probabilities that are to be used in
determining the expected utility of an action must now be the conditional probabilities of the
states given that the action is done. (This is true generally. However when the states are
probability-independent of the actions, the conditional probability of each state given that one
of the actions is done will be equal to the probability of the state, so the latter may be used)'
(Nozick 1990, p. 232). There also, the formula for conditional expected utility was stated for
the cases of the two particular actions being discussed there, though not the general formula
for variable action. The general formula is presented in Jeffrey (1965).
[22] The problem was thought of by William Newcomb, a physicist, told to me by a mutual
friend, and (with Newcomb's permission) first presented and discussed in Nozick (1969).

box you will get just M; if the being has not put the M in the second box, then if you take what is in both boxes you will get $1,000, whereas if you take only what is in the second box you will get no money at all. In either case, whether the M has been placed in there or not, you will receive more money—$1,000 more—by taking what is in both boxes. (Taking what is in both boxes strongly *dominates* taking only what is in the second.) Therefore, you should take what is in both boxes.

Since 1969, when I first presented and discussed this problem, there has been much detailed investigation and illuminating theorizing about it.[23] In my initial essay, I distinguished those conditional probabilities that mark an action's *influencing* or *affecting* which state obtains from mere conditional probabilities that mark no such influence; and I suggested that, when it conflicts with the dominance principle, the principle of maximizing conditional expected utility should not be invoked if its conditional probabilities were of the second sort. I supported this by intuitive examples. (These, because of their attempt to incorporate a needed reflexivity, were somewhat more complicated than some examples discussed afterwards.) Linked genetic predispositions to a disease and to a career choice should not, I argued, lead someone to avoid one career since this raises the estimate of his chances of getting the disease—whether he actually does have that genetic make-up or will actually get the disease is not *influenced* or *affected by* the career choice. It did not occur to me to utilize this theme for the full and systematic development of competing versions of decision theory, causal and evidential, with their differing versions of the expected utility principle and even their differing versions of the dominance principle.[24]

The causal decision theorists too use not simply the unconditional probability of the outcome, but a probability relating the outcome to the action, this time not simply the conditional probability, prob $(0i/A)$, but some causal–probabilistic relation indicating direct causal influence; the corresponding formula with these causal probabilities states the causally expected utility of act A, CEU (A).

In the larger work from which this essay is extracted (Nozick 1993; see also 1992), I argue that neither of these rules alone—to maximize CEU or to maximize EEU—is wholly adequate: each has some legitimacy and must be given its due. So I propose a principle of decision that mandates maximizing a weighted sum of causally expected utility, evidentially expected utility, and symbolic utility. (It is the first two of these that play the major role in my revised discussion of Newcomb's Problem in Nozick (1993, 1992).)

---

[23] For a selection of articles until 1985, and a bibliographical listing of others, see Campbell and Sowden (1985).

[24] On causal decision theory, see Gibbard and Harper (1978); Lewis (1981); and Sobel (1985). Nor did I notice the possibility of specific situations where the states were probabilistically independent of the actions yet causally influenced by them—Gibbard and Harper's Reoboam example—which should have marked a fourth row in my three-rowed chart on p. 132 of my original article.

Let *CEU(A)* be the causally expected utility of act A, the utility of that act as it would be computed in accordance with (some favoured version of) causal decision theory; let *EEU(A)* be the evidentially expected utility of act A, the utility of that act as it would be computed in accordance with evidential decision theory; and let *SU(A)* be the symbolic utility of act A, which incorporates the utility of the various outcomes and actions *symbolized* by the act; let *We, Wc,* and *Ws* be the weights given to each of these kinds of utility. (It is best not to try to incorporate symbolic utility alongside other utilities, since it may well not obey an expected value formula; *also,* we might well want to keep separate track of symbolic utility, because we think it appropriate to give this factor different weights in different kinds of choice situation.) Associated with each act will be a decision-value DV, a weighted value of its causally expected utility, its evidentially expected utility, and its symbolic utility:

$$DV(A) = Wc \times CEU(A) + We \times EEU(A) + Ws \times SU(A).$$

The rule is that a person is to choose an act with maximal decision-value.

There are many different mathematical structures that would give CEU and EEU a role, but the DV formula is especially simple, and it would be premature to look now at anything more complicated. The weighted DV structure by itself, of course, does not give anyone much guidance. What should the weights be? Must a person use the same weights in all decision situations, or might the weights vary for different types of decision situation, or more systematically according to where a decision situation falls along some dimension *D*, the further to the left the more plausible the use of one of the decision criteria (and hence the greater weight it receives), the further to the right the more plausible the use of the other one? I would welcome a theory to specify or restrict the weights, just as I would welcome a theory to specify or restrict prior probabilities within a Bayesian structure and one to specify or restrict the substantive content of preferences within the usual ordering axioms. Yet, still, in each case the general structure can be illuminating. It would be instructive to investigate the formal characteristics of this decision-value structure; it would not be surprising if this principle of weighted combination, like other criteria previously investigated in the literature of decision under uncertainty, sometimes failed to exhibit certain desirable features.[25]

Symbolic utility is not a different kind of utility, relating to standard utility in something like the way metaphorical meaning stands to literal.

---

[25] See Milnor (1954), and Luce and Raiffa, (1957, pp. 275–98). Earlier I said that symbolic meaning need not carry over proportionally into probabilistic contexts. Yet the DV formula includes symbolic utility as one of the weighted components. We might wonder whether symbolic utility will carry over into the weighted DV context. However, shifting to a probabilistic situation is a shift to a *different* situation, while shifting to the DV formula does not shift the choice situation.

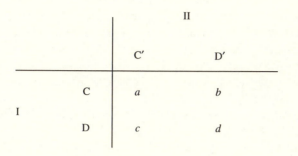

Fig. 2

Rather, symbolic utility is a different kind of *connection*—symbolic—to the familiar kind of utility. It stands alongside the already familiar connections, the causal and the evidential. The symbolic utility of an action A is determined by A's having symbolic connections to outcomes (and perhaps other actions) which themselves have the standard kind of utility, just as the CEU of A is determined by A's causal–probabilistic connections to outcomes with the standard utility.

Should we ensure that these types of connection—causal, evidential, and symbolic—are exclusive? The EEU of an action includes its causal components, since the conditional probabilities of outcomes given actions, prob $(0/A)$, incorporate causal influences when such exist. In our weighted-sum formula, then, should we not interpret the EEU as the expected utility represented by those (portions of) probabilities that are *not* (simply derivative from) causal ones? And, similarly, shouldn't the symbolic utility SU of an action be its symbolic utility which is not (simply) derivative from and represented within its causal and evidential connections?[26]

Let us consider the implications of this decision structure for the Prisoner's Dilemma (see Fig. 2), where each party has a choice between two actions—call them D for the dominant one, C for the co-operative—and the following preferences among the possible outcomes of the combined actions, a, b, c, and d: person I prefers c to a to d to b, while person II prefers b to a to d to c. Since person I prefers c to a, and d to b, action D dominates action C and he chooses to do D. Since person II prefers b to a, and d to c, action D' dominates action C', and he chooses to do D'. Together, D and D' yield the outcome d, while both of them prefer the outcome a (which would result from C and C') to outcome d. Therefore, these simple facts about the structure of the 2×2 matrix and the structure of each person's preference ordering seem sufficient to mark a Prisoner's Dilemma situation.

Some people have argued that a rational person in this situation, knowing the other is also a rational person who knows as much about the situation

[26] The one psychological study I know of that treats both causal and evidential connections, and seeks to disentangle them, is Quattrone and Tversky (1984).

as he himself does, will realize that any reasoning that convinces will be convincing for the other too; so if he himself concludes that the dominant action is best, the other person will also, and if he concludes the co-operative action is best, the other person will too. In this situation, then, it would be better to conclude that the co-operative action is best, and, realizing all this, he therefore (somehow) does so. This type of argument has had a mixed reception.

The Prisoner's Dilemma parallel's Newcomb's Problem, whether or not the two are (as some have argued) identical in all essential features. Both involve two arguments that lead to differing actions: one argument based upon the dominance principle interpreted in a way that is congenial to causal decision theory, the other based upon considering what each act would indicate (and what outcome therefore should be bet upon), in a way that is congenial to evidential decision theory. The argument that in the Prisoner's Dilemma you should expect that the other person will do as you do, even though your action does not causally affect what he does, fits the principle of maximizing the evidentially expected utility, where the conditional probabilities need not represent any causal influence. Causal decision theory recommends performing the dominant action; evidential decision theory recommends performing the co-operative action when you think the other party is relevantly similar to yourself. It is not necessary for you to be certain you both will act alike; it will be enough if the conditional probabilities of the other party's actions, given your own, vary sufficiently. (Notice too that evidential decision theory might lead to performing the dominant action, if you believed the other party was likely to perform a *different* act from yours, or simply if his act was independent of your own but you ascribed sufficiently pessimistic probabilities to his chances of co-operating.)

In the case of Newcomb's Problem, one is motivated to grant legitimate weight to each of the two principles, i.e. attending to CEU and attending to EEU, because of the switching of decisions that occurs when the amount of money in the first box is varied, even though the structure of the problem is kept constant, as judged by the two competing principles of decision which would have maintained their same decision through these changes (see Nozick 1993; 1992). In the case of the Prisoner's Dilemma, proponents of the two differing arguments about what rational agents with the common knowledge should do find that the abstract structure of Fig. 2 is sufficient to give their favoured argument its compelling grip. All the dominance argument needs is that person I prefers c to a, and d to b, while person II prefers b to a, and d to c. All that the evidentially expected utility argument about rational agents seems to need is that each has common knowledge, that each is a rational agent, and that each prefers a to d. If people do lack complete confidence in these arguments, however, we should find that

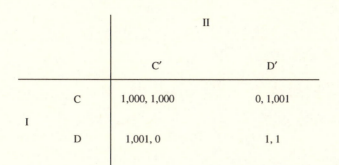

Fig. 3

variations in the amounts[27] of the payoffs within the abstract structure of Fig. 2 (while still maintaining the *order* of the party's preferences) will produce changes in the decision people would make.

Suppose that utility is measured on an interval scale, unique up to a positive linear transformation, with an arbitrary unit and an arbitrary zero point, in conformity to some variant of the standard von Neumann–Morgenstern axioms.[28] In the situation represented by Fig. 3, where the matrix entries are such utility numbers, we would think that co-operation is the rational choice. In general, when the co-operative solution pay-offs are very much higher than the dominance ones, and when the non-matching pay-offs offer only slight gains or losses over these two, then we will strongly think that co-operation is rational, and will find that the dominance argument has little force. Alternatively, as in Fig. 4, when the co-operation solution is only slightly better than the dominant one, and when the extreme values diverge greatly (and when we have no special ties to or particular knowledge of the other party's probabilities of action), then we will think it is rational to perform the dominant action, not running any risk of the other party's performing his dominant action which he has a large incentive to do. (And if I go through this reasoning, and think he also is very likely to be like me, then I may well settle on the dominant action in this case, comfortable with the realization that he will do so also.)

These shifts in the decision one would make, which depend upon the (ratios of the differences in the) particular numerical utility entries in the matrix, are in accordance with the earlier principle of maximizing decision-value, for people who give some weight to each of the particular principles

[27] More exactly—since utility is measured on an interval scale—in the ratios of differences in amounts. When the discussion to follow ignores this complication in the interests of lucidity, it can be suitably rephrased.

[28] See von Neumann and Morgenstern (1947, app., pp. 617–32). An examination of philosophical issues about the von Neumann–Morgenstern and similar sets of conditions is contained in Nozick (1990).

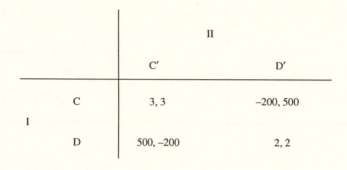

Fig. 4

CEU and EEU. At what precise point their decision will shift as the utilities are varied will depend on how confident they are in each of these principles, i.e. on what weights they (implicitly) assign to them, and also on the probabilities they assign to the other person's action being the same as their own. Notice however that, even if this is given a probability of 1, and even if the agent gives greater weight to the EEU principle than to the CEU principle, he will not necessarily perform the co-operative action. If the utility stakes are big enough and fit the situation in Fig. 4, that fact can combine with the weight that is given to the CEU principle, or with the dominance principle itself (in its causal variant), or with some other principle that gives weight to the security level, to yield a recommendation for the dominant action. Even absolute confidence that the other person will act as you do is not enough to guarantee your performing the co-operative action—in the absence of absolute confidence in, or weight to, the EEU principle.[29] (I have been assuming until now that it is one particular version

---

[29] 'But wouldn't a correct theory *insist* that, when the probability is 1 that the other person will behave as you do, you *should* choose the co-operative action in the Prisoner's Dilemma situation, whatever the magnitude of the utility differences in the matrix? And so isn't this divergence an *objection* to the DV structure?' We might wonder, though, whether the person has (one level up) complete confidence in his probability estimate of 1, and whether that lack of complete confidence might affect his action in this high-risk situation (see Ellsberg 1961). Notice, too, that the argument proceeds too quickly from (1) common rationality, to (2) they will do the same thing, to (3) crossing out the upper-right and lower-left boxes in the matrix, representing divergent actions, to (4) arguing that, given that the choice is between the two remaining boxes, both should choose the one they prefer—that each prefers—i.e. both should perform the co-operative action. Assuming common knowledge of rationality allows us to assume that we will reason in the same way and will end up doing the same thing. But perhaps *that* will result from our each reasoning about all four boxes in the matrix, and each concluding that, in the light of the joint strategic situation presented by the full matrix, including all four boxes, I (and he or she) should take the non-cooperative action, and so we will both end up in the lower-right non-cooperative box—*thus* satisfying the condition that they act identically. Our knowing in advance that we will do the same thing means we know we will not end up in the upper-right or lower-left box, but this doesn't mean we can therefore first delete them and then reason about the remaining situation; for perhaps the reasoning whereby we *will* end up performing the same action depends upon our *not* first deleting those divergent corners.

of the DV principle, with its particular weights fixed, that a person applies in all decision situations. However, it might be that, for a given set of constituent principles of decision, a person assigns different weights to them depending upon the type of decision situation he faces. Still, each type of situation where more than one particular principle received positive weight would be fitted by some DV structure or other.)

Our discussion of the Prisoner's Dilemma thus far has considered only two components of the DV structure. However, the DV structure incorporates the symbolic utility (SU) of performing an action alongside its CEU and its EEU. It might be thought that, if an action *does* have symbolic utility, then this will show itself completely in the utility entries in the matrix for that action; for example, perhaps each of the entries gets raised by a certain fixed amount that stands for the act's symbolic utility, so that there need not be any separate SU factor. However, the symbolic value of an act is not determined solely by *that* act; what the act means or symbolizes can depend upon what other acts are available with what pay-offs, and what acts are also available to the other party or parties. The act symbolizes something when done in *that* particular situation, in preference to *those* particular alternatives. If an act symbolizes 'being a co-operative person', that will not be simply because it has those two possible pay-offs, but because it occupies a particular position within the two-person matrix, viz. being a dominated action that (when joined with the other person's dominated action) yields a higher pay-off to each than does the combination of the dominant actions. Hence its SU is not a function of those features captured by treating an act in isolation, simply as a mapping of states onto consequences.[30]

An act's symbolic value may depend upon the whole decision or game matrix. It is not appropriately represented by some addition or subtraction to the utilities of consequences *within* the matrix. Many writers assume that *anything* can formally be built into the consequences (see e.g. Hammond 1988), for instance how it feels to perform the action, the fact that you have done it, or the fact that it falls under particular deontological principles. However, if the *reasons* for doing an act A affect its utility, then to build this utility into A's *consequences* would thereby alter the act and change the reasons for doing it; on the other hand, the utility of *that* altered action will depend upon the reasons for doing *it*, and to build this into its consequences would alter the reasons for doing the now doubly altered act; etc. Moreover, the utilities of an *outcome* can change if the action is done for certain reasons.[31]

---

[30] This is how L. J. Savage treats acts within the formalism of his decision theory, cf. his *The Foundations of Statistics* (1954). However, an act cannot be reduced in this way, even apart from issues about its possible symbolic value (see Nozick 1990, pp. 184–93).

[31] As a result of Newcomb's Problem, cases have been investigated where the *probability* of an outcome alters with the reasons for doing the action, thus giving rise to the literature on 'ratifiability'.

What we want the utilities of the outcomes to represent, therefore, is the *conditional* utilities of the outcomes, given that the action is done for certain reasons.[32] This creates a problem for consequentialism in dealing with dynamic consistency issues; for it might be that the fact of having reached a particular sub-tree of the decision-tree gives you information that alters the utility of a future outcome. If we attempt to cope with this by insisting that the utilities within the tree always be fully specified conditional utilities, we cannot have the *same* outcomes at any two different places in the decision-tree—to the detriment of stating general normative principles to govern such trees. (We can make this as a point about the order of quantifiers. For *each* fact about an act, there might be a description that enables you to list that fact as a consequence of the act, but it does not follow that there is a description such that, for *all* facts about the act, that description incorporates them within the act's consequences.)

These considerations show that in Prisoner's Dilemma situations an action should be conceived as having a utility of its own, not simply as involving a constant utility addition *within* a row of its matrix;[33] but I wish to claim something stronger, namely that this utility is a *symbolic* utility. This is not simply the usual kind of utility but is applying to a different kind of entity than usual, an action rather than an outcome. It is a different kind of utility, that is, a utility involving a different kind of connection. In some Prisoner's Dilemma situations, performing the dominated action—what usually is called the 'co-operative action'—may have symbolic value for the person. It may stand for his being a co-operative person in interactions with others, a willing and non-carping participant in joint ventures of mutual benefit. Co-operating in this situation then may get grouped with other activities of co-operation that are not embedded in Prisoner's Dilemma situations; not co-operating in this particular Prisoner's Dilemma situation may then come to threaten his co-operating in those other situations—the line between them may not be so salient, and his motivation for co-operation in the others may be partly symbolic also. Giving great utility to

[32] Or even, the conditional utility of the outcome given that the action is done for certain reasons *and leads to the outcome*. In the economic literature on auctions, it is pointed out that a person's estimate of the value of an outcome might change when he discovers that his particular bid was the winning one, when this indicates that other knowledgeable bidders had information, or reached conclusions, that led them to value the outcome less than he did. The ratifiability literature notes that the fact that 'I decide to do A' can affect the estimate of the probability of a consequence C of A, in that prob (C/I decide to do A) is not equal to prob (C), while the auction literature notes that 'My doing A is successful in bringing about C' can affect the utility of C, perhaps by altering the probabilities of other information which affects the utility of C. Thus, a fully formulated decision theory must utilize not only conditional utility—see Nozick 1990, pp. 144–58—but the conditional utility it uses must be, not simply u (outcome O/ the action A is done) but u(outcome O/ the action A is done, for reasons R, and this A done for R leads to O).

[33] It is also worth mentioning that, when the sequencing of the action is strategically relevant, game theorists do not simply concentrate upon the matrix representation of a game and its pay-offs, but need to consider the game-tree.

being a co-operative person, in a particular Prisoner's Dilemma situation the individual performs the dominated act that symbolizes this.[34]

This does not mean that even such a person will look only at that act's SU. He will also consider its particular utility entries, and how these are evaluated by the CEU and the EEU principles. The decision-value of the act for him will depend upon all three—its SU, CEU, and EEU—and upon the weights he gives to them. Thus, merely giving some (positive) symbolic utility to being a co-operative person does not guarantee his performing the co-operative action in a Prisoner's Dilemma situation.

I do not claim that the only possible symbolic meaning relevant to the Prisoner's Dilemma situation is 'being a co-operative person'. Someone might think that performing the *dominant* action in such situations symbolizes 'being rational, not being swayed by sentimentality'; thinking this is quite important, he gives great symbolic utility (within his DV principle) to performing the dominant action, in addition to the weight he gives to the CEU or dominance principle itself. Some writers on Newcomb's Problem who are proponents of the view that taking what is in both boxes is most rational overcome discomfort at the fact that they and people like themselves do worse on this problem than do maximizers of EEU by saying that its 'moral' is: 'if someone is very good at predicting behavior and rewards predicted irrationality richly, then irrationality will be richly rewarded' (Gibbard and Harper 1978, p. 151). I take it that such people give very great utility—is that a symbolic utility?—to being rational according to their best current estimate of what precise principles that involves. (It will be a subtle matter to distinguish between someone who gives weight to only *one* principle, CEU for example, and someone who gives some weight to CEU and also some lesser weight to EEU yet also attaches great symbolic utility—greatly weighted—to following his best *particular* estimate of what rationality involves.) One would guess that, if following a particular decision principle has symbolic utility, or if engaging in a particular kind of decision process or procedure does, new complications will arise.

To say all this about symbolic utility is to say that our responses to the Prisoner's Dilemma are governed, in part, by our view of the kind of person we wish to be, and the kind of ways in which we wish to relate to others. What we do in a particular Prisoner's Dilemma situation will involve all this, and will invoke it to different degrees depending upon the precise (ratios of differences among) utility entries in the matrix and also upon the particular factual circumstances that give rise to that matrix, circumstances

---

[34] Can one build this into the standard decision theory by saying that one constant consequence of his performing the dominant act in the Prisoner's Dilemma situation is that he will think of himself as a non-cooperative person, and then represent this in the game matrix by a negative addition, an addition of negative utility, all across the row for that action? Notice that this component of utility would be a function of his attitude towards that act as it stands within the structure of the whole matrix.

in which an action may come to have its own symbolic meanings, not simply because of the structure of the matrix.

We knew all this already, of course, at least as a psychological point about why people differ in their responses to Prisoner's Dilemma situations. However, the DV principle leaves room for general views about what sort of person to be, as this relates to and groups particular choices, not simply as a possible *psychological* explanation of why (some) people deviate from rationality, but as a legitimate component—symbolic utility—within their *rational* procedure of decision.

We want a sharper result than that the co-operative action will be performed if the symbolic utility of doing so (and the weight attached to this) is high enough. Under what conditions, for what specifications of weights within a DV structure for one (or both) of the participants, will a person choose to perform the co-operative action in the Prisoner's Dilemma situation, in a one-play or iterated game, with or without common knowledge that both parties are maximizers of DV? These are topics for further investigation.

The themes I have discussed above about principles and symbolic meaning apply to ethical principles also. By grouping actions together in a class, one action comes to stand for all, and the weight of all is brought to bear upon the one—any one—giving it a co-ordinate (symbolic) disutility; eating this one dessert symbolizes eating them all. Deontological constraints might exhibit this same phenomenon. By grouping actions together into a principle forbidding them—'do not murder'—an action is removed from separate utilitarian (or egoist) calculation of *its* costs and benefits. The action comes to stand for the whole group, bearing its weight upon its shoulders. This need not happen in a way that makes the constraint absolute, barring the action no matter what, but it constitutes a far greater barrier to performing it, by throwing its greatly increased (symbolic) disutility into any calculation.

Recall now our earlier discussion of the symbolic meaning of ethical action, which can symbolize (and express) being a rational creature which gives itself laws, being a law-making member of a kingdom of ends, being an equal source and recognizer of worth and personality, etc. The utility of these grand things, symbolically expressed and instantiated by the action, becomes incorporated into that action's symbolic utility and hence into that action's decision value. Thus, these symbolic meanings become part of one's reason for acting ethically. A person who maximizes an act's utility, broadly conceived, that is who maximizes its decision value (DV), may be led to perform ethical actions. This person would be pursuing his *own* goals (which need not be *selfish* goals). In terms of the categorization of Amartya Sen (1987, pp. 80–8), therefore he would be engaged in self-goal pursuit, rather than in *not* marginally pursuing *his* own overall individual goal. But note that, if falling into this further category of not marginally pursuing his own overall individual goal itself comes to have symbolic utility to him, then it will enter into his DV. At that point, when he acts, taking account of this symbolic utility, is he once again pursuing his own goal, that is *his* revised DV, so that his attempt (within the DV framework) to enter Sen's other category is doomed to failure? However we decide this, the more general point holds. Being ethical is among our most effective ways of symbolizing (a connection to) what we value most highly. And that is something a *rational* person would not wish to forgo.

References

Ainslie, George (1975), 'Specious Reward: A Behavioral Theory of Impulsiveness and Impulse Control', *Psychological Bulletin*, 82: 463–96.
—— (1986), 'Beyond Microeconomics', in Jon Elster (ed.), *The Multiple Self*, Cambridge University Press, pp. 133–75.
Arkes, H. R. and Blumer, C. (1985), 'The Psychology of Sunk Cost', *Organizational Behavior and Human Decision Processes*, 35: 124–40.
Campbell, Richard and Sowden, Lanning (1985), *Paradoxes of Rationality and Cooperation: Prisoner's Dilemma and Newcomb's Problem*, University of British Columbia Press, Vancouver.
Carson, Ronald (1986), 'The Symbolic Significance of Giving to Eat and Drink', in Joanne Lynn (ed.), *By No Extraordinary Means: The Choice to Forgo Life-Sustaining Food and Water*, Indiana University Press, Bloomington, Ind., pp. 84–8.
Elgin, Catherine (1983), *With Reference to Reference*, Hackett, Indianapolis, Ind.
Ellsberg, Daniel (1961), 'Risk, Ambiguity, and the Savage Axioms', *Quarterly Journal of Economics*, 75: 643–69.
Firth, Raymond (1973), *Symbols: Public and Private*, Cornell University Press, Ithaca, NY.
Fried, Charles (1970), *An Anatomy of Values*, Harvard University Press, Cambridge, Mass.
Geertz, Clifford (1973), 'Deep Play: Notes on the Balinese Cock-fight', in his *The Interpretation of Cultures*, Basic Books, New York.
Gibbard, Allan and Harper, William (1978), 'Counterfactuals and Two Kinds of Expected Utility', in C. A. Hooker, J. J. Leach, and E. F. McClennen (eds.), *Foundations and Applications of Decision Theory*, D. Reidl, Dordrecht, pp. 125–62. Reprinted 1985.
Goodman, Nelson (1968), *Languages of Art*, Bobbs-Merrill, Indianapolis, Ind.
Hammond, Peter (1988), 'Consequentialist Foundations for Expected Utility', Theory and Decision, 25: 25–78.
Herrnstein, Richard (1961), 'Relative and Absolute Strengths of Response as a Function of Frequency of Reinforcement', *Journal of the Experimental Analysis of Behavior*, 4: 267–72.
Jeffrey, Richard (1965), *The Logic of Decision*, McGraw-Hill, New York.

Lewis, David (1981), 'Causal Decision Theory', *Australasian Journal of Philosophy*, 59: 5–30.

Luce, R. D. and Raiffa, Howard (1957), *Games and Decisions*, John Wiley, New York.

Milnor, John (1954), 'Games against Nature', in R. M. Thrall, C. H. Coombs, and R. L. Davis (eds.), *Decision Processes*, John Wiley, New York, pp. 49–59.

Nozick, Robert (1969), 'Newcomb's Problem and Two Principles of Choice', in N. Rescher *et al.* (eds.), *Essays in Honor of C. G. Hempel*, D. Reidl, Dordrecht, Netherlands, pp. 114–46.

—— (1974), *Anarchy, State, and Utopia*, Basic Books, New York.

—— (1981), *Philosophical Explanations*, Harvard University Press, Cambridge, Mass.

—— (1989), *The Examined Life*, Simon & Schuster, New York.

—— (1990), *The Normative Theory of Individual Choice*, Garland Press, New York (written in 1963 as a doctoral dissertation, Princeton University).

—— (1992), 'Decisions of Principle, Principles of Decision', *Tanner Lectures on Human Values*, xiv, University of Utah Press, Salt Lake City.

—— (1993), *The Nature of Rationality*, Princeton University Press, Princeton, NJ.

Quattrone, G. A. and Tversky, Amos (1984), 'Causal versus Diagnostic Contingencies: On Self-Deception and the Voter's Illusion', *Journal of Personality and Social Psychology*, 46: 237–48.

Savage, L. J. (1954), *The Foundations of Statistics*, John Wiley, New York.

Schelling, Thomas (1966), 'The Art of Commitment', in his *Arms and Influence*, Yale University Press, New Haven, Conn., pp. 35–51.

Sen, Amartya (1987), *Ethics and Economics*, Basil Blackwell, Oxford.

Smart, J. J. C. and Williams, Bernard (1973), *Utilitarianism: For and Against*, Cambridge University Press.

Sobel, J. H. (1985), 'Circumstances and Dominance in a Causal Decision Theory', *Synthese*, 63: 167–202.

von Neumann, John and Morgenstern, Oscar (1947), *The Theory of Games and Economic Behavior*, 2nd edn., Princeton University Press, Princeton, NJ.

Williams, Bernard (1976), 'Persons, Character and Morality', in Amelie Rorty (ed.), *The Identity of Persons*, University of California Press, Berkeley, Calif., pp. 197–216.

8

Valued Opinions or Opinionated Values: The Double Aggregation Problem

KEVIN ROBERTS

1. Introduction

Within the realm of social choice, the framework originally developed by
Arrow can be viewed as applying to two different and distinct aggregation
problems. In the first, aggregation takes the form of utilizing information
about individual well-being to generate a social ranking of states. This is
what is done by a social welfare function. In the second, the purpose of
aggregation is to take a collection of social rankings of states that individuals in society may possess and to combine them to create a 'consensus' social
ranking. This could be done by a voting system. In a general problem of
social choice, one could expect to meet both aggregation problems—
individuals in society have (perhaps different) views about the well-being of
all individuals in society and, using this information, a *single* social ranking
of states is desired.

A two-step aggregation exercise can work in two distinct ways. In the first,
each individual's opinions are collapsed into that individual's social ranking—his values. Everybody's social ranking is then aggregated to form a
single social ranking. In the second, individual opinions are first aggregated
across individuals to create a 'consensual' opinion about individual well-
being across states. This single opinion about well-being is then collapsed,
through the operation of a social welfare function, say, into a single social
ranking. There is no reason why this 'double aggregation' should be a
two-step procedure. The general problem involves the movement from a set
of opinions about well-being to a single social ranking; a function that
achieves this operation will be called an *extensive social welfare function*
(ESWF) (see Roberts 1980a). Despite the fact that this problem is central to
the notion of social choice aggregation, almost nothing is known about the
character of ESWFs. This paper attempts to redress this imbalance.

There are at least two difficulties when dealing with ESWFs. First, the
structure of ESWFs is likely to be interesting only when individual opinions
of well-being are sufficiently 'rich', in the sense that they incorporate
interpersonal comparisons of well-being. The aggregation of a single set of
opinions that incorporate interpersonal judgements has been fairly extensively analysed: Sen (1977) provides a fine review of the main results. Here,
though, one is looking at aggregation with different sets of opinions, each

incorporating interpersonal comparisons, and with little or no comparability across opinions. An example of across-opinion comparability would be a situation, say, where some individual i is better off in state x than in state y. If individual j's opinion of i's difference in utility between x and y exceeds individual k's opinion of the difference, then there is across-opinion comparability. Conceptually, this is close to the existence of objective and independent entity—a *util*—which can used by any individual to express interpersonal comparisons. This seems far-fetched, and the most relevant situations to investigate are ones where no such yardstick exists: interpersonal comparisons are within-opinion rather than across-opinion.

Across-opinion comparability may be ruled out, but that does not mean that there are no restrictions on the opinions held by one individual given the opinions held by another individual. This leads to the second difficulty when dealing with ESWFs: a restricted domain for the function. The most obvious restriction comes from the idea of *non-paternalism*. If i's opinion is that he himself is better off in state x than in state y, then this should be incorporated into everybody else's opinions about well-being: an ESWF should not be expected to operate unless individual j's opinion is that i is better off in state x than in state y. A less obvious type of restriction comes from the idea that there may be greater agreement in opinions about particular types of information on well-being. For instance, there may be agreement concerning the ordinal ranking of individual well-being, but no such agreement about the cardinalization of such a ranking—everybody may agree that individual i in state x is better off than j in y, but there may be no agreement about how this difference in well-being compares with the difference between i in state w and j in state z, say. This can be the case even if each individual is clear in his own mind about the relative magnitude of these differences.

The above example illustrates a tension that exists in the aggregation problem captured by an ESWF. In a problem where a single set of opinions is being operated on by a social welfare function, the class of possible social welfare functions is expanded when the set of opinions includes 'richer' information, e.g. comparability of welfare differences as well as comparability of welfare levels. (For those unfamiliar with informational bases in social choice theory, see Sen (1974) and Roberts (1980b).) However, when there are several opinions, the lack of consensus is likely to be greater the 'richer' the information incorporated into opinions. For an ESWF, 'richer' information is a twin-edged sword.

Consider the structure of an ESWF for a problem directly akin to the one originally studied by Arrow (1963). Assume that each individual's opinion consists of an ordering of each social state for every individual in society; and, furthermore, assume that the opinions of one individual impose no restriction on the opinions held by other individuals. With n individuals in society, an ESWF faces the problem of aggregating n^2 orderings into a single ordering. In this context, the conditions used by Arrow to prove his Impossibility Theorem seem appealing, in which case the result will be that one of the n^2 orderings will be dictatorial: there will be two individuals (perhaps the same person) i and j such that, if i's opinion is that j is better off in state x than in state y, then x will be ranked above y in the social ordering. This social ordering is a *double dictatorship*: it is a dictatorship because only individual i's opinions count, and it is a dictatorship because only opinions about j's well-being count.

The purpose of this paper is to see how this double-dictatorship result is tempered by the introduction of richer informational structures, i.e. different forms of interpersonal comparability, and by restricted domain conditions like non-paternalism that were discussed earlier. The largest set of possible ESWFs will emerge when the richest informational structures and the strongest restricted domain conditions are used.

A strong and startling result will be presented. Even in situations where the class of possible ESWFs will be large, one aspect of the double-dictatorship result remains: one individual's opinions are always dictatorial. Work in social choice theory over the last twenty years has shown how, with interpersonal comparisons, different individuals' well-beings can be traded off. This allows a movement away from the straitjacket of the Impossibility Theorem and permits the social ordering to be sensitive to more than one individual's well-being. However, as the present paper shows, no such trade-off is possible when it comes to the aggregation of different opinions about well-being.

The framework of the problem is laid out in the next section and appropriate definitions are given. In Section 3 the structure of ESWFs is analysed when welfare differences are interpersonally comparable but welfare levels are non-comparable. Although the results presented follow from more general results in Section 4, the structure of the proofs throws light on why the general result holds. Section 4 examines ESWFs when both welfare levels and welfare differences are comparable. Sections 3 and 4 concentrate on the case of societies with two individuals; Section 5 extends the results to the general case. Throughout, the general result emerges that only one individual's opinions count—well defined ESWFs reflect opinionated values rather than valued opinions. Concluding remarks are contained in Section 6.

2. The Framework

We are interested in determining a *social ordering R*, assumed to be complete, reflexive, and transitive, defined over the set of feasible social states X; the cardinality of X is assumed to be at least 3. R will denote the set of all possible orderings over X. $N = \{1,..., i, j, k, l, ..., n\}$ is the set of individuals in society and n is assumed finite. Each individual has two roles: as the provider of opinions, and as the receiver of well-being or welfare. U is the set of all real-valued functions that may be defined on $X \times N \times N$. For any $u \in U$, $u(x, i, j)$ denotes the welfare of i in state x in the opinion of j.

An *extensive social welfare function* (ESWF) is a mapping f from a set $D \in U$—the domain of the ESWF—to the set $\mathcal{R}$; i.e. $f: D \to \mathcal{R}$. Given conditions imposed upon possible ESWFs, their power will be felt the most strongly when the domain of the function is largest. This can be achieved by imposing the following Arrow-type condition.

UNRESTRICTED DOMAIN (U). $D = U$; i.e. f is defined for all $u \in U$.

In the present context, where there are different opinions, it may be reasonable to restrict attention to situations where opinions are non-paternalistic.

NON-PATERNALISTIC UNRESTRICTED DOMAIN (NPU):
$D = \{u \in U : \forall\, x, y \in X, y\ \forall i, j, \in N : u(x, i, i) \geqslant u(y, i, i) \Rightarrow u(x, i, j) \geqslant u(y, i, j)\}$.

Thus, if i is of the opinion that he is better-off in x than in y, then f is defined only when everybody else is of the same opinion about i's welfare. A much stronger domain restriction is the following.

ORDINAL AGREEMENT UNRESTRICTED DOMAIN (OAU)
$D = \{u \in U : \forall\, x, y \in X, \forall\, i, j, k, l \in N : u(x, k, i) \geqslant u(y, l, i) \Rightarrow u(x, k, j) \geqslant u(y, l, j)\}$.

This condition implies NPU but it is stronger. The idea behind it is that there may be agreement in opinions about the overall ranking of well-being—who is better-off than whom—but no agreement about the magnitude of differences in welfare.

As well as an unrestricted domain condition, two other Arrow-type conditions will be imposed.

UNIVERSAL AGREEMENT PARETO (P). $\forall\, x, y \in X$: $[\forall\, i, j \in N$: $u(x, i, j) \geqslant u(y, i, j)] \Rightarrow x R y$ where R is the social ordering $f(u)$. If in addition $u(x, i, j) > u(y, i, j)$ for some i, j, then $x\, P\, y$.

For simplicity, P is made an extension of the strong Pareto condition in the sense that indifference at the individual welfare level implies indifference at the social level. This feature ensures that, in the presence of the other conditions that will be used, the social ordering is *neutral* (see below). If a weak Pareto condition had been specified, a property of *weak neutrality* would have held (Roberts 1980*b*), and this is sufficient for the results of this paper.

INDEPENDENCE of IRRELEVANT ALTERNATIVES (I). For any $u, u' \in D$, if, for some $x, i, \in X$,

$$\left. \begin{array}{l} u(x, i, j) = u'(x, i, j) \\ u(y, i, j) = u'(y, i, j) \end{array} \right\} \quad \text{for all } i, j \in N,$$

then $xRy \Leftrightarrow xR'y$ where $R = f(u)$ and $R' = f(u')$.

This differs in two respects to the condition used by Arrow. First, because of the present context, the condition has been extended to allow the ranking over a pair $\{x, y\}$ to be determined by everybody's opinion about everybody's well-being in those two states. Second, Arrow made the social ranking over the pair $\{x, y\}$ sensitive only to the individual ranking over the pair, thereby ruling out other welfare information like cardinality and interpersonal comparability. This can be achieved, if required, by adding an appropriate invariance condition.

ORDINALITY, NON-COMPARABILITY. If $u, u' \in D$ satisfy the condition that, for all $x, y \in X$, $i, j \in N$: $u(x, i, j) \geqslant u(y, i, j)$ if and only if $u'(x, i, j) \geqslant u'(y, i, j)$, then $f(u) = f(u')$.

Thus, ONC combined with I gives Arrow's condition of independence of irrelevant alternatives. Arrow's Impossibility Theorem applied in the present framework gives the 'double-dictatorship' result mentioned in the Introduction.

THEOREM. If f satisfies U, I, P, and ONC, then there exist $i, j \in N$ such that, for all $x, y \in X$,

$$u(x, i, j) \geqslant u(y, i, j) \Rightarrow xPy$$

where P is the strict preference relation underlying $f(u)$.

Without comparability and across-opinion domain restrictions, j's opinion of i's well-being is dictatorial—j's opinions are dictatorial, and i is dictatorial because the social ordering focuses on his well-being.

In this paper, interest will centre on the case where individual welfare is interpersonally comparable. Various invariance conditions could be imposed (Roberts 1980b), but for the development of the argument the following two conditions will suffice.

DIFFERENCE COMPARABILITY (DC). If $u, u' \in D$ satisfy the condition that, for all $x \in X$, $i, j \in N$,

$$u(x, i, j) = \alpha_{ij} + \beta_j u'(x, i, j)$$

for some set of numbers α_{ij} and β_j, $\beta_j > 0$, then $f(u) = f(u')$.

FULL COMPARABILITY (FC). If $u, u' \in D$ satisfy the condition that, for all $x \in X$, $i, j \in N$,

$$u(x, i, j) = \alpha_j + \beta_j u'(x, i, j)$$

for some set of numbers α_j and β_j, $\beta_j > 0$, then $f(u) = f(u')$.

Looking at any one individual's opinions, DC demands invariance with respect to changes in welfare levels but allows the social ranking to be sensitive to a change in the ranking of welfare differences; FC demands less invariance in the sense that a change in the ranking of welfare levels is also allowed to influence the social ranking. The interpretation of FC is that, at the individual opinion level, both welfare differences and welfare levels are interpersonally comparable. With both DC and FC, no across-opinion comparability is built in; across-opinion restrictions come from the restricted domain conditions on D.

We now return to the issue of neutrality and show in Lemma 1 that, under any one of the unrestricted domain conditions U, NPU, or OAU, together with I and P, the social ordering is equivalent to an ordering defined on a subset of Euclidean n^2-space—everybody's opinion of everybody's welfare in any state.

LEMMA 1. Assume that f satisfies U or NPU or OAU, I and P. Consider any $u, u' \in D$ such that, for all $i, j \in N$,

$$u(x, i, j) = u'(w, i, j)$$

$$u(y, i, j) = u'(z, i, j)$$

for some $w, x, y, z \in X$. Then

$$x R y \Leftrightarrow w R' z$$

where $R = f(u)$, $R' = f(u')$.

Proof. Take the case where w, x, y, z are all distinct. (When they are not, the argument is easily amended—see d'Aspremont and Gevers 1977.) Consider u'' such that, for all $i, j \in N$,

$$u''(w, i, j) = u'(w, i, j).$$

$$u''(x, i, j) = u(x, i, j)$$

$$u''(y, i, j) = u(y, i, j)$$

$$u''(z, i, j) = u'(z, i, j).$$

Notice that, if U or NPU or OAU is satisfied with $u, u', \in D$ then $u'' \in D$. Let $R'' = f(u'')$ and assume that $x R y$. By I, $x R'' y$. By P, $w I'' x$, $y I'' z$. Therefore $w R'' z$. By I, $w R' z$. Thus, $x R y \Rightarrow w R' z$. Similarly, $w R' z \Rightarrow x R y$. ∎

The usefulness of this lemma is that it says that to determine the structure of ESWFs it is necessary only to look at orderings defined on the appropriate welfare space—a subset of n^2-space. For the rest of the paper, attention will centre on such orderings.

3. Comparability of Welfare Differences

For social welfare functions to be non-dictatorial, it is necessary to move away from the informational parsimony of the Arrow setup and introduce interpersonal comparisons. What is unclear is how the 'double-dictatorship' result of Theorem 1 will be tempered by the introduction of more information. It is worth noting that, if non-paternalism is assumed, Theorem 1 is automatically tempered because if there are no interpersonal judgements everybody's opinion will be the same, and the fact that one individual's opinion is dictatorial is unimportant.

In this section the informational basis of difference comparability DC will be investigated. If welfare levels are not comparable, then the domain restriction OAU does not make sense; however, given that non-paternalism is important, it will be desirable to work under the domain condition NPU. As will become clear, ESWFs are harder to deal with than conventional one-opinion social welfare functions. For this reason, it will be desirable to limit the problem under consideration to the case where there are only two individuals in society: $n = 2$. In Section 5 it will be shown that results extend to the general case.

Given Lemma 1, the ranking of any two states depends only on individuals' opinions about well-being in those two states. With $n = 2$ there are two opinions, and there are two individuals whose well-being is important. Under non-paternalism NPU, there are two possibilities that arise in the determination of the social ranking of two states: either it is the consensual opinion that both individuals are better off in one of the states (in which case P tells us the social ranking), or there is a consensual opinion that one of the individuals is better off in one of the states and the other individual in the other.

Configuration 1 shows such a situation. Each table is one of the individual's opinions about well-being; for example, individual 1's opinion is that the well-being of individual 2 in state x is α. Later it will be shown that, under the invariance transformation of DC, this configuration exhausts all

Configuration 1

	1	2
x	0	α
y	1	0

	1	2
x	0	β
y	1	0

possibilities (other than those where individual 1 has the same well-being in two states, in which case the social ranking is determined by P) for suitable choices of α and β.

Assume that the set of possible (α, β) under which x is weakly preferred to y is given by U. If i's well-being is dictatorial, then this set will be empty. If it is non-empty, then $(\alpha, \beta) \in U \Rightarrow (\alpha', \beta') \in U$ where $\alpha' \geqslant \alpha$, $\beta' \geqslant \beta$. (This is a simple application of Lemma 1 and P.) If U is non-empty, take two elements (α_1, β_1) and (α_2, β_2) and consider Configuration 2, where $0 < \lambda_1, \lambda_2 \leqslant 1$. What can be said about the social ranking over the triple (x, y, z)? Under DC, the social ranking will remain the same if a constant is removed from 2's welfare. Thus, the ranking of $\{x, y\}$ is the same as the ranking over $\{x,y\}$ in Configuration 3. Given that, by assumption,

Configuration 2

	1			2	
	1	2		1	2
x	0	$\alpha_2 - \alpha_1\left(1 - \dfrac{1}{\lambda_1}\right)$	x	0	$\beta_2 - \beta_1\left(1 - \dfrac{1}{\lambda_2}\right)$
y	1	$-\alpha_1\left(1 - \dfrac{1}{\lambda_1}\right)$	y	1	$-\beta_1\left(1 - \dfrac{1}{\lambda_2}\right)$
z	$\dfrac{1}{\lambda_1}$	0	z	$\dfrac{1}{\lambda_1}$	0

Configuration 3

	1			2	
	1	2		1	2
x	0	α_2	x	0	β_2
y	1	0	y	1	0

$(\alpha_2, \beta_2) \in U$, we therefore have xRy in the social ranking in Configuration 2. Applying DC again, the ranking over $\{y, z\}$ must be the same as the ranking of Configuration 4; thus yRz (as $\alpha_1, \beta_1) \in U$). Transitivity of the social ranking tells us that $x\,R\,z$ in Configuration 2; or, by applying DC yet again, we know that $x\,R\,z$ in Configuration 5. The conclusion is reached that $(\alpha_1, \beta_1) \in U$, $(\alpha_2, \beta_2) \in U$ implies that $[\alpha_1(1 - \lambda_1) + \alpha_2\lambda_1, \beta_1(1 - \lambda_2) + \beta_2\lambda_2] \in U$. In Fig. 1, by letting λ_1, λ_2 vary over their range, the shaded

Configuration 4

1	1	2
y	0	α_1
z	1	0

2	1	2
y	0	β_1
z	1	0

Configuration 5

1	1	2
x	0	$\alpha_1(1 - \lambda_1) + \alpha_2\lambda_1$
z	1	0

2	1	2
x	0	$\beta_1(1 - \lambda_2) + \beta_2\lambda_2$
z	1	0

region is seen to be part of the set U. Note, in particular, that this implies that U is convex.

Returning to Configuration 1, consider now the set L of possible (α, β) under which y is weakly preferred to x. By P, the interiors of L and U are disjoint. The argument presented above for U applies equally to L: $(\alpha_1, \beta_1) \in L$ and $(\alpha_2\beta_2) \in L$ implies that, for all $\lambda_1\lambda_2$, $0 < \lambda_1, \lambda_2 \leqslant 1$, $[\alpha_1(1 - \lambda_1) + \alpha_2\lambda_1, \beta_1(1 - \lambda_2) + \beta_2\lambda_2] \in L$. L is also convex, as thus L and U can be separated by a line in (α, β)-space. More importantly, if $(\alpha_1, \beta_1), (\alpha_2, \beta_2)$ are as in Fig. 1, then they cannot be on the boundary of U because the shaded region lying below a line through $(\alpha_1, \beta_1), (\alpha_2, \beta_2)$ would be in the interior of the set L, contradicting the argument which has

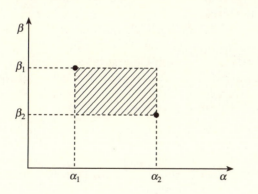

Fig. 1

shown that they are in the interior of the set U. Thus, the line separating L and U is vertical or horizontal: with Configuration 1 there is either an α^* such that $\alpha > \alpha^*$ implies that $x\,P\,y$ and $\alpha < \alpha^*$ implies that $y\,P\,x$ (individual 1's opinions are dictatorial), or there is β^* such that $\beta > \beta^*$ implies that $x\,P\,y$ and $\beta < \beta^*$ implies that $y\,P\,x$ (individual 2's opinions are dictatorial). Finally, if U, say, is empty, then individual 1's well-being is a measure of social welfare, and non-paternalism ensures that in this degenerate case both individuals' opinions are dictatorial.

Configuration 6

	1		2	
	1	2	1	2
x	$u(x, 1, 1)$	$u(x, 2, 1)$	$u(x, 1, 2)$	$u(x, 2, 2)$
y	$u(y, 1, 1)$	$u(y, 2, 1)$	$u(y, 1, 2)$	$u(y, 2, 2)$

Configuration 7

	1		2	
	1	2	1	2
x	0	$\dfrac{u(x, 2, 1) - u(y, 2, 1)}{u(y, 1, 1) - u(x, 1, 1)}$	0	$\dfrac{u(x, 2, 2) - u(y, 2, 2)}{u(y, 1, 2) - u(x, 1, 2)}$
y	1	0	1	0

To make the argument general, it must be shown that Configuration 1 is equivalent to any situation where there is a conflict in well-being between the two individuals. Returning to the notation introduced in Section 2, let x and y be such that 1's well-being is higher in y, 2's well-being is higher in x. The configuration is given in Configuration 6, which is equivalent given DC to Configuration 7, a configuration belonging to the class given by Configuration 1. Applying the dictatorial opinion result to Configuration 7 gives the following ESWF characterization.

THEOREM 2. Let $n = 2$. If f satisfies NPU, I, P, and DC, then there exist two possibilities:

(i) *Either* there exists an $\alpha^* \geq 0$ such that, for all $x, y \in X$,

$$u(x, 2, 1) + \alpha^* u(x, 1, 1) > u(y, 2, 1) + \alpha^* u(y, 1, 1) \Rightarrow xPy;$$

i.e. individual 1's opinions are dictatorial and, using these opinions, the social ordering is weighted utilitarianism.

(ii) *Or* there exists a $\beta^* \geqslant 0$ such that, for all $x, y \in X$,

$$u(x, 2, 2) + \beta^* u(x, 1, 2) \geqslant u(y, 2, 2) + \beta^* u(y, 1, 2) \Rightarrow xPy;$$

i.e. individual 2's opinions are dictatorial and, using these opinions, the social ordering is weighted utilitarianism. (When α^* or β^* tend to infinity, the interpretation is that 1's well-being is dictatorial.)

The most important feature of this result is that one individual's opinions are dictatorial. Given this, an ESWF is a procedure for moving from only one set of opinions to a social ordering—it acts like a standard social welfare function. The weighted utilitarianism feature of the result is unsurprising because, as d'Aspremont and Gevers (1977) have shown, standard social welfare functions must always be of this form under the informational basis of difference comparability (DC).

Finally, if the domain restriction is lifted and paternalistic preferences are permitted—U replaces NPU—then Theorem 2 applies over the domain of the function where opinions are non-paternalistic. It is straightforward to show that, to satisfy transitivity, dictatorial opinions over a subset of the domain must be permitted to be dictatorial over all of the domain. (See the move from OAU to NPU in the next section.) This 'epidemic' of dictatorships is a well-known feature of social choice problems.

4. Comparability of Welfare Levels and Differences

The richer the informational structure underlying opinions, the more opportunity there is for disagreement. Without interpersonal comparability, there can be no disagreement under non-paternalism; however, non-paternalism places very few restrictions on interpersonal judgements. Given a rich informational structure, it is also possible that there is agreement across opinions concerning particular aspects of interpersonal judgements, but not about others. The most obvious example of this is captured by the domain restriction OAU, where there is agreement about judgements concerning welfare levels—who is better off than whom—but, subject to this restriction, there is no agreement about the magnitude of welfare differences. This section pursues the case where opinions are rich in the sense that levels and differences are comparable—the informational basis of full comparability— and starts by looking at the structure of ESWFs under OAU.

The approach taken is similar to that in the last section, but under DC it was shown that in the $n = 2$ case an individual's opinion could be collapsed into a single number (α for individual 1, β for individual 2). But with comparability of both welfare levels and differences, there is less redundant information. Making use of Lemma 1, the ranking of any two states

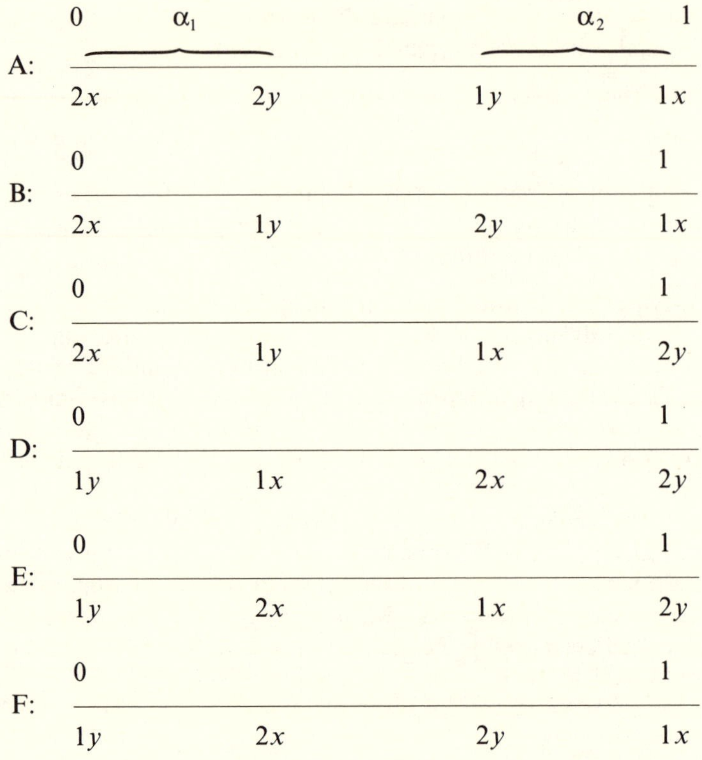

	0	α_1	α_2	1
A:	$2x$	$2y$	$1y$	$1x$
B:	$2x$	$1y$	$2y$	$1x$
C:	$2x$	$1y$	$1x$	$2y$
D:	$1y$	$1x$	$2x$	$2y$
E:	$1y$	$2x$	$1x$	$2y$
F:	$1y$	$2x$	$2y$	$1x$

Fig. 2

$\{x, y\}$, will depend upon opinions of well-being in these states. Consider one such opinion. Taking the $n=2$ case again, individual 1's opinion will be captured by four numbers: $u(x, 1, 1)$, $u(x, 2, 1)$, $u(y, 1, 1)$, $u(y, 2, 1)$. Under FC, an individual's opinion is invariant with respect to a common scaling and addition to welfare. Thus, unless all four numbers are identical—in which case this will be true for all opinions under non-paternalism and the two states will be declared indifferent by invoking P—the lowest number can always be scaled to zero and the highest number to unity. An opinion can therefore be expressed by an ordering of well-being in the two states and two numbers α_1 and α_2. Looking only at cases of strict preference, where individual 1 prefers x to y and 2 prefers y to x, there are six orderings in the $n = 2$ case and these are shown in Fig. 2. For instance, if case A is individual 1's opinion then $u(x, 2, 1) = 0$, $u(y, 2, 1) = \alpha_1$, $u(y, 1, 1) = 1 - \alpha_2$ and $u(x, 1, 1) = 1$.

Under OAU, both individuals will have the same ranking of well-being in the two states. We will start by looking at the structure of the ESWF when both opinions are of type A. Opinions can be captured by Configuration 8.

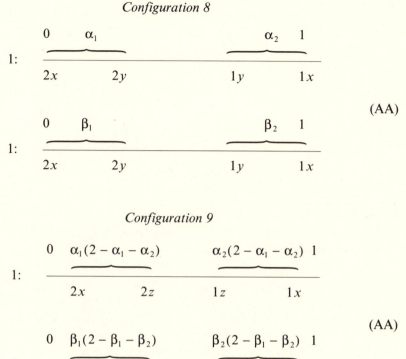

Configuration 8

(AA)

Configuration 9

(AA)

For what values of $(\alpha_1, \alpha_2, \beta_1, \beta_2)$ will x be weakly preferred to y? As in the last section, let this set be U. Let $(\alpha_1, \alpha_2, \beta_1, \beta_2) \in U$. Consider a $u \in D$ such that the configuration over $\{x, y\}$ is as in Configuration 8 and the configuration over the ordered pair $\{y, z\}$ is as in Configuration 8, with $\{y, z\}$ replacing $\{x, y\}$. Then $x \, R \, y$, $y \, R \, z$, and so $x \, R \, z$, and the configuration over $\{x, z\}$ will be as in Configuration 9. Notice that this is an AA configuration with the inferior state z showing less inequality of welfare than in Configuration 8. Now a ranking in Configuration 8 permitted a ranking in Configuration 9; similarly, a ranking in Configuration 9 permits a ranking in a new configuration; and so on. Repeating this indefinitely gives rise to $x \, R \, y$ under Configuration 10. Here, $u(y, 1, \cdot)$ is arbitrarily close to $u(y, 2, \cdot)$, although, because no continuity assumption has been imposed on the function f, $x \, R \, y$ is not guaranteed in the limit. Consider the two-dimensional set U^* defined by

$$U^* = \left\{ (A, B) : A = \frac{\alpha_1}{\alpha_1 + \alpha_2} \quad B = \frac{\beta_1}{\beta_1 + \beta_2} \quad \text{s.t.} \ (\alpha_1, \alpha_2, \beta_1, \beta_2) \in U \right\}.$$

Configuration 10

0	$\alpha_1/(\alpha_1 + \alpha_2)$		$\alpha_2/(\alpha_1 + \alpha_2)$	1

1: _____

$2x$ .... $2y, 1y$ .... $1x$

(AA)

0	$\beta_1/(\beta_1 + \beta_2)$		$\beta_2/(\alpha_1 + \beta_2)$

2: _____

$2x$ .... $2y, 1y$ .... $1x$

Given P, if $A' < A$ and $B' < B$, where $(A, B) \in U^*$ then $(A'B') \in U^*$. It is also easy to see, from the argument giving rise to Configuration 10, that, if $(\alpha_1, \alpha_2, \beta_1, \beta_2) \in U$ and

$$\frac{\alpha_1}{\alpha_1 + \alpha_2} > \frac{\alpha_1'}{\alpha_1' + \alpha_2'}, \qquad \frac{\beta_1}{\beta_1 + \beta_2} > \frac{\beta_1'}{\beta_1' + \beta_2'}$$

for some $(\alpha_1', \alpha_2', \beta_1', \beta_2')$, then $(\alpha_1', \alpha_2', \beta_1', \beta_2') \in U$. Thus, if $(\alpha_1/(\alpha_1 + \alpha_2),$ $\beta_1/(\beta_1 + \beta_2))$ is contained in the *interior* of U^*, then $(\alpha_1, \alpha_2, \beta_1, \beta_2) \in U$; in fact, being in the interior of the set permits one to conclude that the preference ranking over $\{x, y\}$ in Configuration 8 will be strict: x P y. The relevance of the foregoing is that the dimensionality of opinions of an AA-type configuration is reduced from 4 to 2.

The ESWF f will be determined by the structure of the set U^*. Configuration 11 gives an example where opinions over all the pairs $\{x, y\}$, $\{y, z\}$, $\{x, z\}$ are of the A-type. Assume that

$$\left(\frac{\alpha_1}{\alpha_1 + \alpha_4}, \frac{\beta_1}{\beta_1 + \beta_4}\right) \in \text{int } U^* \qquad \text{and} \qquad \left(\frac{\alpha_2}{\alpha_2 + \alpha_3}, \frac{\beta_2}{\beta_2 + \beta_3}\right) \in \text{int } U^*.$$

Configuration 11

0	α_1		α_2		α_3		α_4	1

1: _____

$2x$ ..... $2y$ ..... $2z$ ..... $1z$ ..... $1y$ ..... $1x$

0	β_1		β_2		β_3		β_4	1

2: _____

$2x$ ..... $2y$ ..... $2z$ ..... $1z$ ..... $1y$ ..... $1x$

Then $x\,Py$ and $y\,Pz$ so that $x\,Pz$. Using this gives

$$\left(\frac{\alpha_1 + \alpha_2}{\alpha_1 + \alpha_2 + \alpha_3 + \alpha_4}, \frac{\beta_1 + \beta_2}{\beta_1 + \beta_2 + \beta_3 + \beta_4}\right) \in \text{int } U^*.$$

To see the significance of this, it is appropriate to distort the set int U^*. Let

$$V = \left\{\alpha, \beta : \left(\frac{\alpha}{1+\alpha}, \frac{\beta}{1+\beta}\right) \in \text{int } U^*\right\}.$$

Then simple algebra gives

$$\left(\frac{\alpha_1}{\alpha_4}, \frac{\beta_1}{\beta_4}\right) \in V \quad \& \quad \left(\frac{\alpha_2}{\alpha_3}, \frac{\beta_2}{\beta_3}\right) \in V \Rightarrow \left(\frac{\alpha_1 + \alpha_2}{\alpha_3 + \alpha_4}, \frac{\beta_1 + \beta_2}{\beta_3 + \beta_4}\right) \in V.$$

Defining

$$A_1 = \frac{\alpha_1}{\alpha_4}, \quad A_2 = \frac{\alpha_2}{\alpha_3}, \quad \lambda_1 = \frac{\alpha_4}{\alpha_3 + \alpha_4}, \quad B_1 = \frac{\beta_1}{\beta_4}, \quad B_2 = \frac{\beta_2}{\beta_3}, \quad \lambda_2 = \frac{\beta_4}{\beta_3 + \beta_4}$$

as changes of variable, this becomes

$$(A_1, B_1), \in V \,\&\, (A_2, B_2) \in V \Rightarrow [\lambda_1 A_1 + (1 - \lambda_1) A_2, \lambda_2 B_1 + (1 - \lambda_2) B_2] \in V,$$

which shows that V has the same structure as the set U in the last section (see Fig. 1). Exactly the same arguments apply: corresponding to V, there is a disjoint set M where the strict preference is reversed; both sets are convex and are thus separated by a line, this line being the boundary to both sets (by P); two points on the line cannot be as in Fig. 1 because the interior of the shaded region would be in both sets; the separating line must therefore be horizontal or vertical.

To summarize the argument, it has been shown that, for all situations that correspond to Configuration 8,

(i) *either* there exists an A^* such that

$$\frac{\alpha_1}{\alpha_2} < A^* \Rightarrow x\,Py \quad \text{and} \quad \frac{\alpha_1}{\alpha_2} > A^* \Rightarrow y\,Px,$$

(ii) *or* there exists a B^* such that

$$\frac{\beta_1}{\beta_2} > B^* \Rightarrow x\,Py \quad \text{and} \quad \frac{\beta_1}{\beta_2} > B^* \Rightarrow y\,Px.$$

In the first case, it is individual 1's opinions that are dictatorial, and in the second it is individual 2's opinions. If either of the sets V and M is empty, then one of the individuals' well-being is dictatorial, in which case both opinions are dictatorial.

Finally, assuming, say, that individual 1's opinions are dictatorial in the A-type configuration, consider what can be said about Configuration 12.

Configuration 12

	0				$A^*/(1 + A^*)$	1
1:						
	$2x$	$1y$	$2z$	$1z$		$1x$
		$2y$				

	0					1
2:						
	$2x$	$1y$	$2z$	$1z$		$1x$
		$2y$				

Here, $u(y, 1, \cdot) = u(y, 2, \cdot)$. Assume that $u(y, 1, 1) < A^*/(1 + A^*)$. Then, given OAU, there exists a $u \in D$ such that welfare in $\{x, y\ z\}$ are as shown. As $\{x, z\}$ is an A-type configuration, xPz. By P, zPy. Thus, when $u(y, 1, \cdot) = u(y, z, \cdot)$, 1's opinions are also dictatorial.

So far, what has been shown is extremely limited: when individuals' opinions are of the A-type one individual's opinions are dictatorial. It must now be shown that this is the case for all the other types in Fig. 2. Referring back to that figure, the only other case where one can have a triple $\{x, y, z\}$ such that each of the pairs is of the same type is type D. With a direct relabelling, what has been shown for type A must be true for type D: if both individuals' opinions are of the D-type, then one individual's opinions are dictatorial.

If individual 1's opinions are dictatorial in A-type situations, then are his opinions dictatorial in D-type situations? Assume that 2's opinions are in fact dictatorial. Consider Configuration 13 over pair $\{x, y\}$ and assume that $\beta_1/\beta_2 = B^* + \varepsilon$ for some small ε. Consider a $u \in D$ over $\{x, y, z\}$ as a Configuration 13. Taking $(\alpha_1, \alpha_2, \beta_1, \beta_2)$ fixed, assume that $\alpha_3/\alpha_4 > A^*$ so

Configuration 13

	0	α_1		α_3		α_4		α_2	1
1:									
	$1y$		$2x$		$1z$		$1x$		$2y$
					$2z$				

	0	β_1		β_3		β_4		β_2	1
2:									
	$1y$		$2x$		$1z$		$1x$		$1x$
					$2z$				$2y$

that, as the configuration over $\{x, z\}$ is of an A-type, $z\ P\ x$. Assume that β_3, β_4 are such that $(\beta_1 + \beta_3/(\beta_2 + \beta_4) < B^*$ so that, as the configuration over $\{y, z\}$ is of a D-type, $y\ P\ z$. Transitivity then gives $y\ P\ x$. However, with the same fixed $(\alpha_1, \alpha_2, \beta_1, \beta_2)$, $(\alpha_3, \alpha_4, \beta_3, \beta_4)$ could be such that $\{\alpha_3/\alpha_4 < A^*$ and $(\beta_1 + \beta_3/(\beta_2 + \beta_4) > B^*$, in which case $x\ P\ z$ and $z\ P\ y$. Transivity then gives $x\ P\ y$. But, by I, the ranking over $\{x, y\}$ depends upon opinions only over $\{x, y\}$ and, as these are the same in both situations, one cannot have $x\ P\ y$ and $y\ P\ x$. Thus there is a contradiction, and individual 2 cannot be dictatorial in D-type situations if 1 is dictatorial in A-type situations. Let the critical point for α_1/α_2 be A^{**} in D-type situations.

It can now be shown that, if 1's opinions are dictatorial in A- and D-type situations, then they are dictatorial in the other four situations in Fig. 2. This is accomplished by showing that all the other situations can be created by combining A- and D-type situations. Consider a type-B situation (Configuration 14) over a pair $\{x, y\}$. (Individual 2's opinions are suppressed for clarity.) Assume that

$$\left(\frac{A^{**}}{1 + A^{**}}\right)(1 - \alpha_1 - \alpha_3) > \left(\frac{A^*}{1 + A^*}\right) - \alpha_1$$

and consider some $u \in D$ which conforms to Configuration 14 over $\{x, y, z\}$ where

$$\left(\frac{A^{**}}{1 + A^{**}}\right)(1 - \alpha_1 - \alpha_3) > \alpha_2 > \left(\frac{A^*}{1 + A^*}\right) - \alpha_1.$$

Looking at $\{x, y\}$, the ranking is of type A and, as is easily checked, $(\alpha_1 + \alpha_2)/(1 - \alpha_1 - \alpha_2) > A^*$, so that $z\ P\ x$. Looking at $\{y, z\}$, the ranking is of type D and, as $\alpha_2/(1 - \alpha_1 - \alpha_2 - \alpha_3) < A^{**}$, $y\ P\ z$. Therefore, $x\ P\ y$. Similarly, if

$$\left(\frac{A^{**}}{1 + A^{**}}\right)(1 - \alpha_1 - \alpha_3) < \left(\frac{A^*}{1 + A^*}\right) - \alpha_1,$$

then $y\ P\ x$: individual 1's opinions are dictatorial in type-B situations. A similar exercise can be carried through for the other three situations. The essential point is that the social 'value' of state x, say, in Configuration 13, can be captured by an 'equality' state z where both individuals receive welfare:

$$\frac{A^*}{1 + A^*}\, u(x, 1, 1) + \frac{1}{1 + A^*}\, u(x, 2, 1)$$

and, for states like y, where individual 1 has a lower welfare, the social 'value' is captured by an 'equality' state z where both individuals receive

$$\frac{A^*}{1 + A^{**}}\, u(x, 1, 1) + \frac{1}{1 + A^{**}}\, u(x, 2, 1).$$

Configuration 14

$$
\begin{array}{ccccc}
0 & \alpha_1 & \alpha_2 & \alpha_3 & 1
\end{array}
$$

I:

$$
\begin{array}{ccccc}
2x & 1y & 1z & 2y & 1x \\
 & & 2z & &
\end{array}
$$

This 'equality' state welfare can be viewed as a real-valued representation of social welfare. In a single-opinion problem, Roberts (1980b) characterized social welfare functions under FC: with $n=2$, they must be of this order-dependent weighted utilitarian form. The following ESWF characterization theorem has been proved.

THEOREM 3. Let $n = 2$. If f satisfies OAU, I, P, and FC, then there exist two possibilities:

(i) *either* there exist A^*, A^{**}, $0 \leqslant A^*$, A^{**} such that, if

$$
W(u(x, \cdot, 1)) = \begin{cases}
\dfrac{A^*}{1 + A^*}\, u(x, 1, 1) + \left(\dfrac{1}{1 + A^*}\right) u(x, 2, 1) \\
\qquad\qquad \text{if } u(x, 1, 1) \geqslant u(x, 2, 1) \\[2ex]
\dfrac{A^{**}}{A + A^{**}}\, u(x, 1, 1) + \left(\dfrac{1}{1 + A^{**}}\right) u(x, 2, 1) \\
\qquad\qquad \text{if } u(x, 1, 1) \leqslant u(x, 2, 1),
\end{cases}
$$

then, for all $x, y \in X$,

$$
W(u(x, \cdot, 1)) > U(u(y, \cdot, 1) \Rightarrow xPy;
$$

i.e. individual 1's opinions are dictatorially used in an order-dependent weighted utilitarian welfare function.

(ii) *Or* there exist B^*, B^{**}, $0 \leqslant B^*$, B^{**} such that, if

$$
W(u(x, \cdot, 2)) = \begin{cases}
\dfrac{B^*}{1 + B^*}\, u(x, 1, 2) + \left(\dfrac{1}{1 + B^*}\right) u(x, 2, 2) \\
\qquad\qquad \text{if } u(x, 1, 2) \geqslant u(x, 2, 2), \\[2ex]
\dfrac{B^{**}}{B + B^{**}}\, u(x, 1, 2) + \left(\dfrac{1}{1 + B^{**}}\right) u(x, 2, 2) \\
\qquad\qquad \text{if } u(x, 1, 2) \leqslant u(x, 2, 2)
\end{cases}
$$

then for all $x, y, \in X$,

i.e. individual 2's opinions are dictatorially used in an order-dependent weighted utilitarian welfare function.

This result shows that the class of ESWFs is very restrictive and, of most importance, that one individual's opinions are used dictatorially in the construction of a social ranking. What should be reiterated is the fact that the characterized class is very limited under OAU and FC. Condition FC admits a rich set of interpersonal judgements, and any reduction in the information that may be utilized would further restrict the set of admissible ESWFs. Similarly, OAU limits the domain of ESWFs and a broader domain could be expected only to further limit the admissible class.

Consider the effect of strengthening OAU to allow an ESWF to be defined when the ordinal ranking of welfare does not necessarily coincide across opinions: given non-paternalism, the relevant condition will be NPU. Over the domain of the function covered by OAU, Theorem 3 will continue to apply. The remaining issue is whether the theorem applies when ordinal rankings differ. Consider the case where, over a pair $\{x, y\}$, individual 1's opinions are of type A and individual 2's are of type B (see Configuration 15). Assume that $\alpha_1/\alpha_2 > A^*$, so that if Theorem 3 still applies then $y \, P \, x$. Consider a $u \in D$ with the configuration over $\{x, y, z\}$ as shown in Configuration 15. In particular, assume that in 1's opinion state z is very similar to state y, so that $\alpha_3/\alpha_4 > A^*$. Then over $\{x, z\}$, both individuals' opinions are of type A and Theorem 3 applies, $\alpha_3/\alpha_4 > A^*$, implying that $z \, P \, x$. By P, $y \, P \, z$ so that transitivity implies $y \, P \, x$: Theorem 3 applies in type-AB situations. A similar construction applies in all other cases.

THEOREM 4. Let $n = 2$. If f satisfies NPU, I, P and FC, then the characterization given in Theorem 3 applies.

For completeness, it is noted that a similar argument applies for movements from NPU to U:

THEOREM 5. Let $n = 2$. If f satisfies U, I, P, and FC, then the characterization given in Theorem 3 applies.

Configuration 15

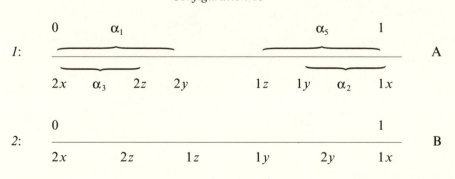

5. Many-Person Societies

The results for two-person societies obtained in the previous two sections are suggestive about what happens in many-person societies. In the two-person society, an individual has a dual role as a receiver of well-being and a supplier of opinions. A many-person generalization can occur in two separate ways. First, the number of opinions can increase beyond two; second, the number of individuals whose well-being is being assessed can be increased beyond two. It is worth noting that in the foregoing the results have not depended upon there being any connection between those individuals who receive well-being and those who supply opinions.

It is useful to start with the case where there is an arbitrary number of opinions n but opinions concern the well-being of only two individuals. The analysis of the last section is structured so that it straightforwardly extends to this more general case.

If opinions concern the well-being of only two individuals, Fig. 2 gives the situations that can arise. Assume that OAU holds so that all opinions must be of the same type in the figure; if they are of type-A then Configuration 8′ applies.

Using the same notation as in the last section, let U be defined as the set of $\{\alpha_1^i, \alpha_2^i\}$ such that, under Configuration 8', $x\,P\,y$; U^* and V are defined as:

$$U^* = \left\{ \{A_i\} : A_i = \frac{\alpha_1^i}{\alpha_1^i + \alpha_2^i} \quad \text{s.t.} \quad \{\alpha_1^i, \alpha_2^i\} \in U \right\}$$

$$V = \left\{ \{\alpha_i\} : \left\{ \frac{\alpha^i}{1 + \alpha^i} \right\} \in \text{int } U^* \right\}.$$

If $\{\alpha_1^i/(\alpha_1^i + \alpha_2^i)\} \in \text{int } U^*$ then $\{\alpha_1^i, \alpha_2^i\} \in U$. The structure of V is uncovered by looking at Configuration 11'. If $\{\alpha_1^i/\alpha_4^i\} \in V$ and $\{\alpha_2^i/\alpha_3^i\} \in V$, then $x\,P\,y$ and $y\,P\,z$ so that $x\,P\,z$. Thus, $\{(\alpha_1^i + \alpha_2^i)/(\alpha_3^i + \alpha_4^i)\} \in V$ or, defining $\lambda_i = \alpha_4^i/(\alpha_3^i + \alpha_4^i)$,

$$\left\{ \lambda_i \left(\frac{\alpha_1^i}{\alpha_4^i} \right) + (1 - \lambda_i) \left(\frac{\alpha_2^i}{\alpha_3^i} \right) \right\} \in V.$$

Configuration 8′

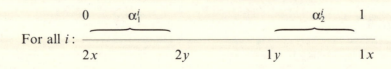

For all i:

Configuration 11'

	α_1^i		α_2^i				α_3^i		α_4^i	
0										1

For all i:

$2x$		$2y$	$2z$	$1z$	$1y$	$1x$

Letting $A_1^i = \alpha_1^i/\alpha_4^i$ and $A_2^i = \alpha_2^i/\alpha_3^i$ then gives $\{A_1^i\} \in V$ and $\{A_2^i\} \in V \Rightarrow$ $\{\lambda_i A_1^i + (1 - \lambda_i) A_2^i\} \in V$. V is a set in n-dimensional Euclidean space with similar qualitative features to the set V of the last section (and the set U of Section 3). It is, for instance, convex. Corresponding to V, there is a set M where the strict preference in Configuration 8' is reversed; this has the same qualitative structure to V and

$$\{A_1^i\} \in M \quad \text{and} \quad \{A_2^i\} \in M \Rightarrow \{\lambda_i A_1^i + (1 - \lambda_i) A_2^i\} \in M.$$

Thus, M is also convex and, as it is disjoint from V, the two sets can be separated by a hyperplane; this hyperplane is the boundary to both sets (by P). Letting the hyperplane be defined by $\sum_{i=1}^{n} A^i c_i = c^*$, where the c_i and c^* are constants, with the notation of Configuration 8':

$$\sum_{i=1}^{n} \left(\frac{\alpha_1^i}{\alpha_2^i}\right) c^i > c^* \Rightarrow yPx$$

$$\sum_{i=1}^{n} \left(\frac{\alpha_1^i}{\alpha_2^i}\right) c^i > c^* \Rightarrow xPy.$$

Here the c_i will be non-negative (by appeal to P and transivity). Assume that $c_i > 0$ and $c_j > 0$ for some i and j, $i \neq j$. Consider $\{A_1^k\}$, $\{A_2^k\}$ such that

$$\sum_{k=1}^{n} A_1^k c_k = \sum_{k=1}^{n} A_2^k c_k = c^*, \quad A_1^k = A_{2k}, \quad k \neq i, j$$

and $A_1^i > A_2^i$, so that $A_1^j < A_2^j$. For any $\varepsilon > 0$ $\{A_1^k - \varepsilon\}$, $\{A_2^k - \varepsilon\} \in V$ so that

$$\{B^k\} = \{A_1^1 - \varepsilon, A_1^2 - \varepsilon, ..., \lambda_i A_1^i + (1 - \lambda_i) A_2^i - \varepsilon, ..., \lambda_j A_1^j$$

$$+ (1 - \lambda_j) A_2^j - \varepsilon, ..., A_1^n - \varepsilon\} \in V$$

for all $\lambda_i, \lambda_j, 0 < \lambda_i, \lambda_j < 1$. But

$$\sum_{k=1}^{n} B^k c_k = \sum_{k=1}^{n} A_1^k c_k - n \varepsilon \in c^* + (1 - \lambda_i)(A_2^i - A_1^i) c_i + (1 - \lambda_j)(A_2^j - A_1^j) c_j$$

so by choosing λ_i close to unity, λ_j close to zero and ε small, for all λ_i, λ_j, $0 < \lambda_i$, $\lambda_j < 1$. But

$$\sum_{k=1}^{n} B^k c_k = \sum_{k=1}^{n} A_1^k c_k - n \in c^* + (1 - \lambda_i)(A_2^i - A_1^i) c_i + (1 - \lambda_j)(A_2^j - A_1^j) c_j$$

so by choosing λ_i close to unity, λ_j close to zero and ε small,

$$\sum_{k=1}^{n} B^k c_k > \sum_{k=1}^{n} A_1^k c_k = c^*.$$

Thus, $\{B_k\} \in M$, which contradicts the fact that M and V are disjoint. Thus, if $c_i > 0$ then $c_j = 0$ for all j, $j \neq i$, and i's opinions are dictatorial when opinions are in type-A configurations.

The rest of the analysis of the last section can be followed through to show that i's opinions are dictatorial in all other possible situations. This gives a result akin to Theorem 3.

THEOREM 6a. Let there be n opinions about the well-being of two individuals. If f satisfies OAU, I, P, and FC, then there exists an individual opinion i and A^*, A^{**}, $0 \leqslant A^*$, A^{**} such that, if

$$W(u(x, \cdot, i)) = \begin{cases} \left\{ \dfrac{A^*}{1 + A^*} u(x, 1, i) + \dfrac{1}{1 + A^*} u(x, 2, i) \right\} \\ \qquad\qquad \text{if } u(x, 1, i) \geqslant u(x, 2, i), \\[2mm] \left\{ \dfrac{A^{**}}{1 + A^{**}} u(x, 1, i) + \dfrac{1}{1 + A^{**}} u(x, 2, i) \right\} \\ \qquad\qquad \text{if } u(x, 1, i) \leqslant u(x, 2, i), \end{cases}$$

then, for all $x, y \in X$,

$$W(u(x, \cdot, i)) > W(u(y, \cdot, i)) \Rightarrow xPy;$$

i.e. individual i's opinions are dictatorial.

The extension to the domain conditions of (NPU) and (U) are straightforward.

It is now possible to examine the case where there are r, $r > 2$, individuals whose well-being is under consideration. The easiest way of proceeding is by induction on r; thus, assume that one individual's opinions are dictatorial when there are $r - 1$ individuals under evaluation. Consider an r-individual society where two particular individuals are restricted to having equal welfare in every state (but not necessarily across states). This is isomorphic to an r-individual society, and OAU, I, P apply in this society if they apply in the r-individual society. Thus, one individual's opinions will be dictatorial under the restriction that i and j, say, have the same welfare. It is relatively states and again there is a dictatorial opinion. If the dictatorial opinion differs in the two cases, then the argument used with respect to Configuration 13 can be applied to obtain a contradiction.

It remains to show that an opinion that is dictatorial when at least two individuals have the same welfare is also dictatorial when all welfares differ. Consider state x in Configuration 16 where individuals have been labelled so that individual 1 has the lowest welfare, individual 2 the second lowest, etc. Assume that 1's opinion is dictatorial when two individuals have the same welfare. It will be shown that 1's opinion is dictatorial when x is compared with some other state y where individuals 1 and 2 have the same welfare level in state y and all individuals other than 1 and 2 receive the same well-being in x and y. If 1's opinions are not dictatorial, then there exist situations where opinions about state y are as y_1 is portrayed in Configuration 16 and xPy_1, but when opinions about y are as y_2 is portrayed, y_2Px. (Notice that under OAU there is no single $u \in D$ which can capture the opinions shown over the triple $\{x, y_1, y_2\}$). Consider an 'equality' state z where everybody has the same welfare. Individual 1's opinions are dictatorial over $\{y_1, z\}$. Consider $u \in D$ which conforms to the portrayed configuration over the triple $\{x, y_1, z\}$ and assume that 1's opinions dictate that y_1Pz but that, if welfares in state y_1 had been more than some small ε lower for individuals 1 and 2, then zPy_1. Thus, xPy_1 and y_1Pz so that xPz. Consider now a $u' \in D$ which conforms to Configuration 16 over $\{x, y_2, z\}$. By I, xPz. But, given how z is defined, zPy_2. This contradicts the fact that zPy_2 and shows that 1's opinions must be dictatorial in the comparison of x with y.

Configuration 16

1:	0							...
	$1x$	$1y_1$	$1y_2$	$2x$	$3x$	$1z$	$4x$	
		$2y_1$	$2y_2$		$3y_1$	$2z$	$4y_1$	
					$3y_2$	$3z$	$4y_2$	
					.			
					.			
					.			

~1:	0							...
	$1x$	$1y_2$	$1y_1$	$2x$	$3x$	$1z$	$4x$	
		$2y_2$	$2y_1$		$3y_1$	$2z$	$4y_1$	
					$3y_2$	$3z$	$4y_2$	
					.			
					.			
					.			

Now consider the comparison between state x and any other state z where two individuals i and j have the same welfare level. By introducing a state y with the properties that have been imposed above, it is known that 1's opinion will be dictatorial in the ranking between x and y and in the ranking between y and z. An argument similar to the one used with respect to Configuration 13 then shows that 1's opinions are dictatorial in the ranking between x and z. Finally, the argument can be extended to the ranking of two states x and y where individual welfares are strictly ordered in each state. By introducing a state z with the property that two individuals have the same welfare level in that state, 1's opinion will be dictatorial in the ranking between x and z and between z and y. Again, the argument used with respect to Configuration 13 shows that 1's opinion is dictatorial in the ranking between x and y. This completes the induction step.

> THEOREM 6. Let there be n opinions about the well-being of r individuals. (In particular, $n = r$ is permitted.) If f satisfies OAU, I, P, and FC, then there exists an individual i and a strictly monotonic function W with r arguments such that, for all $x, y \in X$,
>
> $$W(u(x, \cdot, i)) > W(u(y, \cdot, i)) \Rightarrow xPy;$$
>
> i.e. individual i's opinions are dictatorial.

The class of possible welfare functions W is characterized in Roberts (1980*b*). To see that there exists a function W with the required properties, it is sufficient to note that $W(u(x, \cdot, i))$ can be taken as the critical welfare of an 'equality' state y such that, if welfare in y is below (above) this level, then $xPy(yPx)$.

As in the last section, OAU can be changed to NPU or U to give the same result as stated in Theorem 6. Furthermore, if FC is strengthened to DC, then it can be applied to show that Theorem 2 extends to the case of an arbitrary number of opinions and individual well-beings.

6.   Concluding Remarks

In the past, social choice theory has dealt with the problem of utilizing information about well-being—an opinion—to construct social rankings and with the separate problem of aggregating social rankings—values—into a single ranking. It is clear from Arrow's *Social Choice and Individual Values* (Arrow 1963) that he recognized that the dictatorship result would be applicable to this latter aggregation problem. Information involving interpersonal judgements allows one to move away from a dictatorship result when using an opinion to construct a social ranking. But in a framework where there are many opinions available as 'raw' information, how can one move to a single social ranking without one individual's opinions being dictatorial?

This paper has adopted the Arrow framework in the sense that interest has centred on functions that map available information into social orderings, these functions obeying suitably generalized versions of the original Arrow restrictions. The available information is very much richer than that used in the Arrow problem, or, for that matter, in almost all other social choice problems. It is remarkable that, even in environments favourable to the existence of a wide range of aggregation functions, there must always be an individual whose opinions are dictatorial; the negativism of the Arrow result is more robust than has been previously acknowledged.

References

Arrow, K. J. (1963), *Social Choice and Individual Values*, 2nd ed., Yale University Press, New Haven, Conn.

d'Aspremont, C. and Gevers, L. (1977), 'Equity and the Informational Basis of Collective Choice', *Review of Economic Studies*, 44: 199–209.

Roberts, K. W. S. (1980a), 'Possibility Theorems with Interpersonally Comparable Welfare Levels', *Review of Economic Studies*, 47: 409–20.

—— (1980b), 'Interpersonal Comparability and Social Choice Theory', *Review of Economic Studies*, 47: 421–39.

Sen, A. K. (1974), 'Informational Bases of Alternative Welfare Approaches: Aggregation and Income Distribution', *Journal of Public Economics*, 3: 387–403.

—— (1977), 'On Weights and Measures: Informational Constraints in Social Welfare Analysis', *Econometrica*, 45: 1539–72.

PART II
Welfare and Development

9

Rational Fools and Co-operation in a Poor Hydraulic Economy

PRANAB BARDHAN

I

In the poorest parts of the world, in many ways water is destiny. In South Asia and sub-Saharan Africa—the two regions where mass poverty in the world is geographically concentrated—the life of most peasants continues to be a precarious gamble on the rains (apart from the relentless fact that their children die by the millions from unsafe drinking water and largely water-borne diseases). A controlled supply of water is crucial for agriculture in these areas, which are marked by generally low and highly variable rainfall and by flood-proneness in areas of high rainfall. In 1853, when Marx and Engels first discussed, in correspondence, the problems of 'Asiatic' societies, they immediately agreed on the particular importance of public irrigation in these societies, necessitated by what they called 'climatic and territorial conditions'.[1] Even though their emphasis on the idea of the centralized hydraulic state (particularly its subsequent extension by Wittfogel 1957 in a drastic form) was somewhat misplaced, it was a valuable insight which gave rise to a large anthropological literature on the relationship between irrigation and social and political organization.[2] In this paper, however, we shall keep our focus on the economic–institutional aspects; also, while there are major problems with the management of the main canal systems and with the structure and practices of the irrigation bureaucracy, we shall concentrate instead on the local community-level issues of co-operation which have often been cited as the key to substantially improving the existing levels of utilization of potential in irrigation and flood control.

'Water reform', in the sense of building or promoting genuine broadly based community institutions of co-operation from below (as opposed to government-mandated water-user associations), is at least as important as land reform in rural development. These institutions can have various functions in different irrigation systems: they aim at pooling efforts and resources in constructing and maintaining field channels at the outlet level of the main canal systems; at regulating water allocation and monitoring

---

[1] For an account of the roots of Marx's thinking on this question in earlier European tradition, as well as a critique of the ingredients of the concept of the Asiatic mode of production, see Anderson (1974).

[2] For a review of this literature, see Hunt and Hunt (1976).

violations; in cases of tank irrigation at desilting, weeding, and stopping encroachments on tank beds; at repairing, maintaining, and controlling water allocation from state and community tube-wells; at controlling groundwater over-exploitation with privately owned pumps in areas with fragile aquifers; and so on. But the history of local community-level co-operative organizations of water users in many areas is rather mixed. There are several documented examples of successful local-level co-operation in water management in poor countries[3] (although usually at a rather low level of organizational form), but there are more numerous cases of failure of such co-operation or co-ordination, often leading to an anarchical scramble for water with the inevitable dominance of the rich and powerful farmers.

As an illustration of this 'anarchy syndrome' in the appropriation of water, let me quote from an account by H. C. Hart from his walk along one of the watercourses intended to feed 4,300 acres of canal-commanded land in Shirol, a tail-end village of Karnataka's Ghataprabha project in South India:

Of seven outlet gates at the lower end of the watercourse, six were ripped out of their concrete channels, bent, or otherwise prevented from closing. The seventh was intact, but so hopelessly blocked with sediment that water could never reach it. 'It has been like this for three years', said the junior engineer. 'The cultivators break the gates. They should be severely punished. But what can we do?'

The junior engineer, an exceptional officer, had in fact tried to do something. We saw the need for it, and the difficulties, two kilometers further down the watercourse. At this point water in the channel simply dried up, leaving the last four outlets useless. . . . [The irrigators on the middle reaches of the watercourse], having blocked closure of their outlet gates, had also headed up water into them by means of home-made barriers in the bed of the watercourse. This effectively preempted the already insufficient flows from reaching the tail. The junior engineer had instituted closure of all upper outlets of the watercourse . . . during half of every week, pushing water down to the tail. It was an improvised rotational delivery.

It was not, however, entirely successful. When water began reaching the tail for the first time in many years, part of it was illegally diverted by a large landowner having twenty acres *above* the watercourse. His land was designed to receive canal water from an entirely different channel higher up. But finding water available here he had headed up the little supply one or two feet, dug an entirely unauthorized ditch to his land, and appropriated what he needed. His illegal ditch stood as evidence that the Irrigation Department was impotent. (Hart 1978, pp. 4–125).

Yet from another part of South India, Wade (1987) has reported some cases of village-level corporate irrigation organization with considerable co-operation in water allocation and monitoring, functioning on a day-to-day basis. It is thus important for us to understand the conditions working for and against sustainability of local co-operation in situations of economic and social interdependence.

---

[3] See e.g. Wade (1987), Ostrom (1990), and Tang (1991).

As a young student many years back, my first exposure to the general analytical issues of the incentive problem in group behaviour in situations of a mixed game of conflict and co-operation in the context of economic development was from the early writings of Amartya Sen: the discussion of the isolation paradox and the assurance problem in Sen (1961) and Sen (1967) and of labour allocation in a co-operative enterprise in Sen (1966). These issues have remained matters of abiding interest for me, and in this paper I go back to some of them in the context of local-level co-operation in water allocation and management. I shall first try to draw some lessons from the growing theoretical literature on co-operation in repeated game theory and in evolutionary biology, and then comment upon some limitations of the theoretical literature, particularly in the light of some of the pragmatic insights one can glean from the available field studies on the subject. My purpose in this paper is largely integrative, putting together evidence from disparate sources, both theoretical and empirical.

II

For quite some time, the literature on collective action has been characterized by a pervasive pessimism on co-operation, as, for example, in the widely noted work of Mancur Olson on political economy, or that of G. Hardin on the tragedy of the (open-access) commons. The theoretical underpinning of this literature has been provided by the standard one-shot Prisoner's Dilemma game as in Fig. 1(*a*), in which 'defection' or non-cooperation is the dominant strategy of each player, no matter what the other players do. However, as Taylor (1987) and others have pointed out, the constellation of costs and benefits of collective action on common-pool resources like water is often of a kind that is much more favourable to the possibility of co-operation than the Prisoner's Dilemma game.

Take, for example, the case of what Taylor calls the 'chicken' game (or what evolutionary biologists usually call the 'hawk-and-dove' game), as depicted in the pay-off matrix of Fig. 1(*b*). Suppose two neighbouring farmers are pondering the issue of who will carry out the essential maintenance

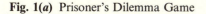

		Farmer II	
		C	D
F a r m e r I	C	3, 3	1, 4
	D	4, 1	2, 2

Fig. 1(*a*) Prisoner's Dilemma Game

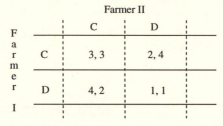

Fig. 1(b) Chicken or Hawk-and-Dove Game

work on the irrigation ditches that both use. Either farmer can do it by himself but each, of course, prefers to 'free-ride' on the other's work. The literature usually jumps to the extreme case of the Prisoner's Dilemma immediately after mentioning the free-rider problem. But in the case of many vital common-pool resources like water, the consequences of 'defection' on the part of both agents may be so bad that either of them would rather do the work himself if the other did not. As Fig. 1(b) shows, (defect, defect) is not the dominant strategy, unlike in the Prisoner's Dilemma game. Of course, in this case precommitment to an aggressive strategy is individually advantageous, and the powerful people in the village may resort to this; but at least the necessary maintenance work will not go by default.

There are, of course, cases in which an individual farmer cannot by himself do the whole work, and the extra benefits from the part of the work done by him do not fully cover his costs, as in the example of Fig. 1(c). In this example, however, each farmer co-operates when the other does, but defects when the other defects. This is an assurance game, which captures a widely observed phenomenon in the field studies: nobody wants to be 'suckered', but each one tends to be co-operative when the others (at least a critical mass of others, in a multi-person game) are, something that the Prisoners' Dilemma game fails to capture.

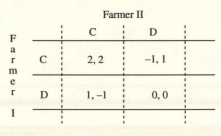

Fig. 1(c) Assurance Game

Even in the case of the Prisoner's Dilemma, the earlier pessimism is modified in the repeated game theory literature, where it is shown that co-operative equilibria can be spontaneously sustained by the long-run interests of foresighted self-interested individuals. The possibility of co-operation will, of course, depend on the future pay-offs not being discounted too heavily, or on the short-run rewards to defection (like stealing water) being not too large. The proofs of the relevant theorems in the literature of discounted many-person repeated games[4] work on the basis of the possibility of administering sufficient punishments over time to outweigh the immediate benefits for the defector and of these punishments being credible. But therein lies a second-order collective action problem, since punishment is costly to the punisher, while the benefits are distributed diffusely in the community. The primary trick here is to devise strategies that punish players who fail to play their part in punishing the defector—i.e. rules of what can be called *meta-punishment*.

Elster (1989) has raised a question about such meta-punishment rules: do people really punish others when they fail to sanction people who fail to sanction people who fail to sanction a defector? In a large community it is quite likely that sanctions run out of steam at two or three removes from the original violation. But in a small community of irrigators meta-punishments may not be unreasonable. (But then, in small communities the social costs of punishment to the punisher as well as the punished may also be larger.)

The theoretical models point to a potentially large number of equilibrium outcomes, facing which players may use observed past behaviour of others as a guide in their choice. In other words, even when costs and benefits of co-operation are otherwise identical, what degree of trust the players have in one another serves a crucial role. In this context, Seabright (1993) has a model of trust where he shows that, when many equilibria can exist in which the players' beliefs about each other's trustworthiness are confirmed by subsequent behaviour, there is a tendency for co-operative behaviour to enhance the prospects for successful further co-operation. As Seabright points out, when trust matters for the possibility of co-operation, the equilibrium is more renegotiation-proof, since the reputation loss in a breach of trust will make it difficult for the violator to persuade the others to let bygones be bygones. This ensures that punishments are more credible.

Conditions under which co-operation survives have also been explored in evolutionary biology. In a framework of limited rationality and learning by trial and error, game theory has been used to explain evolutionary processes. The central concept, as explained by Smith (1982), is that of evolutionary stability. An evolutionarily stable strategy (ESS) is a pattern of behaviour such that, if it is generally followed in the population, any small number of people who deviate from it will do less well than the others: no 'mutant' strategy can 'invade' the population.

---

[4] See Abreu (1988), Fudenberg and Maskin (1986).

Let us consider a large population from which pairs of individuals are repeatedly drawn at random to play a particular two-person symmetric game. If $V(I, J)$ is the expected pay-off to playing I against an opponent who plays J, then the average pay-off to playing I in a large population of others playing I is $V(I, I)$, and the average pay-off to playing J in the population is $V(J, I)$. In this case I is an ESS when either $V(I, I) > V(J, I)$, or $V(I, I) = V(I, J)$ and $V(I, J) > V(J, J)$. In a two-person repeated Prisoner's Dilemma game it can be shown that conditional co-operation (tit-for-tat) is ESS, as long as rates of time discount are not too large, the expected duration of the game is sufficiently long, the rewards to defection are not too great, and the punishment for defection is very costly to the defector. These conditions should be familiar from our discussion in the earlier part of this section.

But, while conditional co-operation is *stable* under these circumstances (i.e. it can defend itself against invasion), it may not be *viable* in the sense of Axelrod and Hamilton (1981); i.e. it may not be able to invade a large population of non-cooperators. If, however, we give up the assumption that agents are randomly paired for contests, and allow for the fact that agents are more likely to be paired with others adopting the same strategy, conditional co-operation may be viable as well as stable. As Bowles (1989) notes, when what he calls the 'degree of community' is sufficiently great (i.e. when the fraction of all contests that are among agents playing the same strategy is large), the likelihood of both stability and viability of the conditional co-operation strategy is enhanced.

III

While the game-theoretic models in general give us important insights into the sustainability of co-operation among self-interested agents in a situation of strategic interdependence in the management of common-pool resources like water, it is at the same time important to recognize that in a way these models divert attention from other salient issues in real-world co-operation which the models are much too mechanical and rigid to be able to cope with any degree of subtlety. For example, they cannot usually handle the impact of ongoing interactions among agents in the updating and contingent modifications of the rules of the game, changes in the pay-off matrix (as non-cooperative choices cumulatively drain a common resource,[5] e.g. in the

---

[5] In a multi-person situation one can imagine the marginal sanction on defectors depending on both the state of the (degrading) resource and the support a co-operator gets from others in the act of sanctioning. If p is the proportion of co-operators, the marginal sanction may then depend on the product $p(1-p)$. If the net benefit from co-operation is linear, then it can be shown in a simple model like that in Brown (1989) that there will be multiple equilibria allowing the possibility of a small amount of 'defection' without a total breakdown of the village co-operative effort.

over-exploitation of groundwater), and the possible evolution of strategy sets as an outcome of successive rounds of a game. The models also ignore the importance of group dynamics, which through deliberation and persuasion may bring about endogenous preference changes and reorientation of values in a community, and the importance of leaders and political entrepreneurs acting as catalysts in initiating co-operation and breaking deadlocks, emphasizing to people how others' efforts are contingent on theirs, and enlarging the shadow of the future.

The language of Prisoner's Dilemma game theory, as Sen (1987) has pointed out, makes it hard to discuss behaviour patterns which, in adapting to the recognition of mutual interdependence, go beyond what Sen calls 'self-goal choice' and work towards the enhancement of the respective goals of the members of a group. Such social norms may be particularly important in a small water community of a village. As Wade (1987) notes in his field study, the villagers were not particularly morally motivated; they were more pragmatic, but their self-interest was usually coupled with the moral capacity to recognize the related claims of others. Such social empathy[6] (the ability to imagine oneself in the shoes of others)—even sympathy and commitment, if it induces reciprocal behaviour—may, of course, be instrumentally useful in the general pursuit of self-goals. Besides, in a world where we often cannot predict each other's reactions, norms provide much-needed rules of thumb and focal points and lend a degree of inflexibility and commitment which form the basis of our binding agreements. As a result, as Elster (1989) points out, we often do better by following norms than by calculation.

Field studies in villages, as well as experimental studies of psychologists and economists, show that quite a large number of people are motivated by the norm of fairness: they don't want to free-ride on the co-operation of others, nor do they want to co-operate when few others do. Sociologists have emphasized what Coleman (1990) calls 'zeal', the opposite of free-ridership: how individuals, particularly in small communities, sometimes incur high costs for what they perceive to be good for their 'team', driven by the human desire for approval from others (positive sanctions). Of course, such team spirit may be rare in faction-ridden villages. Internal sanctions or internalization of social norms (often working through guilt, loss of self-respect, etc.) depends on factors like the degree to which the individual identifies with the group and the degree to which the norm and its sponsors are seen as legitimate. Intra-village conflicts may thus hamper the process of such internalization. On the other hand, if the conflict is perceived as something *vis-à-vis* outsiders or common adversaries, norms solidify more easily. As Wade (1987) comments, 'the [Irrigation

---

[6] I agree with Binmore (1991) that 'empathy', which is different from 'sympathy' in the sense of Hume and Adam Smith, can easily be accommodated in the repertoire of *Homo economicus*.

Department] official who has to be bribed or entreated, the upstream village that has to be stopped from taking too much water, becomes an antagonistic "them", and, being reified, can enhance perception of a reified collective "us" '. As for external sanctions in support of norms and meta-norms, as Axelrod (1986) indicates, they depend on similar structures of punishments and meta-punishments as in our earlier discussion of co-operation in repeated games.

As Ostrom (1990) notes, in actual field settings, unlike in the abstract models, one observes many cases of collectively arranged and financed 'enforcers' of co-operative arrangements (like the 'common irrigators' in Wade's villages in South India) and a great deal of peer monitoring. In cases of violations, the system of sanctions is often quite flexible and graduated, depending on the seriousness and context of the offence. Such contextuality is usually missing in the inexorable trigger strategies of punishment in the theoretical models. Too much flexibility, of course, can give wrong incentives.

Not surprisingly, co-operation works better in small groups with similarity of hydrologic needs and clear boundaries, and shared norms and patterns of reciprocity.[7] In such communities monitoring is easier, the 'common knowledge' assumption of models of strategic decisions is likely to be more valid, and social sanctions are easier to implement through reputation mechanisms and multiplex relationships of face-to-face communities. Migration and mobility possibilities work against co-operation. Contact with outsiders and the exit option reduce the effectiveness of social norms and the validity of the 'common knowledge' assumption. Prolonged repetition of the game also becomes more uncertain, raising incentives for short-run opportunism.

Even with similarity of social norms and of demographic size and composition, different villages can have completely different degrees of success in co-operative irrigation organization, depending crucially on hydrologic circumstances and the extent of ecological stress. Several cases suggest a kind of backward-bending curve relating the success of co-operative organization to (the quantity and reliability of) water supply: when the latter is extremely deficient, co-operation is difficult to organize; then at moderate levels of scarcity chances of success improve, other things remaining the same; then again, when water is much too plentiful, the urge to co-operate diminishes.

As is well known, the models emphasizing opportunism and incentives to break an agreement point to only one aspect of the collective action

---

[7] In a game played by rotating irrigators (turntakers and turnwaiters) with self-enforced rules (i.e. without formal guards), Weissing and Ostrom (1990) show that in the equilibrium an increase in the number of irrigators is associated with an increase in the stealing of water, other things remaining the same. But, of course, in actual field settings other things do not remain the same: in larger systems the irrigators often increase the rate of monitoring.

problem; the other is the bargaining problem where disputes about sharing the potential benefits may lead to a breakdown of the necessary co-ordination. Here an increase in the disparity in private benefits from common property resource management can lead to a situation in which some parties may lose from co-operation (in the usual case of absence of side-payments), and this may erode a pre-existing co-operative arrangement.[8] Intra-group heterogeneity in pay-offs may thus have an adverse consequence for the sustainability of co-operative agreements. This adds to some of the factors we have cited before, to reinforce the conclusion that social heterogeneity and intra-village conflicts and inequality may impede collective action in water management: internalization of co-operative norms is more difficult under such circumstances; the degree of confidence or trust that individuals have in the likelihood that others will play their part in a co-operative agreement, as in Seabright's model (1993), may be low; the 'degree of community' which lends *viability* to conditional co-operation in the evolutionary models we have discussed may be missing.

Field studies confirm these theoretical expectations. From a study of twenty-three community irrigation systems in different countries, Tang (1991) observes: 'a low variance of the average annual family income among irrigators tends to be associated with a high degree of rule conformance and good maintenance'. Jayaraman (1981) notes how the relatively egalitarian structure of the community is an important factor in the farmers' coming together in his case studies of farmers' organizations in surface irrigation projects in Gujarat. A study of ten tank irrigation cases in Tamil Nadu by Easter and Palanisami (1986) shows that the smaller the variation in farm size among the farmers, the more likely they are to form water-user organizations. Some other case studies indicate that, with the increased access to private pumpsets, the powerful people in the village are less interested than before in the maintenance of irrigation channels. Wade (1987) describes how, in villages where the rich farmers are able to get enough water for their land without having to organize corporately and without having to incur large additional expenditures themselves, since they own the land immediately below the canal outlets, they even block the formation of a co-operative water control committee (which might curtail their own irrigation freedom) at the expense of the small cultivators lower down.

Thus, the distribution of control over land in relation to proximity to the outlets strongly influences the nature of corporate response to a given water scarcity situation in a village. Sometimes land fragmentation (which may have adverse effects in other aspects of agriculture) may actually help co-operation, since some of the big farmers may have fragments of land at

---

[8] For an example from fishing with heterogeneous fishermen, see Johnson and Libecap (1982).

disadvantaged locations, away from the outlets, and may thus be induced
to organize co-operation. Boyce (1987) notes how, in tubewell irrigation
co-operatives in Bangladesh, when some powerful individuals manipulate
the location of the tubewell and distribution of water in their favour, the
resentment of those excluded or unfairly treated leads them sometimes to
sabotage the pumpsets. Bandyopadhyay and von Eschen, apart from
generally noting, from their survey some decades back of some villages in
West Bengal, the marked negative effect of economic and social stratification on co-operation, cite instances of village élites frustrating efforts at
co-operation on the part of the poor:

One instance of a deliberate effort to prevent co-operation took place in a village
where several cultivators tried to co-operate informally to irrigate their land by
bringing water from a nearby source. Two of the richer farmers in the area, however,
opposed this idea, claiming that the interest on money they had earlier lent these
cultivators was greater than the amount the latter intended to invest for the
irrigation, and demanding immediate repayment instead. The small cultivators felt
the real reason was that, if their irrigation efforts had succeeded, they would no
longer have been dependent on the richer farmers; nor could the farmers continue to
earn an easy income by loaning money at high interest rates with little risk. The two
rich farmers in question successfully frustrated the efforts at co-operation by first
lodging false charges with the police of theft and trespassing, and then going to court
to seek an injunction against digging irrigation channels on the grounds that these
would pass over land which they owned—land which, in fact, did not belong to them
and which they simply seized. This harassment ultimately led the small farmers to
abandon their efforts. (Bandyopadhyay and von Eschen 1988, p. 134)

This is, of course, a case in which the rich farmers did not themselves
belong to the irrigation community, and thus did not subscribe to its norms
or obey its sanctions. Even when they do belong to the irrigation community, in cases of sharp class antagonism the sanctions may be less
effective if reputation loss beyond one's own class or reference group is
perceived as insignificant. This is why Singleton and Taylor (1992) emphasize the importance for co-operation of 'mutual vulnerability' (to one
another's sanctions).

While the previous points focus on some degree of egalitarianism facilitating co-operation, let us finally note a somewhat contrary factor that one
observes in some case studies. In many local communities some rudimentary
forms of co-operation have been sustained and enforced over the years by
traditional authority structures. While there may have been some bit of a
sharing ethic, the predominant social norm was often that of an unequal
patron–client system, in which the powerful, who might enjoy disproportionate benefits from the institution of co-operation, enforced the rules of
the game and gave leadership to solidaristic efforts. As the advent of
participatory politics and social upheavals erodes the legitimacy of these
traditional authorities, and as modernization improves the options of both

'exit' and 'voice' for the common people, these solidaristic ties loosen and the old co-operative institutions sometimes crumble. Appeals to supra-local authorities for conflict resolution and arbitration become more common; frequent recourse to external political intervention to reverse local sanctions makes them much less effective in punishing defectors from co-operative arrangements; and dependence on the state increases to carry out functions like local water management and repair and maintenance of irrigation structures, which earlier used to be in the domain of locally autonomous, though hierarchical, organizations. Many rural communities in developing countries are now in the difficult transition period between the decline of the traditional co-operative institutions and the rise of the new water-user associations, based on shared reciprocity and defined rights, common lobbying interest, and legal–rationalistic norms (like regular auditing of accounts or checks and balances on arbitrary use of power), yet struggling to be born. With the growing politicization, accountability of the decision-makers in the local community has increased in many places, but sometimes at the expense of loosening enforcement standards on rules and assignments of co-operative arrangements. With increased political and social awareness, however, villagers are increasingly able to differentiate between domains of relationships which formerly used to be lumped in a dense, all-encompassing network. As a result, even in a highly conflict-ridden village people some-times are able to leave their factional disputes or caste conflicts behind when they settle rules of allocation and monitoring in a functionally separate water-user community, enhancing the latter's chances of survival.[9]

References

Abreu, D. (1988), 'On the Theory of Infinitely Repeated Games with Discounting', *Econometrica*, 56/2: 383–96.

Anderson, P. (1974), *Lineages of the Absolutist State*, New Left Books, London.

Axelrod, R. (1986), 'An Evolutionary Approach to Norms', *American Political Science Review*, 80/4: 1095–111.

—— and Hamilton, W. D. (1981), 'The Evolution of Cooperation', *Science*, 27 March.

Bandyopadhyay, S. and von Eschen, D. (1988), 'Villager Failure to Cooperate: Some Evidence from West Bengal, India', in D. W. Attwood and B. S. Baviskar (eds.),

---

[9] In a different context Amulya Reddy, a scientist leader in the alternative technology movement in India, has commented on this ability of villagers to separate domains of conflictual issues by referring to the Indian practice of leaving *chappals* (sandals) outside before entering a temple. Tang (1991) refers to Chiangmai village in Thailand, where the major factional division creates numerous conflicts among farmers, but they are still able to co-operate on irrigation matters.

Who Shares? Cooperatives and Rural Development, Oxford University Press, New Delhi.

Binmore, K. (1991), 'A Liberal Leviathan', University of Michigan Working Paper, September.

Bowles, S. (1989), 'Mandeville's Mistake: The Moral Autonomy of the Self-Regulating Market Reconsidered', mimeo, August.

Boyce, J. (1987), *Agrarian Impasse in Bengal: Institutional Constraints to Technological Change*, Oxford University Press.

Brown, T. (1989), 'The Commons: Tragedy of Practice or of Theory', mimeo, University of California at Berkeley, April.

Coleman, J. (1990), *Foundations of Social Theory*, Harvard University Press, Cambridge, Mass.

Easter, K. W. and Palanisami, K. (1986), 'Tank Irrigation in India and Thailand: An Example of Common Property Resource Management', University of Minnesota Department of Agricultural and Applied Economics Staff Paper, August.

Elster, J. (1989), 'Social Norms and Economic Theory', *Journal of Economic Perspectives*, 3/4: 99–117.

Fudenberg, D. and Maskin, E. (1986), 'The Folk Theorem in Repeated Games with Discounting or with Incomplete Information', *Econometrica*, 54/3: 533–54.

Hart, H. C. (1978), 'Anarchy, Paternalism or Collective Responsibility Under the Canals?' *Economic and Political Weekly*, 23–30 December.

Hunt, R. and Hunt, E. (1976), 'Canal Irrigation and Local Social Organization', *Current Anthropology*, 17/3: 389–411.

Jayaraman, T. K. (1981), 'Farmers' Organizations in Surface Irrigation Projects: Two Empirical Studies from Gujarat', *Economic and Political Weekly*, 26 September.

Johnson, R. N. and Libecap, G. D. (1982), 'Contracting Problems and Regulation: The Case of the Fishing', *American Economic Review*, 72/5: 1005–22.

Ostrom, E. (1990), *Governing the Commons: The Evolution of Institutions for Collective Action*, Cambridge University Press, New York.

Seabright, P. (1993), 'Is Cooperation Habit-Forming?' in P. Dasgupta and K. G. Maler (eds.), *The Environment and Emerging Development Issues*, Clarendon Press, Oxford.

Sen, Amartya (1961), 'On Optimizing the Rate of Saving', *Economic Journal*, 71: 479–95.

—— (1966), 'Labour Allocation in a Cooperative Enterprise', *Review of Economic Studies*, 33: 361–71.

—— (1967), 'Isolation, Assurance and the Social Rate of Discount', *Quarterly Journal of Economics*, 81: 112–24.

—— (1977), 'Rational Fools: A Critique of the Behavioural Foundations of Economic Theory', *Philosophy and Public Affairs*, 6: 317–44.

—— (1987), *On Ethics and Economics*, Basil Blackwell, Oxford.

Singleton, S. and Taylor, M. (1992), 'Common Property, Collective Action and Community', *Journal of Theoretical Politics*, 43: 309–24.

Smith, J. M. (1982), *Evolution and the Theory of Games*, Cambridge University Press.

Tang, S. Y. (1991), 'Institutional Arrangements and the Management of Common-Pool Resources', *Public Administration Review*, 51/1: 42–51.

Taylor, M. (1987), *The Possibility of Cooperation*, Cambridge University Press.

Wade, R. (1987), *Village Republics: Economic Conditions for Collective Action in South India*, Cambridge University Press.

Weissing, F. and Ostrom, E. (1990), 'Irrigation Institutions and the Games Irrigators Play: Rule Enforcement without Guards', in R. Selten (ed.), *Game Equilibrium Models*, ii, Springer-Verlag, Berlin.

Wittfogel, K. (1957), *Oriental Despotism*, Yale University Press, New Haven, Conn.

10

Primary Education and Economic Development in China and India: Overview and Two Case Studies

JEAN DRÈZE and MRINALINI SARAN

1. Introduction

A recent article in *China Daily* quotes Vice-Premier Zhu Rongji as saying that 'the introduction of a market economy does not mean making intellectuals hawk in the streets'. The context, which refers *inter alia* to the well-known story of a 'leading Beijing professor who was selling dumplings in the street', helps us to understand this somewhat mysterious statement. The concern of the Vice-Premier is with recent reports of disquieting trends in China's education sector, including the fact that, owing to the failure of the government to guarantee salary payments, many teachers have to 'scrape about for the basic necessities of life'.[1] These trends may seem surprising, given the extremely rapid growth of the Chinese economy since the reform process was initiated in 1978. But the connections between economic organization and social achievements are far from simple, and some of them can be easily overlooked when dazzling rates of economic growth capture most of the attention. This paper explores some of these connections, with reference to primary education in China as well as in India.

Much of this investigation will be based on a comparative evaluation of the recent experiences of two particular villages—Palanpur in India and She Tan in China—in the field of primary education. These two case studies should not be interpreted as an attempt to assess what is happening in India and China on the basis of a sample of size 1 for each country. The overall contrast between India and China will be examined directly, in Section 3, on the basis of recent statistical evidence. This examination

We are most grateful to Sudhir Anand, Robin Burgess, Mary Ann Burris, Elizabeth Croll, Prachi Desai, Haris Gazdar, Athar Hussain, Zou Lan, Nick Menzies, Peter Nolan, Alan Piazza, Emma Rothschild, Ruizhen Yan, Du Ying, and Duan Yingbi for helpful discussions and comments. We are also indebted to Peter Lanjouw and Jackie Loh for their invaluable help with the analysis of Indian and Chinese data. Sanjay Ambatkar and Rohini Somanathan provided excellent research assistance at various stages of this study, and very insightful comments on an earlier draft.

[1] All the quotes are from *China Daily*, 20 March 1993.

clearly indicates that China is well ahead of India in the field of primary education.[2]

Given that Palanpur is situated in one of the most illiterate areas of India while She Tan is situated in a comparatively advanced region of China, it is not surprising that the Chinese advantage emerges in the village studies presented in this paper. Our purpose is not to stress this advantage, but to probe the mechanisms that have led to these contrasting achievements, as well as to identify important areas of possible concern and further research. Indeed, a number of aspects of the relationship between primary education and economic development emerge more clearly from detailed case studies of this kind than from statistical analysis. The two, of course, are not mutually exclusive.

A few words should be said at the outset about the two villages in question. Palanpur is situated in Moradabad district of Western Uttar Pradesh (North India). This village has been the object of four in-depth surveys (in 1957–8, 1962–3, 1974–5, and 1983–4), and a great deal has already been written about it.[3] The observations reported in this paper are based partly on these four surveys (especially the last one), and partly on further fieldwork carried out by us in February and July 1993.

She Tan belongs to Zhejiang Province, a fast-growing area of eastern China.[4] She Tan is somewhat more prosperous than Palanpur, and other contrasts between the two villages will have to be interpreted in that light. Another important caveat is that we have less detailed information on She Tan than on Palanpur. Our observations on She Tan are based on one month of fieldwork carried out in February 1992, and on a short revisit which took place in March 1993.

The influence of Amartya Sen's ideas on what follows will be obvious to anyone familiar with his extensive writings on development and related subjects. Primary education in developing countries is an issue to which he has been deeply committed for a long time.[5] The scope for learning from the comparative development experiences of India and China is a theme he has often pursued, particularly in his analysis of hunger and famines in the modern world.[6] The distinction between economic growth and the quality of life, the role of public support in supplementing market-based

---

[2] It is not true, of course, that every region of China has achieved higher education standards than every region of India. The issue of regional variations, and other internal diversities within each country, will also be discussed in Section 3.

[3] See in particular Ansari (1964), Bliss and Stern (1982) and Lanjouw and Stern (forthcoming).

[4] 'She Tan' is a pseudonym; 'Palanpur' is not.

[5] This commitment has found expression in a wide variety of writings and lectures, from his Lal Bahadur Shastri Memorial Lecture delivered in New Delhi in 1970 (partly published in Sen 1971) to his recent analysis of 'threats to Indian secularism' (Sen 1993).

[6] See e.g. Sen (1981a, 1982, 1983, 1989).

entitlements, the importance of gender inequalities, the pervasive influence of co-operative conflicts in social living, and the scope for public action to transform living conditions at an early stage of development are other recurrent themes of his writings that have influenced the perspective adopted in this paper.[7] Our own contribution, such as it may be, has been greatly facilitated by these—and other—remarkably clear and powerful guidelines arising from Amartya Sen's thought.

1. Primary Education Economic Development, and Public Action

2.1. General Considerations

Economic development is, ultimately, concerned with improving the quality of life. Among the means that can be used to pursue this objective, the expansion of private incomes is an important one. Lack of income is indeed one of the crucial constraints that prevent many people from acquiring the commodities they need (food, clothing, shelter, etc.) to improve their living conditions.

But lack of income is by no means the only issue. Indeed, the relationship between private income and the quality of life is far from rigid. Essential factors affecting this relationship include the allocation of income between different possible uses, the distribution of resources within the household, the quality of the environment, the availability of public services, etc. To illustrate, the nutritional status of a child is a question not just of household income, but also of consumption patterns, intra-family distribution, epidemiological protection, parental care, hygienic practices, social stimulation, and related factors. Promoting the ability that people have to transform private incomes into better living conditions is an essential part of the development challenge.

Education can play a crucial role, both in enlarging people's income-earning opportunities and in enabling them to achieve a better quality of life at a given level of income. The first of these two considerations has received a great deal of attention in the literature on 'human capital', which suggests that economic returns to primary education in developing countries are typically very high.[8] The second consideration has received special emphasis in the more recent literature on 'human development'. Here again, the basic message of many studies is that the potential benefits of elementary education tend to be extremely large. The powerful influence of female

---

[7] On these different issues, see e.g. Sen (1981*b*, 1984, 1985*a*, 1985*b*, 1988, 1990*a*); also Kynch and Sen (1983), Sen and Sengupta (1983), and Drèze and Sen (1989, 1990, forthcoming).

[8] For reviews of the evidence, see e.g. Colclough (1982), Psacharopoulos (1984, 1985, 1988), and Schultz (1988); see also Alderman *et al.* (1993), and the more recent studies cited there.

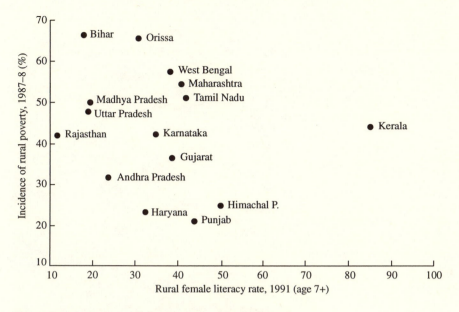

Fig. 1 Rural poverty and female literacy in Indian states
Sources: Minhas *et al.* (1991); Census of India, 1991, series 1, paper 2 of 1992.

literacy on child nutrition and survival, for instance, has been clearly brought out in a large number of empirical studies.[9]

If educational achievements were tightly determined by income levels, the preceding discussion would not matter very much. Income would remain the key variable, and the independent influence of education would be of little practical significance. Education, however, is not just a by-product of income. This point can be illustrated, somewhat crudely perhaps, by comparing the respective achievements of different Indian states and Chinese provinces in terms of adult literacy. As Figs. 1 and 2 indicate, there are enormous diversities in the educational achievements of different states and provinces even at comparable levels of income. In rural India, for instance, the female literacy rate (for women aged 7 and above) varies from 12 per cent in Rajasthan to 85 per cent in Kerala, despite the absence of any significant difference in rural poverty levels between these two states. And Punjab's rural female literacy rate is similar to that of West Bengal, even though the incidence of poverty is almost three times as high in West Bengal

[9] On this, see Caldwell (1979, 1986), Behrman and Wolfe (1984, 1987), Ware (1984), Jain (1985), Cleland and van Ginneken (1987, 1988), Nag (1989), Cleland (1990), Bhuiya and Streatfield (1991), Bourne and Walker (1991), Thomas *et al.* (1991), among others. On the related issue of the link between female education and fertility, see the proceedings of the Workshop on Female Education, Autonomy and Fertility Change in South Asia (New Delhi, April 1993), and the literature cited there.

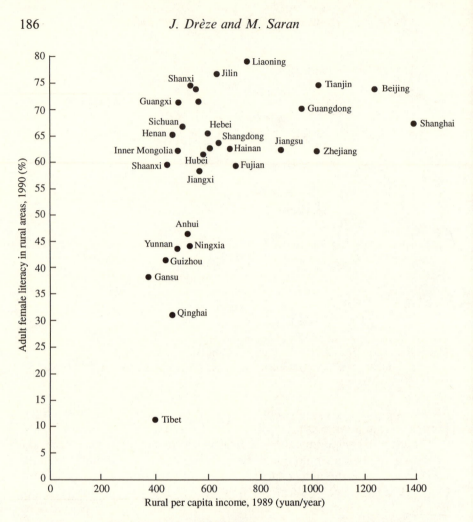

Fig. 2 Rural per capita income and female literacy in Chinese provinces
Sources: World Bank (1992) and Loh (1993)

as in Punjab. Similar contrasts apply between Chinese provinces. For instance, while 18 out of 30 Chinese provinces had a rural per capita income between 400 and 600 yuan per year in 1989, rural female literacy rates in these 18 provinces ranged from 11 to 75 per cent (Fig. 2). Here again, the association between educational achievements and income levels is far from tight.

One important reason for these contrasts is that, aside from private incomes, public action is a crucial determinant of educational achievements. Kerala's success, for instance, clearly relates to its strong record of public commitment to the provision of basic education. Conversely, the educational backwardness of some of the North Indian states (including Uttar Pradesh, where Palanpur is situated) is largely a reflection of the comprehensive neglect of public services in that part of the country, as will be argued further in this paper. The role of public action in some of China's early achievements, including the promotion of mass literacy, has also been quite decisive.[10]

The importance of public action in the field of education is not just a confined empirical observation, contingent on the particular development experiences of India or China. The potential effectiveness of education campaigns in raising literacy levels has been demonstrated in many parts of the developing world (including not only China and Kerala but also Sri Lanka, Cuba, Burma, Vietnam, Tanzania, and parts of north-east India). There are also well-known theoretical considerations, within as well as outside the standard framework of economics, suggesting that market signals and private activity alone rarely provide an effective basis for the promotion of elementary education in developing countries. One of the key issues is that there are pervasive 'externalities' in educational achievements and their uses, which are typically not captured in private calculations of costs and benefits. Other relevant considerations may include: (1) disincentives against long-term investment in education linked with 'imperfections' in credit and insurance markets; (2) the view of education as a 'merit good'; (3) the existence of increasing returns to scale (e.g. in a village school); (4) the notion that basic education is a 'right' to which all citizens are entitled; (5) the fact that the utilization of educational services typically involves one person taking decisions on behalf of another person (e.g. a father or mother deciding on behalf of a child); and (6) the 'diffusion effect' arising from the relation between experience and expectations (on which, more in Section 7). While market processes provide powerful incentives for certain types of activities, they are often inadequate when it comes to the widespread and equitable provision of basic education.

If we begin with these elementary reminders, it is because the preceding observations have not always been reflected in recent assessments of economic trends in China and India. In both countries, the prime concern of government planners is to achieve or maintain high rates of economic growth. This is certainly an important objective. The impressive transformation of living standards in China during the last fifteen years powerfully illustrates the benefits of rapid and broadly based growth in private incomes, just as the *absence* of a similar transformation in India illustrates the penalties of slow and inequitable growth. But there is also a danger of being over-concerned with economic growth, and of losing sight of other possible bases of improvement in the quality of life, including public

---

[10] For further discussion of these diverse experiences, see Drèze and Sen (1989, forthcoming), and the literature cited therein.

involvement in the field of primary education. Trends in the quality of public education and related social services tend to be less visible than the growth or decline of private incomes, and their consequences, being largely of a long-term nature, also tend to be less immediately perceived. As will be argued in this paper, greater vigilance is required in this respect in both countries.

2.2. Factors of Success

A number of conceptual difficulties are involved in studying the provision and utilization of educational services. We have already noted, in the preceding section, how these services possess certain features that make them quite different, as far as economic analysis is concerned, from commodities such as rice or shoes. More can be said along those lines. For instance, the conventional notion of exogenously given 'preferences' evades the whole question of motivation and values, which play a crucial part in educational decisions. The standard tools of consumer theory are quite blunt in this context.

We shall not attempt to propose an alternative, general approach. Before proceeding with our empirical investigation, however, it may be helpful to identify the basic issues that arise in connection with the promotion of elementary education in developing countries. Much of this paper concentrates on four—partly overlapping—sets of issues: (1) resources, (2) values, (3) incentives, and (4) institutions. Table 1 provides some illustrative examples of issues of each type.

The question of resources is of obvious relevance. Indeed, this question often captures most of the attention in policy debates, with the level of government expenditure on education as the main focus. At the household level, income is an important determinant of the affordability of education.

Table 1. *Provision and utilization of primary education: basic issues*

	Provision	Utilization
Resources	Public expenditure	Private income
Values	Public commitment to the promotion of basic education	Parental valuation of male and female education
Incentives	Accountability of teachers	Value of child labour
Institutions	Nature and functioning of responsible public agencies	Ability of parents to organize in pursuit of collective interests

Note: The specific issues mentioned in this table are illustrative, and are not meant to exhaust the range of relevant considerations.

'Values' is used here as something of a short-hand for the subjective basis (motivation, attitudes, norms, etc.) of education-related decisions. The choices that people make when faced with different alternatives (e.g. sending a daughter to school or keeping her at home) do not come out of the blue, and an attempt must be made to understand what influences them. The relevant values, it should be noted, are not just those of individual actors such as a father or mother or teacher: they may also be social values, e.g. the priority that a particular caste, ethnic, or occupation group collectively attaches to female education. The crucial issue of public commitment to the promotion of education also falls largely under this heading.

Incentives are a familiar theme in economic analysis, and have consider-able relevance in the field of education (although not always in the traditional form of pecuniary inducements). The process of education involves many different actors (children, teachers, parents, the village council, the government, etc.), and the incentives that these different actors have to play their part in the system is a crucial factor of success or failure. The quality of teaching, for instance, can be very poor unless some mechanism ensures that teachers are accountable to their pupils' parents, or to the village council, or to government inspectors. The opportunity cost of acquiring education (involving, *inter alia*, the question of child labour) is another incentive problem that will need careful consideration in this paper.

Finally, institutional issues have a major bearing on educational achieve-ments. We have already noted that the market mechanism on its own provides an inadequate basis for the provision and utilization of educational services. This raises the question of whether alternative or supplementary arrangements can succeed in providing the required resources, values, and incentives. It is in this respect that a particularly sharp contrast will emerge between Palanpur and She Tan.

3. India and China: Comparative Achievements in Rural Literacy[11]

Recent censuses conducted in China (1982 and 1990) and India (1981 and 1991) provide useful information on the literacy situation in each country.[12] A brief overview of the census results may help to put the case studies of Palanpur and She Tan in perspective.

The basic census figures (male and female rural literacy rates in Indian states and Chinese provinces for the census years) are presented in Figs. 3 and 4. Table 2 combines census data with related information from other

---

[11] This section draws substantially on collaborative work with Jackie Loh (London School of Economics).

[12] On the methodology of the Chinese and Indian censuses, see Li Chengrui (1992) and Bose (1991*a*, *b*), respectively. The 1990 literacy figures for China presented in this paper are based on the 10% Sampling Tabulation of the 1990 Population Census, as reported in Loh (1993).

sources, not only for China and India but also for the areas where Palanpur and She Tan are situated (Uttar Pradesh state and Zhejiang province, respectively); we have also included the relevant figures for the state of Kerala, which, as we shall see, is a case of great interest.

3.1. The Basic Facts

Before commenting on the census figures presented in Figs. 3 and 4, we should mention three comparability problems that have the net effect of making the gap between India and China look a little *smaller*, in these figures, than it really is.

First, the literacy rates for India and China are based on different age cut-offs. More precisely, the Indian literacy rates apply to persons aged 7 and above, while the Chinese literacy rates apply to persons aged 15 and above (these being the only age groups, other than the whole population, for which 1990–1 information is available at the time of writing).[13] Further, the available information on age-specific literacy rates in India indicates that 7+ literacy rates are typically a little *higher* than 15+ literacy rates.[14] Thus, the gap between Indian and Chinese literacy rates would be slightly larger if an identical age cut-off of 15 had been applied in both countries.[15]

Second, the Chinese and Indian populations have different age structures. In particular, old people represent a somewhat larger share of the population in China than in India, and this has the effect of driving down the average literacy rates in China for a given profile of age-specific literacy rates. This particular feature, of course, has to be considered along with other contrasts between the Indian and Chinese population structures. Taking the whole age structure into account, it can be shown that age-structure effects happen to play a negligible role in the particular contrasts that are being considered here, and can be ignored for our purposes.[16]

---

[13] Sex-specific rural literacy figures for the 7+ age group in Indian states in 1981 have been derived from the published figures applying to the 5+ age group by assuming that, in each state and for each sex, the ratio of 5+ to 7+ literacy is the same in rural areas as in 'rural and urban areas combined' (for which published figures on both 5+ and 7+ literacy rates are available); this is not a far-fetched assumption, since rural areas have a very large weight in 'rural and urban areas combined' in most Indian states. A similar procedure was adopted to derive 15+ rural literacy figures for Chinese provinces in 1982 from (1) published 12+ rural literacy figures, and (2) 12+ and 15+ literacy figures for rural and urban areas combined.

[14] For instance, in 1981 the all-India 7+ literacy rate was higher than the 15+ literacy rate by 2.8 percentage points (calculated from Government of India 1991, table C9). With a few minor exceptions, the 7+ literacy rate in 1981 was a little higher than the 15+ literacy rate in all Indian states.

[15] Using an identical age cut-off of 7 for both countries would make little sense, given that achieving literacy in Chinese at that early age is extremely difficult.

[16] The reasoning is as follows. When 1981 age-specific literacy rates for India are combined with the age structure of the *Chinese* population, they give an average literacy rate of 41.1% for the 15+ age group; this is very close to the corresponding literacy rate of 40.8% (again for the 15+ age group) obtained when the same age-specific literacy rates are combined with the age

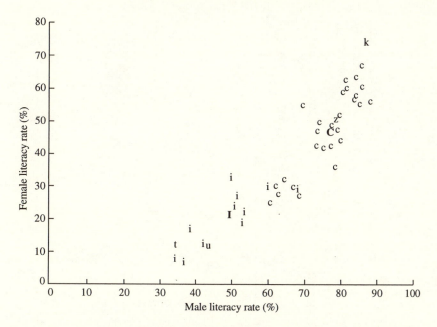

Fig. 3 Rural literacy rates in Indian states (1981) and Chinese provinces (1982)
C = China; *I* = India; *c* = Chinese province; *i* = Indian state; *k* = Kerala (India);
t = Tibet (China); *u* = Uttar Pradesh (India); *z* = Zhejiang (China).

Sources: Loh (1993) and Government of India (1991), based on census data. Indian literacy rates apply to persons aged 7 and above; Chinese literacy rates apply to persons aged 15 and above.

Third, it can be argued that literacy is a more demanding achievement in China than in India. In China, a person is usually considered literate if he or she can read about 1,500 characters.[17] By contrast, the Indian alphabets typically consist of a few dozen letters. (For example, the most widely used among Indian scripts, *devnagiri*, is based on an alphabet of 62 letters.) The number of characters or letters, of course, is not a definitive criterion of comparison, since literacy in Chinese requires only character recognition while alphabet-based reading involves the additional skill of combining

structure of the *Indian* population. Similarly, the Chinese age-specific literacy rates lead to an average of 65.9% (for persons aged 15 and above) when they are combined with the age structure of the Indian population, again very close to the figure of 65.8% obtained by combining these age-specific literacy rates with the age structure of the Chinese population. In other words, differences in age structure account for a very small part of the difference in overall literacy rates between India and China.

[17] In China, people who cannot read at least 500 different characters are officially considered 'illiterate', and those who can read between 500 and 1,500 characters are considered 'semi-literate' (Zhang Shaowen and Wei Liming 1987). All the Chinese census figures used in this paper are based on treating 'illiterate or semi-literate' as a single category, and on considering as 'literate' only those persons who fall outside that composite category (as in Li Chengrui 1992).

Table 2. *Literacy and Related Indicators in Selected Areas of China and India*

	Rural literacy rates (%) 1981[a]		Rural literacy rates (%) 1991[b]		Age-specific literate rates (%) — Literacy rate in 15–19 age group, 1981[c]		Rural literacy rate in 10–14 age group, 1987–88		Literacy rate in 15–19 age group, 1990[d]		Infant mortality rate[d] (per 1,000 live births)		Estimated rural per capita expenditure, 1988[f] (Rs/year)	Estimated rural per capita income, 1989[e] (yuan/year)
	M	F	M	F	M	F	M	F	M	F	1981	1989		
Palanpur	28	6	33	8	35	9	n/a	n/a	50	9	n/a	n/a	2,205 ($159)	n/a
Uttar Pradesh state	41	11	52	19	n/a	28	68	39	n/a	n/a	151	118	1,956 ($141)	n/a
INDIA	47	21	58	31	66	43	73	52	n/a	n/a	110	91	2,064 ($148)	n/a
Kerala	83	72	93	85	(92)[f]	92	98	98	n/a	n/a	38	22	2,448 ($176)	n/a
CHINA	79	51	84	63	96	85	n/a	n/a	97	92	37	40	n/a	602 ($160)
Zhejiang province	80	55	85	62	n/a	n/a	n/a	n/a	n/a	n/a	33	n/a	n/a	1,011 ($269)
She Tan	n/a	n/a	n/a	n/a	n/a	n/a	(close to 100%)		(close to 100%)		n/a	n/a	n/a	n/a

[a] 1982 for China; 1983 for Palanpur; in this column, the reference age group is 5^+ for all Indian figures, and 12^+ for all Chinese figures.

[b] 1990 for China; 1993 for Palanpur; in this column, the reference age group is 7^+ for all Indian figures, and 15^+ for all Chinese figures.

[c] 1982 for China; rural and urban areas combined.

[d] Rural and urban areas combined.

[e] In brackets, value in reference—year US dollars at the official exchange rate.

[f] Figure based on the *assumption* that the absence of any gender bias in literacy, observed in 1987–8, also applied in 1981.

Sources: The Indian figures are compiled from Government of India (1984, 1985, 1988, 1991, 1992), Verma (1988), Bose (1991*a, b*) and National Institute of Rural Development (1991); data relating to Palanpur are based on our own field surveys; the Chinese figures are derived from Banister (1992), World Bank (1992), and Loh (1993). Uttar Pradesh (India) and Zhejiang (China) are the state/province where Palanpur and She Tan are respectively situated.

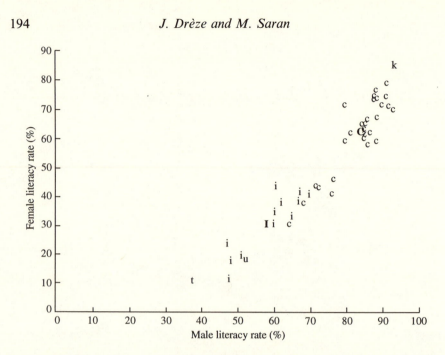

Fig. 4 Rural literacy rates in Indian states (1991) and Chinese provinces (1990)
C = China; I = India; c = Chinese province; i = Indian state; k = Kerala (India);
t = Tibet (China); u = Uttar Pradesh (India); z = Zhejiang (China).

Sources: Loh (1993) and Government of India (1992), based on census data. Indian literacy rates apply to persons aged 7 and above; Chinese literacy rates apply to persons aged 15 and above.

letters into a recognizable word or idea. But the fact remains that literacy skills in Chinese typically take several years to acquire (and can be retained only with regular practice), while literacy in Indian languages can often be achieved within a few months or even weeks.

Despite the fact that the net effect of these three 'biases' is to raise the Indian literacy figures relative to the Chinese ones, Figs. 3 and 4 clearly show that China is well ahead of India in the field of rural literacy. In 1991 China had a lead of 26 percentage points in male literacy, and of 32 percentage points in female literacy. And, while in rural India about 25 per cent of adolescent boys and 50 per cent of adolescent girls remain illiterate, the corresponding proportions for China are only around 3 and 8 per cent, respectively (Table 2).

The 1981–2 figures show that China's considerable lead was already firmly established by the end of the 1970s, when the country embarked on a far-reaching programme of economic reforms. The basis of this early success, achieved at a time when economic growth in China was not much more rapid than in India, was a strong commitment to the direct provision of education at an early stage of development. China has been bolder than India in this respect (building partly on the institutional framework provided by the Communist Party and the communes), and this contrast is reflected in the respective achievements of the two countries.[18]

A comparison between Figs. 3 and 4 indicates that male and female literacy rates have increased in all Indian states and Chinese provinces during the 1980s. It is difficult to say much more than that on the basis of these two figures. Given that there is a large overlap between the populations surveyed in the first and second census in each country, and that the literacy status of the overlapping population is likely to remain more or less constant, changes in average literacy rates between the two references years are driven by a small part of the population (those who die in the intervening period, or enter the relevant age groups). Looking at these average literacy rates is not a very effective way of assessing the progress that has taken place in different states or provinces in the 1980s. Age-specific literacy rates would be far more helpful, but the relevant census figures have not been published in either country at the time of writing.

3.2. Internal Diversities

As was mentioned in Section 2.1, there are large disparities in educational achievements, within India and China, between different states or provinces. Figs. 3 and 4 suggest that in both countries inter-regional disparities in literacy rates are largely driven by differences in *female* literacy rates, which vary over a much wider range than male literacy rates.

These inter-regional contrasts are only one aspect of the internal diversity that can be found in each country. Other relevant disparities (e.g. those relating to age or caste or class) cannot be investigated in any detail here, but it is worth emphasizing that an adequate assessment of the literacy situation in India and China would have to pay serious attention to these disparities, which imply very low levels of education for disadvantaged sections of the population in each country. To illustrate, in India in 1981 the rural female literacy rate was as low as 8 per cent among scheduled castes (which represent 16 per cent of the Indian population), 7 per cent among scheduled tribes (representing 8 per cent of the population), and 4 per cent among women aged above 60. When different sources of inequality are combined, the literacy rates for the most disadvantaged groups come down to minuscule figures; for instance, in 1981 the literacy rate among tribal women in rural Rajasthan was less than 1 per cent.[19]

---

[18] For further discussion of the role of public action in China's early successes, see Drèze and Sen (1989, ch. 11). On China's education system during and after the Mao period see Hsi-en Chen (1981), Hayhoe (1984, 1992), Cleverley (1985), World Bank (1985), Shi Ming Hu and Saifman (1987), Knight and Li Shi (1991).

[19] All the figures cited in this paragraph have been calculated from census data presented in Verma (1988).

Despite the inter-regional contrasts that exist within India and China, the basic pattern emerging from Figs. 3 and 4 is that every Chinese province fares better than every Indian state, with few exceptions. Among these exceptions, two stand out sharply: Kerala and Tibet.

We shall return to Kerala in a moment. Tibet distinguishes itself as having the lowest rural literacy rates among all Chinese provinces *and* Indian states (Fig. 4). It is possible that the interpretation of Chinese census figures requires special care for Tibet, where, for instance, ethnic minorities (for whom the standard literacy criteria may be misleading) represent a particularly large part of the population. But Fig. 3 and 4 indicate that, aside from being very low, literacy levels in Tibet have shown remarkably little *improvement* between 1982 and 1990. (In fact, female literacy rates do not seem to have improved at all over that period.) This further observation cannot be easily dismissed, unless there are serious problems of comparability over time in addition to problems of comparability between Tibet and other Chinese provinces. In any case, the recorded gap between Tibet and other parts of China is so large that Tibet would remain far behind the rest of the country even if substantial upward corrections were made to deal with possible comparability problems. The existence of a serious problem of low educational achievements in Tibet is hard to dismiss.

The causes of this problem cannot be investigated in any detail in this paper, not least because the Chinese government releases very little information on Tibet. Poverty alone is not much of an explanation: while Tibet is certainly one of the poorest provinces in China, its literacy rates are much lower than those of several provinces that have similar levels of per capita incomes (see Fig. 2). A more plausible hypothesis is that the commitment of the Chinese leadership to the promotion of literacy in Tibet has been rather weak. There may even have been some deliberate neglect of literacy in Tibet, aimed at containing the growth of political dissent in that region. This possibility is a useful reminder of the fact that one basic weakness of the Chinese political system is the dependence of social progress on the initiative and commitment of the leadership. When this commitment is strong, the achievements can be quite remarkable, as the progress achieved by 1982 in the other provinces illustrates. But when the leadership, for one reason or another, fails to address a pressing problem, there is little scope for public pressure to challenge that inertia.[20]

3.3   Kerala and China

Kerala is well known for its exemplary record in the field of literacy, and its leading position *vis-à-vis* other Indian states in Figs. 3 and 4 comes as no

---

[20] This political problem played a crucial role in the development of the tragic famine of 1958–61, as Amartya Sen has persuasively argued (Sen 1982).

surprise. What is less well known is that Kerala is also doing significantly better than China in terms of rural literacy. In fact, Fig. 4 suggests that by 1991 Kerala was not only ahead of China in this respect, but also ahead of *every* individual Chinese province. Kerala's lead is particularly pronounced for female literacy.[21]

In interpreting the comparative records of China and Kerala, it should be borne in mind that Kerala made a much earlier start in the promotion of mass literacy. While the widespread provision of basic education became an important concern of the Chinese leadership only after 1949, Kerala has a long history of public commitment in this field, going back to the nineteenth century. This means, *inter alia*, that Kerala enjoys relatively high literacy rates even in older age groups, which is not the case in China (especially for women). For the younger age groups, Table 2 indicates that by 1982 China already had rural literacy rates that were quite close to those applying in Kerala, although the gender bias was significantly larger in China. Further progress occurred in the 1990s, bringing China's literacy rate in the 15–19 age group to the impressive level of 95 per cent by 1990, with a somewhat reduced gender bias. For Kerala, Table 2 indicates that universal literacy in the younger age groups has virtually been achieved, with *no* gender bias. This is an outstanding achievement, especially in view of Kerala's low per capita income.

We conclude by noting that, while China and Kerala are now quite close to each other in terms of rural literacy in the younger age groups, the political basis of their achievements has been radically different. China's success has derived from the ideological commitment of the leadership to the promotion of education at an early stage of development. In Kerala, on the other hand, early state initiatives taken in the nineteenth century have empowered the population to exert an independent pressure on the state at a later stage. High literacy levels have helped the population of Kerala to play a creative part in the pluralist political system of independent India, which is quite responsive to organized popular demands. As many commentators have noted, public pressure has now become the driving force behind the government of Kerala's extensive involvement in the provision of a wide range of social services, including not only education but also health care, social security, and food distribution.[22]

---

[21] With a uniform age cut-off of 15 for Kerala as well as for Chinese provinces, Kerala would retain a strong lead for female literacy, but a few Chinese provinces would be slightly ahead of Kerala in terms of male literacy.

[22] See e.g. Kabir and Krishnan (1992), Jeffrey (1993), Ramachandran (forthcoming), and the literature cited there. The militancy of Kerala's population belies the expectations expressed by the Maharaja of Travancore in 1881: 'No civilized government . . . can be oblivious to the great advantages of popular education . . . *a government which has to deal with an educated population is by far stronger* than one which has to control ignorant and disorderly masses' (cited in Jeffrey, 1993: 56; emphasis added).

2.4. *Uttar Pradesh and Zhejiang*

The age-specific literacy rates presented in Table 2 highlight an important contrast between the current literacy situations in India and China. In China, literacy is still far from universal in the population as a whole, but illiteracy is getting quite close to eradication in the younger age groups, which enjoy literacy rates well above 90 per cent. This encouraging pattern, which promises a relatively rapid convergence to universal literacy, does not apply in India, where much remains to be done to raise literacy rates in the younger age groups. This is particularly the case for girls, only half of whom are literate in the 10–14 age group.

Table 3. *Rural literacy rates among persons aged 10–14 in India, 1987–1988*

State	Rural literacy rate in 10–14 age group (%)	
	Male	Female
Kerala	98.1	98.2
Manipur	94	92
Himachal Pradesh	95	81
Assam	83	78
Meghalaya	74	75
Tamil Nadu	85	71
Punjab	76	69
Maharashtra	86	68
Haryana	87	63
Gujarat	78	61
West Bengal	69	61
Karnataka	74	56
Orissa	70	51
Jammu & Kashmir	79	50
Andhra Pradesh	66	42
Madhya Pradesh	68	40
Uttar Pradesh	68	39
Bihar	59	34
Rajasthan	72	22
INDIA	73	52

Note: The states are arranged in descending order of female literacy rate.

Source: Sengupta (1991), based on National Sample Survey data.

There are, of course, important variations within India in the extent of this problem of low literacy rates in the younger age groups, as Table 3 indicates. Here again, inter-regional variations are particularly sharp for females, with the female literacy rate in the 10–14 age group varying from

22 per cent in rural Rajasthan to 98 per cent in rural Kerala.[23] Four North Indian states, notorious for their neglect of social services and for their poor achievements in the field of education and health, stand out as having particularly low female literacy rates in the 10–14 group: Rajasthan (22 per cent), Bihar (34 per cent), Uttar Pradesh (39 per cent), and Madhya Pradesh (40 per cent). To appreciate the enormity of the problem, it is useful to remember that these four states currently have a combined population of about 350 million—a little below 10 per cent of the entire developing world.

This is the background of our case study of Palanpur, situated in Uttar Pradesh, one of these four 'problem' states. As can be seen from Table 2, literacy rates in Palanpur are particularly low, even by Uttar Pradesh's unexacting standards.[24] A close examination of the experience of this particular village may help to throw some light on the broader problem of educational failure in this 'area of darkness'.

She Tan, on the other hand, is situated in a province (Zhejiang) whose educational record is very close to the Chinese average (see Table 2); this second case study may help to understand the basis of China's achievements. As far as the comparative aspect of these two case studies are concerned, the different backgrounds of the two villages will have to be taken into account, including the fact that She Tan, unlike Palanpur, is situated in a progressive region of the country. While this difference of background complicates some aspects of this comparative investigation, it also has some advantage for our purposes, in so far as it 'magnifies' some of the contrasts that we are concerned to identify.

4. Palanpur and She Tan

Primary education does not happen in a social vacuum. The resources, values, incentives, and institutions that come into play in the educational process are partly derived from, or influenced by, other features of the economy and the society. Among the relevant features are: (1) demographic behaviour, (2) economic organization, (3) social divisions, (4) gender relations, and (5) collective institutions. It may be helpful to comment briefly on these aspects of Palanpur and She Tan before we examine their respective records in the specific field of education. Table 4 presents a few clues in summary form.

[23] As Table 3 shows, the only two Indian states that have (slightly) higher literacy rates for females than for males in the 10–14 age group are Kerala and Meghalaya. It is interesting that both states have a strong tradition of matrilineal kinship for large sections of the population (including the Nayars in Kerala, and the Khasi and Garo tribes in Meghalaya).

[24] It is worth noting that, although literacy rates in Palanpur are significantly lower than in Uttar Pradesh as a whole, they are almost identical to the local district figures, which are themselves not unusual for Utter Pradesh districts. In other words, there are large areas within Uttar Pradesh where literacy rates are just as low as in Palanpur.

Table 4. *Palanpur and She Tan, 1993*

	Palanpur	She Tan
Location	Moradabad District (Western Uttar Pradesh)	Shao Xing County (Zhejiang Province)
Population	1,133	987
Average hh size	5.9	4.0
Life expectancy at birth[a] (male/female)	55/53 [1986–90]	68/72 [1981]
Sex ratio[a] (females per 1,000 males)	882 [1991]	940 [1990]
Infant mortality rate[a] (deaths per 1,000 live births)	97 [1991]	33 [1981]
Birth rate[a] (per 1,000)	36 [1991]	15 [1990]
Adult literacy rate (male/female, age 15+)	32/6 [1983]	87/67[a] [1990]
Usual living arrangements	Nuclear family or patrifraternal joint family	Nuclear family
Land area (acres per person)	0.34	0.11
% of landless households	20	0
Per capita annual income[b]	126 (1,390)	225 (3,600)
Daily wage rate for casual agricultural labour[b]	0.8 (8.2)	0.9 (14.0)
Land ownership and management	Land is privately owned, unequally distributed, and cultivated by owners as well as share-croppers.	Land is collectively owned; the main fields are divided every 5 years on an equal basis between adult village residents, who cultivate or sub-let their plots; other fields (groves, orchards, etc.) are contracted out to the highest bidder by the village government.
Main occupations	Cultivation; wage labour in agriculture; unskilled wage labour in nearby cities	Cultivation; wage labour in village enterprises and cities; skilled non-agricultural self-employment
Sexual division of labour	Women do not engage in wage labour, and do not work outside the village; some low-caste women work on family	Women are engaged in a wide range of economic activities.

Table 4. (*contd.*)

	Palanpur	She Tan
	plots; high-caste women do only domestic work.	
Village government	Elected village headman acts as intermediary between the village and government officials; elected village council is non-functional.	Elected village headman and 'Party leader' (elected by village Party members) work together.
Public services and facilities	School; three handpumps	School; electricity; tap water; irrigation; toilets; road maintenance; community hall; *wu bao*
Social security arrangements	Filial support for the aged	Equal land entitlements; filial support for the aged (mandatory); elderly couples without adult children receive community support (*wu bao*)
Social divisions	Large economic inequalities based on unequal land ownership and differential access to non-agricultural employment; strong caste hierarchy; inequalities of caste and class tend to reinforce each other	Growing economic inequalities based on differential access to non-agricultural employment
Gender relations and social status of women	Patrilineal inheritance, strict patrilocal residence, sharp sexual division of labour, restricted female autonomy, strong boy preference	Patrilocal residence, boy preference; relatively weak sexual division of labour

[a] State/province figure (or district figure, when available), for rural and urban areas combined, from official sources.

[b] In 1993 US$ at the prevailing, unofficial exchange rate; in brackets, money wage/income divided by the local market price (per kg) of staple grain (wheat in the case of Palanpur and rice in the case of She Tan).

Note: A certain amount of guesswork is involved in the estimation of some of the village-level figures (e.g. per capita income in She Tan), and these figures should be taken as indicative. Numbers in square brackets indicate the reference year, when different from 1993.

Sources: World Bank (1992); Loh (1993); Premi (1991); Government of India (1988, 1989, 1993); Bose (1991*a*, *b*); Banister (1992). Field survey data.

4.1. Palanpur

The demography of Palanpur[25] is fairly typical of Uttar Pradesh, where the 'demographic transition' is still at a very early stage. The village had a total population of 960 in 1983–4, with an average household size of a little under 7. The rate of population growth is almost 2.5 per cent per year, corresponding to annual birth and death rates of the order of 40 and 15 per thousand, respectively. The high death rate largely reflects high infant and child mortality rates. A large majority of mothers in Palanpur have lost at least one child, and many have lost three or more. (One mother reports having lost sixteen.)

The main economic activities in Palanpur are agriculture and wage employment outside the village. Agricultural practices are based on the familiar 'Green Revolution' technology, involving an intensive use of modern irrigation devices, chemical fertilizers, and high-yielding seeds. Land is privately owned and its distribution is highly unequal; about 20 per cent of Palanpur households are landless, while households in the top quintile of the land ownership scale own almost 60 per cent of the village land. The farm-household is the basic production unit. Households possessing more land than they can (or wish to) cultivate on their own lease out some of their plots to other households, or hire wage labour to supplement their own labour resources. Wage employment outside the village consists mainly of unskilled work in enterprises located in nearby cities (e.g. cotton-spinning factories, steel-polish workshops, and sugar mills).

The distribution of employment opportunities outside the village tends to replicate or amplify inequalities based on land ownership. The overall distribution of income and wealth in Palanpur, as in most Indian villages, is highly unequal. In 1983–4 per capita income ranged from Rs206 per year for households in the bottom decile of the income scale to Rs2,067 per year for households in the top decile.[26]

Another major source of social inequality is the caste system, which divides the society into endogamous groups arranged in strict hierarchical order, and traditionally attached to specific occupations. Inequalities of caste and class tend to reinforce each other, with 'higher' castes typically having better endowments of land and other productive resources, and achieving higher incomes.

A further source of social division is the unequal position of men and women in society. Patrilineal inheritance and patrilocal residence are major

[25] This section is deliberately brief. For further details on Palanpur, see Bliss and Stern (1982) and Lanjouw and Stern (forthcoming). In this section the reference year is 1983–4 (when the most detailed survey of the village was conducted).

[26] The figure of Rs206 per year for per capita income in the bottom decile (roughly equivalent to 0.5 kg of wheat per day) may seem incredibly low. It should be borne in mind, however, that many households in that decile are experiencing a transient, downward income fluctuation, and have a negative saving rate for the year in question. The distribution of expenditure is less unequal than that of income.

sources of gender inequality and female dependency (Drèze 1990). The dependent position of women is reinforced by a sharp sexual division of labour, which excludes a majority of women from most forms of gainful employment. Parental preference for boys is very strong, one of its symptoms being a high level of excess female mortality among infants and young children.

Collective institutions in Palanpur are poorly developed. Political parties, trade unions, women's organizations, youth clubs, co-operative societies, and similar associations are conspicuous by their absence.[27] As far as village governance is concerned, the village headman essentially acts as an intermediary between the village community and the state. The village headman, who is elected every few years, is invariably a rich (male) landowner from one of the 'higher' castes. The village council (*panchayat*), also formed by election, is, for practical purposes, non-functional. One of the consequences of the defective nature of collective institutions in Palanpur is the poor functioning of public services, including—as we shall see—the village school.

4.2. She Tan

She Tan is situated in a fertile region of eastern China, traditionally known as *yu mi zhi xiang*, or the land of fish and rice. Tucked into a valley, the village has low, terraced hills on three sides and a clear, shallow river on the fourth. A rough gravel road links She Tan with a nearby township and the county capital.

In February 1993, She Tan had a population of 987, with about 250 households. Census data suggest that Zhejiang Province is a relatively 'advanced' province in demographic terms, with, for instance, slightly better life expectancy and infant mortality figures than the national average.[28] In She Tan itself, a significant 'demographic transition' has already taken place, leading to low mortality and fertility rates and a low rate of population growth.

As elsewhere in rural China, the commune system was disbanded in She Tan after 1978 and replaced by the 'household responsibility system'. The land remains collectively owned, but it is now leased to individuals, households, or production teams for management and cultivation. Each adult member, male or female, is entitled to the use of about one *mu* (0.16 acre) of land, equally distributed over good, mediocre, and poor land. Aside

---

[27] Caste councils, which lay down certain social norms applicable to specific castes across villages in a particular area, are still functional, but their concerns are largely confined to marriage arrangements, kinship organization, and related matters.

[28] Life expectancy at birth in 1990 was 67.8 years in China and 69.7 years in Zhejiang. Infant mortality in 1981 was 37 per thousand in China and 33 per thousand in Zhejiang Province (Banister 1992).

from this equal division of the main fields, the village government contracts other plots of village land (e.g. groves and orchards) to the highest bidder. The role of the village government, as far as land is concerned, is confined to the allocation of plots and the collection of contract fees. The household responsibility system has given peasants very effective incentives to increase production, as any surplus not sold to the state at low official prices can be consumed or sold at market rates.

In addition to grain, fruit and vegetable cultivation, post-reform She Tan households engage in a variety of sideline activities that account for a substantial and growing portion of family income. These include raising pigs and ducks for sale or slaughter, and rabbits for their fur which is sheared and sold to clothes factories in the country capital. Some villagers dredge sand from the river bed, sift it and sell it for use in construction. A large number of households also raise silkworms during the summer.

A third major source of income is wage employment in village or township entreprises. She Tan itself has a small brick-making entreprise, but many young people do wage labour outside the village in township and county enterprises like tea and silk processing factories. Migration to urban areas is meant to be strictly controlled, but it does occur in the form of villagers unofficially joining the 'floating population' of larger cities.

While land is quite equally distributed, non-agricultural income varies widely from household to household. This has led to growing inequalities of income and wealth between She Tan families, clearly visible in the range of dwellings observed in the village. Houses vary from modest wood and brick structures with tiled roofs to multi-storied concrete constructions of six rooms with amenities like televisions, gas stoves, ceiling fans, and pink stuffed sofas. We estimate that average per capita income in the village was about 1,800 yuan per year in 1993, or 225 dollars at the prevailing unofficial exchange rate.[29]

In She Tan the nuclear family is the basic social unit. However, informal ties with the extended family are extremely close, with parents, siblings, and in-laws frequently dropping in and out of each other's homes, lending each other money, and even pooling resources to bid for extra land contracts.

The post-Liberation marriage law of 1950, further revised in 1982, was a serious attempt to improve the status of women all over China including the countryside. It made forced, arranged marriages illegal, banned extravagant wedding ceremonies, and raised the minimum legal marriage age to 20 for girls and 22 for boys.[30] Marriages were required to be registered with local

---

[29] This estimate is derived from rough calculations based on the available information on wages, employment, agricultural output, and crop prices. It is quite close to the official estimate of per capita income for rural areas of Zhejiang Province.

[30] The average age at marriage for women in 1987 was 23 in Zhejiang Province, and 22 in China as a whole (Hayase and Kawatama 1990).

village authorities. Other laws formalized women's right to work outside the home and to participate in paid labour.

The results of these legal reforms, combined with effective social mobilization, are clearly visible in She Tan. Women are involved in a wide variety of economic activities outside the home, including working in fields and in enterprises outside the village. Common perceptions of what constitutes 'woman's work', however, remain influential. Raising silkworms, for example, is largely a female activity, although men help with the collection of mulberry leaves. Similarly, women process the silk cocoons both manually and automatically. It is believed that women's fingers are more nimble and therefore better suited to this rather messy job. Women are tacitly barred from jobs that involve a certain level of technological skill, like driving a tractor or handling highly mechanized processes in enterprises. It is believed that these jobs are 'too hard' for women.

Most domestic sideline industries, like raising pigs or rabbits, are in the hands of women. The fact that these activities generate a substantial amount of additional household income (occasionally more than male earnings) gives women greater clout in domestic decisions, including how to spend money. But the double burden of domestic chores and gainful employment is also evident in She Tan. Men do not provide any meaningful help with cooking, cleaning, dish-washing, laundry, or child-care.

The adoption of the household responsibility system, with the nuclear family becoming once again the unit of production, has important implications for women. Under the commune system, for example, women worked mostly in production teams with other men and women, and got paid in workpoints. Now, at least some women report spending a larger share of their time in household chores and domestic sideline industries (despite the overall expansion of employment opportunities). Although further evidence is needed on the precise extent of this emerging trend, the possibility of women returning to traditional roles based in the house cannot be overlooked.[31]

She Tan has a female *ji hua sheng yu gan bu*, or 'birth control cadre', who distributes free contraceptives (mostly IUDs, but also pills and condoms) to couples of child-bearing age. Her duties include monitoring married women's periods and noting which couples are eligible to bear children each year. The marriage bureau in the township administers an examination testing a couple's knowledge of birth control methods before authorizing the marriage certificate.

She Tan has a functioning village government, actively involved in regulating the provision of collective services like water, electricity, irrigation, taxation, education, public announcement systems, and the 'five

---

[31] This issue is discussed in Mak (1989), Aslanbeigui and Summerfield (1989), Kelkar (1989), and Rosen (1992), with reference to rural China as a whole; see also Sun (1993).

guarantees' (*wu bao*) social security system for the aged with no children.[32]
A village head is elected by the villagers every two years; the current village
head has been re-elected five times over a period of ten years. He works
closely with the Party leader, who is elected by the thirty or so Party
members in the village. The village head need not be a Party member,
although She Tan's is. The village head and Party leader appear to take
most decisions concerning village affairs together, and say that they 'work
through' their differences. But we have not had the opportunity to observe
directly the details of the village government's mode of operation and its
relationship with the Party.

The financial resources of the village government have been significantly
eroded by the transition from the commune system to the household
responsibility system. Now that most productive activity occurs in the
private sector, incomes initially accrue to households (rather than to the
collective), and the village government has to raise resources through
indirect means. These include (1) profits from village enterprises, (2)
earnings from land contracts, (3) user charges (e.g. for irrigation water), and
(4) taxes and *ad hoc* 'contributions'. As will be seen further on, the current
system of local public finance provides an inadequate and unreliable basis
for collective activities and services, including the village school.

4.3. Preliminary Contrasts

A number of important similarities and contrasts emerge from the preceding
sketches of Palanpur and She Tan, and from the complementary information provided in Table 4. For our purposes, the following are particularly
noteworthy.

First, parental considerations on educational matters are likely to be quite
different in She Tan's small, nuclear families and in Palanpur's much larger
households. For instance, the importance that parents attach to the educational achievements of individual children is likely to be greater in families
with fewer children.

Second, the economy of She Tan, aside from being somewhat more
prosperous than that of Palanpur, also enjoys a built-in social security
system, in so far as every adult is entitled to an equal share of the village
land.[33] Palanpur has to deal with the special problem of educational
investment on the part of poor parents, for whom the opportunity cost of
schooling can be quite high.

---

[32] She Tan has three elderly villagers with no offspring to look after them. This makes them
eligible for the 'five guarantees'. The village government spends about 1,000 yuan a year on
each of these three people, providing shelter, grain, and personal services as needed; in addition,
these three villagers are entitled to the same share of village land as other adults.

[33] This basic source of social security is supplemented by (1) a strong tradition of filial
support for the aged, now backed by government legislation, and (2) the provision of 'five
guarantees' to old persons without adult children.

Table 5. Selected features of the village primary school in Palanpur and She Tan

	Palanpur		She Tan	
	1983	1993	1978	1993
Location of the school building	Outskirts of the village	Outskirts of the village	Centre of the village	Centre of the village
Description of the school building	Dilapidated 2-room brick structure; no furniture	New, 2-room brick structure; no furniture	Large, furnished brick building (4 rooms)	As in 1978, but quite dilapidated
No. of grades taught	5	5	4	2
No. of teachers	1	2	5	2
No. of female teachers	0	0	n.a.	2
Teachers' village of origin	Palanpur	Nearby villages	2 from She Tan, 3 from elsewhere	Near by village
Teachers' monthly salary[a]	n.a. (460)	82 (900)	n.a.	31 (500)
Enrolment[b]	30 (19%)	54 (39%)	75 (about 100%)	42 (90–100%)
Observed attendance (spot-check)	10–12 (when classes are held at all)	28	n.a.	35
Female enrolment[c]	10 (33%)	11 (19%)	n.a.	12 (29%)
Observed female attendance[c]	1–2 (when classes are held)	9 (15%)	n.a.	6 (17%)
Annual fee per child[d]	(negligible)	0.5 (6)	(negligible)	13 (200)
Source of funding	State government	State government	n.a.	Fees; village enterprises; township support

[a] In 1993 US$ at the prevailing, unofficial exchange rate; in brackets, nominal salary/fee divided by the local market price (per kg) of staple grain (wheat in the case of Palanpur; rice in the case of She Tan).

[b] In brackets, enrolment as a percentage of the number of children in the relevant age group (rough estimates, in the case of She Tan).

[c] In brackets, female enrolment/attendance as percentage of total enrolment/attendance.

Source: Field survey.

Third, the village society in Palanpur is, and has always been, a sharply divided one. Connected with long-standing divisions of caste and class is a traditional view of education as the privilege of particular social groups, and this, too, is a strong obstacle to the universalization of primary education. Another important connection between social inequality and education is that sharp social divisions reduce the extent of common interests in the provision of public goods, including the village school.

Fourth, gender inequalities are pervasive in both villages, but in somewhat different forms. The issue of female education, which is a very important part of the broader problem of primary education, has to be analysed in the light of these inequalities.

Finally, the institutional basis of collective action is quite different in Palanpur and She Tan. Specifically, She Tan has a stronger system of village government, buttressed by the Party, with a proven ability to undertake major tasks such as overseeing the allocation of land and the provision of a range of public goods.

Against this background, the next two sections discuss the issue of primary education in Palanpur and She Tan, with particular attention to the functioning of the village school in each case. A comparative summary of the basic features of the village school in Palanpur and She Tan can be found in Table 5.

5. Primary Education in Palanpur

5.1. Educational Achievements

Educational achievements in Palanpur are extremely low. To illustrate, the literacy rate among persons aged 5 and above was only 18 per cent in 1983–4; for women in this age group the literacy rate was as low as 6 per cent (see Table 6). A more detailed picture for 1983–4 is presented in Table 6. Interestingly, literacy rates in Palanpur were very close to the corresponding census-based figures for Morabadad district in both 1981 and 1991.

As we shall see below, Palanpur's low educational standards reflect a disastrous record of public involvement in the field of education over a long period of time. From 1957–8 to 1983–4 the proportion of the population with at least some schooling increased from 6 to 20 per cent. Equally interesting is the fact that in 1983–4 as many as 56 persons reported being unable to read or write *despite* having been to school.

As Table 6 illustrates, there are sharp disparities in educational achievements based on caste, class, and gender. Literacy rates tend to be particularly low among women, scheduled castes, and poor households. For a poor, low-caste woman, the chances of achieving basic literacy (let alone a higher educational standard) are practically nil.

Table 6. Literary and school attendance in Palanpur, 1983–1984

Caste/ community	No. of persons	% of literates among persons aged 5 and above		% attending school among children aged 6–10[a]	
		Male	Female	Male	Female
Hindus					
Thakur	217	44	8	61	27
Kayasth	14	100	100	100	100
Sudra	492	28	3	48	8
Scheduled castes	118	4	0	6	0
Muslims	119	21	2	8	0
TOTAL	960	28	6	39	14

[a] All schools (including private schools and government schools in nearby villages) are taken into account in these attendance figures.

Note: Caste groups are arranged in descending order of social status (with, for instance, Thakurs being at the top of the caste hierarchy). 'Scheduled castes' are officially recognized as particularly disadvantaged groups, and are entitled to certain forms of positive discrimination in terms of education and public employment. In Palanpur, the social and economic status of Muslims is roughly comparable to that of scheduled-caste Hindus.

Source: Field survey.

The caste factor deserves special mention. It is, indeed, rather striking that educational achievements should vary so much between different castes within a small village where primary education is supposed to be freely available to all. Female literacy rates, for instance, vary from zero for the scheduled castes to 100 per cent among members of the Kayasth caste. The Kayasths, who are traditionally engaged in administrative and related occupations, attach an extremely high value to education; they are prepared to make extraordinary efforts to ensure the education of their children, if need be by organizing private tuition at home.[34] Scheduled-caste persons, on the other hand, largely continue to regard unskilled casual labour as their hereditary occupation, and their view of the importance of education is formed in that light. Of course, it is also the case that scheduled-caste households tend to be much poorer than Kayasth households, and this economic factor helps to explain their low educational achievements. But the sharpness of caste-based contrasts in educational achievements suggests that attitudes and values associated with caste, reflecting *inter alia* the role

[34] The fact that female education is comparatively advanced among Kayasths facilitates the low-cost provision of private tuitions, in so far as these often take the form of adult Kayasth women teaching their own children or relatives at home.

that different castes are expected to play in the village society, exercise an influence of their own.[35] As many commentators have noted, the traditional view of education as a privilege of particular castes remains an important obstacle to the universalization of primary education in India.[36]

It is worth noting that the 'caste factor' is not just a matter of how individuals perceive themselves, or of what they are expected to do or be within the village society. The traditional association between caste and education is also one plausible reason why public commitment to the promotion of education among disadvantaged castes in India is much lower than it ought to be. As a matter of fact, statements to the effect that education is 'not very important' for certain sections of the population are not uncommon among Indian political leaders and policy-makers.[37]

Similar remarks apply with reference to gender. When the social role of rural women is confined to domestic work and child-bearing, female education can easily be regarded as a 'wasteful investment'. This, again, affects (1) the educational aspirations of girls, (2) the parental and social support that they receive in their pursuit of these aspirations, and (3) the strength of public commitment to the promotion of female education.[38] We shall return to these issues in Section 5.5.

5.2. The Village School

Like a majority of Indian villages, Palanpur has a primary school financed and run by the government. The functioning of this village school, however, is extremely poor. We shall briefly describe the state of the school in 1983–4 before commenting on recent developments as well as on alternative educational opportunities.

In 1983–4 the village school in Palanpur was, for practical purposes, non-functional. The total staff of the school consisted of a single male

[35] Probit analysis based on 1983–4 data confirms that caste has a statistically significant influence on school attendance independently of per capita income. Specifically, children from scheduled-caste and Muslim families are less likely to attend school than children from other families, at a given level of per capita income.

[36] It is interesting that, in some areas of India where scheduled castes or scheduled tribes constitute the dominant group in the population, their educational achievements are comparatively high. For instance, as Bara *et al.* (1991) point out, 'the tribals in the North-East have been able to surge ahead of the Central Indian and dispersed tribes because political control and much of their education is in their own hands . . . Where education is in the hands of outsiders, tribal literacy is low, since upper-caste attitudes as well as vested interest in their cheap labour go against their education' (pp. 411–12). Similarly, K. N. Nair *et al.* (1984) describe a mono-caste Harijan village of Tamil Nadu where adult literacy rates (male and female) are above 99 per cent.

[37] On this point, see particularly Weiner (1991). A recent newspaper article quotes the Vice-President of the Bharatiya Janata Party (the main opposition party in India at the time of writing) as saying: 'Education is not very important for farmers. Do you expect them to have to write to anybody?'

[38] On the related issue of female 'socialization' and educational achievements, see Chanana (1988, 1990), Dube (1988) and Karlekar (1988).

teacher; this feature, incidentally, is quite common for primary schools in rural India.[39] Since the salary of the teacher was not related to his work performance, and since his appointment was technically a 'permanent' one, he had little incentive to take his job seriously. In fact, he rarely took the trouble of turning up at all. When he did, he was usually accompanied by ten or twelve children at most, mainly sons and daughters of his own close relatives. If government inspectors happened to visit the school, a suitable bribe was sure to make them look the other way.

Given this virtual breakdown of primary education at the village level, it is not surprising that literacy rates in Palanpur are so low. The main problem, it appears, is persistent absenteeism on the part of the teacher, connected with the lack of effective supervision and accountability. It should be mentioned, however, that, even in the absence of this particular problem, the provision of primary education in Palanpur would suffer from a number of other shortcomings.

First, the physical facilities available are very poor. For instance, the two-room brick structure built in the 1960s to accommodate the school was completely dilapidated by 1983–4 (largely due to vandalism and pilferage). When the school functions at all, teaching takes place in the shade of a nearby tree.

Second, a single teacher cannot possibly answer Palanpur's needs for primary education, even with the highest commitment. In 1983–4, Palanpur had as many as 160 children in the 6–10-year age group, roughly corresponding to the five grades of schooling a village school is supposed to provide. Achieving universal school attendance in that age group would require at least four teachers. Even in relation to the actual attendance figures of ten or twelve children, the single-teacher formula is highly problematic, in so far as the children in question belong to several (up to five) different grades.[40]

Third, Palanpur's single teacher is a male member of the 'highest' caste in the village.[41] The absence of female teachers in the village school is likely to discourage at least some parents from sending their daughter(s) to school, given the common perception that girls are more appropriately taught by women than by men. Similarly, the fact that the schoolteacher belongs to a caste (Thakur) that has traditionally dominated and often oppressed other

[39] For rural and urban areas combined, the proportion of primary schools consisting of a single teacher in 1986 varied from less than 1 per cent in Kerala to 59 per cent in Jammu and Kashmir, with an all-India figure as high as 28 per cent (Tyagi 1991: 82). It can be safely assumed that most teachers in these schools are men.

[40] Apparently, the village teacher deals with this situation by addressing himself to children of different grades in turn. We leave it to the reader to consider the likely effect of this method on the quality of teaching.

[41] The village teacher also happens to be the son of the village headman. We were unable to ascertain whether this factor had played a role in helping him (1) to secure the position of schoolteacher, and (2) to get away with persistent absenteeism.

castes in Palanpur is likely to reduce his sensitivity to the needs of low-caste children.

Finally, the failure of the 'supply side' of Palanpur's educational facilities tends to hide a possible problem of low 'effective demand' for primary education in this village. One source of this problem, which we have already commented on in the preceding section, is the tradition of attaching limited importance to the educational achievements of particular groups, particularly girls and low-caste children. Another important factor is that many parents consider the real cost of sending children to school to be quite high. This is not so much because the fees are high or the books expensive (in fact, fees and other financial requirements are very low); more important consideration is that school attendance has a high 'opportunity cost' in the form of child labour.[42] In Palanpur, a majority of children in the school-going age group spend a good deal of their time minding younger siblings, helping with agricultural tasks, or looking after farm animals. Poor parents cannot afford to overlook the loss of family labour (and, in some cases, wage labour) involved in sending their children to school.

5.3. Alternative Opportunities

Given the deplorable functioning of the village school, many parents in Palanpur have explored alternative means of providing some education for their children. The two main alternatives are (1) government schools in other villages, and (2) private schools.[43]

Most nearby villages have government schools. One of them, situated in Akroli (about 2 km from Palanpur), functions relatively well. Akroli is a large village, and this school has as many as eight grades and ten teachers; it also has a director. The size of the school, its public visibility, and the fact that the director, on the whole, has an interest in ensuring that the teachers do their job probably help to reduce the problem of teacher absenteeism and shirking. Be that as it may, the fact is that the school functions and is considered to provide satisfactory education. Many parents in Palanpur send their young sons to Akroli. However, girls are very rarely sent to school there, as it is considered unsafe or unwise for young girls to travel outside the village without being accompanied by an adult.[44] While the government school in Akroli represents an important alternative source of basic education, therefore, this opportunity is available almost exclusively to male children.

[42] The notion that, for a majority of parents, forgone labour is by far the most important component of the total opportunity cost of schooling is confirmed by econometric studies (Alderman *et al.* 1993) as well as anthropological studies (J. C. Caldwell *et al.* 1985).

[43] We have also mentioned, earlier in this section, how Kayasth households sometimes organize private tuitions in their own homes. This is an exceptional initiative, of which we have observed no other example in Palanpur.

[44] In 1983–4, only three Palanpur girls in the 5–14-year age group were attending school outside the village (compared with 29 boys). All three were Kayasth.

Private educational institutions spring up from time to time in Palanpur and the surrounding villages. This usually takes the form of a well-educated member of the village offering to teach village children under a tree or in some unused public building in return for school fees, or of frustrated parents co-operating to find a suitable teacher and asking him or her to set up an informal 'school' for their children (again, of course, in return for fees).[45] In 1985 Palanpur had a private school of some importance, launched and supervised by the main village doctor, a well-educated Kayasth who came from a nearby town. This school closed down after a few years for unknown reasons.[46]

Private schools have the advantage of being 'incentive-compatible', in the sense that it is in the interest of parents to keep an eye on the teachers, *and* in the interest of teachers to be responsive to parental demands (unlike in the government primary school, where the teacher is paid irrespective of his performance). The drawback of private schools, of course, is that they charge substantial fees. This consideration is very serious for poor parents, who rarely send their children to private schools. And here again, the limitations of alternative educational arrangements are particularly important for girls, since even relatively well-off parents in Palanpur would hesitate to pay substantial school fees for the education of a girl child. In rural India, there is no plausible substitute for an efficient system of public education.

5.4. Recent Developments

The situation described so far applied, by and large, throughout the 1980s. Some new developments took place in the early 1990s, which deserve brief mention.

In 1991 the government constructed a new school building in Palanpur. The new building was placed next to the old one, and its structure was quite similar. By the time we visited the village in January 1992, this new building was already quite dilapidated, and seemed vulnerable to the same fate as the old one. The sudden appearance of a new building did not affect the mode of operation of the village school, which remained virtually non-functional.

In January 1993 a more substantive development took place. The government of Uttar Pradesh introduced a new rule, stipulating that a government-appointed teacher was no longer allowed to teach in his or her own village.

---

[45] 'Venture schools' of this kind have been part of the Indian tradition for a long time; see e.g. Matthai (1915, ch. 2).

[46] One serious problem faced by private schools in this area is that, unless they succeed in obtaining official 'recognition' (*maantee*), they are not entitled to issue primary school certificates. Many private schools deal with this by 'associating' themselves with a government school, and transferring children to that school during their final year, on payment of a bribe. In effect, this amounts to 'sub-contracting' of education by the public sector to the private sector. Another form of sub-contracting that prevails in the area, including in the Akroli school, consists of government schools hiring private teachers to mind the children.

As a result, the earlier village teacher was transferred to a nearby village, and an experienced Brahmin teacher from Akroli was put in charge of Palanpur's primary school. A second teacher was also appointed, again from a different village.

We visited the village school on four occasions in February and July 1993. On each occasion, one of the two newly appointed teachers (usually the Brahmin teacher from Akroli) was present. He was actively teaching in only one instance, but even on other occasions he was found to maintain a semblance of order and to encourage the children to do exercises. There had, in other words, been some improvement in the functioning of the village school, although the overall standard of teaching remained low. This was also the view of many parents; one of them summarized the current state of the school as 'pachaas per cent sahi hai' ('it's 50 per cent alright').

The improved functioning of the school led to some increase in attendance. There were, on average, 28 pupils present when we visited the school (19 boys and 9 girls), and 54 were enrolled (43 boys and 11 girls), out of 140 children in the 6–10-year age group. The girl–boy ratio in the village school is significantly higher than the overall ratio of girls to boys attending schools, because almost all the children attending schools in other villages are boys. But the absolute number of girls going to school remains small—19 per cent of the relevant age group are enrolled, and 15 per cent were observed to attend.

These developments had clearly been triggered by the new government policy, which disturbed the original equilibrium. In so far as recent changes simply reflect the different personalities of the old and new teachers, the improvements observed in Palanpur may have been compensated by a deterioration in the village where the original Palanpur teacher was sent. But it is also possible that the new policy of preventing teachers from being employed in their own villages has led to an overall improvement. Absenteeism is certainly more of a temptation when a teacher is within walking distance of his house and fields; and the ability of a teacher to ignore parental demands may be weaker when he is seen as a vulnerable, isolated 'outsider' rather than as a member of one of the most powerful families in the village. Having said this, the new policy also has some negative features that require careful consideration. In particular, this policy may have dramatically reduced the scope for appointing female schoolteachers: in rural North India, married women's freedom of movement is highly restricted, and very few of them are likely to be willing or allowed to commute every day to another village.

5.5.   On Female Education

As we saw earlier in this section, very few girls in Palanpur are enrolled in a primary school, and even fewer actually attend classes (see Tables 5 and

6 for details). Further, female school attendance has shown little responsiveness to recent improvements in the functioning of the village school. This strongly suggests that lack of interest in female education on the part of parents is the root of the problem. The possible reasons for this lack of parental motivation call for further comment.

To start with, the perceived value of female education obviously depends on the role that adult women are expected to play in society. In Palanpur, the 'ideal' woman (*sati*) is a dutiful housewife devoted to the welfare of her husband and children. The vast majority of girls are expected to spend most of their adult life in domestic work and child-rearing (and possibly some family labour in agriculture), irrespective of their educational achievements. It is in the light of these social expectations about the adult life of women that female education appears to many parents to be 'pointless'. The situation might be quite different in a society where the sexual division of labour is less stringent and where women spend a greater part of their adult life in activities for which education is perceived to be important.[47]

But this is not the end of the story. Indeed, it may be argued that the sexual division of labour is not very different in many areas of India where female educational achievements are much higher than in Uttar Pradesh. Also, education can be of great benefit even for 'domestic' activities, especially child-rearing, and, if nothing else, one might have expected female education to be valued from that point of view. An important feature of the North Indian kinship system, however, is that a woman is 'transferred' at the time of marriage from her parents' patrilineal family to that of her husband, usually in a different village.[48] Marriage is viewed as *kanyadaan*, 'the gift of a daughter', and the links that a married woman retains with her parental family are extremely weak. Relations between in-laws tend to be confined to certain social obligations, with the 'wife-givers' occupying an inferior position. This means that the benefits of female education largely accrue to a different, distant and alien household. It is this combination of a sharp sexual division of labour with an emphasis on patrilineal kinship and patrilocal residence that strongly reduces the perceived value of female education, at least from the point of view of parental self-interest.[49]

---

[47] It is interesting that, while the educational achievements of a wife have little value in the North Indian tradition (in fact, they are often perceived as a potential 'threat' to male authority), the same tradition has often shown great appreciation of the intellectual qualities of courtesans and high-class prostitutes, whose companionship was expected to be pleasing and stimulating (see e.g. Altekar 1956, Leslie 1989, and the *Kamasutra*). The story 'Revenge Herself' (Antarjanam 1993) skilfully builds on this paradox.

[48] On the North Indian kinship system, see Altekar (1956), Karve (1965, 1974), Kapadia (1966), Shah (1973), Sharma (1980), Dyson and Moore (1983), Kolenda (1984), MacDorman (1986), and Caldwell and Caldwell (1987), among others. What we are referring to, and what represents the focus of most of these studies, is really the kinship system of *Hindu* North India. Even within the Hindu community, there are some important inter-caste and inter-regional differences, but these need not concern us here.

[49] The situation is neatly summed up in popular sayings such as 'bringing up a daughter is like pouring water in sand' and 'bringing up daughters is like watering a plant in another's

The North Indian kinship system has another feature which can reduce parental interest in female education. This is the emphasis on hypergamous marriage and dowry. In North India, a bride is expected to be married into a family, and to a man, of 'higher' status; and the higher the status of the groom and his family, the larger the dowry to be paid by her parents to her future in-laws. For a poor farmer or labourer, therefore, a well-educated daughter is a serious liability: she can only be married to an even better-educated boy, whose family is likely to demand a substantial dowry.[50]

All these considerations are very different in the case of male children. The sexual division of labour enhances economic returns to male education. The educational achievements of a son entail long-lasting benefits to his parents, in so far as he is likely to support them in their old age and perhaps even to continue living in the same household.[51] And a well-educated son can be the source of a large dowry. Parents in Palanpur are quite explicit about the influence of economic considerations—especially better employment prospects and improved old-age support—on educational decisions relating to their sons.[52]

To conclude, the interests and motives of parents with respect to male and female education tend to be very different. In the case of male education, economic returns are perceived to be large, and this perception is probably correct.[53] Economic returns and parental self-interest, on the other hand, provide very weak incentives for female education, given current marriage practices, property rights, and the sexual division of labour. Concern for the well-being of a daughter in her own right, and perceptions of the contribution that education can make to the quality of her life, are likely to be more

courtyard' (Dube 1988, p. 168). Similarly, in her study of female education in rural Maharasthra, Vlassoff (1993, p. 8) reports: 'The most common objection to education . . . was that it was not useful in the village context where women *become the property of others* and "have only to manage the kitchen" ' (emphasis added).

[50] This problem has been noted by the Committee on the Status of Women in India (1974, p. 74), Almeida (1978, p. 264) and van Bastelaer (1986, p. 61), among others. Even in rural South India, some parents are reported to be worried that education 'would make daughters unmarriageable', because a woman 'must be married to a male with at least as much education' (J. C. Caldwell *et al.* 1985, pp. 39, 41).

[51] We have observed on several occasions how good education for at least one son is regarded by some parents as a more important objective than basic education for all their sons or children. (Basu, 1992, reports a similar observation in a Delhi slum; see also Berreman, 1972, p. 331.) One possible motivation for this priority arises precisely from considerations of old-age support.

[52] For very similar findings in a group of villages in Karnataka, see J. C. Caldwell *et al.* (1985). The authors find that 'education is certainly seen as a route to jobs' (p. 46), and that 'some parents emphasize immediate returns, but many more stress delayed returns and the provision of security' (p. 40). The information presented clearly suggests that these views apply with particular force to male education; for instance, while the motivation to send a son to school is 'to equip the child for a job' in 65% of the cases surveyed, the corresponding percentage for daughters is only 29% (p. 38).

[53] Probit analysis based on 1983–4 data indicates that education has a positive (and highly significant) effect on individual chances of obtaining a job in the formal sector, holding other assets constant.

important factors. This basic contrast has to be borne in mind in the planning of public policy.[54]

6. Primary Education in She Tan

6.1. Background: Primary Education and Recent Reforms

There is little doubt that the household responsibility system has led to a substantial expansion of private incomes and economic opportunities in She Tan. This is certainly a positive development from the point of view of education, in so far as it makes schooling more affordable and also raises the economic returns to education. But the fundamental reform of economic organization also has other possible implications for the future of primary education, which require careful scrutiny.

One of these possible implications is an increase in the incidence of child labour. The responsibility system, which is based on strengthening the link between reward and effort, enhances the value of family labour, including the productive activities of children. A household faced with the choice between extra help to increase family income and sending a child to school may be tempted to assign more importance to the immediate monetary benefits. This is particularly likely in the case of a poor household, for which even small increases in income can mean a great deal.

A similar reasoning applies to teachers and the value of their time. Given the strengthened link between reward and effort in the private economy, teachers now have an incentive to spend time in productive activity rather than in teaching, preparing classes, undergoing training, etc. This problem was less acute during the commune period, when teaching was rewarded on the same basis as other occupations.

In addition, the household responsibility system tends to make it more difficult to ensure that the teaching profession attracts talented individuals. Under this system, teachers' salaries become a crucial parameter, and it is generally acknowledged that these have lagged behind earnings in other occupations in recent years. Teachers in She Tan now earn wages comparable to those of a casual agricultural labourer (see Tables 4 and 5). Elsewhere in rural China, there have even been reports of teachers not being paid at all for extended periods.[55] The fact that teachers are usually assigned to particular positions, rather than being able to make their own occupational

---

[54] Several studies have noted how attitudes towards female education in rural India can change very substantially over a relatively short period of time; see e.g. J. C. Caldwell *et al.* (1985), Chanana (1993), and Vlassoff (1993).

[55] 'It is not uncommon for teachers in a number of rural counties to go without pay because of inadequate local funding. "The central government must pay enough attention to the problem", the Vice-Premier stressed' (*China Daily*, 20 March 1993). On the growing problem of teacher recruitment in China, see World Bank (1985) and Henze (1992).

choices, reduces the impact of these emerging incentive problems. But in the long term economic pressures are likely to make themselves felt; enforced restrictions of choice may not prove an adequate solution.

This problem ties in with the crisis of local public funding. The shift to the household responsibility system, under which incomes derived from production are earned by households rather than by the collective, has eroded the financial basis of social services at the village level. Currently, there are stringent official limits on the extent to which village governments are allowed to tax peasants' annual incomes.[56] Village governments resort to 'contributions' (sometimes misleadingly translated from the Chinese term as 'voluntary contributions') to ease the financial crunch, but this system is clearly unsatisfactory. It is often regressive, leaves too many loopholes for corrupt cadres, outlines no clear policy for priorities, and fails to provide a secure financial basis for public services.

This crisis of local public funding has several practical implications for education. We have already mentioned the low level of teachers' salaries. Equally serious is the increasing reliance on school fees; in She Tan these have risen from 4 yuan per child per year in the early 1980s to 100 yuan in 1993. Lack of long-term investment in educational facilities is another likely consequence. Finally, the current system of decentralized funding with an eroded tax base creates a great deal of uncertainty for the education sector: expenditure on primary education is largely at the discretion of local leaders, and the link between public resources and the profitability of local private enterprises puts primary schools at the mercy of economic fluctuations.

Another implication of the household responsibility system relates to women's work and the value of female education. As mentioned in Section 4, there are some indications of women in She Tan reverting to traditional roles based in the household. If education is not seen as important for domestic work, this development may lead to a decline in the perceived value of female education relative to that of male education. (This phenomenon has been documented for higher education, see Rosen, 1992.)

A further offshoot of the responsibility system that could affect education is increasing inequality within the village. As some peasant families have better access than others to non-agricultural income (e.g. from domestic sideline industries or township enterprises), the distribution of wealth is rapidly polarizing. These growing inequalities can undermine the foundation of common action based on shared needs. For instance, if the richer sections of a village are unconcerned about increases in school fees, the demands of poorer households for subsidized education may be consider-

---

[56] In She Tan, the annual expenditure of the village government amounts to 30,000 yuan—less than 2% of the estimated annual income of the village. Village and township governments together are officially allowed to tax up to 5% of rural incomes. By contrast, the proportion of total income assigned to collective purposes in rural China during the 1958–78 period was in the range of 13–28% (Ling 1992, p. 11).

ably weakened. A more extreme version of this situation is the emergence of a division between a subsidized, low-quality system of public education and a higher-cost, higher-quality system of private education geared to the needs of the richer sections of the population.[57]

Recent reforms in rural China include not only the household responsibility system, but also a stringent family planning policy (introduced in the late 1970s), and it might be asked how this policy is likely to affect primary education. To start with, a reduction in fertility is likely to increase the ability and incentives that parents have to take care of individual children, and to invest in education. If the number of teachers remains constant, fewer children also means a reduction in teacher–pupil ratios, and an opportunity for some improvement in the quality of education. On the other hand, a sharp decline in fertility may also lead to some reduction of collective interest in educational services: if the number of children attending the village school decreases, the number of households directly concerned with the quality of schooling also declines.[58] This, like the emergence of economic inequalities, can reduce the strength of collective demand for public education services.

Clearly, the effects of recent reforms on education in rural China (taking into account not only the expansion of private incomes and economic opportunities, but also the changing opportunity cost of educational activities, the crisis of local public funding, the consequences of demographic change, etc.) are quite diverse, and their overall impact is a matter for careful empirical investigation. Despite some important informational limitations, an attempt will be made to pursue this investigation for She Tan.

6.2. Educational Standards

As we saw in Section 3, China has achieved commendable standards of rural literacy, with particularly high literacy rates in the younger age groups. This pattern clearly applies in She Tan, where average literacy rates are high but with sharp variations between gender and age groups. Although precise figures for She Tan are not available, casual observation and informal enquiries suggest that women above 40 are rarely literate, although their husbands usually are. Among adolescents of both sexes, literacy seems to be close to universal.

The perceived value of education is remarkably high in She Tan. This applies to both male and female education. Invariably, mothers interviewed envisioned a high level of education for their sons and daughters; they hoped for the complete twelve years of education, and some even mentioned college.

[57] It is likely that this type of dualism has already developed in some urban areas, where private education establishments are not uncommon (see e.g. Anon. 1989*a*; Economist 1993).

[58] According to the village teachers, only 6 children were born in She Tan in 1992. This means that, in 6 years' time, at most 6 households (out of about 250) will be directly concerned with the quality of first-grade education in the village school.

Nevertheless, we encountered common doubts about girls' ability to do well beyond a certain level. Parents, teachers, and daughters alike believe that girls can study well, but that their intellect deteriorates after they 'mature' (reach puberty). Thereafter, a girl's attention 'gets unfocused' and she is only 'concerned with her appearance'.

Another pervasive belief is that primary schoolteaching is a woman's job, because a woman is simply better at it. This may be seen as a positive factor (especially if the belief in question is well founded), in so far as it encourages the participation of women in teaching. On the other hand, the perception that primary instruction is a 'female job' may also be connected with the devaluation of the teaching profession that has apparently taken place in recent years.[59]

6.3. The Village School

The annals of the village school show clear signs of an early commitment to education. The school and its surrounding playground, built during the commune period, are placed right in the centre of the village. The T-shaped construction has an office for teachers and three spacious classrooms with tall windows, blackboards, and desks.

The school was at its peak in 1978, with five functioning grades and as many as five full-time teachers. Of the five teachers, two were from outside the village, while the remaining three were recruited from She Tan itself. The school fees at that time were negligible (less than 4 yuan per year per child).

The current functioning of the village school remains quite good in many ways. Classes start on time and the teachers are (despite their very low salaries) qualified. All children are equipped with schoolbags, notebooks, textbooks, and pencils. Child absenteeism is low. (Enrolment in the register closely corresponds with actual attendance.) But, along with these positive signs of continued commitment to primary education, there are also serious indications of decline.

Physical facilities

The school's physical condition has deteriorated steadily since 1978. The walls have not been whitewashed for years. The mud floors badly need repair, and one of the ceiling beams is propped up with a bamboo support. Numerous window panes are broken: a cause of serious hardship during the winter when chilly winds blow through the rooms.

Readily acknowledging this lack of investment in the school, the village head explained that the village government had spent large resources on building a road the previous year, and therefore had nothing left for the school. The state of the village school, however, reflects many years of neglect. When financing is tight, there is a danger of other public investments taking precedence over primary education.

---

[59] On this trend, see e.g. Wu (1987).

Attendance

Along with the physical deterioration that has taken place over the past fifteen years, the village school has also seen a sharp drop in the number of children attending classes. According to popular opinion in She Tan, including that of the teachers, the declining number of students is a consequence of effective birth control: fewer children are born, therefore fewer pupils attend the village school.

This explanation, however, is not corroborated by the village birth records.[60] If school attendance closely reflected the lagged effect of birth rates in the relevant years, then the number of students should have been fairly constant from 1977 to 1988 with a sharp increase around 1989 and after. This is because the annual number of children born between 1983 and 1987 happens to be higher than for earlier years; from 1989 onwards, children born during that period would enter the school-going age group, and if each child in that group attended school, enrolment would be increasing instead of decreasing.

Grades and teachers

A more plausible explanation for this recent decline in attendance is the recent reduction in number of grades taught: from five operating grades in 1978, since 1993 there have been only two, first and second, plus a *xue gian ban* or pre-school. After grade 2, children who wish to continue their studies have to travel to the township (about 3 km away) which can accommodate them. The staff of the village school is down to two teachers, compared with five in 1978.[61]

The decision to reduce the number of grades and teachers over the years was taken at the township level. According to the village head, plans are afoot to scrap She Tan's school altogether, the official aim being to improve the quality of schooling by conglomerating village schools. It is far from clear, however, how exactly this conglomeration would improve the quality of schooling.[62] This new policy may simply be a response to growing difficulties in finding and paying enough qualified teachers to staff village schools.

[60] We have no reliable indication of the quality of these birth records. Our impression is that the records are fairly accurate, given (1) She Tan's high standards of literacy and administration, and (2) the fact that the figures for birth rate and sex ratio at birth derived from these records closely correspond to the rural provincial figures. Although there is a possibility of some under-reporting of female births (as elsewhere in rural China), our argument is unaffected as long as the extent of under-reporting remains fairly constant over time.

[61] Both teachers are women from other villages. One of them has been teaching in She Tan for seven years; she is married and has a child. The other teacher is a younger, unmarried woman.

[62] If conglomeration takes place with a constant number of teachers, the only plausible source of quality improvement would be a reduction in school attendance (resulting from children having to travel longer distances), leading to a drop in pupil–teacher ratios. But this would amount to a questionable strategy of raising quality by reducing attendance. An alternative form of quality improvement would be to use conglomeration as an opportunity to discard the less qualified teachers. Aside from the difficulty of observing the quality of teachers, it is doubtful that such a step has been taken at a time when the ability of the schooling system to retain better qualified teachers has probably come under strain (see Sec. 6.1). Even if an improvement of teaching quality can be achieved by taking that step, this improvement has to be weighed against the more obvious disadvantage of children having to travel longer distances.

The decline of schooling facilities at the village level, and the prospect of the village school being closed down altogether, are causes of serious concern for the people of She Tan. The need to send young children longer distances to attend classes in the township worries many parents, who are naturally concerned about the safety of their offspring.

Drop-out rates

Current attendance figures have two additional features that are worth mentioning. First, there is a sharp drop in the number of pupils from grade 1 (28 students) to grade 2 (14 students). Second, less than one-third of the children attending are girls; the first grade has only 5 girls compared with 23 boys.

These figures suggest the possibility of a substantial drop-out rate, particularly for girls. In the absence of detailed information on the village population, we cannot directly verify this hypothesis. The schoolteachers explained both features of the attendance figures in demographic terms. Last year's grade 1, they said, had only 14 students. They also said that they did not know of any school-age children in She Tan not attending class. The demographic explanation cannot be refuted on the basis of the available evidence, though it does imply a somewhat unlikely combination of male and female births, deaths, and migration in recent years. (For instance, not a single year during the 1977–93 period had a female–male ratio at birth as low as the ratio observed in the first grade.) The possibility that some children have migrated with their parents to urban areas would help to reconcile the birth and attendance figures with the teachers' assertion that all children living in She Tan go to school.[63]

School fees

As mentioned earlier, school fees have increased from 4 yuan per child per year in the early 1980s to 100 yuan in 1993. Exactly how the proceeds of these fees are used is not entirely clear. Teachers reported that their salaries were paid by the township, and that fees were used to pay for notebooks and related supplies. But the amount of money gathered in fees (about 4,200 yuan in 1993) is many times larger than the likely cost of these supplies. There is also little evidence of any expenditure on maintenance. The possibility that school fees are used for purposes unrelated to primary education cannot be ruled out. This would be in line with the current tendency of village governments in China to tax whatever can be taxed in order to solve the problem of an eroded financial base.

In any case, the sharp increase of school fees in She Tan is a serious matter. In this particular village, private incomes and the general value attached to education are probably high enough for school fees to remain a

---

[63] Access to education for the 'floating population' of illegal immigrants in urban areas is an important issue of its own, which cannot be addressed in this paper.

minor consideration in parental decisions to send children to school, at least at the primary level. But in less prosperous villages, and at higher levels of schooling, the disincentive effects of school fees may be substantial. In fact, there is much evidence that school attendance in rural China, especially for girls, is quite responsive to the level of fees.[64]

6.4. Assessment

Several conclusions emerge from the observations reported in this section.

First, the development of primary schooling in She Tan during the last fifteen years has lagged far behind that of the private economy. The available facilities have shrunk and become more expensive, and their utilization may also have declined.

Second, the most evident and firmly established signs of strain are those that derive from a lack of financial resources: the absence of investment in school buildings, the sharp decline in relative salaries of teachers, the increase in school fees, the reduction in the number of grades taught, and the recent proposal to close down the village school altogether.

Third, whether the decline of educational facilities has led to a decline in educational achievements is less clear. Parents remain firmly committed to the pursuit of high educational standards for their children, and their incomes have also increased very substantially during the last fifteen years; these parallel developments may have prevented a deterioration of educational achievements despite the decline of facilities. The available data, unfortunately, do not enable us to settle this issue. At the level of China as a whole (or of Zhejiang Province), there is no sign of any deterioriation in literacy rates during the 1980s; in fact, census data indicate continued improvement, as we saw in Section 3.[65] But this is not to say that education levels have improved as rapidly as they might have improved had a substantial expansion of public schooling facilities taken place along with the rapid growth of the private economy.

Fourth, the growing financial strain experienced in the education sector may be primarily a reflection of the crisis of local public finance, discussed earlier. But it is also worth asking whether the lack of financial means to sustain school facilities at the village level might be a symptom of a deeper problem of reduced commitment to state-based provision of basic education to all. The growing insistence on charging user fees to cover the costs of

[64] See e.g. World Bank (1992) and the accompanying background papers.

[65] While census data indicate that age-specific school attendance has increased between 1982 and 1990 (Loh 1993), Colletta and Sutton (1989) note a significant decline in net enrolment during the 1977–81 period, particularly for girls, with 1977 enrolment levels being recovered only in 1985. The authors also mention that 'the decline in net enrollment following 1977 is thought to be connected to the introduction of the responsibility system on collectives, which raises the opportunity costs of schooling rural children' (Colletta and Sutton, 1989, p. 17). Similar observations are made in World Bank (1985).

education, health, and related public services is a widespread phenomenon in rural China (World Bank 1992). It is hard to avoid the impression that the 'enterprise responsibility' model of economic organization, which currently shapes government policy for public-sector enterprises, is effectively being extended to social services. This extension is, in fact, sometimes explicitly advocated in official circles.[66]

7. Comparative Evaluation

In this section we compare the experiences of Palanpur and She Tan in the field of primary education. Specifically, we discuss the role played by the different constraints identified in Section 2 (resources, values, incentives, and institutions) in these contrasting experiences. The discussion will be somewhat selective: we cannot, obviously, cover all the relevant issues, and we have chosen to concentrate on what appear to us to be the main factors of success or failure in these two villages.

7.1. Resources

As discussed in Section 6, resource constraints have played a crucial role in the stagnation of educational facilities in She Tan over the past fifteen years. The stringency of resource constraints arises from a somewhat contradictory policy in the field of local public finance. On the one hand, public services are expected to be funded from local sources (contrary, one might argue, to the basic principles of equitable distribution and risk pooling). On the other hand, the government imposes exacting limits—perhaps for good reasons— on the extent of taxation at the village and township levels.

Even when these official limits can be violated, the transition from collective to household-based production in rural China has itself considerably reduced the scope for social appropriation of the surplus generated by economic activity. In China as elsewhere, heavy taxation of private incomes poses considerable problems of incentives and administration. In particular, lenient taxation policies can be important in attracting or retaining enterprises—a common concern of local authorities in rural China.

The fact that resources constraints have played a key role in the recent stagnation of educational facilities in She Tan is particularly striking if we remember that this village is situated in one of the more prosperous areas of China. The problem of resources is likely to be particularly acute in poor

---

[66] See e.g. Lo (1984), Anon. (1989*a*). Recent reforms in education include the introduction of a 'principal's responsibility system', which 'follows the trend established in the industrial sector' (World Bank 1991, p. 14). On the problems associated with 'the adoption of cost recovery as the foundation of health care financing', see World Bank (1992). See also Yu Dezhi (1992), whose analysis of recent trends in China's health sector bears some striking similarity to our own findings on education.

areas, where the local tax base is weaker than in She Tan. Whether She Tan's experience is in any sense typical of Zhejiang Province and other prosperous areas of China is harder to say. It is quite possible, of course, that this particular village has faced special problems in raising resources for public services, or that it has given unusually low priority to education in its spending programme. But it is precisely one of the weaknesses of the current structure of local public finance in China that the quality of education is closely tied up with the profitability of village enterprises, the priorities of village leaders, and other undependable parameters. The precise nature and extent of financial constraints in the education sector in different parts of China is a matter that deserves further empirical investigation. Meanwhile, there are already good grounds for serious concern, based not only on our own case study but also on the independent studies and informal reports cited earlier in this paper.

The role of resource constraints in Palanpur's disastrous record in the field of primary education is not so obvious. We observed, in Section 5.2, that the facilities available in Palanpur (including the number of teachers) are well below what would be required to ensure universal primary educa-tion—a declared objective of the Indian government—on the basis of existing arrangements. It is also worth noting that the inadequacy of resources for primary education in Uttar Pradesh is *partly* the outcome of a problem of fiscal decentralization which bears some resemblance to the issue of local public finance in rural China. In India, the bulk of public expenditure on education is incurred by state governments. As a result, there are large inter-state variations in levels of per capita expenditure on education. Further, states with lower educational achievements, and with a greater need for public investment in education, also tend to be those where government resources are more limited and expenditure levels much lower.[67] Uttar Pradesh is one of those states, with the second-lowest level of per capita expenditure on education among all Indian states as well as the third-lowest literacy rate (Tyagi 1991).[68]

Having said this, it is doubtful that lack of financial resources is the main reason for Palanpur's failure. The ineffective utilization of the resources that *are* available is at least as important. Indeed, the village teacher in Palanpur is extremely well paid by local standards; and he is also much better paid than his counterpart in She Tan, despite the fact that Palanpur is much

[67] Per capita public expenditure on education in a particular state can be seen as the product of (1) per capita income in that state, (2) the ratio of government expenditure to state income, and (3) the proportion of state government expenditure allocated to education. By and large, each of these parameters tends to be low in states with higher levels of poverty and illiteracy. For a very helpful overview of education expenditure in India, see Tilak (1993).

[68] These inter-state inequalities are further compounded by a bias in favour of urban areas and higher education. The financial resources actually available for primary education in rural areas of the poorer states are very small indeed. Much the same can be said of human resources, in so far as better-qualified teachers are rarely prepared to work in poor rural areas.

poorer than She Tan (see Table 5). The reasons for his low motivation to teach have to be sought elsewhere. Similarly, *two* school buildings were constructed in Palanpur in recent decades, and their systematic dilapidation has little to do with lack of funds. The promotion of universal primary education in rural India undoubtedly requires an expansion of public expenditure, but a great deal more is involved.

7.2. Values

Education is valued very differently in She Tan and Palanpur. In She Tan, parents have high expectations for the educational achievements of their sons and daughters, and do not lightly compromise that objective for the sake of short-term economic gains. This strong parental commitment to education has helped to prevent a significant deterioration of educational standards since 1978 despite a reduction in available facilities and a large increase in school fees.

A more complex picture applies in Palanpur. Villagers frequently express a clear recognition of the economic and other benefits which better-educated members of the society are able to secure for themselves and their families, and a general lack of awareness of the value of education may not be the basic issue.[69] But, as we saw in Section 5.5, there is, at the very least, a specific problem of undervaluation of female education, partly connected with the fact that the education of girls is of little material benefit to their own parents. We have also discussed how the tradition of seeing education as a high-caste privilege can undermine individual motivation, social stimulation, and public commitment when it comes to the educational advancement of disadvantaged sections of the population.

Ultimately, what requires attention is not only the nature of the attitudes and values that influence educational decisions, but also where these attitudes and values come from. We have seen, for instance, how the valuation of female education in Palanpur connects with basic features of the kinship system and the organization of production. Along similar lines, it could be argued that the more symmetric valuation of male and female education in She Tan partly reflects a higher degree of gender-symmetry in employment opportunities, ownership rights, and marriage practices.[70] It would also be interesting to probe the material, cultural, and political foundations of the high level of general commitment to education observed in She Tan. This commitment

---

[69] It is, of course, difficult to identify the separate effects of low parental motivation and poor educational facilities on schooling decisions. For an innovative econometric estimation of these effects in rural Pakistan, see Alderman *et al.* (1993). The results of that study corroborate the notion that general lack of parental interest in education is not the main issue.

[70] It is possible that the one-child policy has also led to greater gender-symmetry in care for old parents (since many parents now have no sons to depend on in their old age); this, in turn, may reduce an important source of asymmetry in the valuation of male and female education (see Sec. 5.5).

may have deep historical roots; but it may also reflect recent developments, including (1) a sustained experience of free and universal primary education, and/or (2) the impact of many years of active propaganda.

In this connection, two remarks are due. First, the link between experience and expectations is a crucial consideration for the promotion of primary education. The standards of public provisioning that people are used to has an important effect on what they expect and demand. Similarly, their assessment of the benefits of education derives largely from the observation of other people's experiences in this regard. This 'diffusion effect' adds to other arguments for early and active government promotion of primary education. Second, the role of persuasion and propaganda may be particularly important in relation to female education. As was discussed in Section 5.5, economic incentives and parental self-interest alone cannot provide an adequate basis for the expansion of female education in North India, given the prevailing kinship system and relations of production. While it is quite possible to challenge these features of economic and social organization, the promotion of female education should not wait for these profound changes.

7.3. Incentives

As far as incentives are concerned, we have noted a number of important weaknesses of the educational system in Palanpur. The opportunity cost of child labour deters many poor parents from sending their sons or daughters to school. School fees make private educational institutions particularly unaffordable. The distance factor discourages many parents from making use of educational facilities in other villages, given their reluctance to allow young children (and especially daughters) to wander on their own outside Palanpur. The sexual division of labour and the kinship system lead to a devaluation of female education in terms of economic returns and parental self-interest. Last but not least, the village teacher has very little incentive to teach, since there is no relation between remuneration (or job security) and performance, and no effective supervision.

We have laid particular stress on the last point, since frequent teacher absenteeism over a prolonged period seems to be one of the chief causes of Palanpur's educational backwardness. It may be asked whether Palanpur is an 'extreme case' in this respect. We submit that it is not, at least for Uttar Pradesh. In fact, a field investigation carried out in February and March 1994 in three other districts of that state (one each in the Eastern, Central, and Southern regions) indicates that teacher absenteeism and shirking in government primary schools are endemic.[71] We have also had many occasions

---

[71] The findings of this investigation are reported in Drèze and Gazdar (forthcoming). See also Weiner (1991, ch. 4) for a number of relevant testimonies, including that of a senior official at the Ministry of Education, who candidly stated: 'The teachers aren't any good. Often they don't even appear at the school . . . our schools are trash!' (Weiner 1991: 57).

to observe this phenomenon in other educationally backward states of North India (including Bihar, Madhya Pradesh, and Rajasthan). Besides, low levels of teacher absenteeism would be hard to square with the amazing fact that literacy rates remain so low in a region of India where most villages are supposed to have been equipped with a free primary school for a long time.

The incentive problems that have undermined the educational system in Palanpur are less acute in She Tan, but some of them appear to have resurfaced with the transition to the household responsibility system. We noted in Section 6.1 a number of incentive problems that might arise, or intensify, in the course of this transition. These include (1) the rising value of child labour, (2) the expansion of alternative employment opportunities for teachers, (3) the increase of school fees (linked with the erosion of the local tax base), and (4) a possible decline in the perceived value of female education as the sexual division of labour intensifies. We have no firm evidence that any of these incentive problems has had a major impact on primary education in She Tan independently of the resource constraints discussed earlier (although there is a strong possibility of the reduction in grades taught at the village school being linked with the growing difficulty of retaining qualified teachers). Our observations, however, do give grounds for concern about the effects of these incentive problems in areas with lower incomes or a weaker commitment to education. Each of the four basic incentive problems mentioned above has, in fact, been noted in a number of other recent reports on primary education in rural China.[72]

7.4. Institutions

The resources, values, and incentives that come into play in the provision and utilization of education services depend partly on the institutional framework within which the education sector operates. We cannot hope to deal here with all the relevant institutional issues. Instead, we shall briefly comment on the specific role of collective institutions at the village level.

One of the most remarkable aspects of Palanpur's experience with primary education is the virtual absence of any organized demand for improvement. The fact that the village school has remained non-functional for so many years has generated a great deal of private resentment and idle grumbling, but very little collective pressure for change. The schooling establishment, including the village teacher, seems to have no difficulty in getting away with persistent abdication of its responsibilities.

---

[72] See e.g. Lo (1984), Shi Ming Hu and Seifman (1987), Wu (1987), Anon. (1989*b*), Colletta and Sutton (1989), Levy (1989), Mak (1989), Ma Yijun (1989), Shi Lei (1989), Wang (1989), Jee-Peng Tan (1990), Mei and Li (1990), Henze (1992), Rosen (1992), World Bank (1985, 1992), and The Economist (1993), among others. The introduction of a compulsory Education Law in 1986 may have been, in past, a response to some of these incentive problems.

One basic cause of this inertia is the absence of any institutionalized means through which parents might be able to put pressure on the village teacher or the government bureaucracy. Unlike teachers in private schools, the government-appointed teacher is not accountable to the village community in any meaningful sense.[73]

It may be argued, however, that if parents were able to organize they would have no difficulty in *creating* some means of putting pressure on the schooling establishment. A deeper problem is the amorphous nature of political institutions at the village level, and in particular the absence of credible institutions (e.g. trade union, village council, or party committee) that might give expression to the collective demands of parents. As mentioned in Section 4.1, collective institutions in Palanpur are poorly developed, and the lack of debate and action on the question of education is one reflection of the atomized nature of the village society. Individual parents have little ability to change things on their own.[74]

It might be asked why the village headman does not take action. As explained earlier, the headman in Palanpur essentially acts as an intermediary between the state and the village community, and is expected to deal with government-related matters. If the functioning of the village school were a lively electoral issue, he might have a strong incentive to prevent the teachers from shirking. But the distant prospect of an election campaign, involving many other issues than education, has little motivational force in the absence of additional pressure from organized interest groups. As long as the headman remains, effectively, the only recognized political institution at the village level, a large gap will remain between electoral politics and participatory democracy.[75]

The weakness of participatory politics at the village level may seem surprising, given India's reputation for vibrant democratic institutions. In this connection, it should be remembered that education is a helpful tool of

[73] Aside from the institutional issue, a 'selection effect' reinforces the accountability problem: individuals who manage to get themselves appointed as village teachers are usually well-connected, affluent, high-caste persons who are particularly able to resist pressure and ignore the disapproval of the community.

[74] In one village situated in the state of Gujarat (where there is a much stronger tradition of collective action than in rural Uttar Pradesh), we heard the story of how a collective decision had been made to beat up the village teacher if he continued to shirk. He didn't.

[75] Areas of India where a serious effort has been made to reform political institutions at the village level have witnessed significant improvements in the functioning of local public services, including village schools. In West Bengal, for instance, a reformed *panchayat* system has recently provided a relatively effective basis for literacy campaigns; on this, see e.g. Lieten (1992), Banerjee (1992). In Karnataka, *panchayat* reforms have had a less profound impact than in West Bengal (largely because they have failed to alter the rural power structure), but it is nevertheless reported that 'after the *panchayati raj* system was implemented . . . attendance of primary school teachers and health workers went up by 91%' (L. C. Jain, cited in Ford Foundation, 1992, and based on the recent Krishnaswamy Report; see also Vyasulu 1993). Village-level collective institutions have also played a major role in Kerala's educational success (see Santha 1994, and Ramachandran, forthcoming).

creative participation in the political system. If parents in Palanpur were better educated, they would have a greater ability to articulate their demands and to challenge the village teacher. They would be more likely to succeed in making an issue of the functioning of the primary school at the time of village-level elections. They might even take their grievances to higher levels of government, if the village headman failed to support their demands. Instead, widespread illiteracy among adults contributes to an attitude of passive acceptance of the status quo.

Interestingly, we have encountered some examples of effective challenge of the schooling establishment in She Tan. On one occasion, for instance, parents complained that classes often started late at the village school. The Party leader took up this matter with the township authorities, as a result of which the responsible teachers were transferred and replaced; from then on, classes started on time.

This anecdote is noteworthy for several reasons. First, parents thought it important to take action on something that would have been regarded in Palanpur as a trivial matter—the fact that classes started late. This confirms the high degree of parental concern for education in She Tan; it also shows some confidence in the possibility that things can be changed. Second, the relevant authorities actually responded to the complaints that were conveyed by the Party leader. Third, a mechanism existed to induce the village teachers to conform with parental demands.

This is an instance where the authority of the Party has lent itself to popular demands. But this is not to say that village-level political institutions in She Tan are generally more responsive to public pressure than in Palanpur. Indeed, She Tan villagers have found no means of resisting the reduction of grades in the village school, or, for that matter, the much-resented proposal to close the village school altogether. While the Party may be responsive to popular demands when these do not conflict with its own interests or policies, villagers have no effective means of opposing the Party's own programme.

The respective experiences of Palanpur and She Tan point to an important aspect of the institutional basis of village-level public services. The effective functioning of these services often depends crucially on combining local information (e.g. on the performance of village teachers) with a control mechanism that makes it possible to deal with observed problems. The relevant information is available primarily to village residents, and if the control mechanism is also in their own hands, or at least highly responsive to their demands, local public services are more likely to function satisfactorily.[76] In

[76] This statement may not be valid when different members of the village community have sharply divided interests in the quality of public services in question (as with some recent 'anti-poverty programmes' in India). In that case, much would crucially depend on who controls what within the village community. For an empirical illustration with reference to education, see Narain (1972).

Palanpur there is no effective control mechanism, with the result that popular complaints do not get translated into action for change. In She Tan (and perhaps in much of rural China), the Party is the ultimate control mechanism, and it has the ability to implement radical changes. But the Party also has its own interests and priorities. The effective combination of local information and Party authority depends on a convergence of popular interests with those of the Party. In that sense, the institutional basis of the system remains somewhat undependable, as the recent decline of village-level educational facilities in She Tan illustrates.

8. Concluding Remarks

In this paper, we have presented two case studies of primary education in India and China, and we have tried to identify the key factors of achievement and failure in each case. We have also attempted to relate educational achievements to various aspects of economic and social organization.

The background to these case studies was a brief overview of recent trends in rural literacy in both countries (Section 3). The conclusions emerging from that overview include the following.[77]

First, recent census data for both countries indicate that China is well ahead of India in the field of rural primary education. In 1991 China had a lead of about 30 percentage points over India in terms of adult literacy rates in rural areas.

Second, age-specific literacy rates bring out a crucial feature of the Chinese advantage. While nearly 40 per cent of rural Indian children fail to learn to read and write, the corresponding figure for China is only around 5 per cent. This implies that China can be expected to move fairly rapidly towards universal literacy, as the younger cohorts gradually replace the older age groups. In India, by contrast, there is still a massive problem of illiteracy among young boys and girls.

Third, China's lead was achieved during the pre-reform period, on the basis of a strong commitment to the widespread provision of elementary education in rural areas. During the 1980s both India and China made further progress in rural literacy, with their relative position remaining more or less unchanged.

Fourth, female literacy rates are well below male literacy rates in both countries. The gender bias is particularly striking in rural India, where 70 per cent of females above the age of 7 are illiterate, and where only one girl in two learns to read and write. The gender gap is rapidly narrowing in rural

---

[77] The reader who has skipped earlier sections of this paper may wish to refer to Table 2 and Fig. 4, which capture most of the statistical information on which the present conclusions are based.

China (owing to near-universal literacy in the younger age groups), but not in rural India.

Fifth, there are wide inter-regional disparities in rural literacy rates in both countries. The regional contrasts are largely driven by differences in female literacy. The persistence of high levels of female illiteracy in particular states or provinces is a matter of special concern in both countries.

Sixth, in spite of sharp regional contrasts within each country, most Chinese provinces have much higher rural literacy rates than most Indian states. The state of Kerala in India stands out as the main exception to this pattern. With universal literacy among adolescent males *and* females, and near-universal literacy in the adult population, Kerala is well ahead not only of all Indian states but also of all Chinese provinces. This remarkable achievement reflects more than a hundred years of creative interaction between state commitment to, and public demand for, the widespread provision of elementary education.

Seventh, the other striking exception to the general lead of Chinese provinces over Indian states is Tibet. Literacy rates in rural Tibet are not only abysmally low (even lower than in the educationally backward states of North India), they also show little sign of significant improvement over time. While the interpretation of census data for Tibet requires further scrutiny, there is a strong possibility that Tibet has been comprehensively neglected in the efforts of the Chinese leadership to promote elementary education in rural areas.

Against this background, we have examined the record of primary education in two villages, Palanpur in India and She Tan in China. An important difference between these two villages emerges from this comparative investigation.

She Tan can be said to have developed a credible educational system, based on a strong parental demand for education, the accountability of the schooling establishment to local government institutions, and a long-standing government commitment to the widespread and equitable provision of elementary education. The main issue, at the moment, is one of financial resources: with the transition from collective economic organization to the household responsibility system, the financial basis of public provisioning at the village level has become more fragile. The obvious way to address this problem is through an expansion of central government funding for public services in rural areas. There is a case for that, independently of the preceding considerations, on standard grounds of equity and risk-pooling. But the Chinese government seems to be reluctant to take bold steps in that direction, for a somewhat unclear mixture of practical reasons (financial crisis at the central level) and ideological predilections (emphasis on 'enterprise responsibility' throughout the public sector).

In Palanpur, on the other hand, lack of financial means does not appear to be the main issue. A more important cause of persistently low educational achievements is the basic failure of the schooling establishment to provide credible educational services.[78] The government-funded village school is in the hands of a poorly motivated and effectively unaccountable teacher, and the quality of its services is deplorably low—when it functions at all. Other government schools are too distant, and private schools too expensive, to represent an attractive alternative, especially for poor households. In the circumstances, many parents who would be glad, in principle, to send their children to school choose to make use of their labour services instead.

In the case of female education, there is an additional problem of extremely low parental motivation. The fact that recent improvements in the functioning of the village school have led to a significant increase in female enrolment highlights this lack of parental interest in female education. We have discussed how this attitude derives, at least partly, from deep-rooted features of gender relations in North India. In light of these connections, it is not surprising that areas of India with low levels of female education also tend to be those where the position of women has traditionally been one of comprehensive subordination.[79]

The persistent neglect of education in North India relates to the fact that elementary education is not an issue that gets naturally highlighted in the democratic political process. Indeed, those who are in greatest need of elementary education are also—by the same token—in a particularly weak position to translate their needs into coherent and effective political demands. This is in striking contrast with, for instance, the recent ability of university students to make a dramatic issue of caste-based reservation policies, in which they happen to have a strong stake. It is also in contrast with the ability of the privileged sections of the Indian population to press for continued expansion of subsidized higher education. It can be argued that a central aspect of the educational challenge in India is to make elementary education a more lively political issue—as it has been in Kerala for a long time.

In the concluding sentences of his Lal Bahadur Shastri Memorial Lecture on 'Aspects of Indian Education', delivered in Delhi more than twenty years ago, Amartya Sen already stressed this political dimension of the educational challenge:

The most important characteristic of public policy on Indian education has been one of drift—a drift in response to the wind from whichever direction it might be blowing.

[78] As was mentioned in section 7.3, a more recent field investigation (Drèze and Gazdar, forthcoming) suggests that the failures observed in Palanpur are common elsewhere in Uttar Pradesh.

[79] These areas of sharp gender inequalities and low female literacy include Uttar Pradesh, Madhya Pradesh, Rajasthan, and Bihar. Even in Punjab and Haryana (where traditional gender inequalities have also been very strong), female literacy levels remain strikingly low, bearing in mind the relatively high level of income in these two states (see Fig. 1). On regional patterns of sex bias in literacy in India, and their relation to gender inequalities in general, see Sopher (1980) and Raju (1988).

The direction of the wind has largely been determined, naturally enough, by the existing stratification of Indian society. Bending to the pressures of vocal groups and powerful classes has contributed to the perpetuation—and indeed intensification—of the social inequities. The rot in Indian education is, thus, ultimately related to the structure of Indian society.

. . . The most spectacular deficiency [in educational planning] has been one of commitment. The failure of leadership in policy-making is as much due to this deficiency as due to technical errors and mistakes. In the last analysis educational transformation in India is not merely a matter of clear thinking but also of courage and determination . . . To ignore this will be escapism. (Sen 1971, p. 159)

This diagnosis has not lost its relevance.

References

Alderman, H., Behrman, J. R., Khan, S., Ross, D. R., and Sabot, R. (1993), 'Public School Expenditures in Rural Pakistan: Efficiently Targeting Girls in a Lagging Region', mimeo, World Bank, Washington, DC.

Almeida, A. (1978), 'The Gift of a Bride: Sociological Implications of the Dowry System in Goa', mimeo, Université Catholique de Louvain, Louvain-la-Neuve, Belgium.

Altekar, A. S. (1956), *The Position of Women in Hindu Civilization*, Motilal Banarsidass, Delhi.

Anon. (1989*a*), 'Society, Private Sector Urged to Run Schools', *Guangming Ribao*, no. 95, 13 September.

Anon (1989*b*), 'Elementary, Middle School Dropouts Increase', *Zhongguo Jiaoyu Bao*, no. 36, 26 April.

Ansari, N. (1964), 'Palanpur: A Study of its Economic Resources and Economic Activities', Continuous Village Survey no. 41, Agricultural Economics Research Centre, University of Delhi.

Antarjanam, Lalitambika (1993), 'Revenge Herself', in L. Holstrom (ed.), *The Inner Courtyard: Stories by Indian Women*, Rupa, Delhi.

Arriaga, E., Banister, J., and Hao, H. (1988), 'China: Provincial Patterns of Mortality', mimeo, prepared for presentation at a seminar on Mortality and Morbidity in South and East Asia, Beijing, 29 August–2 September 1988.

Aslanbeigui, N., and Summerfield, G. (1989), 'Impact of the Responsibility System on Women in Rural China', *World Development*, 17: 343–8.

Banerjee, S. (1992), 'Uses of Literacy: Total Literacy Campaign in Three West Bengal Districts', *Economic and Political Weekly*, 29 February.

Bangladesh Rural Advancement Committee (1992), 'The Neglected Outpost: A Closer Look at Rural Schools in Bangladesh', mimeo, BRAC, Dhaka.

Banister, J. (1992), 'Demographic Aspects of Poverty in China', background paper prepared for the World Bank (1992) report.

Bara, D., Bhengra, R., and Minz, B. (1991), 'Tribal Female Literacy: Factors in Differentiation among Munda Religious Communities', *Social Action*, 41: 399–415.

Basu, Alaka Malwade (1992), 'Family Size and Child Welfare in an Urban Slum', mimeo, Institute of Economic Growth, New Delhi.

Behrman, J. R., and Wolfe, B. L. (1984), 'More Evidence on Nutrition Demand: Income Seems Overrated and Women's Schooling Underemphasized', *Journal of Development Economics*, 14: 108–28.

—— —— (1987), 'How Does Mother's Schooling Affect Family Health, Nutrition, Medical Care Usage, and Household Sanitation?' *Journal of Econometrics*, 36: 185–205.

Berreman, G. D. (1972), *Hindus of the Himalayas: Ethnography and Change*, 2nd edn., University of California Press, Berkeley.

Bhatty, Z. (1988), 'Socialising of the Female Muslim Child in Uttar Pradesh', in K. Chanana (ed.) (1988).

Bhuiya, A., and Streatfield, K. (1991), 'Mothers' Education and Survival of Female Children in a Rural Area of Bangladesh', *Population Studies*, 45: 253–64.

Bliss, C. J., and Stern, N. H. (1982), *Palanpur: The Economy of an Indian Village*, Oxford University Press.

Bose, A. (1991*a*), *Demographic Diversity of India*, B. R. Publishing, Delhi.

—— (1991*b*), *Population of India: 1991 Census Results and Methodology*, B. R. Publishing, Delhi.

Bourne, K., and Walker, G. M. (1991), 'The Differential Effect of Mothers' Education on Mortality of Boys and Girls in India', *Population Studies*, 45: 203–19.

Caldwell, J. C. (1979), 'Education as a Factor in Mortality Decline: An Examination of Nigerian Data', *Population Studies*, 33: 395–413.

—— (1986), 'Routes to Low Mortality in Poor Countries', *Population and Development Review*, 12: 171–220.

—— Reddy, P. H., and Caldwell, P. (1985), 'Educational Transition in Rural South India', *Population and Development Review*, 11: 29–51.

Caldwell, P. and Caldwell, J. (1987), 'Where There is a Narrower Gap between Female and Male Situations: Lessons from South India and Sri Lanka', paper presented at a workshop on Differentials in Mortality and Health Care, BAMA-NEH/SSRC, Dhaka.

Chanana, K. (ed.) (1988), *Socialisation, Education and Women: Explorations in Gender Identity*, Orient Longman, New Delhi.

—— (1990), 'Structures and Ideologies: Socialisation and Education of the Girl Child in South Asia', *Indian Journal of Social Science*, 3: 53–71.

—— (1993), 'Educational Attainment, Status Reproduction and Female Autonomy: Case Studies of Punjabi Women', paper presented at a workshop on Female Education, Autonomy and Fertility Change in South Asia, New Delhi, 8–10 April.

Cleland, J. (1990), 'Maternal Education and Child Survival: Further Evidence and Explanations', in J. Caldwell *et al.* (eds.), *What We Know About Health Transition: The Cultural, Social and Behavioural Determinants of Health*, Health Transition Centre, Australian National University, Canberra.

—— and van Ginneken, J. (1987), 'The Effect of Maternal Schooling on Childhood Mortality: The Search for an Explanation', paper presented at a conference on Health Intervention and Mortality Change in Developing Countries, University of Sheffield, September.

——— ——— (1988), 'Maternal Education and Child Survival in Developing Countries: The Search for Pathways of Influence', *Social Science and Medicine*, 27: 1357–68.

Cleverley, J. (1985), *The Schooling of China*, George Allen & Unwin, London.

Colclough, C. (1982), 'The Impact of Primary Schooling on Economic Development: A Review of the Evidence', *World Development*, 10: 167–85.

Colletta, N. J., and Sutton, M. (1989), 'Achieving and Sustaining Universal Primary Education: International Experience Relevant to India', PPR Working Paper no. 166, Population and Human Resources Department, World Bank, Washington, DC.

Committee on the Status of Women in India (1974), *Towards Equality*, Ministry of Education and Social Welfare, New Delhi.

Drèze, J. P. (1990), 'Widows in Rural India', Discussion Paper no. 26, Development Economics Research Programme, London School of Economics.

—— and Gazdan, H. (forthcoming), 'Uttar Pradesh: The Penalties of Inaction' in Drèze and Sen (forthcoming).

—— and Sen, A. K. (1989), *Hunger and Public Action*, Clarendon Press, Oxford.

——— ——— (eds.) (1990), *The Political Economy of Hunger*, 3 vols. Clarendon Press, Oxford.

——— ——— (eds.) (forthcoming), *India: Economic Development and Social Opportunity*, Clarendon Press, Oxford.

Dube, L. (1987), 'Kinship, Family and Socialisation in South and South East Asia: A Comparative View', mimeo.

—— (1988), 'On the Construction of Gender: Socialisation of Girls in Patrilineal India', in Chanana (1988).

Dyson, T., and Moore, M. (1983), 'On Kinship Structure, Female Autonomy, and Demographic Behavior in India', *Population and Development Review*, 9: 35–60.

Economist (1993), 'Silver Spoons, Silver Classrooms: The Price of Chinese Education', *The Economist*, 15–21 May.

Ford Foundation (1992), *Perspectives on India's Development in the 1990s: Symposium Review*, Ford Foundation, New Delhi.

Government of India (1984), *Sample Registration System 1981*, Ministry of Home Affairs, New Delhi.

—— (1985), *Sample Registration System 1982*, Ministry of Home Affairs, New Delhi.

—— (1986), *The Teacher and Society: Report of the National Commission on Teachers*, Ministry of Education, New Delhi.

—— (1988), 'Child Mortality Estimates of India', Occasional Papers, no. 5, Demography Division, Office of the Registrar General, Ministry of Home Affairs.

—— (1989), *Sample Registration System 1989*, Ministry of Home Affairs, New Delhi.

—— (1991), *Family Welfare Yearbook*, Ministry of Health and Family Welfare, New Delhi.

—— (1992), 'Final Population Totals: Brief Analysis of Primary Census Abstracts', Census of India 1991, Series-1, Paper 2 of 1992, Office of the Registrar-General, New Delhi.

—— (1993), *Sample Registration System, 1991*, Ministry of Home Affairs, New Delhi.

Hayase, Y., and Kawatama, S. (1990), *Population Statistics of China*, IDE Statistical Data Series no. 55, Institute of Developing Economies, Tokyo.

Hayhoe, R. (ed.) (1984), *Contemporary Chinese Education*, Croom Helm, London.

—— (ed.) (1992), *Education and Modernization: The Chinese Experience*, Pergamon, Oxford and New York.

Henze, J. (1992), 'The Formal Education System and Modernization: An Analysis of Developments since 1978', in Hayhoe (1992).

Hsi-en Chen, T. (1981), *Chinese Education since 1949*, Pergamon, New York.

Jain, A. K. (1985), 'Determinants of Regional Variations in Infant Mortality in Rural India', *Population Studies*, 39: 407–24.

—— and Nag, M. (1985), 'Female Primary Education and Fertility Reduction in India', Working Paper no. 114, Center for Policy Studies, Population Council, New York.

—— —— (1986), 'Importance of Female Primary Education for Fertility Reduction in India', *Economic and Political Weekly*, 6 September.

Jee-Peng Tan (1990), 'Education in China: Comparative Perspectives on Cost and Financing Issues', paper presented at an international symposium on the Financing of Education, Beijing, March 1990.

Jeffrey, R. (1993), *Politics, Women and Well-Being: How Kerala Became 'A Model'*, Indian edn., Oxford University Press, Delhi.

Kabir, M., and Krishnan, T. N. (1992), 'Social Intermediation and the Health Transition: Lessons from Kerala', paper presented at a workshop on Health and Development in India, 2–4 January 1992; to be published in M. Das Gupta, T. N. Krishnan, and L. Chen (eds.), *Health and Development in India*, Oxford University Press, Delhi.

Kapadia, K. M. (1966), *Marriage and the Family in India*, 3rd edn., Oxford University Press, Bombay.

Karlekar, M. (1988), 'Woman's Nature and the Access to Education', in Chanana (1988).

Karve, I. (1965), *Kinship Organisation in India*, Asia Publishing House, Bombay.

—— (1974), *Yuganta: The End of an Epoch*, Orient Longman, Hyderabad.

Kelkar, G. (1989), '. . . Two Steps Back? New Agricultural Policies in Rural China and the Woman Question', in B. Agarwal (ed.), *Structures of Patriarchy*, Zed, London.

Knight, J., and Li Shi (1991), 'The Determinants of Educational Attainment in China', Applied Economics Discussion Paper Series, No. 127, Institute of Economics and Statistics, Oxford.

Kolenda, P. (1984), 'Woman as Tribute, Woman as Flower: Images of "Woman" in Weddings in North and South India', *American Ethnologist*, 11: 98–117.

Kurien, J. (1983), *Elementary Education in India: Myth, Reality and Alternative*, Vikas, New Delhi.

Kynch, J., and Sen, A. K. (1983), 'Malnutrition of Rural Children and the Sex Bias', *Cambridge Journal of Economics*, 7: 363–80.

Lanjouw, P., and Stern, N. H. (eds.) (forthcoming), *Economic Development in Palanpur 1957–1993*, Oxford University Press.

Leslie, J. (1989), *The Perfect Wife: The Orthodox Hindu Woman according to the Shridharma Paddhati of Tryambakayajvan*, Oxford University Press, Delhi.

Levy, R. J. (1989), 'Trouble in the Schoolyard: Crisis and Reform in the Chinese Educational System', mimeo.

Li Chengrui (1992), *A Study of China's Population*, Foreign Languages Press, Beijing.

Lieten, G. K. (1992), 'Literacy in Post-Land Reform Village', *Economic and Political Weekly*, 18 January.

Ling, Zhu (1992), 'On Poverty Studies in China', mimeo, Economic Research Institute (Chinese Academy of Social Sciences), Beijing.

Lo, B. L. C. (1984), 'Primary Education in China: A Two-track System for Dual Tasks', in Hayhoe (1984).

Lockheed, M. E. (1992), *Improving Primary Education in Developing Countries*, World Bank/Oxford University Press.

Loh, J. (1993), 'A Summary of Literacy in China', mimeo, STICERD, London School of Economics.

Ma Yijun (1989), 'Decade of Suffering: A Chronicle of 300,000 Temporary Workers in Shenzhen', *Beijing Zhongguo Zuojia*, no. 3.

MacDorman, M. (1986), 'Contemporary Marriage Practices in North India: Evidence from Three Uttar Pradesh Villages', Ph.D. thesis, Australian National University.

Mak, G. C. L. (1989), 'Women's Education in the People's Republic of China: Progress and Contradictions in Revolution and Modernization', in Jing Wang and Yenbo Wu (eds.), *Perspectives on Contemporary Education in China*, Comparative Education Center, State University of New York at Buffalo.

Matthai, J. (1915), *Village Government in British India*, T. Fisher Unwin, London.

Mei, Z., and Li, Y. (1990), 'Child Labour Flourishes Along Ancient Silk Road', *Shehui* (Shanghai), no. 2, 20 February.

Miller, B. (1981), *The Endangered Sex*, Cornell University Press, Ithaca, NY.

Minhas, B. S., Jain, L. R., and Tendulkar, S. D. (1991), 'Declining Incidence of Poverty in 1980s: Evidence versus Artefacts', *Economic and Political Weekly*, 6–13 July.

Nag, M. (1989), 'Political Awareness as a Factor in Accessibility of Health Services: A Case Study of Rural Kerala and West Bengal', *Economic and Political Weekly*, 25 February.

Nair, K. N., Sivanandan, P., and Retnam, V. C. V. (1984), 'Education, Employment and Landholding Pattern in a Tamil Village', *Economic and Political Weekly*, 16–24 June.

Narain, I. (1972), 'Rural Local Politics and Primary School Management', in Rudolph and Rudolph (1972).

National Institute of Rural Development (1991), *Rural Development Statistics 1990*, NIRD, Hyderabad.

Pandey, G. D., and Talwat, P. P. (1980), 'Some Correlates of Literacy and Educational Attainment among Children in Rural Areas of Uttar Pradesh', *Demography India*, 9:

Population Census Office under the State Council and Department of Population Statistics, State Statistical Bureau, PRC (1991), *10 Percent Sampling Technique on the 1990 Population Census of the People's Republic of China (Computer Tabulation)*, China Statistical Publishing House, Beijing.

Premi, M. K. (1991), *India's Population*, B. R. Publishing, Delhi.

Psacharopoulos, G. (1984), 'The Contribution of Education to Economic Growth: International Comparisons', in J. W. Kendrick (ed.), *International Comparisons of Productivity and the Slowdown*, Ballinger, Cambridge, Mass.

—— (1985), 'Returns to Education: A Further International Update and Implications', *Journal of Human Resources*, 20: 583–97.

—— (1988), 'Education and Development: A Review', *World Bank Research Observer*, 3.

Radhakrishnan, M. P. (1991), 'Kerala: The First Fully Literate State', *Yojana*, 30 June.

Raju, S. (1988), 'Female Literacy in India: The Urban Dimension', *Economic and Political Weekly*, 29 October.

Ramachandran, V. K. (forthcoming), 'The Experience of Kerala', in Drèze and Sen (forthcoming).

Rosen, S. (1992), 'Women, Education and Modernization', in Hayhoe (1992).

Rudolph, S. H., and Rudolph, L. I. (eds.) (1972), *Education and Politics in India: Studies in Organization, Society, and Policy*, Harvard University Press, Cambridge, Mass.

Santha, E. K. (1994), 'Local Self-Government in Malabar (1800–1960)', Occasional Paper No. 12, Institute of Social Sciences, New Delhi.

Schultz, T. P. (1988), 'Education Investments and Returns', *Handbook of Development Economics*, i., North-Holland, Amsterdam.

Sen, A. K. (1970, 1971), 'Aspects of Indian Education', Lal Bahadur Shastri Memorial Lecture, New Delhi, 1970; partly reprinted in P. Chaudhuri (ed.) *Aspects of Indian Economic Development*, Allen & Unwin, London, 1971.

—— (1981a), *Poverty and Famines*, Clarendon Press, Oxford.

—— (1981b), 'Public Action and the Quality of Life in Developing Countries', *Oxford Bulletin of Economics and Statistics*, 43: 287–319.

—— (1982), 'How is India Doing?' *New York Review of Books*, 21.

—— (1983), 'Development: Which Way Now?' *Economic Journal*, 93: 745–62.

—— (1984), *Resources, Values and Development*, Basil Blackwell, Oxford.

—— (1985a), *Commodities and Capabilities*, North-Holland, Amsterdam.

—— (1985b), 'Women, Technology and Sexual Divisions', *Trade and Development*, UNCTAD, New York, no. 6.

—— (1988), 'The Concept of Development', in H. Chenery and T. N. Srinivasan (eds.), *Handbook of Development Economics*, i, North-Holland, Amsterdam.

—— (1989), 'Food and Freedom', *World Development*, 17: 769–81.

—— (1990a), 'Gender and Co-operative Conflicts', in I. Tinker (ed.), *Persistent Inequalities*, Oxford University Press.

—— (1990b), 'Food, Economics and Entitlements', in Drèze and Sen (1990).

—— (1993), 'The Threats to Secular Indian', *New York Review of Books*, 40: 26–32.

—— and Sengupta, A. (1983), 'Malnutrition of Rural Children and the Sex Bias', *Economic and Political Weekly*, Annual Number, 18: 855–64.

Sengupta, S. (1991), 'Progress of Literacy in India during 1983 to 1988', *Sarvekshana*, April–June.

Shah, A. M. (1973), *The Household Dimension of the Family in India*, Orient Longman, New Delhi.

Sharma, U. (1980), *Women, Work and Property in North-West India*, Tavistock, London.

Shi Lei (1989), 'Complete Bankruptcy of Compulsory Education', *Pai Hsing* (Hong Kong), no. 193, 1 June.

Shi Ming Hu, and Saifman, E. (1987), *Education and Socialist Modernization*, AMS Press, New York.

Shukla, S. (1992), 'Litaracy and Development: Retrospect and Tendencies', *Economic and Political Weekly*, 21 September.

Sopher, D. (1980), 'Sex Disparity in Indian Literacy', in D. Sopher (ed.), *An Exploration of India: Geographical Perspective on Society and Culture*, Cornell University Press, Ithaca, NY.

Sun, L. H. (1993), 'Free-Market Wave Revives Old Bias on "Woman's Place" ', *International Herald Tribune*, 17 February.

Thomas, D., Strauss, J., and Henriques, M. H. (1991), 'How Does Mother's Education Affect Child Height?' *Journal of Human Resources*, 26: 183–212.

—— (1992), 'Education, Health, Nutrition and Demographic Changes: A Review of Evidence on Asia', *Indian Journal of Labour Economics*, 35.

—— (1993), 'Costs and Financing of Education in India: A Review of Issues, Problems and Prospects', mimeo, National Institute of Educational Planning and Administration, New Delhi.

Tyagi, P. N. (1991), *Education for All: A Graphic Presentation*, National Institute of Educational Planning and Administration, New Delhi.

van Bastelaer, T. (1986), 'Essai d'analyse des systèmes de paiements de mariage: le cas de l'Inde', unpublished M.Sc. thesis, Facultés des Sciences Economiques et Sociales, Université de Namur, Belgium.

Verma, V. S. (1988), *A Handbook of Population Statistics*, Office of the Registrar General, New Delhi.

Vlassoff, C. (1980), 'Unmarried Adolescent Females in Rural India: A Study of the Social Impact of Education', *Journal of Marriage and the Family*, 42: 427–36.

—— (1993), 'Against the Odds: The Changing Impact of Education on Female Autonomy and Fertility in an Indian Village', paper presented at a workshop on Female Education, Autonomy and Fertility Change in South Asia, New Delhi, 8–10 April.

Vyasulu, V. (1993), 'Management of Poverty Alleviation Programmes in Karnataka: An Overview', paper presented at a workshop on Poverty Alleviation in India held at the Institute of Development Studies, Jaipur, February.

Wang, J. (1989), 'Compulsory Nine-Year Education in China: Issues and Prospects', in Jing Wang and Yenbo Wu (eds.), *Perspectives on Contemporary Education in China*, comparative Education Center, State University of New York at Buffalo.

Ware, H. (1984), 'Effects of Maternal Education, Women's Roles, and Child Care on Child Mortality', in W. H. Mosley, and L. C. Chen, (eds.), *Child Survival: Strategies for Research*, Population Council, New York.

Weiner, M. (1991), *The Child and the State in India: Child Labor and Education Policy in Comparative Perspective*, Oxford University Press, Delhi.

—— (1991), 'China: Provincial Education Planning and Finance', Report no. 8657–CHA, World Bank, Washington, DC.

—— (1992), *China: Strategies for Reducing Poverty in the 1990s*, World Bank, Washington, DC.

Wu, Yen-bo (1987), 'Policies and Realities: Why High School Teachers Do Not Want to Teach', in Jing Wang and Yenbo Wu (eds.), *Perspectives on Contemporary Education in China*, Comparative Education Center, State University of New York at Buffalo.

Yu Dezhi (1992), 'Changes in Health Care Financing and Health Status: The Case of China in the 1980s', Innocenti Occasional Papers, Economic Policy Series, no. 34, International Child Development Centre, Florence.

Zhang Shaowen and Wei Liming (1987), 'Combating Illiteracy in China', *Beijing Review*, 16 February.

World Bank (1985), *China: Issues and Prospects in Education*, World Bank, Washington, DC.

11

Children and Intra-Household Inequality:
A Theoretical Analysis

RAVI KANBUR

1. Introduction

The issue of intra-household inequality has received increasing attention over the past decade. A number of authors (e.g. Sen 1984) have argued that resources within the household are not distributed according to need, and this has led to attempts by others to model intra-household allocative behaviour (see e.g. the discussion in the recent survey by Behrman and Deolalikar, 1989). The question of what happens to intra-household inequality when total household resources increase has been raised by Haddad and Kanbur (1990c). They argue, on the basis of empirical evidence on calorie adequacy from the Philippines, that as households become better off intra-household inequality first increases and then decreases; in other words, there appears to be an intra-household Kuznets curve. The behaviour of intra-household inequality as the household becomes better off is clearly important for policy, since interventions are often restricted to the household level while the objective is to improve the welfare of the least well-off individuals. It is also important as a reduced-form test of alternative models of intra-household allocation.

It turns out that many of the tractable derivations of the reduced-form relationship between intra-household inequality and total household resources, and indeed many of the other tractable implications of intra-household allocation, are available only in what might be described broadly as the 'linear expenditure systems' framework. The objective of this paper is to lay out a generic analysis in this framework, and to show how a number of formulations of intra-household allocation essentially lead to special cases of the framework. This includes (1) household welfare maximization, (2) intra-household allocation viewed as the outcome of a Nash co-operative bargain, and (3) intra-household allocation as a Nash non-cooperative game, with children as public goods. Each of these structural models has

The Policy, Research, and External Affairs Complex (PRE) distributes PRE Working Papers to disseminate the findings of work in progress and to encourage the exchange of ideas among Bank staff and all others interested in development issues. These papers carry the names of the authors, reflect only their views, and should be used and cited accordingly. The findings, interpretations, and conclusions are the author's own. They should not be attributed to the World Bank, its Board of Directors, its management, or any of its member countries.

been suggested as an explanation for intra-household allocation. We start, however, by setting out the framework of linear expenditure systems.

2. Linear Expenditure Systems and the Behaviour of Intra-Household Inequality

We will conduct the discussion in terms of a variable x which depicts total household resources. The index $i = 1, 2, ..., n$ will identify each of the n individuals in a household, so that x_i is the flow of resources to the ith individual, and $\sum_{i=1}^{n} x_i = x$. At this level of generality x can have several interpretations. The most convenient way is perhaps to think of it as some measure of welfare. More concretely, it can be thought of as calorie intake relative to requirement (as in Haddad and Kanbur 1990*a*, *c*). Our focus is on how the allocation x_i ($i = 1, 2, ..., n$) changes with x. In reduced form, we can write

$$x_i = x_i(x), \qquad i = 1, 2, ..., n \tag{1}$$

as the functional relationship derived from the structural model of intra-household allocation. A measure of inequality of the intra-household allocation can then be written as

$$I = I(x_1(x), x_2(x), ..., x_n(x)). \tag{2}$$

Given the reduced form (1), we can therefore derive the relationship between intra-household inequality and total household resources.

Consider the following special case of (1):

$$x = \bar{x}_i + \alpha_i \left(x - \sum_{j=1}^{n} \bar{x}_j \right), \qquad i = 1, 2, ..., n$$

$$\alpha_i > 0 \ \forall \ i \tag{3}$$

$$\sum_{i=1}^{n} \alpha_i = 1.$$

In the next two sections we will discuss structural models that lead to this reduced form. For now, notice that (3) is nothing but a linear expenditure system for the n 'commodities', $i = 1, 2, ..., n$, with intercepts $\bar{x}_i$, total expenditure x, supernumerary expenditure $x - \sum_{j=1}^{n} \bar{x}_j$, and marginal propensity to spend on commodity i given by x_i. How does intra-household inequality behave as total household resources change in this framework?

Before answering this question, let us rewrite

$$x_i = \left(\bar{x}_i - \alpha_i \sum_{j=1}^{n} \bar{x}_j \right) + \alpha_i x$$

$$= (\bar{x}_i - \alpha_i \bar{x}) + \alpha_i x \qquad (4)$$

$$= \beta_i + \alpha_x$$

where

$$\bar{x} = \sum_{j=1}^{n} \bar{x}_j \; ; \quad \beta_i = \bar{x}_i - \alpha_i \bar{x}; \quad \sum_{i=1}^{n} \beta_i = 0.$$

The share of x_i in x, s_i is given by

$$s_i = \frac{x_i}{x} = \alpha_i + \beta_i x^{-1}. \qquad (5)$$

Thus, the squared coefficient of variation of x_i, which is the same as the variance of s_i, is given by

$$\sigma_s^2 = \sigma_\alpha^2 + 2\sigma_{\alpha\beta} x^{-1} + \sigma_\beta^2 x^{-2}, \qquad (6)$$

where σ_s^2, σ_α^2, and σ_β^2 are the variances of the subscripted variables, and $\sigma_{\alpha\beta}$ is the covariance of α and β.

We will focus on σ_s^2 as our measure of intra-household inequality. We are interested in its behaviour as a function of x. It is easily shown that this function has a unique minimum at

$$x^* = \frac{-\sigma_\beta^2}{\sigma_{\alpha\beta}}.$$

Of course, the economically relevant range for x is $x \geqslant \bar{x} > 0$. Thus, if $\sigma_{\alpha\beta} \geqslant 0$, then $d\sigma_s^2/dx < 0$ for all x in the relevant range, as shown in Fig. 1. If $\sigma_{\alpha\beta} < 0$, then there are two cases to consider. If $\bar{x} \geqslant x^* > 0$, i.e. if $\sigma_{\alpha\beta} \leqslant -\sigma_\beta^2/x$, then $d\sigma_s^2/dx > 0$ for $x > \bar{x}$, as shown in Fig. 2. But if $x^* > \bar{x}$,

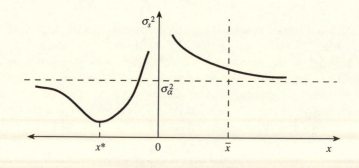

Fig. 1

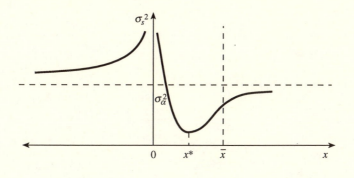

Fig. 2

i.e. if $0 > \alpha_{\alpha\beta} > -\sigma_\beta^2/x$, then σ_s^2 follows a U shape in the relevant range of $x > \bar{x}$, as shown in Fig. 3.

Translating these conditions on α_i and β_i into conditions of α_i and x_i, after making the normalization assumption that $\bar{x} = 1$, we get the following, complete characterization:

$$\sigma_{x\alpha} \geq \sigma_\alpha^2 \Rightarrow \frac{\mathrm{d}\sigma_s^2}{\mathrm{d}x} < 0 \qquad \forall x > \bar{x} \tag{7a}$$

$$\sigma_{\bar{x}}^2 \leq \sigma_{x\alpha} < \sigma_\alpha^2 \Rightarrow \frac{\mathrm{d}\sigma_s^2}{\mathrm{d}x} > 0 \qquad \forall x > \bar{x} \tag{7b}$$

$$\sigma_{x\alpha} < \min(\sigma_\alpha^2, \sigma_{\bar{x}}^2) \Rightarrow \frac{\mathrm{d}\sigma_s^2}{\mathrm{d}x} \qquad \text{has a U shape in the range } x > \bar{x}. \tag{7c}$$

Figs. 4(*a*) and (*b*) characterize the different ranges of $\sigma_{\bar{x}\alpha}$ for the cases where $\sigma_{\bar{x}}^2 < \sigma_\alpha^2$ and where $\sigma_{\bar{x}}^2 > \sigma_\alpha^2$.

The behaviour of intra-household inequality in a linear expenditure system framework depends, therefore, on the pattern of covariance between

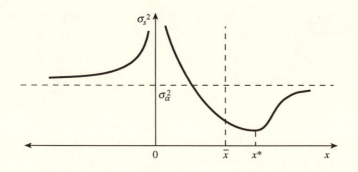

Fig. 3

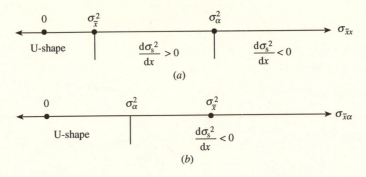

Fig. 4

the parameters $\bar{x}_i$ and α_i of the system. But we already have an important result in (7). Notice that in no circumstances can the linear expenditure system generate the inverse-U shape of the Kuznets curve, for which there is some evidence in the data (Haddad and Kanbur 1990c). This would seem to be a strong argument against models of intra-household allocation that lead to a linear expenditure system as a reduced form. The next two sections consider some applications of this general characterization.

3. Two Simple Applications

3.1. Household Welfare Maximization

Suppose that the intra-household allocation (1) is the result of the maximization of a household welfare function:

$$\max_{x_2, x_2, ..., x_n} W(x_1, x_2, ..., x_n) \quad \text{s. t} \sum_{i=1}^{n} x_i = x. \tag{8}$$

If the welfare function were specialized to the following case of the Stone–Geary utility function,

$$W(x_1, x_2, ..., x_n) = \sum_{i=1}^{n} \alpha_i \ln(x_i - \bar{x}_i); \; \alpha_i > 0 \qquad \forall i,$$

$$\sum_{i=1}^{n} \alpha_i = 1, \tag{9}$$

then it is well known that the optimal solution to (8) is exactly as given by (3).

Hence the behaviour of intra-household inequality is determined by the pattern of the minimum consumption levels $\bar{x}_i$ and the weights α_i given to the individuals in the welfare function. If, for example, $\bar{x}_i$ and α_i are negatively correlated, then case (7c) obtains and intra-household inequality follows a U shape, *not* the inverse-U shape of the Kuznets curve that is found empirically by Haddad and Kanbur (1990c). If, on the other hand, all α_i are the same, then case (7a) obtains and inequality decreases continously. If $\sigma_{\bar{x}\alpha}$ is positive, case (7c) may still obtain, provided the covariance between $\bar{x}$ and α is not too high. If $\sigma_{\bar{x}\alpha}$ is high enough, in particular if it is higher than σ_{α}^2, then intra-household inequality will decrease as the household's resources increase.

3.2 Two-Person Nash Co-operative Bargaining

Haddad and Kanbur (1990b) have investigated the behaviour of intra-household inequality for a two-person household where allocations are determined as outcomes to a Nash bargain. As is well known, if we specify the total resources being bargained over as x, the threat points of the two individuals as $\bar{x}_1$, and $\bar{x}_2$, and their 'bargaining strength' parameters as α_1, and $\alpha_2 (\alpha_1 + \alpha_2 = 1)$, then the Nash solution to the co-operative bargain is given as the solution to the following problem:

$$\max_{x_1, x_2} (x_1 - \bar{x}_1)^{\alpha_1} (x_2 - \bar{x}_2)^{\alpha_2} \quad \text{s.t. } x_1 + x_2 = x. \tag{10}$$

But a logarithmic transform of the maximand in (10) gives us (9) for $n = 2$ and hence (3) as the solution with $n = 2$.

We are back, therefore, to the results in (7) for the case of $n = 2$, which we have already discussed in Section 3.1. The two-person Nash bargaining model with fixed $\bar{x}_1$, $\bar{x}_2$, α_1, and α_2 leads to one of the three patterns for intra-household inequality, shown in (7a), (7b), and (7c) as total household resources increase. In the symmetric bargaining model, with $\alpha_1 = \alpha_2$, we have $\sigma_{\bar{x}\alpha} = \sigma_{\alpha}^2 = 0$ and therefore case (7a)—inequality decreases continuously. Since none of these outcomes is like the Kuznets curve observed in the data (Haddad and Kanbur 1990c), this model will have to be modified. Haddad and Kanbur (1990b) consider endogenizing $\bar{x}_1$ and $\bar{x}_2$ as x changes and find that, under certain conditions, intra-household inequality does indeed follow a Kuznets curve.

4. A Further Application: Children as Public Goods

The two-person Nash bargaining framework is clearly inappropriate when there are children involved, unless we assume that the welfare of children is subsumed under the objective function of one of the two players. When children are present, one way of modelling their role in the household is as public goods, from which adults get utility but towards the maintenance of which each adult makes a voluntary contribution. This perspective, which is reflected, for example, in the policy debate on whether welfare payments intended for children should be given through the father or the mother, leads to a model of non-cooperative Nash equilibrium between the players, in a game over contributions for child upkeep. What are the implications of this model for intra-household inequality?

Consider the case where there are two adults, indexed 1 and 2, and a child, indexed 3. The consumptions of the three individuals are x_1, x_2, and x_3. The two adults have individual resources y_1 and y_2, which they decide to split between own consumptions, x_i, and contributions to the child's consumption, c_i. Clearly, $c_1 + c_2 = x_3$. The child's consumption is a public good; i.e. x_3 enters both adults' utility functions (along with their own respective consumptions). Each adult decides on his or her contribution to child consumption conditional upon the other adults' contribution.

Let adult i's utility function be given by

$$u_i = \gamma_i \ln (x_i - \bar{m}_i) + (1 - \gamma_i)\ln(c_1 + c_2 - \bar{x}_3) \qquad i = 1, 2. \tag{11}$$

This is a Stone–Geary form with minimum consumptions for the adult and $\bar{m}_3$ for the child. The weights on the contribution of own consumption and child consumption (after logarithmic transformation) are γ_i and $(l - \gamma_i)$. For simplicity, we assume that neither adult's own consumption affects the other's utility. The two adults solve the problems:

$$\max_{x_i, c_i} \gamma_i \ln(x_i - \bar{m}_i) + (1 - \gamma_i) \ln(c_i + c_j - \bar{m}_3)$$

$$\text{s.t.} \qquad x_i + c_i = y_i \qquad i = 1, 2; \qquad j = \begin{cases} 1 \text{ if } i = 2 \\ 2 \text{ if } i = 1 \end{cases} \tag{12}$$

This leads to the following solutions for $i = 1, 2$:

$$x_1 = \bar{m}_1 + \gamma_1 \left[y_1 - (\bar{m}_1 + \bar{m}_3 - c_2) \right] \tag{13a}$$

$$c_1 = [\bar{m}_3 - c_2] + (1 - \gamma_1) \left[y_1 - (\bar{m}_1 + \bar{m}_3 - c_2) \right] \tag{13b}$$

$$x_2 = \bar{m}_2 + \gamma_2 \left[y_2 - (\bar{m}_2 + \bar{m}_3 - c_1) \right] \tag{14a}$$

$$c_2 = [\bar{m}_3 - c_1] + (1 - \gamma_2) \left[y_2 - (\bar{m}_2 + \bar{m}_3 - c_1) \right] \tag{14b}$$

A number of authors have considered the utility function (11) for public good games (e.g. Ulph 1988, Woolley, 1988) and have derived the Nash equilibrium solution to c_1 and c_2. Solving for c_1 and c_2 simultaneously in (13b) and (14b), we get the following as interior solutions to the Nash game:

$$c_1 = \frac{(1 - \gamma_1)\,y_1 - \gamma_1(1 - \gamma_2)\,y_2 + \gamma_1(1 - \gamma_2)\,\bar{x}_3 - (1 - \gamma_1)\,\bar{x}_1 + \gamma_1(1 - \gamma_2)\,\bar{x}_2}{1 - \gamma_1\gamma_2}, \quad (15)$$

$$c_2 = \frac{(1 - \gamma_2)\,y_2 - \gamma_2(1 - \gamma_1)\,y_1 + \gamma_2(1 - \gamma_1)\,\bar{x}_3 - (1 - \gamma_2)\,\bar{x}_2 + \gamma_2(1 - \gamma_1)\,\bar{x}_1}{1 - \gamma_1\gamma_2}. \quad (16)$$

Using these in (13a) and (14a), and noting that $x_3 = c_1 + c_2$, we have a complete characterization of consumption allocation in the interior Nash equilibrium:

$$x_1 = \frac{\gamma_1(1 - \gamma_2)\,(y_1 + y_2) + (1 - \gamma_1)\,\bar{m}_1 - \gamma_1(1 - \gamma_2)\,\bar{m}_2 - \gamma_1(1 - \gamma_2)\,\bar{m}_3}{1 - \gamma_1\gamma_2};$$

$$x_2 = \frac{\gamma_2(1 - \gamma_1)\,(y_1 + y_2) + (1 - \gamma_2)\,\bar{m}_2 - \gamma_2(1 - \gamma_1)\,\bar{m}_1 - \gamma_2(1 - \gamma_1)\,\bar{m}_3}{1 - \gamma_1\gamma_2}; \quad (17)$$

$$x_3 = \frac{(1 - \gamma_1)\,(1 - \gamma_2)\,(y_1 + y_2) + [\gamma_1(1 - \gamma_2) + \gamma_2(1 - \gamma_1)]\,\bar{m}_3}{1 - \gamma_1\gamma_2}$$

$$\frac{-(1 - \gamma_1)\,(1 - \gamma_2)\,(\bar{m}_1 + \bar{m}_2)}{1 - \gamma_1\gamma_2}.$$

It will be seen that the equations in (17) are in fact in the form of a linear expenditure system. If we define the following:

$$x = y_1 + y_2;$$

$$\alpha_1 = \frac{\gamma_1(1 - \gamma_2)}{1 - \gamma_1\gamma_2}; \qquad \alpha_2 = \frac{\gamma_2(1 - \gamma_1)}{1 - \gamma_1\gamma_2}; \qquad \alpha_3 = \frac{(1 - \gamma_1)\,(1 - \gamma_2)}{1 - \gamma_1\gamma_2} \quad (18)$$

$$\bar{x}_1 = \bar{m}_1; \qquad \bar{x}_2 = \bar{m}_2; \qquad \bar{x}_3 = \bar{m}_3,$$

then it is seen that (17) is nothing other than (3) for $i = 1, 2, 3$. Thus, the reduced form of the children as a public goods model of intra-household allocation, where preferences of adults as between own consumption and child's consumption are given by Stone–Geary utility functions, leads once again to the linear expenditure system.

Equations (17) and (18) can be used to discuss intra-household inequality in this model. Notice first of all that the allocation depends only on $x = y_1 + y_2$, i.e. on total household resources. The division of income does not matter. This is a strong result which has immediate policy implications. It suggests that in this framework the policy debate on targeting of child payments to the mother or the father is irrelevant—the public goods game serves as a perfect aggregator, and what matters is the total level of resources.

As discussed by Bergstrom and Varian (1985), the above is a general result for public goods, and does not depend on the Stone–Geary utility function.

However, what the linear expenditure specialization allows us to do is to consider explicitly the behaviour of inequality as a function of total household resources. We know from the discussion in Section 3 that only one of three outcomes is possible: inequality always increasing, inequality always decreasing, or a U shape where inequality first decreases and then increases. To the extent that the empirical evidence points to an inverse-U shape where inequality first increases and then decreases, this is an argument against the children as a public goods model—at least against the interior Nash equilibrium solution of this model.

Consider now possible corner solutions. Following Woolley (1988), consider the case where one adult, say adult 2, is constrained to set $c_2 = 0$. Using this in (13) and (14), we get the following allocation as solution:

$$x_1 = \bar{m}_1 + \gamma_1 [y_1 - (\bar{m}_1 + \bar{m}_3)] \tag{19a}$$

$$x_2 = y_2 \tag{19b}$$

$$x_3 = \bar{m}_3 + (1 + \gamma_1)[y_1 - (\bar{m}_1 + \bar{m}_3)] \tag{19c}$$

It is seen immediately that the distribution of total household resources between the adults now *does* affect the intra-household allocation. Most particularly, increases in y_1 increase x_1 and x_3, but increases in y_2 only increase x_2. If we think of individual 2 as the male adult, this model does provide a rationalization of targeting extra resources to the female, since at least some of these will get to the child.

The allocation in (19) allows a richer variety of shapes in the relationship between intra-household inequality and total household resources, but it depends on how exactly the increase in resources is divided between y_1 and y_2. If increments are distributed in constant proportion, so that $y_1 = \delta x$ and $y_2 = (1 - \delta)x$, then we get the allocation

$$x_1 = (1 - \gamma_1)\bar{m}_1 - \gamma_1 \bar{m}_3 + \gamma_1 \delta x$$

$$x_2 = (1 - \delta)x \tag{20}$$

$$x_3 = \gamma_1 \bar{m}_3 - (1 - \gamma_1)\bar{m}_1 + \delta(1 - \gamma_1)x.$$

This is, of course, another linear expenditure system, so that a similar characterization to the one in (7) obtains. The only chance for a variation is if, after a certain level of x, the interior solution comes into play. This switch in regimes between two different linear expenditure systems can lead to a richer pattern of behaviour.

If the increment in x comes solely from y_2 (say, male income), then the behaviour depends on the position of x_2 relative to x_1 and x_3. If x_2 is already greater than x_1 and s_3, the inequality will increase inexorably. Consider now the case where x increases through increases in y_1 (female income). Unit increments in this are divided according as γ_1 to x_1 and $(1 - \gamma_1)$ to x_3. In this case both x_1 and x_3 will increase relative to x_2. Thus, inequality will decrease. It should then be clear that, if initial increments to household resources go to the male and subsequent increments to the female, then we will indeed get the Kuznets relationship of inequality first increasing and then decreasing as total household resources increase.

5. Conclusion: The Need for Nonlinear Extensions

We have seen that models of intra-household allocation that lead to linear expenditure system allocations imply very specific relationships between intra-household inequality and total household resources. We have derived these relationships and have argued that they can be used as reduced-form tests of particular models. Of course, this procedure has well-known problems, but it is hoped that this way of proceeding will give guidance on how the structural models should be modified. The essential message is that they have to be modified so as to make intra-household allocation *nonlinear* in total household resources, as follows.

1. In the household welfare maximization models this means using utility functions that are more general than the Stone–Geary form. It should be noted, however, that most generalizations of demand systems in the income dimension essentially involve introducing the logarithm of income as an independent variable. This monotonic transformation will not of course affect our conclusions on the *shape* of the relationship between intra-household inequality and total household resources. In any event, most attention in generalized demand systems is given to the cross-price effects (e.g. the 'Almost Ideal Demand System' of Deaton and Muellbauer, 1980) across commodities, an issue that is not relevant to the models developed here.

2. In the Nash co-operative bargaining models, the modifications must involve endogenizing the threat points as total household resources increase. This is done by Haddad and Kanbur (1990*b*), who find that with this modification a Kuznets curve *is* possible.

3. In the children-as-public-goods model, departures from the Stone–Geary utility function are likely to make the solution intractable. An alternative is to examine corner solutions of the Nash game, as a way not only of possibly generating the Kuznets curve, but also of rationalizing policy concerns about the need to target incremental resources to female adults.

All three of these avenues hold out interesting possibilities for further research.

References

Behrman, J. and Deolalikar, A. (1989), 'Health and Nutrition', in H. Chenery and
T. N. Srinivasan (eds.), *Handbook of Development Economics*, North-Holland,
Amsterdam.

Bergstrom, T. C. and Varian, H. R. (1985), 'When Are Nash Equilibria Independent
of the Distribution of Agents' Characteristics?' *Review of Economic Studies*, 52:
715–18.

Deaton, A. and Muellbauer, J. (1980), 'An Almost Ideal Demand System', *American
Economic Review*, 100: 866–81.

Haddad, L. and Kanbur, R. (1990a), 'How Serious is the Neglect of Intra-Household
Inequality?' *Economic Journal*,

———— (1990b), 'Are Better Off Households More Unequal or Less Unequal?'
PRE Working Paper, no. 373, World Bank, Washington, DC.

———— (1990c), 'Is There an Intra-Household Kuznets Curve?' PRE Working
Paper, no. 466, World Bank, Washington, DC.

Sen, A. K. (1984), 'Family and Food: Sex Bias in Poverty', in A. K. Sen, *Resources,
Values and Development*, Oxford, Basil Blackwell.

Ulph, D. (1988), 'A General Non-Cooperative Nash Model of Household Consumption Behavior', mimeo, University of Bristol.

Woolley, F. (1988), 'A Non-Cooperative Model of Family Decision Making',
Working Paper no. TIDI/125, London School of Economics.

12

The Entitlement Approach to Famine:
An Assessment

SIDDIQ OSMANI

1. Introduction

Nothing excites intellectual curiosity more than the overturning of a time-honoured belief. This is specially so when that overturning is accomplished by scholarly analysis, as distinct from Messianic rhetoric. So when as highly acclaimed a scholar as Amartya Sen challenged the popular belief that famine means shortage of food, it inevitably caused a stir.

The famine that had killed two to three million people and brought starvation to millions more in Bengal in 1943 was not, he maintained, a result of shortage of food (Sen 1976, 1977). What's more, he went on to argue, the Bengal famine was by no means unique in this regard. He showed that many contemporary famines in Asia and Africa shared this property of not being caused by reduced availability of food (Sen 1981*b*). Famine, he concluded, is a case of people not having enough food to eat, but not necessarily of there not being enough food to go around. From this emerged what has come to be known as the 'entitlement approach' to hunger and famine—an approach that focuses attention on people having or not having enough command over food, as distinct from there being or not being enough food to be eaten.

Over the years, Sen and others following his lead have extended the reach of the entitlement approach from its initial concern with the genesis of famine. In a more recent treatise, for example, Drèze and Sen (1989) have skilfully utilized the insights of this approach to shed radically new light on the policy issues relating to famine relief and the more widespread problem of combating endemic hunger. To many, these insights have for ever changed the way they perceive the problems of hunger and famine.[1]

But, for all the adulation it has received, the entitlement approach has not gone unchallenged. Although it is perhaps fair to say that those who have delved into Sen's copious writings on this matter have generally come out impressed with his arguments, a significant strand of critical reaction has persisted to this day. A major objective of this paper is to assess the merit

I have benefited from helpful comments of Derseh Endale and Amartya Sen on an earlier draft, but I am alone responsible for the views and interpretations contained in the paper.

[1] As Robert Solow remarks in his review of the Drèze–Sen book, 'It has changed the way I will think about famine relief from now on' (Solow 1991, p. 23).

of this critical literature with a view to forming a judgement as to where exactly the entitlement approach now stands.

I am not going to attempt a comprehensive assessment of the whole of the critical literature. It is convenient to divide this literature into two parts: one that questions the *analytical* merit of the entitlement approach as a tool for understanding famines in general, and one that takes issue with Sen's *empirical* analysis of particular famines. The two parts are not necessarily independent, but they are nevertheless distinct. I shall concentrate on the first part, delving into the empirical literature only in so far as issues relating to particular famines are relevant for understanding disputes at the analytical level.

I begin in Section 2 by sketching out the conceptual apparatus of the entitlement approach. In doing so, I draw attention to a certain transition that seems to have occurred between Sen's earliest formulation and the later ones. I attach some importance to this transition, because I believe that the failure to notice it may be responsible at least in part for some of the confusion surrounding the entitlement approach. An attempt is then made in Section 3 to reach a clear understanding of what the entitlement approach really claims, and what it does not. In Section 4 I take up the major criticisms of the entitlement approach, and evaluate their merit in the light of the preceding account of what I believe the entitlement approach to be really about. Section 5 provides a brief summary and some concluding remarks.

2. The Conceptual Apparatus of the Entitlement Approach

The basic unit of analysis is an individual person. For practical purposes, however, the analysis can also be conducted at collective levels such as household, group, or class by using the standard device of assuming a 'representative individual'.

2.1. The Basic Concepts

The analysis is built upon three basic conceptual categories: the endowment set, the entitlement set, and the entitlement-mapping (or E-mapping, for short).

The *endowment set* is defined as the combination of all resources legally owned by a person. In this definition, 'resources' include both tangible assets, such as land, equipment, and animals, and intangibles, such as knowledge and skill, labour power, or membership of a particular community. Furthermore, the word 'legally' has to be interpreted broadly to mean conforming to established social norms and practices, and not merely to what is sanctioned formally by the state.[2]

---

[2] The need for adopting such a broad interpretation arises from the fact that, while legal ownership in the modern sense is often non-existent in traditional societies, especially in relation to landed property, some notion of ownership none the less exists based on conventions.

The *entitlement set* is defined as the set of all possible combinations of goods and services that a person can legally obtain by using the resources of her endowment set. This cryptic definition calls for a little elaboration, however. First, the definition recognizes that from any given set of resources one may be able to obtain many different combinations of final goods and services, although at any point in time a person will be seen to be enjoying only one of those possible combinations, depending on her tastes and preferences. The entitlement set refers to all the possible combinations, not just the one actually being enjoyed. Second, resources may be used in many different ways to obtain the final goods and services. For example, a farmer may use his land, labour, and other resources to produce the food he wants; a labourer may exchange his labour power to secure his food; a fisherman may first use his labour, equipment, and fishing boat to produce a catch of fish and then exchange it to get the rice he wants; an unemployed person may use his resource of 'citizenship of a welfare state' to claim a transfer of state funds in the form of unemployment benefit. These acts of production, exchange, and transfer are all different ways of using one's resources. Third, the manner in which a person uses his resources must have the sanction of the law of the land, again interpreted in the broadest sense of the term; thus, the commodities that can be obtained through looting (by using muscle power in an illegal fashion) are not counted as part of a person's entitlement set.

The *entitlement mapping*, or *E-mapping*, is simply the relationship between the endowment set on the one hand and the entitlement set on the other. Roughly speaking, it shows the rates at which the resources of the endowment set can be converted into goods and services included in the entitlement set. For example, an E-mapping includes, for the farmer, the input–output ratios in farm production; for the labourer, the ratio between money wage and the price of food, i.e. the real wage rate; for the fisherman, both the input–output ratio in fishing and the relative price of fish and rice; and for the unemployed person, the rate of unemployment benefit. Thus, an E-mapping would in general have three broad components: a production component containing various input–output ratios (or, more generally, production functions), an exchange component[3] made up of rates of exchange involved in trading,[4] and a transfer component.[5]

---

[3] Note that wage employment, i.e the trading of labour-power, is a part of the exchange mapping. Ghose (1982) seems to have overlooked this point when he suggested that Sen's framework of 'exchange entitlement' needs to be broadened to include analysis based on 'employment entitlement'.

[4] Strictly speaking, the exchange mapping includes, in addition to rates of exchange, any restriction that may exist on trading, such a quantity rationing, involuntary unemployment, etc.

[5] It is worth noting that the transfer component includes only those transfers to which a person is legally entitled—for example, social security provisions of the state. This leaves out not only illegal transfers (such as stealing and looting), but also non-entitlement transfers, such as charity. Although there is nothing illegal about receiving charity, it is not counted as part of entitlement mapping for the simple reason that one is not legally entitled to charity, whatever may be one's view about the poor's moral entitlement to it. The general point is that entitlement analysis is concerned with legal as distinct from moral entitlement.

The following diagram shows the relationship among the three basic concepts:

$$\text{Endowment} \xrightarrow{\text{E-mapping}} \text{Entitlement}$$

Next follows the concept of *entitlement failure*, which is derived from the three basic concepts and plays a crucial role in the analysis of famines. A person is said to suffer from the failure of food entitlement when her entitlement set does not contain enough food to enable her to avoid starvation in the absence of non-entitlement transfers, such as charity; it means that, no matter how a person may reallocate resources to obtain the food she wants, she cannot get the minimum amount needed to escape starvation. A *famine* occurs when a large number of people within a community suffer from such entitlement failures at the same time.

It is useful to note at this stage one important aspect of the causal structure that binds these concepts together. A moment's reflection will show that, while all three basic categories can in principle affect each other, there nevertheless exists an important asymmetry between entitlement on the one hand and endowment and E-mapping on the other. In the case of both endowment and E-mapping, the definitions allow for the effect of exogenous factors; that is, it is granted that either of them may change without any prior change in any of the other two categories,[6] but the same is not true of entitlement. Since the entitlement set is derived by applying E-mapping on the endowment set, it is only through changes in either endowment or E-mapping that any change in entitlement can occur. Note that this is not a theory or a hypothesis, but simply a logical implication of the definitions. It then follows that 'entitlement failure', and thus famine, can occur only through some adverse change in either endowment or E-mapping or both. This leads to the useful organizing principle that all possible causes of famines can be classified into two broad groups: one that affects the endowment set and the other that affects the entitlement mappings. In a sense, this organizing principle can be regarded as the core of the entitlement approach. We shall come to appreciate its significance as we proceed further.

For some purposes, a slightly different way of classifying the causal factors may be useful. Noting that E-mapping consists of three different kinds of relations, i.e. production, exchange, and transfer, one can identify four distinct sources of entitlement failure: endowment loss, production failure, exchange failure, and transfer failure. For people who do not rely primarily on exchange to obtain their staple food, entitlement failure would occur through the first two of the four channels. This case is described by

---

[6] For example, endowment may change exogenously when a farmer happens to inherit the land of his father, or E-mapping can change exogenously when, for instance, adverse weather reduces the crop output, or the government raises the price of rationed food.

Sen as *direct entitlement failure*. When exchange is involved, then any one of the first three channels may act as the conduit of entitlement failure. For example, a fisherman may lose his boat (an endowment loss), which will prevent him from catching the fish that he must exchange in order to get his staple food, rice; or his boat may be intact but his catch of fish may still be too inadequate (production failure) to be exchanged for the minimum amount of rice he needs; or both endowment and production may remain intact, and yet he may not get enough rice because the relative price of fish has slumped (exchange failure). In all these cases, a *trade entitlement failure* will be said to have occurred.[7]

The point of this dichotomy between direct and trade entitlement failures is to draw attention to the fact that the genesis of famines may be very different as between subsistence and exchange economies. Direct entitlement failures have traditionally been the major cause of famine in the subsistence-oriented peasant economies of the past. But in the modern exchange economies, famine caused by trade entitlement failures is a very distinct possibility. Indeed, one of Sen's major contributions to our understanding of hunger has been to demonstrate how this distinctive mechanism has been at work in modern-day famines.

2.2. Transition in the Conceptual Framework

The preceding discussion has been based on the formulation presented by Sen in his book *Poverty and Famines* (Sen 1981*b*) and in his subsequent writings. In both terminology and content, this formulation differs somewhat from Sen's earliest presentations of the entitlement approach (e.g. in Sen 1977). The newer framework is, in my view, more complete and consistent. But it is my impression that the transition that has taken place in the conceptual framework has gone largely unnoticed, so that, while commenting on the entitlement approach, people still often cling to the older framework. This has sometimes resulted in a misunderstanding about the nature and objective of the entitlement approach, leading also to unwarranted criticisms. It is therefore necessary to clarify how the formulation has changed over time.

It is useful to begin by considering the term 'exchange entitlement'—a term we have not used so far (for reasons to be explained below). It was in the language of 'exchange entitlement'—rather than 'entitlement', without the qualifier 'exchange'—that Sen originally launched his analysis of

---

[7] It should be noted that, unlike the dichotomy between endowment failure and mapping failure, this dichotomy between direct and trade entitlement failures is neither disjoint nor exhaustive. It is not disjoint because both direct and trade entitlement failures can occur as a result of endowment loss or production failure. And it is not exhaustive because it leaves out the possibility of transfer failure.

famines. Specifically, famine was described as the failure of exchange entitlement. The term was defined as follows:

With an initial endowment x of commodities (including labour), the exchange entitlements offered by a particular set of market configurations (in addition to direct production possibilities) can be seen as the set $S(x)$ of all commodity bundles that can be acquired starting from x. (Formally, therefore, the set of exchange entitlements can be seen as a mapping $S(\cdot)$ from a given person's endowment vectors to availability sets of commodity vectors.) (Sen 1977, p. 34)

Two features of this definition are worth noting. First, Sen seems to suggest that 'exchange entitlement' stands for both $S(x)$ and $S(\cdot)$—the entitlement set and the entitlement mapping respectively, as we have called them. The first sentence points to entitlement set, but the second sentence, within parenthesis, seems to point to entitlement mapping. Secondly, the definition of exchange entitlement seems to exclude the 'production' channel of converting endowments into entitlements.

Although formally both the set and the mapping were implied by the term, it is clear from Sen's subsequent remarks that his stress was on the mapping interpretation. One of the clearest examples is the following statement: 'Even in an exchange economy, starvation can result from the loss of assets (including health) *rather than* exchange entitlement variations' (Sen 1977, p. 35; emphasis added). Sen is drawing a distinction here between starvation caused by loss of assets and starvation caused by exchange entitlement variation. But the need for this distinction would not arise if the term 'exchange entitlement' were to refer to the set $S(x)$, for in that case starvation caused by loss of assets would also be called starvation caused by exchange entitlement variation. By making this distinction, then, Sen must be implying that exchange entitlement variation refers only to the shift in $S(\cdot)$. In other words, the term 'exchange entitlement' is to be equated with the mapping $S(\cdot)$, as distinct from the set $S(x)$.

The second feature of the definition—namely, the exclusion of the production channel—also gets further support from various remarks of Sen. For example, 'famines *can* certainly take place *without* shifts in exchange entitlement. An example is a famine affecting people who typically eat what they produce, e.g. hunters, or peasants in an economy with little exchange' (Sen 1977, p. 35; emphasis original).

These two features of the original formulation imply a certain restriction on the concept of 'failure of exchange entitlement' (FEE). In so far as exchange entitlement refers only to the mapping, starvation caused by the loss of assets would not qualify as a case of FEE; similarly, in so far as the production channel is excluded from the mapping, starvation suffered by direct producers of food as a result of a crop failure would not count as FEE. Accordingly, when famine is said to be caused by the failure of exchange entitlement, some categories of famine will be left out of reach of the entitlement approach. As we shall see later in the paper, this implicit restriction has been responsible for a good deal of confusion about the real message of the entitlement approach.

It should be noted that the restrictive nature of this formulation had a certain redeeming logic in the particular context in which it arose. The context was the great Bengal famine of 1943, and Sen was arguing that the proximate cause of this famine was neither loss of production nor loss of assets, but adverse shift in people's command over food in the market-place. Given this hypothesis, there was no great harm in excluding produc-tion loss from the analytical framework. Also, it made sense to stress the mapping interpretation of exchange entitlement, even though formally one could refer to both the set and the mapping in the same breath. There was no inconsistency in doing the latter, because if loss of assets (x) is disregarded, then any variation in $S(x)$ must come solely from variation in $S(\cdot)$, and any variation in $S(\cdot)$ must be reflected fully in a corresponding variation in $S(x)$. So, for the purposes of that specific empirical analysis, Sen's formulation of exchange entitlement was not particularly problematic.

But, as Sen later extended his analysis to other instances of famine, where the loss of both production and assets had played a more prominent role, the need for a more general framework became obvious. It was then no longer possible to exclude production; moreover, if entitlement variation caused by loss of assets was to be allowed, then it would have been singularly confusing to describe both $S(x)$ and $S(\cdot)$ by the same term. Both these concerns are taken care of in the formulations presented in Sen's later writings, beginning with Sen (1981a, 1981b). In the first place, production is explicitly included, along with exchange and transfer, in the definition of mapping. Secondly, two distinct terms are now employed to refer to the set and the mapping. The precise manner of making this distinction itself seems to have undergone some change over the years. The latest position, as spelt out in Drèze and Sen (1989, pp. 9–10, 23), seems to be as follows. The set is now described as the 'entitlement set' or just 'entitlement' (leaving out the qualifier 'exchange'), while the mapping is described by 'exchange entitle-ment', or 'exchange entitlement mapping', or simply 'E-mapping'. Famine is now defined as 'entitlement failure', rather than 'exchange entitlement failure' as in the past, thus leaving no room for doubt that famines caused by both endowment loss and mapping failure belong to the domain of entitlement analysis.

I have followed this formulation closely in this paper, with the exception that the qualifier 'exchange' has been eliminated not only from the descrip-tion of the set but also from that of the mapping. This has been done mainly to avoid any confusion that might arise from the term's original association with a more restricted framework of analysis.[8]

---

[8] There is also a second, essentially semantic, reason for avoiding it. Since exchange is only one of the three components of mapping (the other two being production and transfer), it does

To recapitulate, the original framework was restricted in two ways: (1) entitlement failure was seen to arise solely from variation in entitlement mapping; and (2) entitlement mapping was defined so as to exclude production. Both these restrictions were removed in the subsequent generalized framework, in which (1) entitlement failure was seen to arise from changes in both endowment set and entitlement mapping; and (2) entitlement mapping was defined comprehensively to include production, exchange, and transfer.

3.   The Entitlement Approach to Famine: What Does It Say?

The entitlement approach was designed initially to investigate the causes of famine. But what exactly does it say about causation? Put most succinctly, it says: famines are caused by entitlement failure. But this does not help matters much, because different people seem to attach different meanings to this statement. Underlying these differences are alternative interpretations of what the entitlement approach is supposed to be about.

3.1.   Three Interpretations of the Entitlement Approach

Broadly speaking, one can distinguish three different levels of interpretation of the entitlement approach: as a specific hypothesis which stresses the non-importance of food availability for modern famines; as a general hypothesis which lays stress on the failures of entitlement mapping for understanding famines in exchange economies; and as a general framework for analysing famines in any economy. More fully, we may set out these alternatives as follows.

1. *Specific hypothesis.* Modern famines are caused not so much by reduced availability of food as by adverse changes in the entitlement mapping of the poor—in particular, by deterioration in the exchange component of the mapping.

2. *General hypothesis.* In an exchange economy, famines are caused not so much by endowment failure as by adverse changes in the entitlement mapping of the poor—in particular, by deterioration in the exchange component of the mapping.

3. *General framework.* By seeing famines as entitlement failure, and by noting that entitlement failure can occur only because of an adverse change in either endowment or entitlement mappings, the entitlement approach

---

not seem very illuminating to use 'exchange entitlement' as a synonym for 'entitlement mapping'. Sen of course argues that production can also be seen as an exchange—to wit, an exchange with nature; but that still leaves out transfer, which is typically unilateral in character and thus rather hard to be seen as an act of exchange.

offers a useful organizing framework for studying the causes of famines in any kind of economy.

The first interpretation places the entitlement approach in direct contradiction with the popular notion that famines are caused by reduced availability of food—a notion that has been dubbed by Sen as 'FAD' (food availability decline). To accept the entitlement approach is thus taken to imply the denial of the FAD hypothesis.[9]

The second interpretation, by contrast, does not deny that famines can be caused by food availability decline; but it insists on three things. (1) If food availability does play a role, it will do so mainly by worsening the entitlement mapping of a person (for example, by raising the price of food). (2) Factors other than food availability decline can also cause famines by worsening the entitlement mapping; for example, a general inflationary pressure fuelled by excessive monetary expansion can do so by raising the price of food. (3) Whatever it is that causes famine in an exchange economy will typically do so by worsening the entitlement mapping as opposed to depleting the endowment set. It is this interpretation that seems to lie behind one strand of opinion which takes the entitlement approach to mean that famines are all about loss of purchasing power.[10]

This is clearly a more general hypothesis than the previous one, in so far as it allows that famines can be caused by food availability decline as well as by other factors. Although very general, this is still an empirical hypothesis, however, in the sense that it is a falsifiable proposition. It denies something that is in principle testable—specifically, it denies that depletion of endowment sets is a major cause of famines in the modern world.

By contrast, the third interpretation is not really a hypothesis at all. In this interpretation, to say that famines are caused by entitlement failure is not, strictly speaking, a causal statement but a definitional one. That is to say, entitlement failure defines rather than causes famines. It is, however, a very useful definition for the purpose of organizing the search for causes; it immediately focuses the mind of the analyst searching for causes, since by definition entitlement failure can occur only through endowment loss or through the breakdown of entitlement mapping. The rationale of the entitlement approach is then not to suggest, or to deny, any particular hypothesis about what causes famines, but rather to direct the search for causes into two broad channels, one involving the endowment set and the

---

[9] Rangasami is not alone in accepting this interpretation when she says, 'Amartya Sen's contribution that famine *is not* caused by a "fall in food availability" is of critical importance' (Rangasami 1985, p. 1797; emphasis added).

[10] See e.g. Kula (1989, p. 13): 'the so-called entitlement approach, which attributes famines primarily to decline in purchasing power amongst sections of the population'.

other involving the entitlement mapping. The entitlement approach is thus essentially a framework of analysis.[11]

I shall argue that it is the third interpretation—which I shall call the *approach-view*—that can be ascribed to Sen himself. He is in fact quite categorical about this, as the following statements would testify: 'the entitlement approach provides a general framework for analysing famines rather than one particular hypothesis about their causation' (Sen 1981*b*, p. 162); and, again, 'the main interest in the approach does not, I think, lie in checking whether most famines are related to entitlement failures, which I suspect would be found to be the case, but in characterizing the nature and causes of entitlement failures where such failures occur' (Sen 1981*b*, p. 164).

But we don't have to taken Sen's words for it; as we shall see below, the approach-view is also the only interpretation that is consistent with the generalized conceptual framework developed in *Poverty and Famines*. In spite of that, the first two interpretations—which together I shall call the *hypothesis-view*—continue to be popular, long after the publication of that book. Why? Without first answering this question, one cannot make a fully convincing case for accepting the third interpretation. So that is what I try to do below. I first speculate why the hypothesis-view has seemed plausible to so many people, then explain why this view has to be rejected despite its apparent plausibility, and in the process establish the case for the approach-view.

I believe there are two main reasons for the continued popularity of the hypothesis-view. First, it is partly a legacy of Sen's initial formulation of the entitlement approach, which appeared to give some support to the first two interpretations. Secondly, the nature of Sen's criticism of FAD has been widely misunderstood. Parallel to the distinction between entitlement hypothesis and entitlement approach, there is also a distinction between FAD hypothesis and FAD approach. Sen's objective was to criticize the FAD approach; but this was misinterpreted as a rejection of the FAD hypothesis, which in turn led to the view that he was trying to propose an alternative hypothesis.

3.2.   Legacy of the Initial Formulation

We have seen earlier how the term 'exchange entitlement' was given a dual meaning in Sen's original formulation of the entitlement approach. Accord-

---

[11] Actually, in a very weak sense it too represents a hypothesis, since it too denies something that is in principle testable. Recall that the entitlement set is defined as the bundle of goods and services that can be legally obtained starting from the endowment set, which is itself defined as having the sanction of the law. So a crisis originating from extra-legal claims on resources will not be recognized as such by the entitlement approach. Furthermore, by insisting that famines are caused by entitlement failure, one denies also that famines can be a matter of wilful starvation. However, since both these are very unusual circumstances (at least as a mass phenomenon), their denial does not constitute much of a hypothesis. For more on this point, see Sen (1981*b*, p. 164).

ing to one of its two meanings, 'exchange entitlement' referred to the mapping from endowments to food availability, excluding the production channel. So the failure of exchange entitlement (FEE) would refer only to those instances of starvation that are not induced by adverse changes either in endowments or in production mapping.

It is possible that this restriction on the meaning of FEE has contributed to the popularity of the hypothesis-view of entitlement theory. Suppose a famine strikes by reducing the subsistence production of food for a large number of farmers. Then the restriction implies that this will not be a case of failure of exchange entitlement (FEE), but will certainly be a case of food availability decline (FAD). FEE and FAD can thus be seen as alternative explanations of famine. From here it is a small step to argue that holding the view that famines are caused by FEE implies a denial of FAD, which is precisely what is argued in the first interpretation of the entitlement approach.

The second interpretation also follows from the same restriction, specifically from that part of the restriction that excludes starvation resulting from adverse changes in endowments. Because of this exclusion, the act of equating famines with FEE can be seen as tantamount to proposing the hypothesis that famines are caused only by adverse changes in entitlement mappings. This is of course precisely what is suggested by the second interpretation of the entitlement approach.[12]

Thus, both variants of the hypothesis-view of entitlement theory can be seen to derive their sustenance from the restrictive nature of its initial formulation. But this interpretation can no longer be sustained as soon as one embraces the general conceptual framework developed in *Poverty and Famines*. The crucial distinguishing feature of this framework, as contrasted with the initial formulation, is that entitlement failure now becomes a comprehensive concept, without any restriction whatsoever on the kind of starvation it is allowed to encompass.[13] Entitlement, it may be recalled, is defined in this framework as the entitlement set, not as the entitlement mapping; and in defining the entitlement set all possible mappings are considered, including the production mapping. So any adverse change in the endowment set, or in any of the mappings—including the production mapping—will have its repercussions on a person's entitlement. Accordingly, entitlement failure (FEE) will now refer to any kind of starvation, whether originating from endowment loss, production failure, or the failure of any other mapping.[14]

---

[12] Sen himself appears to lend support to this interpretation by saying, 'The exchange entitlement approach focuses on shifts in the mapping $S(\cdot)$, which depends on relative values, rather than shifts in x (i.e. amounts of physical endowments)' (Sen 1977, p. 35).

[13] Save the minor, and rather unlikely, exceptions mentioned in the fn. 12.

[14] Note that, although by entitlement failure we are now referring to the contraction of the entitlement set, rather than the failure of exchange entitlement mapping, we continue to use the acronym FEE for entitlement failure in deference to the currency it has gained in the literature.

Since FEE now embraces all kinds of starvation, the statement that famines are caused by FEE must be definitionally true; as such, it cannot contain any causal hypothesis. Specifically, since starvation resulting from endowment loss is also now included in FEE, it is no longer possible to say that the entitlement theory deals only with the hypothesis that famines are caused by the failure of entitlement mapping. Thus, the second interpretation can no longer be sustained.

The same is true about the first interpretation: one can no longer interpret entitlement theory as the denial of FAD. Once again, it is the comprehensive nature of the concept of FEE that rules out this interpretation. Think of any conceivable way in which FAD can cause starvation—this will be seen as a case of entitlement failure. For example, if FAD occurs as a result of loss of production, then the subsistence producers will face what has been described earlier as 'direct entitlement failure'. If the loss of production also causes starvation to wage-labourers by forcing them out of employment, or by reducing their wages, this will entail the failure of exchange mapping, leading to 'trade entitlement failure'. If the reduced availability of food causes distress to purchasers of food by raising its price, then this will be another case of 'trade entitlement failure'. Thus, one way or the other, FAD can operate only by causing entitlement failures, so that any case of FAD-induced starvation must count as a case of FEE. As a result, when the entitlement theory defines famine as FEE, it cannot logically rule out the FAD hypothesis. The true relationship between FAD and FEE is then one of subsumption rather than contradiction.

Thus, neither of the two hypothesis-view interpretations is consistent with the comprehensive framework of entitlement analysis. The only valid interpretation is the third one, which purports to advance no causal hypothesis, only an organizing framework within which various causal influences can be systematically explored.

It is now easy to see why the entitlement approach has been subject to a variety of interpretation. At least in part, this has been due to the transition that has taken place in the framework of entitlement analysis. In one of the earliest responses to Sen's work, Alamgir (1980) popularized the contest between FEE and FAD as the essence of the entitlement approach. For this, he was later chastised by Reutlinger (1984), who argued that this contest was invalid because 'The attribution of a famine to FEE is not a hypothesis at all . . . By definition, a famine is a Fee . . .' (p. 885). This exchange neatly reflects the transition mentioned above. Alamgir was referring to the restricted formulation given in Sen (1977); and, as we have seen, this formulation did make it tempting to see FEE an alternative to FAD. Reutlinger, on the other hand, was reviewing the book *Poverty and Famines*; and, having absorbed the book's message that the entitlement approach was to be seen as a general framework of analysis which subsumes FAD, he went on to criticize Alamgir.

Since the framework of *Poverty and Famines* has superseded Sen's earlier writings, all those who, unlike Alamgir, wrote after its publication ought to have shared Reutlinger's understanding. Yet, many of them did not; the hypothesis-view, and especially the anti-FAD interpretation of entitlement theory, has continued to hold sway.[15] One can only suspect that the striking novelty of Sen's earliest writings on this matter had left such a lasting imprint on his readers' minds that many of them failed to notice the subsequent transition.

But I believe there is also another, perhaps more important, reason. This has to do with a misunderstanding about exactly what Sen was up to when he was lambasting the FAD view of famine.

3.3. FAD versus FEE: Hypothesis or Approach?

In all of his writings on famines and related matters, especially in his early writings, Sen has been utterly scathing in his criticism of FAD.[16] This has helped foster the notion that Sen's objective was to debunk the FAD hypothesis and to advance his own entitlement approach as an alternative hypothesis of famine causation. But, in my view, this is a misreading of his work. What Sen was actually doing was to pose a contest between the entitlement *approach* and the FAD *approach*, not between some entitlement *hypothesis* and the FAD *hypothesis*.

To see the contrast between these two contests, one first has to see the distinction between the FAD hypothesis and the FAD approach. To an extent, this distinction is the one between the specific and the general, though there is more to it than that. To say that a particular famine has been caused by serious shortfall in food availability is to advance the FAD hypothesis; to say that many a famine is caused by sudden decline in food availability is to express a judgement that the FAD hypothesis has wide applicability—but one is still talking about a hypothesis. However, to say that the best way to understand famines—all famines—is to look at what has happened to aggregate food availability is to propound the FAD *approach*.

It is the FAD *approach* whose usefulness Sen has so vehemently denied. There are two reasons for this denial, which also constitute the reasons for preferring the entitlement approach. These reasons can be described as plurality of causes and asymmetry of impact.

---

[15] Thus, for instance, even as late as in 1988, seven years after the publication of *Poverty and Famines*, Arnold finds it a weakness of the entitlement approach that it is not 'difficult to find examples of famines where there is clear evidence of a serious shortfall in food availability' (Arnold 1988, p. 45).

[16] So much so, that even such a sympathetic commentator as Reutlinger (1984, p. 885) was led to conclude: 'Sen himself, in my view, has overreacted to the excesses of those who hold that famines are caused by a food availability decline.'

1. *Plurality of causes.* Famines can occur without any decline in food availability; in such cases the FAD approach is evidently useless, while the entitlement approach is eminently suitable. Recall the organizing principle of the entitlement approach: it directs the search for causes into two broad channels—endowment loss and mapping failure—because whatever it is that causes a famine must work through either of these channels so as to impinge eventually on the entitlement set. So, if a famine happens to be caused by something other than food availability decline, the entitlement approach should in principle be able to identify the cause, while the FAD approach will have no clue about it.

2. *Asymmetry of impact.* Whether or not availability decline plays a causal role, the FAD-ist way of focusing on aggregate availability is not terribly illuminating, because famines typically affect some groups of people more than others, and some not at all; and we shall never know why this is so by looking simply at aggregate availability of food. By contrast, the entitlement approach should be able to explain such asymmetries by looking separately at the entitlement sets of different socio-economic classes.

These arguments are good enough to establish the superiority of the entitlement approach at the conceptual level. But Sen was not content merely to conduct the argument at an abstract level; he was also concerned to show that these analytical grounds were not empirically empty. This is what his four case studies in *Poverty and Famines* were meant to achieve. In each of these cases, he attempted to show that the FAD hypothesis did not hold. As a result, his empirical studies have an unmistakable flavour of being against the FAD hypothesis.

It is this that has led many to believe that Sen's objective was to debunk the FAD hypothesis and to put some entitlement hypothesis in its stead. But actually, the denial of the FAD hypothesis in those specific cases was only a means of justifying the general denial of the FAD approach, which was the real goal. In order to establish the first ground for rejecting the FAD approach—i.e. plurality of causes—he had to show that famines could occur without food availability decline; and that is what his case studies purported to show.

The 'means–goal' distinction between the two denials has an important implication for the kind of attitude an entitlement analyst ought to have towards the FAD hypothesis. In order to achieve the goal of debunking the FAD approach, it is not necessary to debunk the FAD hypothesis generally; that is to say, it is not necessary to claim that the FAD hypothesis can never be valid. All one needs to show is that the FAD hypothesis did not hold in some instances of famine, for this is good enough to establish the 'plural cause' ground for debunking the FAD approach. To put it differently, while the entitlement analyst will deny that food availability decline is a necessary condition of famine, he does not have to deny that it may be sufficient in particular instances.

It is also important to note that, by allowing the sufficiency of FAD in particular cases, the entitlement analyst does not have to face any contradiction with his own approach, because, as we have seen, his approach is comprehensive enough to subsume the cases of FAD-famine. That is why the entitlement approach has no real quarrel with the FAD hypothesis; its quarrel is only with the FAD approach.

Once it becomes clear that Sen's argument was not with the FAD hypothesis as such, it also becomes obvious that he was not proposing any alternative entitlement hypothesis. The argument was against the FAD approach, and his proposal was to replace it with the entitlement approach. Unfortunately, this distinction between hypothesis and approach has been lost on many a commentator, leading to a good deal of confusion as to what the entitlement analysis is all about and also, as we shall see in the next section, a good deal of misplaced criticism of the entitlement approach.

There is also a related confusion that persists even among those who seem to appreciate the fact that Sen's argument is really with the FAD approach. The following statement contains a typical expression of this confusion: 'Sen's immediate aim throughout *Poverty and Famines* is to discredit the traditional supply-side views of famines, which he labels the Food Availability Decline (or FAD) approach . . .' (Baulch 1987, p. 195). The confusion here consists in thinking that the essential feature of the FAD approach is its focus on the supply side, which the entitlement approach supposedly rejects in favour of demand side.[17]

In fact, the entitlement approach has nothing against the supply side; but it insists that the supply-side effects ought to be analysed not in terms of what they mean for aggregate food availability, but in terms of what they mean for the entitlement sets of different socio-economic groups. That is to say, it requires us to undertake a detailed and disaggregated study of how the supply side, as well as the demand side, affects the endowments sets and entitlement mappings of different people. In doing so, moreover, the entitlement approach insists that the supply–demand considerations must not be limited to the market for food alone. Instead, it requires us to look at all related markets, including the market for labour and the market for whatever a person may be selling in order to acquire food, and also at macroeconomic variables such as inflation, exchange rate, etc., all of which may affect a person's command over food. In short, the entitlement approach calls for the use of the general equilibrium method.

However, even the contrast between supply-side focus and general equilibrium does not fully capture the difference between the FAD approach and

---

[17] See also Devereux (1988, p. 272): 'entitlement is usually seen as a theory which focuses on demand failure, as contrasted with FAD, which emphasizes food supply failure'.

the entitlement approach. A crucial difference lies in the level of aggregation used. What the entitlement analyst finds particularly inadequate about the FAD approach is not so much its concern with supply as its focus on aggregate availability. By the some token, an aggregative general equilibrium analysis at the level of the whole economy would hardly be satisfactory from his point of view. What he demands is a general equilibrium analysis of the various forces affecting the disaggregated entitlement of different social classes.

Therefore, the real contrast between the FAD approach and the entitlement approach is not one between supply side on the one hand and demand side on the other, or even supply-and-demand combined on the other, but one between aggregate availability on the one hand and disaggregated entitlements on the other. Disaggregation is an essential feature of the entitlement approach.[18]

3.4   What the Entitlement Analysis is All About: In Five Capsules

To recapitulate, I shall sum up in the form of five brief propositions what, in my view, the entitlement approach to famine claims and what it does not.

First, the entitlement approach does not offer any hypothesis—either specific or general—about the causes of famine. In particular, when it is said that famines are caused by entitlement failures, this is not really meant to be a causal statement but rather a definitional one; that is, entitlement failure on a massive scale is to be seen as a definition rather than a cause of famine. The restrictive nature of Sen's earliest formulation of his analysis may have helped in part to promote the idea that he was suggesting a causal hypothesis, one that pits itself against the traditional hypothesis of food availability decline (FAD). But the framework of analysis developed in *Poverty and Famines* makes it abundantly clear that he was really proposing a general approach—i.e. an organizing framework for analysing famines, or

---

[18] It is therefore surprising to find that Patnaik should accuse the entitlement approach of lumping together such diverse social classes as property-owners and wage-labourers: 'The theoretical attempt to incorporate both social types under a generic concept appears to underlie the notion of exchange entitlement; for in this attempt, possession of means of production (enabling the production of commodities) and possession of labour power alone, are treated on par conceptually and subsumed under a single idea of "endowment" ' (Patnaik 1991, p. 2). She is apparently forgetting here that an analysis can be conducted at different levels of abstraction. What is a 'single idea' at the highest level of abstraction may need to be differentiated at a lower level. To draw an analogy from a field with which Patnaik should be thoroughly familiar, 'mode of production' is a single idea at the highest level of abstraction in the Marxist theory of history; but this does not mean that at the level of analysing concrete societies one can treat feudal and capitalist modes of production at par conceptually. In exactly the same way, endowment and entitlement may be expressed as single ideas at the highest level of abstraction, but this does not mean that, at the level of empirical analysis of famines, entitlements of those possessing means of production are to be treated at par with entitlements of those possessing only labour power. In fact, the very idea that these two cannot be treated at par is part of the motivation behind moving away from the aggregative FAD approach.

a framework for investigating many possible causal hypotheses—without being committed to any particular hypothesis. As a result, there is no such thing as an entitlement *hypothesis*; all we have is the entitlement *approach*.[19]

Secondly, the essence of the entitlement approach to famine is to explore the causes of entitlement failure by undertaking a disaggregated analysis of the entitlement sets of different socio-economic classes. Since the entitlement set is determined entirely by the endowment set and the entitlement mapping, such an analysis immediately directs our search for causes towards forces affecting endowments on the one hand and mappings on the other. In so doing, this approach allows us to evaluate a rich variety of causal hypotheses, which may include food availability decline as one of the contenders but need not be restricted to it.

Thirdly, just as the entitlement analysis does not offer any particular hypothesis, so it does not deny any either. Specifically, contrary to a common misconception, it does not deny that famines can sometimes be caused by food availability decline. But it does deny two things. First, it denies that famines are necessarily preceded by availability decline; in other words, it denies the necessity of the FAD hypothesis, without questioning its sufficiency. Secondly, the entitlement approach altogether denies the usefulness of the FAD *approach*, which refers to the traditional practice of regarding aggregate food availability as the focal variable for famine analysis. The contest is therefore between two approaches, not between two hypotheses. The entitlement approach subsumes the FAD hypothesis, but rejects the FAD approach.

Fourthly, the contrast between the entitlement approach and the FAD approach should not be seen, as it has sometimes been, as a contrast between demand-side and supply-side focus. The real contrast lies in the fact that the FAD approach focuses on aggregate availability, while the entitlement approach looks at disaggregated entitlements of different individuals or classes. In doing so, the entitlement approach considers supply, demand, and all other relevant variables within a general equilibrium framework.

Finally, the entitlement approach claims superiority over the FAD approach on two grounds:

1. *Plurality of causes.* There are famines that are not caused by food availability decline; in such cases, the FAD approach is totally useless, if not dangerously misleading, whereas the entitlement approach is in principle capable of identifying and analysing any such non-FAD famine.

2. *Asymmetry of impact.* Regardless of whether or not food availability decline acts as a causal mechanism, the focus on aggregate availability cannot explain why and how certain specific classes fall victim to famine

---

[19] We may also speak of the entitlement theory, so long as we interpret 'theory' broadly to mean a theoretical approach, not narrowly in the sense of a causal hypothesis.

while others escape; the entitlement approach, by contrast, is ideally suited for such disaggregated analysis.

4. Criticisms of the Entitlement Approach

In the light of the preceding discussion, we can now proceed to evaluate the various criticisms that have been made of the entitlement approach. For analytical convenience, we may group most of these criticisms under a number of headings.

One set of criticisms interprets the entitlement approach as a specific hypothesis, and then goes on to show that this hypothesis is not always valid. I have grouped them under the heading 'The Entitlement Approach Has Limited Applicability'. There follows a set of criticisms which purport to expose certain weaknesses of the entitlement approach as an analytical tool for famine analysis. These are classified under two headings: 'The Entitlement Approach Is Not Sufficiently Backward-Looking' and 'The Entitlement Approach Is Not Sufficiently Forward-Looking'. Finally, there is yet another set of criticisms which question whether there is anything new in the entitlement approach. These also are classified into two groups: 'The Entitlement Approach Says Nothing New: Conceptually', and 'The Entitlement Approach Says Nothing New: Historically'.

4.1. The Entitlement Approach Has Limited Applicability

Several authors have contested Sen's claim that some of the major famines he has examined were of non-FAD origin. The argument has raged mostly over the great Bengal famine of 1943 and the African famines of the 1970s. Who has had the better of the argument, though an important issue in its own right, is not something we shall be concerned with in this paper. What concerns us here is the claim of several of these critics that, by refuting Sen's empirical analysis, they have discredited the entitlement approach.

A typical example is Bowbrick, who, in an extended debate with Sen, has claimed to have refuted Sen's diagnosis of the great Bengal famine.[20] In his view, food availability decline was, after all, the most important cause of this famine, and not the loss of entitlements arising from war-induced inflationary pressure, as suggested by Sen. Although his empirical arguments relate to this particular famine, he goes on to draw a general analytical conclusion, which is our main concern here. He argues that 'Sen's theory of famine will lead to the wrong diagnosis and the wrong remedies for famine and will therefore worsen the situation' (Bowbrick 1986, p. 105).

This conclusion has two parts. There is first the claim that it was no accident that Sen misdiagnosed the Bengal famine, because his theory was

---

[20] See Bowbrick (1986, 1987) and Sen (1986, 1987); see also Allen (1986).

such that it could not but lead to the wrong diagnosis. Secondly, such misdiagnosis will worsen the situation further by suggesting the wrong remedies. We shall see that both of these analytical conclusions are false, even if one grants for the sake of argument that Sen did actually misdiagnose the Bengal famine.[21]

The first part of the claim, asserting the inevitability of misdiagnosis, is based on two premises. The first premiss holds that 'one cannot discuss famines without constantly taking into account aggregate food supply' (Bowbrick 1986, p. 106), the implication being that reduction in food supply necessarily plays a part in all famines. Bowbrick, however, simply asserts this proposition, because he nowhere establishes the necessity of food shortage as a precondition of famine. He does however make a case for its sufficiency, in the following manner. He defines three different degrees of food shortage: the first-degree shortage is defined as the situation in which, despite food shortage, widespread starvation can be avoided by redistributing food in the appropriate way, but the second- and third-degree shortages are such that not even a perfect distribution can avoid famine. Thus, famines will inevitably occur in the event of second- and third-degree shortages, and may very well occur even in the case of first-degree shortage owing to practical constraints on redistribution, especially if the population is already living close to the level of bare subsistence. It therefore follows that food shortage of whatever degree will often be sufficient to spark off a famine in a barely subsisting economy.

The second premiss lies in Bowbrick's interpretation of Sen's theory as a specific hypothesis that stands in opposition to the FAD hypothesis. He suggests that the entitlement theory proposes a 'redistribution hypothesis', according to which famines are caused simply by redistribution of command over food (away from the poor and the vulnerable), unaccompanied by any reduction in aggregate food availability.

He then goes on to argue that an approach that explains famines in purely distributional terms will inevitably misdiagnose cases involving second- and third-degree shortage. For, even if these cases are accompanied by adverse redistribution of food, such redistribution in itself cannot be blamed for the famine because even in the absence of any redistribution famine would still have occurred. The situation is slightly different for first-degree shortage, because it is now conceivable that unless some adverse distribution had occurred the shortage alone might not have been enough to induce famine. Accordingly, Bowbrick is willing to concede some ground to the entitlement approach in the case of first-degree shortage. But even in this case he would prefer to take a shortage-focused view, because, even though redistribution

---

[21] Apart from Bowbrick, Alamgir (1980), Basu (1986), and Goswami (1990) have also questioned Sen's belittling of food availability decline as a contributory factor in the Bengal famine of 1943. In my judgement, Goswami's argument, based on an imaginative reconstruction of availability data, comes closest to being convincing.

may have been the original culprit, there may not exist any feasible method of reversing that redistribution, so that for practical purposes shortage will remain the only operative problem that can be dealt with. Following such reasoning, Bowbrick comes to the conclusion that the entitlement approach will tend to misdiagnose famines in most situations.

His argument would have had some merit if his interpretation of the entitlement approach were valid. But therein lies the problem; as I have explained at some length earlier, it is wrong to think of this approach as proposing a specific hypothesis of famine, let alone a hypothesis that focuses only on distribution. It is of course true that Sen's explanation of the Bengal famine was a purely distributional one; but that does not mean that the entitlement approach as such is to be equated with a distributional explanation of famine. The essence of the entitlement approach is its versatility. If inflationary redistribution was the main factor behind the Bengal famine of 1943, loss of assets was the main cause of the famine that befell the African pastoralists in the 1970s, and dramatic shortfall in food production played a major role in the Chinese famine of 1959–61. Indeed, the whole point of Sen's examination of different famines with the help of this approach was precisely to demonstrate that many different types of causation can be illuminated by this approach—inflationary redistribution was one of them, but by no means the only one.

Bowbrick's mistake was to seize upon a particular illustration of this versatility as the sole content of entitlement theory. This is what led him to fear that this theory would misdiagnose shortage-induced famines. But, once the entitlement theory is seen as a general approach, and not as a specific hypothesis, any such fear should immediately disappear. As has been noted earlier, the entitlement approach does not deny that FAD may be sufficient to induce a famine; only its necessity is denied. The repercussions of food shortage, of whatever degree, can be fully accommodated within the comprehensive framework of the entitlement approach. The only difference with Bowbrick would be that, instead of linking famine with different degrees of shortfall in aggregate availability, the entitlement analyst will explore how the shortage has affected the entitlements of different groups of people via their endowment sets and entitlement mappings.

Turning now to the second part of Bowbrick's general criticism, one finds an additional error. Not only that, Bowbrick misinterprets Sen's theory; even on his own interpretation, he cannot be right in his claim that Sen's theory will lead to the wrong remedies.

Bowbrick contends that, by focusing exclusively on distribution and ignoring aggregate shortage, the entitlement theory will fail to recommend food imports. Presumably, this failure will occur because a theory that explains famines in purely distributional terms will have to recommend that the famine be cured solely by reversing the initial redistribution. But such a strategy, Bowbrick fears, will have disastrous consequences, especially in those instances of famines that are caused by second- and third-degree shortage, because by definition such shortages are so severe that no amount of redistribution of existing food supply can prevent large-scale distress.

The problem with this argument lies in the presumption that, if redistribution causes famine, then the only viable policy of famine relief is to reverse that redistribution. This is no less absurd than the suggestion that when an earthquake causes distress the only way to help the victims is to 'undo' the earthquake! An entitlement theorist who believes that a famine has happened because of adverse redistribution of an otherwise adequate food supply is not in fact obliged to rule out the need for bringing in additional supply. He may often find that it is easier to help the victims by augmenting total supply and giving the extra food to the needy than by trying to restore the original distribution of the existing supply. After all, the problem, as he sees it, is that the victims have lost their command over food; so anything that can restore their command would be of help, be it by restoring the original distribution or by bringing extra food to the needy.

Logically, therefore, the necessity of food imports at times of famine should be appreciated no less by those who think that only a redistribution has taken place than by those who think that aggregate availability has declined. So even if the entitlement approach were purely 'distribution-focused', Bowbrick would not need to worry that the entitlement analyst would refuse to recommend importation of food.[22] The fact that in reality the entitlement approach is not so narrowly focused, and that it can see a FAD-famine for what it is, should allay his fears completely.

Another instance of criticism born out of misinterpretation is that by Devereux (1988). The dispute involves the famine that occurred in 1972–4 in the Wollo province of Ethiopia. Sen (1981*b*) had earlier suggested that the Wollo famine, like the great Bengal famine, was not caused primarily by food availability decline. This view has come to be challenged recently, as new studies have tended to indicate that the decline in food availability may have been more severe than Sen had thought.[23] Devereux has tried to

---

[22] There might be a problem if, in addition to holding an exclusively distribution-focused view, the analyst also happens to entertain an unjustifiably strong faith in the redistributive capacity of the state. He might then be tempted to recommend reversal of distributional change as an alternative to augmenting food supply; and this would indeed be disastrous in the event of second- and third-degree FAD famines. But then, an undue confidence in the redistributive capacity of the state would be disastrous in any case, i.e. even in the event of a purely redistributive non-FAD famine. So if the policy advice turned out to be wrong, the fault would lie in overconfidence in the state, not in the use of entitlement approach as such. Once it is understood that there are fairly narrow limits to the state's capacity to reverse large-scale distributional changes, a sensible adherent of the entitlement approach will not shrink from recommending food imports as a good famine-relief policy, regardless of whether or not aggregate food supply has declined. In fact, Sen himself has repeatedly pointed out that food imports may be necessary or at least helpful in most famine conditions, FAD or no FAD. See e.g. Sen (1986, 1987, 1990).

[23] See, among others, Seaman and Holt (1980) and Cutler (1984). Kumar (1990) contains a useful review of the literature.

reconcile the two contending views by arguing that this famine had elements of both FAD and FED (food entitlement decline), the richer of the famine victims being affected by FAD and the poorer by FED.

We shall not go into the empirical question of whether the two segments of famine victims were indeed subject to two different kinds of pressure. What concerns us here is the implication that, in so far as only a part of the distress was due to entitlement failure, this famine demonstrates that entitlement failure cannot be a complete explanation of famines.

The problem with this implication should be obvious by now. To say that the distress was due partly to FED and partly to FAD is to assume that FED refers only to those entitlement failures that do not originate from food availability decline. This is simply a legacy of the view that the entitlement approach is meant to be an alternative to the FAD hypothesis. But, as we have seen, this view is mistaken. Entitlement is a comprehensive concept, incorporating the effects of diverse factors, including food availability. So if anyone suffers because of availability decline, he also suffers an entitlement decline. It therefore makes no sense to divide up the famine victims into two groups—one suffering from FAD and the other from FED—implying thereby that the entitlement analysis applies only to the latter. It is of course conceivable that one group suffers only from the repercussions of aggregate FAD on their individual entitlement sets while another group suffers because of forces that are independent of FAD. But even in that case both groups would be said to be suffering from an entitlement loss (only the source of the loss would be different); so the entitlement analysis would apply to both.

An extreme form of misunderstanding is revealed by Kula (1988, 1989). He not only interprets the entitlement approach as a specific hypothesis, but also gets the very meaning of entitlement wrong, by identifying entitlement with money income. He notes that during the Chinese famine of 1959–61 the urban people had higher incomes (compared with rural people), and still they suffered more because there was not enough food in the towns—either in the market-place or in the public distribution system. Kula interprets this to mean that famine was more severe where entitlement was higher, thus reaching the verdict that 'The Chinese famine of 1959–61 offers powerful evidence to contradict Sen's entitlement approach . . .' (Kula 1989, p. 16).

But Kula fails to note that higher money income does not mean higher entitlement if the income cannot be translated into command over food. In his own thinking, famines are linked primarily with wars and political turmoils, which either prevent food from being grown or prevent the available food from reaching the needy. But if, for these reasons or for any other, a person cannot get hold of food, then his entitlement to food vanishes no matter how large a money income he may have. So the fact that famine was more severe among people with higher money incomes in no way contradicts the entitlement approach.

Kula does, however, make a related point which cannot be disposed of by referring to definitions. He questions the adequacy of the entitlement approach because 'the drop in entitlements is not the *original cause* for most famines mentioned in Sen's writings' (Kula 1988, p. 115; emphasis added). The original cause lies, in his view, in wars and political turmoils (leaving aside unforeseen natural disasters), so that 'the entitlement issue is far from being the major clue to contemporary famines'. He accordingly recommends that a policy of famine anticipation should be concerned more with potential political conflicts than with potential entitlement failures. This line of reasoning has a family resemblance to the group of criticisms that I take up next.

4.2. The Entitlement Approach Is Not Sufficiently Backward-Looking

The point made by Kula that entitlement failure is often not the 'original cause' of famines has been made by others as well, though in a slightly different way. For example, Arnold (1988), Muqtada (1981), Patnaik (1991), and Rangasami (1985) have all found it a weakness of the entitlement approach that it is not sufficiently cognizant of history. By focusing on entitlement failure, this approach takes a snapshot of the moment when the entitlement set lapses from adequacy to inadequacy, ignoring the long drawn-out processes that have led to that crucial moment. But since a famine cannot be properly understood without understanding those antecedent processes, the critics argue that the entitlement approach fails to give a proper account of famines. This shared judgement is however reached by different critics from slightly different perspectives.

Rangasami (1985) locates the problem in the very concept of famine used by Sen: a situation of widespread starvation leading to abnormally high mortality. She feels that, by accepting this common definition of famine, Sen has fixed his attention to the very end of a process, because starvation and mortality can become excessive only at the end of a long process of social, economic, and biological pressures causing gradual erosion of the staying power of a large number of people. For Rangasami, famine is the whole of this process, not merely its terminal point. Any analysis of famine must therefore consider the totality of the process. But since the very concept of entitlement failure (i.e. lapsing into starvation) relates to the terminal point, this approach is alleged to be incapable of dealing with famine as a process. Thus she writes: 'I will suggest by referring to accounts of historians, nutritionists and others that the perceptions of famine we have today only relate to the terminal phase and not of the entire process . . . Consequently, Sen's work which is based on such a definition is inadequate' (Rangasami 1985, p. 1748).

Patnaik (1991) follows a slightly different line. She argues that in debunking FAD the entitlement approach takes an unduly short-run view of food availability. She is referring here to Sen's empirical analyses, in which he had shown that some of the biggest famines of modern times had occurred without any decline in food availability during the period of famine or the period immediately preceding it. Patnaik agrees that what happens to availability during such short periods may well be unimportant for explaining famines, but at the same time she attaches utmost importance to the long-term trend of per capita food availability. As she puts it, 'It would be a grave error to ignore or discount long-term decline in food availability for, as we argue below, and as is indeed obvious on a little reflection, these trends can set the stage for famine even though famine does not thereby become inevitable' (Patnaik 1991, p. 3).

Patnaik illustrates this point by undertaking a re-examination of the great Bengal famine. While concurring with Sen that war-related inflationary pressure was the immediate cause of the famine, she stresses that the magnitude of the disaster can be explained only when one notes how utterly vulnerable the peasants of Bengal had become as a result of a 30 per cent decline in per capita food availability during the inter-war decades. She alleges that, in its preoccupation with the debunking of short-run FAD, the entitlement approach loses sight of this important historical process whereby vulnerability to famine is created over a long period.

A similar point was made earlier by Arnold (1988). Noting that Sen had said little about the historical trends of declining food availability, growing debt burden of the peasants, etc., leading up to the great Bengal famine, Arnold seemed to suggest that this bypassing of history was something that was inherent in Sen's theoretical system. As he put it, 'Even the system of "exchange entitlements" *begs questions* as to why certain sections of society were placed in such dependent and precarious relationships that even without a real decline in the actual availability of food they could still be left without either work or food' (Arnold 1988, p. 46; emphasis added).

The common concern of all these critics is to enter a plea for history. And quite rightly so, because it is undeniable that almost all famines (barring those arising from some unexpected natural disaster) have their roots in the history of a society. A sudden shock, such as the inflationary pressure of the kind experienced in Bengal in the war period, may well be enough to push a lot of people beyond the precipice, but one still has to ask how those hapless people got to the precipice in the first place. For that, one must look back into history, to delineate the socio-economic processes which rendered certain sections of the society vulnerable to sudden sharp shocks. The critics are right in pointing to this need for bringing a historical dimension to the analysis of famine.

What can be questioned, though, is their belief that the entitlement approach is somehow incapable of doing this job. Especially curious to note is Rangasami's methodological objection. Since the entitlement approach highlights the final denouement of a long process of destitution by defining famine as entitlement failure, it allegedly disqualifies itself from looking back into history. This is like saying that, by defining the winner of a race as the runner who reaches the finishing tape first, one is obliged not to enquire what has happened before the final moment of victory!

However, the fact is that in both cases one ignores the past only for the purpose of defining a phenomenon, not for explaining it. If one wishes to analyse why and how the winner beat others to the finishing tape, one is compelled to look back—to see, for example, how he paced himself throughout the race, and even further back, to see how he had prepared himself for the race. In just the same way, by defining famine as the terminal event of entitlement failure, one is obliged to look back into history to see why at that particular point in time a part of the society fell victim to acute starvation.

The essence of the entitlement approach, it will be recalled, is to look closely into a person's endowments and mappings, in order to understand why her entitlement failed or didn't fail, as the case may be. But nothing short of a proper historical analysis can fully explain how the endowments and mappings of different segments of the society came to be what they were at the moment of final denouement. Therefore, not only is the entitlement approach consistent with a careful analysis of history, it very much demands such an analysis. Far from begging the historical question, as Arnold would have us believe, the entitlement approach actually invites it.

This argument should suffice to satisfy those who stress the need for historical analysis, generally. But Patnaik also has a specific point that needs to be addressed. She goes beyond the general plea for history by picking up the trend of food availability as an especially important piece of historical information, one that the entitlement approach allegedly ignores at its peril. In doing so, she appears to be according a privileged position to the trend of long-run availability in the scheme of explanation. It is this privileged position that Sen had tried to deny to short-run FAD; Patnaik seeks to restore it to the long-term trend.

I believe the correct response of the entitlement analyst would be to agree with Patnaik that it would be a 'grave error' to ignore long-run trend of availability, but to disagree with her that Sen's approach ignores it, and to disagree also with her attempt to accord it a privileged status in the scheme of explanation. Indeed, at the general conceptual level, the status of long-term FAD is no different from that of short-run FAD—in both cases the entitlement approach will take into account the impact of availability decline, but without in either case according it a privileged status, a priori.[24]

---

[24] This does not imply that the entitlement approach would regard short- and long-run availability as equally important or unimportant in all instances of famines; it only implies that at the general analytical level there is no basis for thinking that one is more important than the other—their relative importance will vary from case to case.

The logic of denying the privileged status can be illustrated from the same empirical context, namely the Bengal famine of 1943, which Patnaik uses to advance her case. According to her own account, the sharp decline in per capita food production that had occurred in the inter-war period was accompanied by a sharp increase in the production of commercial crops. Two opposing forces were thus operating on the entitlements of the peasants. While the reduced production of foodgrains had a potentially adverse effect on their entitlements, the increased production of commercial crops could conceivably have offset this effect. But this did not happen, as the offsetting effect turned out to be too weak owing to an iniquitous structure of rewards in the production of commercial crops. The result was that the peasantry was left dangerously vulnerable to external shocks by the time the Second World War was breaking out. But since one finds in this account two distinct forces at work in creating famine-vulnerability, there is no a *priori* reason for picking up one of them for privileged consideration.

The general point is that the 'availability-focused' view is no more defensible in the long run than in the short. However, this does not mean that the long-term trend of food availability will be ignored by the entitlement approach. To think otherwise, as Patnaik seems to do, is to succumb to the common confusion that the entitlement approach advances some specific hypothesis in contrast to FAD. But once it is realized that what is being proposed is a general approach which subsumes FAD along with other possible influences on the entitlement set, it becomes clear that the question of ignoring availability cannot simply arise—be it in the long run or in the short.

So neither Patnaik, who is particularly anxious to see that long-term food availability trends are given due weight, nor others such as Arnold and Rangasami, who wish to bring in a historical dimension more generally, need have any fear that the entitlement approach is unequal to the task. Yet all of them have expressed deep scepticism, and in support of their view they have pointed out, not without some justice, that Sen's own analyses of actual famines are lacking in historical depth.[25] One must therefore face the question: if the entitlement approach is so eminently suitable for historical analysis, why didn't Sen himself go deep into history? A couple of points are worth noting in response.

First, it is arguable that for his immediate purpose it was not necessary for Sen to look deeply into history. His immediate purpose, it will be recalled, was to demonstrate the power of the entitlement approach over the FAD approach, rather than to provide a comprehensive etiology of particular famines. In order to achieve this limited objective, all that was necessary for him was to show that the entitlement approach can allow for *plural*

---

[25] This is not to suggest that Sen did not consider the historical background at all; the point is rather that he laid much more stress on proximate causes than on historical processes.

causes and *asymmetric impact*, neither of which can be explored through the FAD approach. To show this, it was enough to identify the proximate forces that shaped the entitlement sets of different social classes at the moment of final denouement; and this is what Sen did.

Secondly, even if one considers the lack of historical depth to be an inadequacy of Sen's empirical analyses, it does not thereby follow that the entitlement approach as such suffers from this inadequacy. As we have seen, far from being intrinsically ahistorical, the approach itself invites deep historical analysis; it does so by asking the analyst to delineate the forces that have shaped the endowments and entitlement-mappings of different social classes. If Sen has failed, in the eyes of some, to respond adequately to that invitation, this does not detract anything from the capability of the approach itself.[26]

4.3. The Entitlement Approach Is Not Sufficiently Forward-Looking

While some have accused the entitlement approach of not being sufficiently backward-looking, others have accused it of not being sufficiently forward-looking, either. Here we shall take up the views recently expressed by de Waal (1990). Based on the insights gained from his extensive studies on famines in Africa (especially the Sudan), de Waal has come to believe that the entitlement approach has serious problems in accounting for some important aspects of famines, especially famines of the kind that have plagued Africa in the recent decades. He has two distinct arguments which imply that this weakness of the entitlement approach arises from its inability to be sufficiently forward-looking.[27]

The first argument follows from the observation that when the threat of famine looms large the poor and the vulnerable do not resign themselves passively to the fate, but rather try to confront the adversity by using various 'coping strategies'. One such strategy is to try and preserve the productive assets they own, even at the cost of great temporary distress, so that when the worst is over they can get on with their lives again. This resolve to preserve assets often means that they accept starvation in the short run which could have been avoided, or at least mitigated, if they had decided to trade assets for food. De Waal contends that this is the kind of starvation that is typically observed in African famines. In other words, we have famines in which people are seen to be starving because they 'choose to starve'.

De Waal suggests that accounting for such famines—where people 'choose to starve'—is outside the pale of the entitlement approach. The

[26] Indeed, Patnaik's own analysis of the Bengal famine can be seen as a fine example of historical entitlement analysis, ignoring of course her inclination to accord a special status to the trend of food availability.

[27] For a comprehensive critique of de Waal's views, see Osmani (1991). See also de Waal's rejoinder (de Waal 1991).

reason is apparently a simple one. According to the entitlement approach, a famine occurs when a lot of people 'have to starve' because their entitlement sets have shrunk in such a way that starvation cannot be avoided no matter how the resources are allocated. But there are famines in which people did not have to starve—rather, they chose to starve. So apparently, the entitlement approach doesn't work; and the reason for its failure seems to lie in its inability to be forward-looking, i.e. in its inability to recognize that people can choose to starve with a view to protecting their future livelihood.

But a little reflection will show that there is really no such failure. It is true that the standard presentation of the entitlement approach—of the kind given earlier in this paper—assumes a single-period context; and when a single-period analysis is confronted with an essentially intertemporal phenomenon, problems are bound to arise. But there is nothing intrinsic about the entitlement approach which is bound to confine it to the single period. It is possible to extend the approach intertemporally, and it is easy to show that such an extension can fully accommodate famines of the kind described by de Waal.[28]

In the intertemporal context, we shall have to think of a multi-period entitlement set, defined as the set of alternative time-profiles of food consumption that can be obtained from current endowments and current and future entitlement mappings. Now consider the situation where the intertemporal entitlement set defined over the two periods—present and future—has contracted in such a way that a person can have adequate food in at best one of the two periods, but not in both. In this situation, he will have to choose between starving now and starving in future. This is obviously the situation facing the famine victims described by de Waal. If they sell their assets they can possibly avoid starvation now, but this will means starvation in future; and if they wish to avoid starvation in future they must accept starvation now. So if de Waal is right in observing that people chose to starve in famine conditions, it means they chose the second of the two options. But the very fact that they chose this option implies that their intertemporal entitlement sets did not contain any time-profile of consumption that could save them from starvation in both periods. This is nothing other than 'entitlement failure'—in the intertemporal sense.

In other words, what appears to be a case of 'choosing to starve', from the myopic perspective of the present, is really a case of 'having to starve', from the perspective of intertemporal decision. So the framework of entitlement failure is equally applicable to those famines in which people apparently 'choose to starve'.

De Waal has a second line of criticism which also points to an alleged myopia of the entitlement approach. The problem, as he sees it, stems from

---

[28] Sen himself has noted this possibility, in passing; Sen (1981*b*, p. 50 n.).

its preoccupation with food. The very concept of entitlement—in the context of famine, at least—refers to command over food. But, as de Waal rightly observes, command over food cannot explain a lot of what happens during a famine. For example, he marshals convincing evidence to show that the incidence of excess mortality during famines bears little correlation with the extent of entitlement failure across regions and socio-economic groups. This lack of correlation suggests the presence of other significant explanatory variables. De Waal lays particular stress on the effects of social disruptions related to wars, etc., leading to mass migration, unhygienic living conditions, and the outbreak of disease, which have a profound impact on morbidity and mortality.

These features of 'social disruption, migration, and disease are all part of famine', and yet 'the entitlement account makes no room for these, and instead concentrates only over command over food through production and exchange' (de Waal 1990, p. 473). Consideration of these features will involve a dynamic analysis of how famine evolves over time. But the entitlement approach is deemed incapable of such a dynamic analysis, focused as it is on the failure of food entitlement at a point in time. As a result, it is argued, the entitlement approach cannot but give a thoroughly inadequate account of famines.

This argument has considerable force. It is indeed undeniable that morbidity and mortality do not depend on food consumption alone. To that extent, the entitlement approach is bound to give an inadequate account of famines. But I shall none the less argue that this inadequacy cannot be seen as a criticism of the entitlement approach. To think otherwise is to misunderstand the objective of this approach.

There are two distinct aspects of any comprehensive understanding of famines; one relates to its cause and the other to its dynamics (i.e. the evolution of the plight and behaviour of famine victims once the famine is on its way). Sen developed his entitlement approach to study the causation of famine, while de Waal is primarily concerned with its dynamics. Since famine is initially about the lack of food, and only subsequently about disease and death, a study of causation can legitimately focus on food as the point of departure for looking back at the chain of events that have led to the crisis. This is precisely what the entitlement approach intends to do.

However, any analysis of how the famine evolves, once it is on its way, must go beyond the focus on food, and bring in events such as social disruption, migration, and disease, which de Waal rightly regards as very important factors shaping the eventual pattern of morbidity and mortality.[29]

---

[29] It is of course conceivable that in some cases an initial social disruption or mass migration, caused for example by a war, may enter the story of causation as well. But if such disruptions do cause famine, they can do so only by causing a failure of food entitlement at some point in the chain of events. So, it would still be legitimate to focus on food as the point of departure for looking back into the chain of causation; thus, the entitlement approach is perfectly capable of accounting for famines caused by social disruptions, etc.

This obviously means that the entitlement approach cannot on its own serve as the theory of famine dynamics.[30] This is a genuine limitation, but not a ground for criticism because the limitation follows from the very nature of the task enjoined upon the entitlement approach—it was designed to shed light on causation, not on dynamics.

4.4. The Entitlement Approach Says Nothing New: Conceptually

The point that the entitlement approach offers nothing new at the conceptual level has been made by a number of both sympathetic critics and hostile opponents. Among the former category, Srinivasan (1983, p. 200) remarks, for example, that 'The "entitlement approach" is a fancy name for elementary ideas fairly well understood by economists, though not necessarily by policy-makers.' Despite this perception of a lack of novelty in the realm of ideas, however, these commentators still feel that Sen's lucid exposition is a great help in clarifying our understanding of famines.

A genuinely hostile critic is Ashok Mitra. Not only does he not find anything new in the concepts, he also insinuates that Sen may be deliberately trying to hide the ugly truths behind poverty and starvation by presenting old ideas in a new garb.[31] This insinuation does not deserve to be dignified with a response, but the general point about the lack of conceptual novelty needs to be addressed.

The case of the critics, both sympathetic and hostile, seems to rest on the following observation: the basic conceptual categories used by Sen are only slight variations of older concepts familiar to economists. For instance, endowment sets are a close relative of the 'distribution of property and incomes' (Mitra 1982, p. 488); the idea of entitlement mapping 'can be easily fitted into the terms of trade paradigm' (p. 488); and the entitlement set 'is not different in essence from purchasing power in the broadest sense' (Patnaik 1991, p. 2). So 'entitlement failure'—the central concept of famine analysis—can be translated into more familiar terms as follows: loss of purchasing power in the broadest sense arising from adverse changes in either the distribution of property and incomes or in the terms of trade defined in the broadest sense. Of course, as the critics themselves recognize, in each of these cases the old concepts have to be stretched a little to conform to Sen's categories. But surely, such stretching at the margin can

---

[30] Sen himself is keenly aware of this: for example, 'the entitlement approach focuses on starvation, which has to be distinguished from famine mortality, since many of the famine deaths—in some cases most of them—are caused by epidemics, which have patterns of their own. The epidemics are, of course, induced partly by starvation but also by other famine characteristics, e.g. population movement, breakdown of sanitary facilities' (Sen 1981b, p. 50).

[31] 'It is not immediately obvious that by presenting the analysis in the manner he has presented it, Amartya Sen has helped to clarify the underlying realities; a few at least would be led to assert that he is desperately anxious to obfuscate realities' (Mitra 1982, p. 489).

hardly justify the attribution of any breathtaking conceptual innovation to the entitlement approach.[32]

This argument is valid as far as it goes, but to go on from here to claim that the entitlement approach is devoid of conceptual novelty is going too far. Such a claim amounts to adopting a very crudely reductionist view: one looks at each of the building blocks in isolation, finds it to be only a slight variation of more orthodox concepts, and thus concludes that there is nothing new in the theory at the conceptual level. But the innovative features of a theory do not reside merely in the individual building blocks, but also in the manner in which they are put together. For, by putting together familiar ideas in a novel manner, it may often be possible to ask new questions and to find new answers to old questions. It is precisely in this way that, I believe, the entitlement approach makes a fundamental conceptual contribution to our understanding of famines.

The crucial innovation here is to make the notion of entitlement failure the central concept of famine analysis. By taking it as the point of departure, and by defining entitlement in such a way that it becomes a function solely of endowment sets and entitlement mappings, this approach invites the analyst searching for causes to look for changes in endowments and mappings. We have already noted the attractive features of this invitation. In the first place, it prepares the analyst for *plural causes*, i.e. for the possibility that there may exist a variety of causes behind a famine, in contrast to the traditional approach which directed attention to a single cause in food availability decline.[33] Secondly, it allows the analyst to trace the *asymmetric impact* of famines on different social classes by enabling him to study their entitlement sets at a disaggregated level—something that is not possible under the food availability approach.

So the novelty of the entitlement approach does not lie primarily in the individual concepts it employs; it lies rather in the manner in which these concepts are brought together so as to pave the way for studying plurality of causes and asymmetry of impact. It is the possibility of studying these two features that is novel, and the contribution of the entitlement approach lies in creating this possibility.

4.5. The Entitlement Approach Says Nothing New: Historically

We shall finally consider a line of criticism that goes even further than the preceding one. It has been suggested that, whatever may be the conceptual

---

[32] But I do believe this is justification enough for introducing new terminology—a view evidently not shared by many critics. This is, however, more a matter of semantic taste than of substance.

[33] Reutlinger (1984, p. 884) makes this point forcefully when he says; 'his food entitlement approach should inevitably lead to a better understanding of famine-related issues than has been the case. This is so because his approach defines a famine in a way which immediately draws attention to a multiplicity of possible causes. . . . the alternative approach of attributing a famine to a single cause, while having the virtue of simplicity, will usually be wrong.'

novelty of the entitlement approach, Sen's contribution does not represent any real advance, since all this was known before. Note that the point here is not merely that Sen used concepts that were already familiar to economists—a point we have already discussed above—but that the way he used those concepts to supposedly create a new way of understanding famines was also nothing new. Mitra (1982, p. 488) makes this suggestion in the most trenchant manner: 'Amartya Sen, I am afraid, has not said anything beyond what our great-grandmothers were already aware of.' In a more scholarly vein, Rangasami (1985) has made the same point by claiming that the late nineteenth-century literature on Indian famines was based on the spirit, if not the language, of the entitlement approach. Since we have rather more evidence on what this literature had to say than what our great-grandmothers used to know, I can only deal here with the former.

The second half of the nineteenth century witnessed a sharp increase in the recurrence of famines in India. This prompted the British administration to set up a series of official inquiries and to develop a code of administrative actions to be taken for the purpose of relieving distress at times of famine. The resulting Reports of various Famine Enquiry Commissions (FECs) and the successive refinements of Famine Codes present a rich picture of contemporary thinking about famines. It is this literature that Rangasami refers to in support of her claim.

She begins by acknowledging a certain ambivalence in official views, as reflected in the FEC Reports on the one hand and the Famine Codes on the other. The Reports, she notes, often take the typical FAD view, but the Codes appear to exhibit a keen awareness of entitlement-based thinking. She explains this duality in the following manner. The Reports were designed to exonerate the administration from any blame for the famines; and by attributing famines to the stinginess of nature, the FAD view fitted nicely in this design. In contrast, the framers of the Codes, whose business it was to organize relief, presumably took a more pragmatic approach; they recognized that 'the coming of famine was due to a number of causes; the decline of food availability, for whatever reason, was one of them', and that, even when such decline occurred, 'it had to be considered within its social and economic context' (Rangasami 1985, p. 1798). Rangasami suggests that such pragmatism not only led to the adoption of what was essentially an entitlement-based approach in the Codes, but also influenced the later Reports to come round to this approach.

I shall argue that Rangasami's reading of the nineteenth-century literature is only partially right. It is indeed true that this literature displays a keen awareness of entitlement-based thinking, and in this sense can legitimately claim to be a precursor of Sen. But it would be going too far to suggest that Sen made no advance on earlier thinking, apart from giving a formal language to incipient ideas. The truth is that Sen's formalization of the entitlement approach allowed a new idea to emerge which was conspicuously missing in the earlier literature: it is the idea that famine can strike even when there is no decline in the production of food. For all its achievements in moving towards an entitlement-based approach, the earlier literature never escaped from the age-old view that famines are invariably connected with decline in food production. It was only with Sen's formulation of the entitlement framework that this escape was finally possible.

It would however be illuminating to begin by noting how close the nineteenth-century literature came to grasping the essence of the entitlement approach. As early as in 1862, Baird Smith had made the uncannily Sen-like remark that 'our famines are rather famines of work than food'.[34] The Famine Codes that were developed in the last two decades of the nineteenth century and in the first decade of the twentieth urged close monitoring of prices, wages, and employment—in addition to crop output—as a method of anticipating impending famines. This shows that the framers of the Codes were conscious that famines could follow the breakdown of what Sen was later to call the entitlement mapping. Building on the insights contained in all the FEC Reports and Famine Codes, as well as other related literature of that period, Loveday (1914) wrote a book on the economics of Indian famines that remains a classic example of entitlement-based thinking. He not only shows clear awareness that when a famine strikes it usually does so by breaking down what would now be called entitlement mappings, but he also gives a rich historical account of how British policies over the decades had made the Indian population vulnerable to famines by eroding their entitlements in various ways.[35]

There is thus unmistakable evidence of the existence, one might even say pervasiveness, of entitlement-based thinking in the earlier literature on Indian famines. But it is equally true that this thinking co-existed with the view that the origin of famine lies necessarily in nature, i.e. in climatic disturbances causing disruption in food production. Furthermore, this co-existence was not a sign of ambivalence, as Rangasami tends to think, but one that was organically linked to form a single consistent approach. The analysis always started from the premise of reduced food production; but, instead of confining the focus on aggregate availability, an attempt was made to trace the effect of reduced production on the entitlements of different social classes by noting the repercussions on prices, wages, and employment.

There was in this respect no difference in the views of FEC Reports and Famine Codes, as suggested by Rangasami. She is much impressed by the

[34] Quoted in Loveday (1914, p. 46), from Smith's 1962 Report on Famine in the North-West Province.
[35] On this aspect of the impact of British policies, Loveday's views were very similar to those of contemporary nationalist thinkers of India, with the important difference however that, unlike the nationalist thinkers, he considered these problems to be no more than temporary dislocations caused by the socio-economic transformation being carried out by the British rulers.

stress laid by successive Famine Codes on the monitoring of prices, wages, and employment as being the embodiment of entitlement-based thinking. But a closer scrutiny shows that, in the thinking of the authors of these Codes, such monitoring was always causally linked with prior disturbance in food production. A good example is the following excerpt from the Madras Code of 1883, which Rangasami herself quotes:

'It is at all times an essential part of the duty of the collectors to scrutinise carefully the returns of rainfall and prices and to bring promptly to the notice of the Board in the Department of Land Records and Agriculture whenever there is any general failure of crops of abnormal rise in prices. A rise of forty per cent above normal in the price of the second sort of rice and of fifty per cent above normal in the price of dry grain is a sure sign of severe scarcity. . . . [However,] When wages ordinarily rise high, a rise of 40 or 50 per cent in prices may be borne with comparative ease, the wages still covering an ample supply of necessary food, but when they are low a much smaller rise may produce privation.' (Rangasami 1985, p. 1798)

The clear link between rainfall, scarcity, prices, and wages drawn above demonstrates that, while the Codes did take an entitlement perspective, they saw the origin of entitlement failure in an initial loss of agricultural production.

Similarly, the FEC Reports too combine a production-centred view of famine with the entitlement-based analysis of its effects. For example, the Report of the 1880 famine, from which Rangasami quotes to demonstrate its FAD view,[36] also elsewhere makes the following exemplary analysis of entitlement failures:

The first effect of famine is to diminish greatly, and at last to stop, all field labour, and to throw out of employment the great mass of people who live on wages of such labour. A similar effect is produced next upon the artisans, the small shop-keepers, and traders, first in villages and country towns, and later on in the larger towns also, by depriving them of their profits, which are mainly dependent on dealings with the least wealthy classes; and lastly, all classes become less able to give charitable help to public beggars, and to support their dependants. (Famine Commission 1980, p. 49)

Here is a classic analysis of how famine spreads through a chain reaction of entitlement failures: first goes the employment of agricultural labourers, setting off a chain of knock-on effects on artisans, traders, and beggars. But notice how the analysis begins; it does so by taking employment failure as the first *effect* of famine, not as its cause. Famine is obviously identified with the loss of food production in the first place, and only then does the analysis proceed by tracing its effects through an entitlement-based reasoning.

---

[36] This is the quotation she cites: 'The devastating famines to which the Provinces of India have from time to time been liable, are in all cases to be traced directly to the occurrence of seasons of drought, the failure of the customary rainfall, leading to the failure of food crop on which the subsistence of the population depends' (Rangasami 1985, p. 1798, quoting from the Report of Famine Enquiry Commission of 1880).

There is thus no justification for postulating any duality between the allegedly FAD-ist FEC Reports and the 'pragmatic' Famine Codes which alone are supposed to have embodied the real intellectual advance that was made in the development of entitlement-based reasoning. Such advance as was made was shared by both Reports and Codes, and they both equally linked entitlement-based reasoning with a production-centred view of famines. Writing in the second decade of the twentieth century, when the insights of all the Reports and Codes had become part of the received wisdom, Loveday spelt out this linkage succinctly as follows:

It would at the present day be more accurate to describe these calamities [famines] as temporary dislocation of employment amongst large numbers of the population *consequent upon failure in the crops of the season.* (Loveday 1914, p. 1; emphasis added)

It was in fact no accident that the contemporary thinking about famine should be so inextricably linked with the idea of shortfall in food production. The Malthusian doctrine was reigning supreme at the time. The British officials had of course long since held the Malthusian theory of population, but it was only in the second half of the nineteenth century that it was applied vigorously in the Indian context. The reason was primarily a political one. It was a bit of an embarrassment for the British Raj that famines had begun to recur at an unprecedented frequency just after the rule of India had passed over from the East India Company to the Crown. The Malthusian theory came in handy at the time to save the Raj the embarrassment. In fact, it did more than that; it turned a potential embarrassment into an occasion for boasting.

It began to be argued that if famine was less frequent in the earlier era it was only because population was then held back by two other Malthusian checks: war and pestilence. But now that the British rule had eliminated these two checks, by bringing peace and stability in the country and by improving living conditions of the people, famine remained the only other check available to nature for keeping population in line with the fertility of soil. By using this ingenious argument, the apologists were able to explain the increased frequency of famines as an unfortunate by-product of the economic and political revolution initiated by the British rule! Ambirajan (1976) has shown that not only was this idea very widely shared at the time by most British observers (with some rare exceptions), but it also held sway over many influential Indians.[37] Given this climate of opinion, it was little surprise that the authors of the FEC Reports and Famine Codes of the late nineteenth century should equate famine with shortfall in food production.

---

[37] There were however differences of opinion on whether crises were inevitable or could be averted with the help of appropriate policies. For more on this, see Ambirajan (1976).

But, to their credit, these authors were far from being crude Malthusians. It is true that their Malthusian perspective inclined them towards the contemporary view that excessive population growth had led to a precarious balance between man and nature; but starting from this premiss they went on to develop a rich analysis of famines. In particular, they drew two implications from this supposedly precarious balance, which had far-reaching consequences for liberating their analyses from the traditional mould.

First, they argued, since too many people lived off land, even a slight disturbance to the normal level of food production could set off a big crisis by throwing a lot of people out of employment and thus setting off a chain of entitlement failures in the manner described earlier. Secondly, they noted that, when famines were indeed set off by such slight disturbances, the aggregate availability of food was not in itself such a big problem, especially since the improvement of communications effected by the British had made it possible to make up small shortfalls in production in affected regions by importing food from other regions of this vast land.

The second implication constituted in effect a liberation from the FAD-view of famines.[38] It is this intellectual triumph that is reflected in statements such as Baird Smith's 'our famines are rather famines of work than food'. This was a great leap forward towards the entitlement approach, but the transition was not complete; for, as can be seen from the first of the two implications drawn, the liberation from a production-centred view (as distinct from the availability-centred view) had yet to occur. Taking this final step was not easy in the prevailing climate of opinion, which generally accepted the Malthusian paradigm as the basic conceptual framework.

The final liberation became possible only when Amartya Sen provided an alternative conceptual framework in which entitlement failure was made the point of departure for famine analysis. The nineteenth-century authors took loss of production as the point of departure, and then proceeded to analyse its effect in terms of a chain of entitlement failures. Sen in effect inverted this process, by making entitlement failure the starting-point, and directing backwards the search for causes. Only then was it possible to see that famines need not originate from production failure; varieties of other causes—for example inflationary pressure as in the Bengal famine of 1943, or a speculative spree encouraged by a weakened public distribution system as in the Bangladesh famine of 1974—can equally cause a chain of entitlement failures culminating in a famine. Amartya Sen's advance over earlier thinking consisted precisely in opening up this possibility of exploring plurality of causes, by making entitlement failure the analytical point of departure.

---

[38] Ghose (1982) presents statistical support for the view that most of the famines in the nineteenth century indeed occurred at times when there was no serious decline in overall food availability.

5. Summary and Conclusions

The aim of this paper was to evaluate the various criticisms that have been made of Amartya Sen's entitlement approach to famine. The assessment was limited to the class of criticisms that relate to the analytics of the entitlement approach in general, rather than to the specific applications of the approach. The major conclusion that emerges from this assessment is that none of the criticisms appears to hold good once the true nature of the entitlement approach is clarified.

I have shown that the criticisms arise mostly from misunderstandings of one sort or another. The most persistent misunderstanding has been the notion that the essence of entitlement theory was to debunk the traditional food-availability-decline (FAD) hypothesis of famine, and to replace it by the alternative hypothesis of entitlement failure. It is this hypothesis-view—i.e. the notion that the objective was to substitute one hypothesis of famine causation for another—that is responsible for a good deal of confusion and a lot of unwarranted criticism.

In fact, what Sen was trying to substitute was not one hypothesis for another, but one approach for another. While debunking FAD, his concern was to discredit the FAD *approach*—an approach towards understanding famines which focuses on aggregate food availability as the crucial analytical variable. A general debunking of the FAD hypothesis was not his aim; that is to say, it was not his contention that famines were seldom, or never, caused by food availability decline. The failure to see this distinction between approach and hypothesis has led to the erroneous notion that the main purpose of entitlement theory was to propose an alternative hypothesis of famines.

I have suggested that, at least in part, the root of this misunderstanding may lie in the restrictive nature of Sen's original formulation of the approach. However, the more general formulation presented in his later writings, especially in his *Poverty and Famines*, lends no support to the hypothesis-view of entitlement theory. What we have there is rather an approach-view. According to this view, the entitlement theory provides an organizing framework for searching for the causes of famine, and claims that this framework is superior to that of the traditional FAD approach.

The framework suggested by this approach takes entitlement failure as the analytical point of departure by defining famine as widespread failure of food entitlement. The search for causes is then directed backwards to identify the forces that have led to this failure. The framework also provides a neat organizing principle for conducting this search, because by definition entitlement failure can be caused only by forces that belong to either of two categories—one involving the endowment set and the other involving the entitlement mapping. The task of the analyst then reduces to searching for forces that might have impinged upon either endowments or entitlement mappings, or both.

An important implication of taking the approach-view is that the entitlement theory cannot be seen to be either proposing or denying any specific hypothesis of famine causation. In particular, one must discard the popular view that the *raison d'être* of the entitlement theory is to debunk the FAD hypothesis. The fact is that the entitlement approach subsumes the FAD hypothesis while rejecting the FAD approach. This means that this approach allows for the possibility that famines can be caused by food availability decline, but it insists that, instead of confining the focus to the level of aggregate availability, the analyst should explore the various mechanisms through which the reduction in availability affects the entitlements of different social classes.

The reasons for proposing the entitlement approach in preference to the FAD approach are twofold. First, the entitlement approach allows for plurality of causes, as opposed to the single-cause focus of the FAD approach. In other words, it allows one to see that famines can occur even when nothing unusual happens to the production or availability of food. Secondly, the entitlement approach can account for the familiar observation that famines typically have asymmetric impact on different social classes, something that cannot be accounted for in the aggregative framework of the FAD approach.

Once the approach-view is accepted as the correct interpretation of entitlement theory, the weaknesses of its criticisms become immediately transparent. One set of criticisms alleges that the entitlement approach has only limited applicability because there are instances of famine that were actually caused by food availability decline. This line of criticism fails to appreciate that the FAD hypothesis is subsumed by the general framework of the entitlement approach—only the necessity of the FAD hypothesis is denied, not its sufficiency.

The second set of criticisms contends that the entitlement approach is incapable of providing a rich historical account of the origins of famine. An important part of understanding any famine is to learn how the vulnerability to famine was historically created. But it is alleged that the entitlement approach cannot achieve this understanding because, by defining famine as entitlement failure, it fixes its gaze on the final denouement of the historical process. This criticism stems from a simple misunderstanding about the strategy of the entitlement approach. The logic of defining famine as entitlement failure is not to keep one's eyes fixed on the moment of final denouement, but rather to direct backwards the search for the causes of failure. Historical analysis is therefore an essential feature of the entitlement approach to famine.

The opposite allegation, that the entitlement approach is not sufficiently forward-looking, has also been made. I have discussed two variants of this criticism. One argues that, by defining famines as situations where people 'have to starve', the entitlement approach fails to account for those instances of famine in which people 'choose to starve', for example by refusing to sell their assets in order to protect their future livelihood. All that is required to counter this criticism is a simple intertemporal extension of entitlement analysis, because what appears to be a case of 'choosing to starve' is really a case of 'having to starve' from an intertemporal perspective.

The second variant of the criticism points out that, by focusing on food, the entitlement approach fails to explain fully the complex dynamics of famine, in which factors other than food also come into play to determine the pattern of famine mortality. Unlike most other criticisms, this one correctly identifies a genuine limitation. But that is how it has to be seen—as a limitation, rather than a criticism—because the entitlement theory was meant to be a theory of causation, not a theory of dynamics. A theory cannot be criticized for not being what it was not meant to be.

The next set of criticisms takes an altogether different line. It argues that there is really nothing new in the entitlement approach, because the concepts it uses are only slight variations of familiar concepts long used by economists. The problem with this criticism is that it is unduly reductionist, judging, as it does, the conceptual novelty of an approach solely by the novelty of the concepts considered in isolation. The real novelty of the entitlement approach lies in the manner in which familiar-looking concepts are brought together to create a new way of understanding famines—a way which, unlike the traditional way of thinking, allows for plurality of causes and asymmetry of impact.

The final set of criticisms goes one step further. It contends that the entitlement approach cannot even claim to have opened up a new way of understanding famines, because people knew it all before. Reference, for example, is made to the nineteenth-century literature on Indian famines to prove the point. I have argued that, while this literature had indeed gone a long way towards adopting the entitlement approach, in one crucial respect it was still bound to the traditional way of thinking. It had learnt to analyse famine as a chain of entitlement failures, and it had also managed to liberate itself from exclusive concern with aggregate food availability, but it was still to liberate itself from the idea that famines necessarily started with some disruption in food production. The analysis always started from loss of production; its effect was then traced through a chain of entitlement failures. Only when Amartya Sen inverted the analytical process, by making entitlement failure the point of departure and directing backward the search for causes, did it become possible to see that factors other than production failure can also cause famine by precipitating entitlement failures. It is this analytical innovation, which allowed the exploration of plural causes, that constitutes Amartya Sen's advance over earlier thinking.

In my judgement, therefore, the entitlement approach comfortably survives all the criticisms it has been subjected to at the general analytical level. But a few qualifications are worth bearing in mind. First, when we speak of the entitlement approach, we ought to think of the general formulation as developed in *Poverty and Famines*, instead of clinging to the restricted formulation as presented in Sen's earliest writings. Secondly, while the entitlement approach is ideal for studying the causation of famine, it cannot claim to provide a complete account of famines; the consideration of famine dynamics, for example, will have to involve many other factors besides entitlement to food. Thirdly, even in the study of causation, the adoption of the entitlement approach is in itself no guarantee that a correct understanding will be achieved; in particular, one is liable to get a rather distorted picture if the analyst fails to take a sufficiently historical view of how the entitlements of different social classes evolve over time.

One final remark remains to be made. In this paper I have concentrated only on famine-related issues, which was of course the original terms of reference for the entitlement approach. But there is also a great potential for applying this framework in the study of long-term endemic hunger. When economists study the impact on hunger and poverty of secular forces such as population growth or technological change or institutional innovations, etc., there is often a tendency to judge the effect in terms of aggregate output. But the entitlement framework offers a different, and richer, framework of studying these impacts. By urging the study of the disaggregated entitlements of different social classes, this approach alerts the analyst to the asymmetries that may exist in the impact of these secular changes; and it turns out that these asymmetries are often very crucial in assessing the impact on hunger and poverty. A complete assessment of the entitlement approach cannot be done without bringing in this dimension of endemic hunger; but this exercise must be left for another occasion.

References

Alamgir, M. (1980), *Famine in South Asia: Political Economy of Mass Starvation*, Oelgeschlager, Gunn & Hain, Cambridge, Mass.

Allen, G. (1986), 'Famines: The Bowbrick–Sen Dispute and Some Related Issues', Letters to the Editor, *Food Policy*, 11: 259–63.

Ambirajan, S. (1976), 'Malthusian Population Theory and Indian Famine Policy in the Nineteenth Century', *Population Studies*, 30: 5–14.

Arnold, D. (1988), *Famine: Social Crisis and Historical Change*, Basil Blackwell, Oxford.

Basu, D. R. (1986), 'Sen's Analysis of Famine: A Critique', *Journal of Development Studies*, 22: 593–603.

Baulch, B. (1987), 'Entitlements and the Wollo Famine of 1982–1985', *Disasters*, 11: 195–204.

Bowbrick, P. (1986), 'The Causes of Famine: A Refutation of Professor Sen's Theory', *Food Policy*, 11: 105–24.

—— (1987), 'Rejoinder: An Untenable Hypothesis on the Causes of Famine', *Food Policy*, 12; 5–9.

Cutler, P. (1984), 'Famine Forecasting: Prices and Peasant Behaviour in Northern Ethiopia', *Disasters*, 8: 48–56.

de Waal, A. (1990), 'A Re-assessment of Entitlement Theory in the Light of Recent Famines in Africa', *Development and Change*, 21: 469–90.

—— (1991), 'Logic and Application: A Reply to S. R. Osmani', *Development and Change*, 22: 597–608.

Devereux, S. (1988), 'Entitlements, Availability, and Famine: A Revisionist View', *Food Policy*, 13: 270–82.

Drèze, J. and Sen, A. K. (1989), *Hunger and Public Action*, WIDER Studies in Developing Countries, Clarendon Press, Oxford.

—— —— (eds.) (1990), *The Political Economy of Hunger*, WIDER Studies in Development Economics, Clarendon Press, Oxford.

Famine Commission (1980), *Report of the Indian Famine Commission*, Part I, Famine Commission, Calcutta.

Ghose, A. K. (1982), 'Food Supply and Starvation: A Study of Famines with Reference to the Indian Sub-Continent', *Oxford Economic Papers*, 34: 368–89.

Goswami, O. (1990), 'The Bengal Famine of 1943: Re-examining the Data', *Indian Economic and Social History Review*, 27: 445–63.

Kula, E. (1988), 'The Inadequacy of the Entitlement Approach to Explain and Remedy Famines', *Journal of Development Studies*, 25: 112–17.

—— (1989), 'Politics, Economics, Agriculture and Famines: The Chinese Case', *Food Policy*, 14: 13–16.

Kumar, B. G. (1990), 'Ethiopian Famines 1973–1985: A Case Study', in Drèze and Sen (1990, vol. ii).

Loveday, A. (1914), *The History and Economics of Indian Famines*, A. G. Bell & Sons, London; reprinted: Usha, New Delhi; page references are to the reprint).

Mitra, A. (1982), 'The Meaning of Meaning', *Economic and Political Weekly*, (Reviews), 27 Mar.

Muqtada, M. (1981), 'Poverty and Famines in Bangladesh', *Bangladesh Development Studies*, 9: 1–34.

Osmani, S. R. (1991), 'Comments on Alex de Waal's "Re-assessment of Entitlement Theory in the Light of Recent Famines in Africa"', *Development and Change*, 22: 587–96.

Patnaik, U. (1991), 'Food Availability Decline and Famine: A Longer View', *Journal of Peasant Studies*, 19: 1–25.

Rangasami, A. (1985), '"Failure of Exchange Entitlements" Theory of Famine: A Response', *Economic and Political Weekly*, 12 and 19 October.

Reutlinger, S. (1984), review of Sen (1981*b*), *Economic Development and Cultural Change*, 32: 881–6.

Seaman, J. and Holt, J. (1980), 'Markets and Famines in the Third World', *Disasters*, 4: 283–97.

Sen, A. K. (1976), 'Famines as Failures of Exchange Entitlements', *Economic and Political Weekly*, Special Number, August.

—— (1977), 'Starvation and Exchange Entitlements: A General Approach and its Application to the Great Bengal Famine', *Cambridge Journal of Economics*, 1: 33–53.

—— (1981a), 'Ingredients of Famine Analysis: Availability and Entitlements', *Quarterly Journal of Economics*, 95: 433–64.

—— (1981b), *Poverty and Famines: An Essay on Entitlement and Deprivation*, Clarendon Press, Oxford.

—— (1986), 'The Causes of Famine: A Reply', *Food Policy*, 11: 125–32.

—— (1987), 'Reply: Famine and Mr. Bowbrick', *Food Policy*, 12: 10–14.

—— (1990), 'Food, Economics and Entitlements', in Drèze and Sen (1990, vol. i).

Solow, R. (1991), 'How to Stop Hunger', *New York Review of Books*, 5 December.

Srinivasan, T. N. (1983), review of Sen (1981b), *American Journal of Agricultural Economics*, 65: 200–1.

13

Household Vulnerability to Aggregate Shocks: Differing Fortunes of the Poor in Bangladesh and Indonesia

MARTIN RAVALLION

Two themes—one substantive, one methodological—have been prominent in Amartya Sen's recent writings on development. The substantive theme concerns social security in developing countries, and the role of public action in achieving it.[1] The methodological theme is that, in exploring the first theme, much can be learnt from cross-country comparative analysis, drawing on the wide range of experiences—successes and failures—among developing countries.[2]

The extent to which poor households are vulnerable to economy-wide shocks such as famines and recessions can provide a good indication of a country's performance in attaining social security. Indeed, under certain conditions—notably, if risk-sharing arrangements (both market- and non-market based) work well enough—vulnerability to covariate shocks will be the most important determinant of social security at the household level.[3] This paper will use the cross-country comparative approach to look at household-level impacts of two aggregate shocks, one in Bangladesh and the other in Indonesia. Those experiences will be used to illustrate some simple, but none the less important, points about the various ways that public policies influence social security, both positively and negatively.

These are the views of the author, and they should not be attributed to the World Bank or any affiliated organization. For their comments on this paper, I am grateful to Shubham Chaudhuri, Gaurav Datt, Samuel Lieberman, Steve Tabor, Peter Timmer, and Dominique van de Walle.

[1] Following Sen and others, 'social security' is defined here as *avoiding poverty by social means*. This definition does not restrict the proximate cause of that poverty to a single factor, such as old age (as is still common in US usage of the term 'social security'). Similarly, a broad view of what constitutes 'poverty' recognizes that deprivation may occur in more ways than an inadequate command over market goods. The broader definition is desirable. For a selection of Sen's writings on social security in developing countries, see Sen (1981*a*; 1984, ch. 13; 1985; 1987; 1989*a,b*).

[2] One finds marked differences in social outcomes at similar levels of GDP per capita (such as between Sri Lanka and other countries at similar or even far higher average income levels; see Sen 1981*b*). Attainments of the multiple objectives of social security also differ widely (such as between China and India; see Sen 1989*b*; Drèze and Sen 1989). While much can be learnt by looking at the residuals around the regression of social outcomes on national income, there are also a number of issues raised by the interpretation of the regression itself; see Anand and Ravallion (1993).

[3] For overviews of the theory and evidence on this and related issues, see Besley (forthcoming), and Lipton and Ravallion (1994).

Maintaining social security in the presence of aggregate shocks can be a compelling motive for government intervention.[4] Two broad types of policies will be discussed here: those that aim directly to reduce the vulnerability of the poor to shocks—*protecting* the poor, in the terms of Drèze and Sen (1989)—and those that endeavour to foster a longer-term reduction in poverty—*promoting* the poor, in their terms.[5]

These two types of public policies need not go hand in hand. Sen (1981*b*) and Drèze and Sen (1989) have argued convincingly, in my view, that poor countries can do a great deal to achieve social security through direct public intervention; they need not wait for growth to facilitate such support.

However, there are reasons to believe that, when successful, these two types of policies can be mutually reinforcing; promoting the poor facilitates their protection, by both private and social means, while protecting the poor facilitates their longer-term promotion. Then it is far better when these two types of policies *do* go hand in hand. That, I shall argue, is an important lesson that can be drawn from the comparison of Bangladesh and Indonesia.

Like all cross-country comparisons, there are risks in this one. Although the impacts on national income were of a similar magnitude, the aggregate shocks being compared here are qualitatively quite different: severe flooding and crop damage in Bangladesh, and an external terms-of-trade shock in Indonesia. The initial point at which the shock hit was very different: in Indonesia it first hit public revenues, while in Bangladesh its initial impact was at the household level. This difference would tend to make it easier for the government of Indonesia to protect the poor.

While recognizing this difference, I will argue that the *history* of economic performance (depending in part on past public policies), and the specific *policies* adopted in response to the shock, were both far more favourable to buffering the poor from the effects of the shock in Indonesia than in Bangladesh. The shock for Bangladesh came after a period of increasing impoverishment. Furthermore, neither political nor economic institutions were able to provide the poor with effective protection from that shock. Indeed, the way those institutions worked probably made matters worse. The final outcome was one of the worst famines of recent times. By contrast, the shock to Indonesia came after a period of sustained promotion of the poor through a process of relatively equitable growth. Furthermore, economic and political institutions helped buffer the poor. The final outcome was that poverty continued to decline.

---

[4] See e.g. Sen (1981*a*), World Bank (1986; 1990*a*, ch. 6), UNDP (1990), Drèze and Sen (1989), Burgess and Stern (1991), Besley (forthcoming), and Lipton and Ravallion (1994).

[5] 'It is useful to distinguish between two different aspects of social security, viz. *protection* and *promotion*. The former is concerned with the task of preventing a decline in living standards as might occur in, say an economic recession, or—more drastically—in a famine. The latter refers to the enhancement of general living standards and to the expansion of basic capabilities of the population, and will have to be seen primarily as a long-run challenge' (Drèze and Sen 1989, p. 16).

1. Bangladesh and Indonesia: Looking Back Thirty Years

As a stylized fact, the poor tend to have access to fewer physical and human resources (savings, credit, good health, skills) to help buffer their consumption from an income loss, and the poor tend also to value a given change in consumption more highly than do the non-poor. Thus, poor households tend to be more vulnerable than the non-poor to a given income loss, in that they have a harder time avoiding an adverse effect on their current welfare.

There are also a number of reasons for believing that the history of deprivation *prior* to a shock is an important determinant of the vulnerability of the poor to that shock. The effects of poverty on vulnerability are likely to be *cumulative*; the longer the period of deprivation, the less chance there will be for physical and human resources to be built up enabling the poor to buffer themselves from the shock.[6] A prior history of chronic and widespread poverty also jeopardizes societal risk-sharing arrangements; while such arrangements may be able to work well even without formal contracts (through repeated interaction in a village society, for example), poverty raises the chance of defection, particularly when faced with a large covariate shock (Coate and Ravallion, 1993). Thus, an obvious place to start analysing the vulnerability of the poor to an aggregate shock is the circumstances of the poor prior to that shock.

While there are a number of problems of comparison, there is some evidence to suggest that thirty years ago average living standards may well have been higher in Bangladesh than Indonesia.[7] There can be no doubt that the reverse is now true. Fig. 1 gives GNP per capita for each country over the period 1962–89. These data suggest that Indonesia overtook Bangladesh in the early 1970s. A different method of comparison suggests that the two countries had quite similar average real incomes thirty years ago. In 'Kravis dollars' (adjusted for differences in the purchasing power of their currencies at official exchange rates), Indonesia's GDP per capita was only a few percentage points higher than that of Bangladesh in 1960, a difference that could hardly be considered significant, given the likely measurement error. Over the last thirty years, real GDP per capita has grown at an average rate of about 4 per cent per annum in Indonesia, while in Bangladesh it has grown at barely one-tenth of that rate. At purchasing power parity for 1985, Indonesia's GDP per capita is now about double that of Bangladesh.[8]

---

[6] With only limited access to credit, savings will be very important for consumption-smoothing. However, with an extended period of relatively low incomes, savings will be depleted. Nutritional deprivation over an extended period can also impede ability to resist a shock, through its effects on health status and productivity.

[7] Unless otherwise stated, the World Bank's Economic and Social Data Base is the source of all data quoted in this paper.

[8] This calculation uses the Summers and Heston (1988) estimate of the purchasing power parity exchange rate.

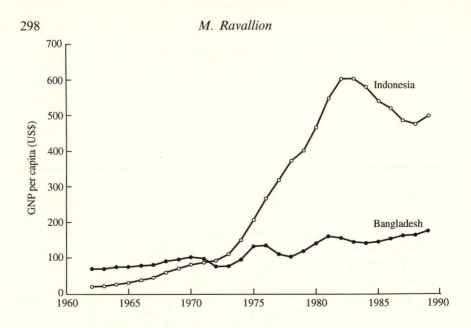

Fig. 1 GNP per capita, Bangladesh and Indonesia, 1960–1990 (Atlas method)
Source: World Bank National Accounts Data Base.

Starting from a similar base, average living standards are now very much higher in Indonesia.

The sectoral composition of aggregate production was also quite similar thirty years ago, with agriculture accounting for slightly more than half of GDP in both countries. By the end of the 1980s, it still accounted for a little less than half of Bangladesh's GDP, but for only one-quarter of Indonesia's GDP. The last thirty years have seen considerable industrialization in Indonesia, while Bangladesh remains heavily reliant on agriculture.

Over the same period, average food energy supply has been on a rising trend in Indonesia, having overtaken Bangladesh in about 1970 (Fig. 2). In Bangladesh, food energy availability has changed little over the last twenty years. The same trends are evident in food production per capita, which has declined in Bangladesh, while it has increased in Indonesia.

Rising average food availability and other forms of aggregate prosperity need not, of course, mean that the poor are better off. For example, there can be no presumption that increasing food production, and hence attainment of national food security, will guarantee that there is not a great deal of food insecurity at the individual level (Sen 1981*a*). Food and other commodity aggregates are only a sub-set of the relevant parameters determining individual food entitlements and other forms of material well-being. So we must also ask: has this dramatic difference in economic growth rates and aggregate food availability between these two countries (having started

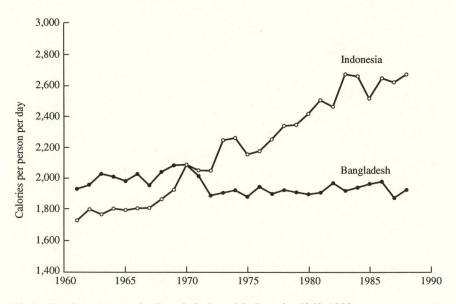

Fig 2. Food energy supply, Bangladesh and Indonesia, 1960–1990
Source: UN Food and Agricultural Organization.

from similar bases) been reflected in greater gains to the poor in Indonesia than in Bangladesh?

This is not an easy question, as we do not have comparable household surveys across these countries covering this period. But from other information it seems clear that the answer is 'yes'. For example, life expectancy at birth was also about the same in the two countries in 1960, at slightly over 40 years. Around 1990 it was over 60 years in Indonesia, about ten years more than in Bangladesh. Fig. 3 gives the time series of life expectancy over the last thirty years. Indonesia overtook Bangladesh in the mid-1960s. The rate of infant mortality (IMR) in Indonesia has been lower than in Bangladesh since the 1950s. In 1960 the IMR was 155 deaths per 1,000 live births in Bangladesh, as opposed to 138 in Indonesia. The rate of improvement has been higher in Indonesia: by 1990 Indonesia's IMR was 63, while in Bangladesh it was 115.[9] Similarly, while the rate of illiteracy fell by nearly 60 per cent in Indonesia over this period (from a 1961 rate of 61 per cent

---

[9] The only comparable data over this period on health services that I can find are for access to doctors. (Nurses would probably be a better indicator, but we do not appear to have pre-Independence data separating Bangladesh—then East Pakistan—from Pakistan.) The number of doctors per capita increased at a far higher rate between the mid-1960s and the mid-1980s in Indonesia than in Bangladesh, though it remained higher in Bangladesh than in Indonesia over the period; around 1965 there were 1.23 doctors per 10,000 persons in Bangladesh and only 0.32 doctors per 10,000 persons in Indonesia; by about 1985 the figures were 1.48 and 1.06 for Bangladesh and Indonesia respectively.

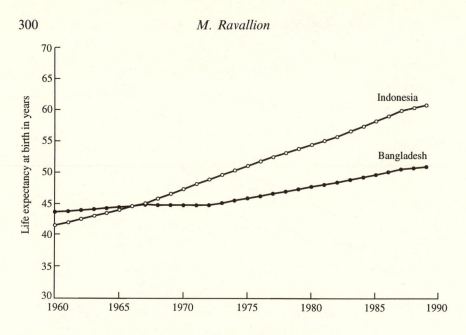

Fig. 3 Life expectancy, Bangladesh and Indonesia, 1960–1990
Sources: UN Population Division and World Bank.

of the population over 15 years of age, to 26 per cent in 1985), Bangladesh
has seen a more modest improvement of 15 per cent, and from a higher level
at the beginning of the period (78 per cent in 1961; 67 per cent in 1985).

While we do not have comparable data for the 1960s, given the similar
average incomes and social indicators of the two countries thirty years ago,
it would be surprising if the incidence of poverty was much different then.
Nor can there be much doubt that the situation is now a good deal better
in Indonesia than Bangladesh. For example, using India's poverty line, and
reasonably comparable household consumption surveys for the mid-1980s,
I have estimated that the proportion of poor in Bangladesh is at least twice
as high as in Indonesia.[10]

However, these long-term cross-country comparisons hide quite a lot
about the economic and political institutions and mechanisms linking
national aggregates (whether of food production or GDP) to well-being at
the household level. That is illustrated well by the two important sub-
periods in the economic history of these two countries over the last thirty
years, to which I now turn.

The aggregate shocks to be looked at below were quite different—severe
flooding and crop damage in the case of Bangladesh, and a sharp fall in
external terms of trade in the case of Indonesia. However, in terms of the

---

[10] This calculation uses the results of Ravallion *et al.* (1991).

effect on national income they are actually quite comparable. In neither case did the shock result in a fall in GNP per capita in constant domestic prices; rather, it resulted in virtual stagnation. Bangladesh's real GNP per capita increased by only 0.5 per cent between 1974 and 1975, having increased by 9 per cent between 1973 and 1974.[11] For Indonesia, the quite robust economic growth rates experienced for many years prior to the oil price shock fell to virtually zero by 1985; real GNP per capita increased by only 0.8 per cent between 1984 and 1985, having averaged about 5 per cent per year over the previous decade. But it is in the effects of these shocks on the poor that the more striking difference emerges.

2. Bangladesh

2.1. The 1974 Famine

The most important, and most devastating, event in the history of food problems in Bangladesh (at least since it has been known by that name) is the famine of 1974, following record flooding and crop damage.[12] Although food-staple production statistics for that year are not beyond question, it cannot be convincingly argued that the 1974 famine was associated with a decline in aggregate food availability *prior* to the famine (Sen 1981*a*). Indeed, aggregate production of the main food-staple, rice, reached a peak in the harvest of the preceding winter; the main effects of the crop damage on output were not felt until the following winter's harvest. What we did see, however, is a sharp contraction during the summer and spring of 1974 in the food-purchasing power of the incomes of certain vulnerable groups, notably agricultural workers and food-deficit peasants (Alamgir 1980; Sen 1981*a*; Ravallion 1987). This, when coupled with the spread of disease, led to a sharp increase in mortality during 1974.

However, one cannot look at this period of Bangladesh's history in isolation from events prior to the onset of famine. There can be little doubt that Bangladesh's rural poor had been experiencing stagnant or falling living standards for at least a decade prior to the famine, associated with agricultural stagnation and rapid population growth. The decline from about 1970 was marked, and can be seen in both the GNP per capita series in Fig. 1 and the food energy supply series in Fig. 2. This alone will increase vulnerability to famine, and the further deterioration may be dramatic even if it is not associated with a similarly dramatic fall in current incomes (Ravallion 1987). When the sudden decrease in the rice purchasing power of rural incomes, particularly agricultural wages, during 1974–5 was

---

[11] While the famine occurred mainly in 1974, the loss of output was mainly in 1975, as will be explained below.

[12] On the Bangladesh famine of 1974 see Alamgir (1980), Sen (1981), and Ravallion (1987).

superimposed on this steady period of impoverishment, one can readily understand the dreadful outcome.

What caused the sharp fall in real incomes of vulnerable households? Here one must understand the way in which economic and political institutions intervene in the relationship between aggregate food availability and the well-being of the poor. Markets are very important in that relationship, though they can be both a positive and negative factor. For example, I have argued elsewhere that there is compelling evidence of very harmful destabilizing speculation in rice markets during the Bangladesh famine (Ravallion 1987). Traders' price forecasting errors appear to have been positively correlated with readily available information on damage to the future harvest. Thus, rice-hoarding prior to anticipated production losses was excessive when compared with the likely outcome with informationally efficient and competitive markets. Rice prices rose to record levels in the months between the flooding and the arrival of the next (depleted) harvest, and prices fell sharply in the week or two preceding the arrival of that harvest. Agricultural wages adjusted very sluggishly to this change, and this, associated with certain changes in labour market conditions, led to a sharp fall in the real wage (Ravallion 1987). The severe contraction in the food entitlements of the poor led to a sharp increase in mortality, which also peaked *before* the decline in aggregate food availability as a result of the flooding.

Nor were the poor offered much protection by the government's own food distribution system. As in many developing countries, this was biased in favour of urban areas and less needy groups, notably the military and civil service (Lipton 1977; Sobhan 1990). Matters were not helped by a diminished food supply into the public distribution system in 1974, the result of procurement failures and external political factors (Alamgir 1980).

In relieving such a famine, the challenge is to make the best use of what markets do well, rather than (as is often the case) to restrict their performance even further. Governments should not ban foodgrain 'hoarding', as they so often try to do. It is unlikely to work, for it is not difficult to hide stocks, and may even make matters worse by fuelling excessive price expectations, premised on a lack of confidence in the government's credibility (Ravallion 1987). Rather, public action should be geared to supporting public confidence in future food availability and the stability of prices, through open market operations and food distribution policies, backed up by adequate stocks and/or the stabilization of external food trade or aid policies.

2.2. Progress since the Famine?

The events of the mid-1970s in Bangladesh have threatened to be repeated a few times since then (and have been relived in not dissimilar fashion in

Ethiopia and Sudan in the mid-1980s). However, some important lessons have been learnt in Bangladesh about how better to protect the living standards of the poor from collapse during famine. The Food for Work Programme introduced soon after the 1974 famine appears to be quite well targeted to the poor, and at relatively modest cost (Ravallion 1991). The maintenance of adequate emergency food stocks through both domestic and external procurement has also helped (Osmani 1991). The first major test of these policies came ten years later in 1984, when the threat of famine was averted after a similar aggregate shock. The goal of effective public action should be to facilitate early protection against entitlement loss, as Drèze and Sen (1989) have emphasized; the poor should not have to wait for the onset of severe malnutrition before help arrives.

Rising real incomes in the longer term can also help cushion the poor against shocks. Has this happened in Bangladesh since the famine? There have been some recent claims of a decline in absolute numbers of poor in Bangladesh during the 1980s. However, a close examination of that evidence suggests it is quite unconvincing.[13] A more plausible assessment is that the proportion of the population deemed to be poor has remained fairly stable over recent years, while absolute numbers of poor have increased. While there were some signs of improvement around the mid-1980s (due in large part to a sharp but short-lived increase in real agricultural wages), this has not been sustained. Instead what we have seen in Bangladesh over the period 1983-92 is generally low growth combined with rising inequality, associated (in part) with a sectoral imbalance in the growth process, at the expense of the rural sector (Ravallion and Sen, 1994).

A sustained long-term impact on the prevalence of chronic poverty and hunger in Bangladesh will almost certainly require a dramatically higher growth rate. The prevalence of poverty can fall at a reasonable rate even if that growth is not combined with falling inequality, though any bias in the growth process against the poorest, particularly in rural areas, must clearly be avoided. One does not want to see a growth process that only reaches the many people hovering just below the poverty line; as Amartya Sen has also emphasized in his contributions to poverty measurement (Sen 1976; 1981a), it is the poorest of the poor that we must be most concerned about.

Unfortunately, the limited growth of the last decade has not favoured the sectors where returns to the poor from growth would be highest, notably agriculture and labour-intensive manufacturing. There are clear policy alternatives for Bangladesh; for example, the country could probably gain greatly from the policies of agricultural and rural development which Indonesia has pursued since the mid-1970s, which I will discuss later. Water control remains a pressing need, for irrigation, drainage, and the control of floods (Boyce 1987). There is ample scope for improving the distribution of

---

[13] The following discussion draws on Ravallion (1990), and Ravallion and Sen (1994).

the benefits of public expenditures (including social services) in Bangladesh (World Bank 1989). There is continuing optimism about recent policy reforms and future prospects in some quarters, though many other observers remain sceptical that these will help greatly without significant changes in the political and administrative environment within which those reforms are to be implemented.

In summary: future famines in Bangladesh can probably be avoided without any reduction in poverty, by further concerted public action to avoid life-threatening down-side variability in the real incomes of the poor. There is no need to wait for prosperity to do the job (Drèze and Sen 1989). But that fact does not in any way diminish the need to make a sustained impact on chronic hunger and poverty, both to promote and to protect the poor. Unfortunately, the (limited) progress in buffering the poor from aggregate shocks through direct public intervention in Bangladesh has not been accompanied by longer-term poverty alleviation. Bangladesh's poor continue to rely heavily on that intervention, and without it they are probably not much less vulnerable now than they were in 1974.

3. Indonesia

3.1. *Macroeconomic Shocks in the 1980s*

Indonesia's economy experienced various external shocks during the early to mid-1980s, chiefly as a result of declining prices of the country's main export good, oil. Public revenues had been heavily dependent on oil exports and so were severely affected. The government's rapid and self-initiated adjustment programme in response to these shocks included aggregate budgetary contraction (with planned outlays cut by about one-fifth), rapid and sizeable currency devaluations, continuing monetary restraint, and trade, finance, and regulatory reforms (Thorbecke 1990; World Bank 1990*b*). GDP per capita growth rates fell sharply over the period, though remaining (barely) positive. The aggregate sectoral structure of output and employment remained fairly static, slowing the aforementioned historical decline in agriculture's share.

We have the advantage of being able to look quite closely at how the poor in Indonesia fared during this period, using two large and comparable household-level data-sets for 1984 and 1987.[14] These data suggest that poverty continued to decline over this period despite the macroeconomic shocks and ensuing adjustments that Indonesia faced. The *qualitative* conclusion that poverty decreased proved to be robust with respect to alternative welfare measures, poverty lines, and poverty measures, although

[14] The following discussion draws on Ravallion and Huppi (1991), Huppi and Ravallion (1991), and World Bank (1990*b*).

the precise *quantitative* magnitudes of the poverty measures and their rate of decline are more sensitive to measurement assumptions.

Gains within the rural sector were important to the country's success at reducing poverty during this period. In Indonesia, the highest concentrations of poverty (both incidence and absolute numbers of poor) are found in the rural farming sector, and this sector accounted for more than a proportionate share of the reduction in aggregate poverty between 1984 and 1987 (Huppi and Ravallion 1991). Gains to other sectors helped, as did population shifts, generally from rural to urban areas.

The gains to the rural poor were due largely to growth in the sector's mean income and consumption rather than improved distribution within that sector. Over half of the gain to the rural farming poor is accountable to gains to the poor in two key provinces, Central and East Java. For them, gains to *both* farm incomes and wage earnings contributed to poverty alleviation, with the latter being particularly important in Central Java. The picture is much more varied among the Outer Islands, with increases in poverty among farmers in a few provinces, though rarely significant (Huppi and Ravallion 1991).

Some features of the government's policy response to the shock played a role in maintaining the country's momentum in alleviating aggregate poverty. For example, agriculture appears to have accounted for a large share of the rise in non-oil exports during the mid-1980s, attributable to the devaluations. Comparisons of the composition of income by source from the household surveys of 1984 and 1987 confirm that there were sizeable gains in cash crop incomes, and that the poor participated in those gains (Huppi and Ravallion 1991). The rate of growth in manufacturing employment during 1985–8 was also substantially higher than had been the case over the previous three years, and this has been attributed in part to trade and industrial deregulation, as well as to changes in the real exchange rate (World Bank 1990*b*).[15]

It also appears that the government made a serious attempt to protect fiscal allocations to programmes that directly benefited the poor, including the rural poor. This is evident in the sectoral composition of public outlays over the period (World Bank 1990*b*). For example, modest positive real growth in public investment in the agricultural sector was maintained, while public non-agricultural investment contracted. Among both routine and development expenditures, certain programmes with probable benefits to the poor were sheltered, such as current transfers to the provinces and the more labour-intensive rural infrastructure projects, with the latter being encouraged in the attempt to expand rural employment opportunities

---

[15] The gains in real earnings of the poor appear to have been largely due to growth in employment, as there was little growth in the real wage rate of agricultural or industrial workers (World Bank 1990).

during the adjustment period. The severest cuts in development expenditures tended to be in the more capital-intensive industrial and mining projects. A successful effort was made to avoid a fall in private consumption during the adjustment period. Compared with a uniform cut in public spending, it is clear that the government's selective pattern of retrenchment helped protect the poor.[16]

3.2. Before the Shocks

While the government's immediate policy response to the shock helped, Indonesia also faced relatively favourable initial conditions at the time of the shock and subsequent adjustment period. Sustained and fairly equitable growth for a number of years prior to the shock meant that Indonesia's poor were in a good position to protect themselves. By the time of the shock, the distribution of household consumption was such that the incidence and severity of poverty would be quite responsive to further growth (Ravallion and Huppi 1991). Conversely, the momentum of poverty alleviation could be maintained at lower growth rates. It can also be argued that much of the stimulus to rural infrastructure development from the late 1970s would have begun to yield substantial returns to the sector by the mid-1980s (World Bank 1990*b*).

What role did public policy play in creating Indonesia's favourable circumstances at the time of the shock? Over recent decades Indonesia has relied little on direct redistributive policy instruments to reduce poverty. Programmes such as labour-intensive rural public works have existed since the early 1970s, though on a more modest scale than found in Bangladesh since the mid-1970s. Government intervention in the physical distribution of food is also minor, compared with the subcontinent, including Bangladesh. (Although, as in Bangladesh, public food distribution has also been biased in favour of the civil service and military). The largest direct intervention aimed explicitly at rural poverty alleviation is probably the transmigration programme, which has voluntarily resettled well over two million families from Java to certain outer islands since 1970. The beneficiaries have tended to be rural landless or marginal farmers, and they gained land titles and generally better social services in their new locations.[17]

But this particular policy is the exception rather than the rule. The direct targeting of public expenditure towards the poor does not appear to have

---

[16] Although that does not mean that protecting the poor was the sole objective; protecting the civil service appears also to have been a consideration (see Thorbecke 1990).

[17] From what we know about this policy, it seems that the benefits are quite well targeted; virtually all participants are poor, as judged by Indonesia's poverty line (World Bank 1988). Though few explicit criteria for eligibility are applied, the cost of moving (particularly forgone income) may well be lower as a rule for the rural poor, thus making this policy an example of a *self-targeted* poverty alleviation scheme, not unlike (in principle) certain rural public employment schemes, as discussed in Ravallion (1991).

been a matter of high priority for the government of Indonesia. While numerous transfer schemes exist (such as subsidies on credit and inputs to agricultural production, notably fertilizers), they are generally not targeted on the poor. The gains to the poor appear to have come primarily out of the growth process. This is not because of a lack of redistributive policy options. As in Bangladesh, there appears to be unexploited scope for better targeting of public expenditures in Indonesia. For example, there is some potential for better regional targeting of central government disbursements (Ravallion 1992*b*).

However, the fact that the poor have participated quite fully in Indonesia's growth process does reflect (in part) successful public policy interventions, such as the government's efforts at rural development and in social-sector policies. It would be quite wrong to say that Indonesia is an example of a country that has made great inroads on the problem of absolute poverty without substantial and supportive governmental action.

To elaborate, over the last twenty years or so there have been a number of specific policy interventions in the Indonesian economy which have had the effect (if not always the explicit intention) of both reducing chronic poverty and reducing the vulnerability of the poor. The government had come to realize in the mid-1970s that national food security was a very high priority, not least for maintaining social stability, and staying in power. It began to pursue this goal through agricultural policies and rural development. Oil revenues provided the resources to do so. Pricing policies (at both macro level and commodity level) and public investment policies promoted agricultural development, most particularly rice production in Java, which has seen an impressive rate of growth in output since the mid-1970s. This was due in large part to growth in yields per acre, attributable to rapid expansion in the use of new seed varieties, helped by price subsidies on inputs, notably chemical fertilizers.[18]

While these policies facilitated national food security and political stability, they also raised and protected the real incomes of a large sub-set of the poor.[19] And, in the context of an increasingly diversified and integrated rural economy, the beneficiaries were not just rice producers. The protection of the rice purchasing power of the poor—many of whom were net consumers, even in rural areas—was also aided by a combination of an evolving public capability for stabilizing rice prices in the 1970s (mainly

---

[18] For a useful overview of Indonesian agricultural development, see Booth (1989). On the specific role played by pricing policies, see Timmer (1989). On the fertilizer subsidies, see Hedley and Tabor (1989).

[19] The extent to which this should be viewed as an objective of the government or a by-product of its policies is quite unclear. The need to maintain support from the rural rich may well have been more important politically (see e.g. Collier 1978). But the important point here is not about intentions but about outcomes.

through open market operations)[20] and the simultaneous development of
rural infrastructure, facilitating (among other things) greater domestic
market integration. The central government's now quite well developed
administrative capability for channelling public resources through to the
village and even sub-village level provides an important policy instrument
for both protecting and promoting the poor.

In contrast to the Bangladesh experience, it is also believable that the way
the relevant markets work in Indonesia has probably helped, rather than
hindered, the protection of the poor from aggregate shocks. For example,
as a stylized fact, Indonesia's poor (in both urban and rural areas) are
thought to face relatively few constraints on their mobility across sectors.
This is particularly so in rural Java, which accounts for a large share of
aggregate poverty in Indonesia. Ease of diversification in income sources
will undoubtedly help the poor adjust to external shocks and macroeconomic policies. Such aspects of market performance are not of course
unconnected to other aspects of the development of physical and human
resources, and the way in which public policies foster, or hinder, that
development.

3.3. Future Prospects

It is likely that the future prospects for the poor in Indonesia will depend
far more on the extent and nature of growth in the urban and non-farm
rural sectors than has been the case over the last fifteen years or so. There
are now clear limits to the extent of further gains from agricultural
development; there seems to be little scope for significant further benefits to
the poor from policy intervention to stimulate the Javanese rice economy,[21]
though there is more potential in other food-crops and tree-crops, for which
productivity among smallholders is still low (World Bank 1990b). However,
sustainable growth in the secondary and tertiary sectors is probably essential
if Indonesia's excellent past record in poverty alleviation is to be maintained. And the extent to which future non-agricultural growth increases the
demand for relatively unskilled labour will undoubtedly remain a key factor
for some time.[22] Future anti-poverty policies will then be much more
concerned about industry and trade issues than has been the case in the past.

---

[20] On rice price stabilization policies in Indonesia, see Mears (1981) and Timmer (1989).
External foodgrain trade has not been used as a rice price stabilization instrument, though it
may well have helped. For example, after the drought of 1987 Indonesian consumers had to
pay more for rice than necessary, associated with the government's reluctance to allow rice
imports.

[21] If only because the policies used to do so in the past (notably input subsidies) are becoming
increasingly less effective (Hedley and Tabor 1989).

[22] While industrial output has grown quite rapidly over the last quarter-century, the
proportion of the labour force employed in that sector has increased only slightly; from about
9% in the mid-1960s to 10% in the mid-1980s (UNDP 1990). Agriculture and services continue
to account for the bulk of the labour force.

Future prospects for the poor will also depend on continuing progress in improving their access to social services, particularly health care. Despite the gains of the last two decades, Indonesia still has quite high infant and maternal mortality rates, judged by the standards of other countries in its region, at similar average income levels (World Bank 1991). Utilization of basic social services by the poor has certainly improved, though progress has been uneven across regions, and the poor are still gaining less from public provisioning than the non-poor (van de Walle 1992). Improvements in both the quantity and quality of social services in Indonesia will be needed both to ameliorate the direct consequences of income poverty and to sustain current long-term progress.

4. Conclusions

The two aggregate shocks studied here were not dissimilar in terms of their impact on national income; both created virtual stagnation for just a year or so. However, they had very different effects on the poor. The flooding and crop damage in Bangladesh during 1974 precipitated a chain of events that brought impoverishment and death to large numbers. By contrast, the collapse in Indonesia's external terms of trade in the mid-1980s left little adverse effect on that country's poor; indeed, Indonesia's momentum in poverty alleviation was maintained through the aggregate shock. The different initial point of impact of the two shocks made it easier for the Indonesian government to contain the shock's transmission to the household level than was the case in Bangladesh. Also, the geography of Bangladesh makes the country uncommonly vulnerable to climatic shocks. But there were other factors underlying the difference in final impacts on the poor.

In both cases, the history of poverty prior to an aggregate shock appears to have greatly influenced the outcome. The bulk of Bangladesh's poor had probably seen little or no improvement in their living standards for a number of years before the 1974 famine, while Indonesia's poor had generally been seeing steady gains for a decade or so before the macroeconomic shock of the mid-1980s. Oil revenues helped finance this favourable history of poverty alleviation in Indonesia, but public policies also played an important role. Effective policies on two key fronts—rural development (both direct support for agriculture and the creation of rural infrastructure) and human resource development—have been instrumental in attaining a pattern of growth in Indonesia conducive to longer-term poverty alleviation. There has been less progress on either front in Bangladesh.

The way markets work also has a bearing on the outcome for the poor. Market performance magnified how the initial shock was transmitted to the poor during the Bangladesh famine, while if anything it probably helped dampen the effect of the external shock on Indonesia's poor. The experiences of both countries also illustrate how market performance can be influenced by public action, both positively and negatively. The Bangladesh government's actions at the time of the 1974 famine helped fuel the speculative crisis in rice markets which was instrumental in the collapse in food entitlements of the poor. Nor did the government's interventions in the spatial movements of rice help. By contrast, the Indonesian government's rapid exchange rate and fiscal adjustments to the external shock, and contemporaneous external trade and industrial deregulations, probably facilitated market adjustments which were, on balance, pro-poor.

Public action can also exercise a positive direct influence on the way in which the shock is transmitted to the household level. Public action in Indonesia during the mid-1980s directly influenced how the external shock was transmitted to the household level, such as through pro-poor shifts in public expenditures. While we have seen little improvement in the incidence of chronic poverty and household food insecurity in Bangladesh, better public policies in response to the threat of famine—aiming to protect the food entitlements of the poor—have allowed an improvement in the ability of the poor to avoid the extremes of transient food insecurity in the 1980s. Progress in poverty alleviation has been slow, but at least famine in Bangladesh can be avoided in the future by public action which protects the poor from a decline in their command over food.

An important overall lesson from the experiences of these two countries is the need to take a holistic view of the set of public actions that matter to social security. Longer-term success in promoting the poor through the right sort of economic growth and human resource policies also has an important role in protecting them from shocks. Similarly, it can be conjectured (though it is not a topic I have dealt with here) that successful public action in helping poor households protect themselves can also facilitate their promotion out of poverty, by reducing the cost they bear in avoiding down-side risk. 'Promotion' and 'protection' are the joint products of effective public action against poverty.

References

Alamgir, M. (1980), *Famine in South Asia: Political Economy of Mass Starvation*, Oelgeshlager, Gunn and Hain, Cambridge, Mass.

Anand, Sudhir and Ravallion, Martin (1993), 'Human Development in Poor Countries: On the Role of Private Incomes and Public Services', *Journal of Economic Perspectives*, 7: 133–50.

Besley, Timothy (1994), 'Savings, Credit and Insurance', in Jere Behrman and T. N. Srinivasan (eds.), *Handbook of Development Economics*, iii, North-Holland, Amsterdam.

Booth, Anne (1989), 'Indonesian Agricultural Development in Comparative Perspective', *World Development*, 17: 1235–54.

Boyce, James K. (1987), *Agrarian Impasse in Bengal: Agricultural Growth in Bangladesh and West Bengal 1949–1980*, Oxford University Press.

Burgess, Robin and Stern, Nicholas (1991), 'Social Security in Developing Countries: What, Why, Who, and How?' in Ehitisham Ahmad, Jean Drèze, John Hills, and Amartya Sen. (eds.), *Social Security and Welfare in Developing Countries*, Oxford University Press.

Coate, S., and Ravallion, M. (1993), Reciprocity without Commitment: Characterization and Performance of Informal Insurance Arrangements', *Journal of Development Economics*, 40: 1–24.

Collier, W. L. (1978), 'Food Problems, Unemployment, and the Green Revolution in Rural Java', *Prisma* (English edn.), 1: 38–52.

Drèze, Jean and Sen, Amartya (1989), *Hunger and Public Action*, Oxford University Press.

Hedley, Douglas D. and Tabor, Steven R. (1989), 'Fertilizer in Indonesian Agriculture: The Subsidy Issue', *Agricultural Economics*, 3: 49–68.

Hossain, Mahabub and Sen, Binayak (1992), 'Rural Poverty in Bangladesh: Trends and Determinants', *Asian Development Review*, 10: 1–34.

Huppi, M. and Ravallion, M. (1991), 'The Sectoral Structure of Poverty during an Adjustment Period: Evidence for Indonesia in the mid-1980s', *World Development*, 19: 1653–78.

Lipton, Michael (1977), *Why Poor People Stay Poor*, Maurice Temple Smith, London.

—— and Ravallion, Martin (1994), 'Poverty and Policy', in Jere Behrman and T. N. Srinivasan (eds.), *Handbook of Development Economics*, iii, North-Holland, Amsterdam.

Mears, L. A. (1981), *The New Rice Economy of Indonesia*, Gadjah Mada Press, Yogyakarta.

Osmani, S. R. (1991), 'The Food Problems of Bangladesh', in Jean Drèze and Amartya Sen (eds.), *The Political Economy of Hunger, iii. Endemic Hunger*, Oxford University Press.

Ravallion, M. (1987), *Markets and Famines*, Oxford University Press.

—— (1990), 'The Challenging Arithmetic of Poverty in Bangladesh', *Bangladesh Development Studies*, 43: 35–53.

—— (1991), 'Reaching the Rural Poor through Public Employment: Arguments, Evidence, and Lessons from South Asia', *World Bank Research Observer*, 6: 153–75.

—— (1992*a*), 'On Hunger and Public Action: A Review Article on a Book by Jean Drèze and Amartya Sen', *World Bank Research Observer*, 7: 1–16.

—— (1992*b*), 'Poverty Alleviation through Regional Targeting: A Case Study for Indonesia', in Karla Hoff, Avi Braverman, and J. E. Stglitz (eds.) (1992), *The Economics of Rural Organization*, Oxford University Press for the World Bank.

—— and Huppi, M. (1991), 'Measuring Changes in Poverty: A Methodological Case Study of Indonesia during an Adjustment Period', *World Bank Economic Review*, 5: 57–84.

Ravallion, M. and Sen, B. (1994), 'When Method Matters: Towards a Resolution of the Debate over Bangladesh's Poverty Measures', Policy Research Working Paper, World Bank, Washington, DC.

—— Datt, G. and van de Walle, D. (1991), 'Quantifying Absolute Poverty in the Developing World', *Review of Income and Wealth*, 37: 345–61.

Sen, A. K. (1976), 'Poverty: An Ordinal Approach to Measurement', *Econometrica*, 46: 437–46.

—— (1981*a*), *Poverty and Famines: An Essay on Entitlement and Deprivation*, Oxford University Press.

—— (1981*b*), 'Public Action and the Quality of Life in Developing Countries', *Oxford Bulletin of Economics and Statistics*, 43: 287–319.

—— (1984), *Resources, Values and Development*, Basil Blackwell, Oxford.

—— (1985), *Commodities and Capabilities*, North-Holland, Amsterdam.

—— (1987), *The Standard of Living*, Cambridge University Press.

—— (1989*a*), 'Development as Capability Expansion', in *Human Development in the 1980s and Beyond, Journal of Development Planning*, Department of International Economic and Social Affairs, United Nations, no. 19: 41–58.

—— (1989*b*), 'Food and Freedom', *World Development*, 17: 769–81.

Sobhan, Rehman (1990), 'The Politics of Hunger and Entitlement', in Jean Drèze and Amartya Sen (eds.), *The Political Economy of Hunger, i, Entitlement and Well-Being*, Oxford University Press.

Summers, R. and Heston, A. (1988), 'A New Set of International Comparisons of Real Product and Price Levels Estimates for 130 Countries, 1950–1985', *Review of Income and Wealth*, 34: 1–26.

Thorbecke, Erik (1990), 'Adjustment, Growth and Income Distribution in Indonesia', mimeo, Cornell University, Ithaca, NY.

Timmer, C. Peter (1989), 'Food Price Policy in Indonesia', in Terry Sicular (ed.), *Food Price Policy in Asia*, Cornell University Press, Ithaca, NY.

United Nations Development Programme (UNDP) (1990), *Human Development Report*, Oxford University Press.

van de Walle, Dominique (1992), 'The Distribution of the Benefits from Social Services in Indonesia, 1978–87', Policy Research Working Paper 871, Public Economics Division, World Bank, Washington DC.

World Bank (1986), *Poverty and Hunger: Issues and Options for Food Security in Developing Countries*, World Bank, Washington DC.

—— (1987), *Bangladesh: Promoting Higher Growth and Rural Development*, World Bank, Washington, DC.

—— (1988), *Indonesia: The Transmigration Program in Perspective*, a World Bank Country Study, World Bank, Washington, DC.

—— (1989), *Poverty and Public Expenditures: An Evaluation of the Impact of Selected Government Programs*, Asia Country Department 1, World Bank, Washington, DC.

—— (1990*a*), *World Development Report 1990: Poverty*, Oxford University Press.

—— (1990*b*), *Indonesia, Strategy for a Sustained Reduction in Poverty*, a World Bank Country Study, World Bank, Washington, DC.

—— (1991), *Indonesia: Health Planning and Budgeting*, a World Bank Country Study, World Bank, Washington, DC.

14

Mass Unemployment as a Social Problem

ROBERT M. SOLOW

It may be possible to learn something new about the normal functioning of social institutions by observing what happens in extreme situations. Presumably that was one of Amartya Sen's reasons for studying severe famine. It was probably not the only reason, however. Infrequent famine is an important enough event to be worth studying for its own sake, even if there were nothing to be learned from it about the distribution of food in normal circumstances.

In this brief note I want to have a look at mass unemployment, in the same spirit. The 1930s were an extreme case, with high and persistent unemployment, the rate reaching above 30 per cent in some places for non-trivial intervals. That event provides a rugged proving-ground for any general picture of the functioning of the labour market. It may be too rugged. Just as hard cases are said to make bad law, it is possible that extreme cases make bad models. A model that works well for unemployment rates of between 3 and 15 per cent could be forgiven for failing outside that range; and trying to repair the model might make it worse. Nevertheless, one would be surprised if there were no general lessons to be learned from the experience of mass unemployment.

The analogy with famine goes a bit further. Very high unemployment is an event worth studying for its own sake. I have read descriptions of Liverpool in the 1980s that make it seem little different from Marienthal—more about that in a moment—in the 1930s. For example, I remember reading, though I do not have the reference, that secondary-school graduates in the North of England are or were routinely equipped with booklets explaining how to apply for unemployment benefits. Even today, high unemployment is not an empty category.

I propose to make my points through a commentary on a pioneering work of social field investigation that I read first as a college student more than fifty years ago, in 1941. It was called *Die Arbeitslosen von Marienthal* (The Unemployed People of Marienthal) and was carried out by Marie Jahoda, Paul Lazarsfeld, and Hans Zeisel in 1931 (see Jahoda *et al.* 1971). I cannot remember what I thought then about *Marienthal*'s demonstration that apathy and the attenuation of social interaction were the main consequences of the experience of prolonged mass unemployment. It is plain, however, that the lesson made a deep impression on me and has haunted me ever since. I do remember that I was stimulated to read E. Wight Bakke's two books (1940*a*, *b*) which studied the same problem and found essentially the same result.

Unemployment is still with us as a fact of life and as a phenomenon to be understood. But there is a sharp divergence in the angle of vision of different academic disciplines. As far as I can tell, most of the sociological and social–psychological literature follows *Marienthal* in treating unemployment primarily as an event that has consequences for those to whom it happens or as a status that has consequences for those who occupy it. This is certainly the case in a recently published book called *Unemployed People* (Fryer and Ullah 1987), which begins, appropriately enough, by printing for the first time a study of a mining valley in South Wales, carried out in 1938 by Marie Jahoda. The same is true of a body of (mostly) Swedish research on the relation between unemployment and the mental health of the unemployed (wherein, by the way, I have learned that there has been a strong positive correlation over time between unemployment rates and the number of published articles concerning the unemployment–health relationship).

Economists are not at all interested in that aspect of unemployment (though I will suggest that maybe they should be). They investigate instead the causes of unemployment, and whether it is functional or dysfunctional for the economic system. The two disciplines come within hailing distance of one another only because economists observe that the incidence of unemployment varies widely across socio-economic groups and wonder why that should be so, and what it says about underlying causes.

This disjunction of interests is brought to life in a story related in a talk given two years ago in Austria by Paul Neurath (son of Otto Neurath) and shown to me by Robert K. Merton (father of Robert C. Merton). Neurath is talking about the origins of the Marienthal study. He related that Jahoda, Lazarsfeld, and Zeisel, these three young social scientists and young socialists, went to Otto Bauer, the great Austro-Marxist and leader of the Austrian Social Democratic Party, with a research proposal. They could use their social-scientific training to do something valuable for the working class by studying how workers use their new-found leisure time, and perhaps by suggesting how they might use it better. Bauer blew up at them and replied: 'How can you talk about investigating leisure when what the people need is work? Why don't you investigate the effects of prolonged unemployment?' (Lazarsfeld tells the same story himself, only less colourfully.) The irony is that one of the hot topics in economics today is a—frustratingly obtuse— dispute as to whether measured unemployment is really voluntary leisure or involuntary unemployment, an efficient or a pathological response of the economic system. Bauer already knew the answer.

Jahoda, Lazarsfeld, and Zeisel are true to type in treating unemployment as something like a natural catastrophe, something that just happens, whose cause is irrelevant to its effects. It has to be said that the case of Marienthal comes pretty close to fitting that description. In its better days, Marienthal had been a one-industry, essentially one-employer, town. The textile mill closed in 1929, and closed irrevocably. By 1931 most of it had been physically demolished. Three-quarters of the families in Marienthal had no employed member. A metaphor like flood or fire seems entirely appropriate.

There is one important respect in which the sociologist's focus on the attitudinal and behavioural consequences of unemployment makes contact with the economist's focus on the systemic causes of unemployment. Any satisfactory theory of the causes of persistent involuntary unemployment in a market economy has to provide a credible answer to a key question. If employment is better than unemployment—as Otto Bauer knew it was—why do we not see more action by the unemployed intended to displace employed workers, either by wage-cutting or in some other way? The current standard theories all provide some sort of answers, but I am not sure they pass the credibility test. Usually the answer takes the form of a reason why the *employer* would reject an offer by an unemployed person to work for less than the wage now being paid someone else. Maybe that is enough, although the suspicion persists that one would see more attempted wage competition if that were in fact the prime answer. There is at least a possibility that a better answer could be found that depends more on the perceptions of the unemployed themselves.

Now it happens that *Marienthal* provides a possible answer to the question. The authors show that prolonged unemployment leads to resignation and aimlessness in its victims. It is perhaps even more revealing that, in spite of all this 'leisure', Marienthalers had very little to do with one another. Unemployed men would stand around in silence. People in that condition are not likely to compete for jobs, or to organize themselves purposefully in any way. The record shows that, whenever the opportunity for a day's work turned up—with a local farmer, say—the Marienthalers would grab it, even walking long distances to do so. But that is nevertheless compatible with a general picture of passivity. Perhaps this passivity explains how a labour market can be at rest even in the presence of unemployment.

Another very clear example of the loss of personal drive that accompanies long and widely shared unemployment comes from a more celebrated case of mass unemployment, the Welsh coal mines in the 1930s. In his *Grass on the Slag Heaps*, Eli Ginzberg observes:

The capacities and morale of the unemployed had been so greatly impaired by years of enforced idleness that the prospect of returning to work was frightening. . . . Men in work do not throw up their jobs in order to live in idleness; but men out of work, especially men who have been out of work for many years, are badly frightened by the responsibilities that attach to working for a living and shy away from assuming them. (Ginzberg 1942, p. 49)

If that observation is anywhere near the mark, it is not hard to see why a pool of long-term unemployed can coexist with a sticky wage structure.

It may be a possible explanation, but it is not really convincing. Marienthal is after all an extreme case. Unemployment was almost universal. The textile mill was in ruins. The few jobs that remained were isolated and casual. Resignation and passivity would seem to be a rational reaction to those circumstances. In industrial Europe a few years ago, national unemployment rates were running from a little less than 10 per cent of the labour force to a little more. That had been the state of the labour market for a dozen years or so. At the time, most projections suggested that unemployment would increase slightly. By the standards of the 1960s that is a lot of unemployment, but it comes nowhere near Marienthal in the 1930s.

It may be significant, however, that nearly everywhere the existing unemployment is becoming more concentrated on a class of long-term unemployed, distinguished demographically or ethnically or regionally or occupationally. A little apathy might not be out of order. Nevertheless, for most of industrial Europe, it would seem that some other explanation besides sheer apathy is required for how the labour market can achieve something close to equilibrium with high, but not catastrophic, unemployment.

I want to spell out in greater detail the odd fact that, in the most popular theories of involuntary unemployment, it is the behaviour of the *employer* that locks the unemployed into their inferior status. In the efficiency–wage model, for instance, the threat of unemployment is needed to induce employed workers to provide adequate effort. If there were no unemployment, layoff would be no threat. Each employer would then find it worth while to pay a little more than the others; being fired would then be costly to a worker because the next job would be a less good job. But what each employer will do, all employers will do, and the outcome must be a situation in which wages are so high that enough unemployment results to provide the requisite threat.

Now comes the key point: an employer would find it best to refuse an offer by an unemployed but capable person to work for less than the going wage. Once employed, such a person would rationally decide to shirk along with the others; that is exactly why the going wage is as high as it is. It is a neat theory, and I think it has a piece of the truth. If it were all or most of the truth, however, one would expect to see more aggressive competition for jobs by the unemployed, at least whenever employment has been falling recently, so that there is some point in testing the market.

Much the same can be said of insider–outsider theories. In that story, too, employers are deterred from hiring the unemployed, even at slightly lower wages. That should not stop the unemployed from trying, at least not in the early stages of a slack period in the labour market. By the very definition of involuntary unemployment, the unemployed would definitely gain from changing places with employed workers of comparable skill at the going wage. They would still gain, therefore, from finding employment at slightly lower wages, and—given greed and rationality—they should try. It does not seem to happen much. (It certainly does not happen much in the academic labour market, the one we all know best.) Mere pessimism about the willingness of employers to accept such offers does not seem like an adequate reason for not trying. I have argued that Marienthal-like apathy would be an extraordinary over-reaction even in today's depressed labour markets. But something must be holding them back.

So far as I know, no one seems to have asked unemployed workers why they do not try to displace employed workers by slightly undercutting the current wage. If asked, I suppose most would reply that it would be demeaning or improper or unfair to do so. One could take that to mean that there is some norm, some internalized standard of behaviour, that would be violated by aggressive competition for jobs. One might also fear that any such reply is a rationalization. Many economists would have that suspicion. A rationalization of what? Perhaps a rationalization of the fact that the unemployed worker is not significantly worse off than his employed fellow worker and therefore would not gain from even small-scale wage-cutting. That seems implausible to me, and incompatible with some observed behaviour, but it is not a point I want to argue.

It is convenient to think of an unemployed worker as having a 'reservation wage', the lowest wage at which he or she would be willing to accept a job if one were offered. (This wage should be thought of as corrected for the unpleasantness of the job in question.) There is some research to show that an unemployed person's reservation wage diminishes as a spell of unemployment gets longer. This observation is not incompatible with an unwillingness to compete for one's normal sort of job by displacing incumbents. If Jahoda, Lazarsfeld, and Zeisel were right that prolonged unemployment induces demoralization, then perhaps a falling reservation wage is a sign of demoralization. That would fit with the 'social-norm' explanation of the rarity of wage-cutting, but in a slightly unconventional way.

It would suggest the hypothesis that 'wage stickiness'—the weakness of wage competition from the unemployed—is a sign of social cohesion. It may be a vehicle of 'market failure' but the symptom of another kind of success. Frank Hahn and I (and, independently, Jörgen Weibull) have thought of formalizing this notion as the equilibrium of a sort of game. The implicit strategy chosen by workers is one in which any defection from the high-wage-cum-unemployment strategy is met by a general reversion to all-out competition. From then on, therefore, wages will be low for everyone and the original defector will have gained only a one-period advantage. The reward for not defecting is that the wage remains high and the unemployed have the normal chance of gaining or regaining employment in the future at something better than the competitive wage. Of course, the 'game' is mostly metaphorical, and one imagines that people perceive the injunction not to rock the boat as an internalized norm of acceptable behaviour.

Metaphor or not, this way of looking at the situation has two plausible implications. A high degree of social cohesion will make the norm self-sustaining, and the breakdown of social cohesion will more likely lead to wage-cutting. Similarly, but not identically, one sees that the persistence of the norm depends on an expected reward, in the form of a sufficient probability of (future) employment at a high wage. Sufficiently high unemployment rates combined with poor prospects for improvement may reduce the probability of reward to the point that the temporary gain from wage-cutting becomes the preferred strategy. Wage resistance may thus break down in deep depressions. This strikes me as plausible, though I must admit that Marienthal offers the possibility that sheer apathy might take over *in extremis*.

It is a good idea not to go overboard for this kind of explanation. Your average economist—I know because I am one—will respond to this sort of notion sceptically and suspiciously. You can explain any kind of behaviour (and its opposite) by postulating a social norm that says 'Do this' (or its opposite). It is hardly an explanation at all, because it raises exactly as many questions as it answers—namely, one—and the new question is no easier than the old. That is why economists like to deduce everything from greed, rationality, and as little additional baggage as possible, however ridiculous that effort may appear to other students of society.

What is needed here is a theory of the dynamics of social norms: their emergence, evolution, solidification, and/or decay. A good theory is one that can produce a lot of implications from a few plausible assumptions. The probabilist and statistician L. J. Savage once remarked, after looking at a particular body of social–psychological work, 'This theory has the highest ratio of axioms to theorems I ever saw.' That is not an Olympic record worth holding. Is it possible to do better? I emphasize that I am asking a question, not leading up to an amateur's answer. Is there a theory out there—a model of the formation of social norms—that can explain why unemployed but unorganized workers do not bid for jobs by wage competition? Could such a theory *predict* whether prolonged unemployment would lead to a breakdown of the restraint and the emergence of competition or would lead instead to the sort of apathy observed in Marienthal? (I should say that we do not know whether Marienthalers would have competed for jobs if some source of partial industrial employment had remained or appeared. The observation was not there to be made in 1931.)

At any moment of time, there is a pool of unemployed men and women. Some of them will have been unemployed for only a short time; some, indeed, were laid off just yesterday. Some will have been unemployed for longer, and some for a very long time. Let us agree to describe as the 'long-term unemployed' those who have been unemployed for more than a year. (I think I might prefer the cut-off point to come after a somewhat longer spell of unemployment, but the data do not permit it.) Now, on the whole, you would expect the share of long-term unemployment in total unemployment to be higher when the unemployment rate is itself high; and that is what generally seems to happen in actual fact. In 1973, when the US unemployment rate was 4.8 per cent, 3.3 per cent of the unemployed had been out of work for more than a year; in 1982, when the overall unemployment rate was 9.5 per cent, 7.7 per cent of the unemployed were long-term unemployed.

But that is not an algebraic necessity. The incidence of long-term unemployment depends also on the inflow into unemployment and the outflow from unemployment. Instead of working out the mathematics, let me give you a commonplace example. Imagine a bathtub with water in it, and with water flowing into it at a certain rate and water draining out of it at a certain rate. If the rate of inflow and the rate of outflow are equal, the level of water in the tub, whatever it may be, will be unchanging. Think of each molecule of water in the tub as an unemployed person. The length of a (completed) spell of unemployment is the length of time that a molecule spends in the bathtub, from the moment it comes in through the faucet until the moment it goes out through the drain. For given but equal rates of inflow and outflow, the average residence time in the bathtub will pretty obviously be greater the more water there is in the tub. That is like saying—as I did a moment ago—that there will be a greater incidence of long-term unemployment the higher the unemployment rate happens to be. But, for any given amount of water in the tub, the average residence time will obviously be longer the slower the inflow and outflow rates. If both are zero, for instance, the residence time will be very long indeed, even if there is not much water in the tub at all. So the incidence of long-term unemployment depends not only on the rate at which people enter the overall unemployment pool (by being laid off or by entering the labour force) and the rate at which they leave the unemployment pool (either by finding jobs or by leaving the labour force altogether). There is another, very important, qualification: all water molecules look alike, but an unemployed computer programmer does not have the same prospects as an unemployed high-school dropout whose last job was working at a filling station.

It is a striking fact that the incidence of long-term unemployment in 1982 was very different from country to country, even between countries with roughly the same overall unemployment rate. For example, the overall unemployment rate was then 9.5 per cent in the United States and 10.2 per cent in the Netherlands; but 7.7 per cent of the American unemployed and 31.6 per cent of the Dutch unemployed had been out of work for more than a year. Germany and Finland both had unemployment rates of 6.1 per cent; but the incidence of long-term unemployment was 11.4 per cent in Finland and 21.2 per cent in Germany. Belgium had an unemployment rate of 13.0 per cent and Great Britain, 12.7 per cent; but about 33 per cent of British unemployment was long-term and fully 60 per cent of Belgian.

It seems to me that the emergence of a substantial class of chronically unemployed people poses intellectual problems for sociologists and economists. For sociologists it is a milder version of the Marienthal problem. What happens to people who remain unemployed for long periods and see themselves as having a relatively small probability of finding work? How do they feel and behave, and what significance do their feelings and behaviour have for the rest of their society? Is there anything to be done that will increase their likelihood of employment, or improve their situation in some other way? A broader issue is hidden here: what is the full social cost of unemployment, especially of long-term unemployment? Is there something to be added on to the narrowly economic cost of the useful output forgone?

It is easier for me to see the questions posed for economics by the emergence of a class of chronically unemployed people. The most obvious one is: why does it happen? Why is unemployment not more evenly distributed over the labour force? There is a trap to be avoided here. If the long-term unemployed turn out to be disproportionately young, or old, or black, or unskilled—especially unskilled—it is tempting to presume that (say) the unskilledness is the basic cause of their unemployment, in the sense that the institution of training programmes would make the unemployment go away. It might; but it is equally possible that the total amount of unemployment at any time is determined by some quite other mechanism, and then the unskilled (or the old or the young or the black) are singled out to bear more than their share of it.

That is a straightforward and natural question to ask. Then there is another that comes naturally only to economists: why do the unskilled or the old not price themselves into employment? Their technological disadvantage, if they have any at all, is presumably not absolute. At some lower wage there must be employers who would hire them. After all, that is, in effect, what happens to last season's shoes. The economist's knee-jerk answer to that question is that the productivity-wage, i.e. the wage at which it would just be worth while to hire a less skilled or older worker instead of a more skilled or younger worker, is less than the reservation-wage of the unemployed; that is to say, the unemployment is 'voluntary'. The chronically unemployed would then not be better off actually working at jobs they can do at the wage now prevailing for such jobs. That is not a foolish argument in any place where the welfare state is strong and the marginal tax rate is high. Nevertheless, I think there is enough evidence that goes against this account of apparent 'market failure' to make a reasonable person look for some other explanation. Now I have connected up with my earlier analytical remarks: what is there in this situation that keeps competitive wage behaviour from breaking out?

There are at least four possible stories one might tell about the failure of wage competition to emerge in the context of mass unemployment. One, of course, is that the welfare state provides well enough for workers in Liverpool that they have no incentive to compete their way back into employment. The second is that the ablest and most aggressive of the unemployed of Liverpool and Birmingham will eventually seep down to the south and find jobs in expanding sectors; the ones who remain are more or less unemployable so that it is no wonder that mobile businesses do not seek them out. A third possibility is that the tacit prohibition against wage-cutting is still holding up, although it might well weaken with time and with unimproving prospects. Finally, Liverpool might be Marienthal, give or take the cultural differences, and it might be anomy, not cohesion, that suppresses any kind of organized competition for jobs.

It is in the back of my mind that a few *Marienthal*-like studies might tell us something about 'Die Arbeitslosen von Liverpool'. It is also in the back of my mind that there might actually exist such studies by sociologists but they escape the attention of even a sympathetic economist like me. They might not even make a dent on an unsympathetic economist who happened to see them.

Is it strange that there should have been, should still be, this disjunction of interest; that economists are interested in the dynamics of unemployment but not in what the experience of unemployment is like, while sociologists and social psychologists are just the reverse? It would not be so surprising to learn that virologists and immunologists who study the AIDS virus have no particular interest in the dynamics of the transmission of the virus, while other research workers care only about the dynamics of the epidemic and pay no attention to the biochemistry. I think there is one important respect in which the parallel fails. In the second case, the epidemiology would be the same even if the biochemistry were different, and the biochemistry would be unchanged if the disease were transmitted in drinking water. But it seems unlikely that the experience of unemployment is unconnected with the way it arises in the labour market; and it is simply not credible that the dynamics of unemployment should have nothing to do with the experience of being unemployed. That leaves us with two modes of thought; the nature of a useful imaginative bridge between them is far from clear.

References

Bakke, E. Wight (1940a), *Citizens Without Work: A Study of the Effects of Unemployment upon the Worker*, Yale University Press, New Haven, Conn.
—— (1940b), *The Unemployed Worker: A Study of the Task of Making a Living without a Job*, Yale University Press, New Haven, Conn.

Fryer, David and Ullah, Philip (eds.) (1987), *Unemployed People: Social and Psychological Perspectives*, Open University Press, Philadelphia, Pa.

Ginzberg, Eli (1942), *Grass on the Slag Heaps*, Harper Brothers, New York.

Jahoda, Marie, Lazarsfeld, Paul F., and Zeisel, Hans (1971), *Marienthal: The Sociography of an Unemployed Community*, Aldine, Atherton, Chicago. Originally published as *Die Arbeitslosen von Mariental* (Vienna, 1933).

Professor Amartya K. Sen
Biographical Data

Birth

Born 3 November 1933 at Santiniketan, India

Citizenship

Indian (permanent resident in the USA)

Education

Presidency College, Calcutta (BA 1953), where Bhabatosh Datta and Tapas Majumdar introduced Sen to welfare economics

Trinity College, Cambridge (BA 1955, MA 1959, Ph.D. 1959), where Maurice Dobb, Dennis Robertson, and Piero Sraffa were among influential teachers who instructed Sen. In his second year, Sen also wrote essays for Joan Robinson. Sen's Ph.D. thesis was on the 'choice of techniques' in developing economies

Cambridge University prizes and awards: Adam Smith Prize 1954, Wrenbury Scholarship 1955, Stevenson Prize 1956

Trinity College prizes and awards: Senior Scholarship 1954, Research Scholarship 1955, Prize Fellowship 1957

Professional appointments

Professor of Economics, Jadavpur University, Calcutta, 1956–8

Fellow of Trinity College, Cambridge, 1957–63

Visiting Assistant Professor, Massachusetts Institute of Technology, 1960–1

Visiting Associate Professor, Stanford University, summer term 1961

Professor of Economics, Delhi School of Economics, University of Delhi, 1963–71

Visiting Professor, University of California at Berkeley, 1964–5

Visiting Professor, Harvard University, 1968–9

Professor of Economics, London School of Economics, University of London, 1971–7

Professor of Economics, Oxford University, and Fellow of Nuffield College, 1977–80

Andrew D. White Professor at Large, Cornell University, 1978–84.

Drummond Professor of Political Economy, Oxford University, and Fellow of All Souls College, Oxford, 1980–8.

Lamont University Professor, Harvard University, and Professor of Economics and of Philosophy, Harvard University, 1988–.

Professional elections

Fellow of the British Academy
Fellow of the Econometric Society
Honorary Fellow of Trinity College, Cambridge
Foreign Honorary Member, American Academy of Arts and Sciences
President of the Development Studies Association, 1980–2
President of the Econometric Society, 1984
President of the International Economic Association, 1986–9
Honorary Vice-President of the Royal Economic Society, 1988–.
President of the Indian Economic Association, 1989
President-elect of the American Economic Association, 1993

Professional awards

Mahalanobis Prize, 1976
Frank E. Seidman Distinguished Award in Political Economy, 1986
Senetor Giovanni Agnelli International Prize in Ethics, 1990
Alan Shawn Feinstein World Hunger Award, 1990

Honorary degrees and titles

D.Litt., University of Saskatchewan, Canada, 1979
Honorary D.Litt., Visva-Bharati University, India, 1983
Honorary DU, Essex University, UK, 1984
Honorary D.Sc., University of Bath, UK, 1984
Docteur Honoris Causa, University of Caen, France, 1987
Dottore ad Honorem, University of Bologna, Italy, 1988
Doctor of Letters Honores Causa, Georgetown University, USA, 1989
Docteur Honoris Causa, Catholic University of Louvain, Belgium, 1989
Doctor of Laws Honoris Causa, Tulane University, USA, 1990
Honorary D.Litt., Jadavpur University, India, 1990
Honorary D.Litt., Kalyani University, India, 1990
Honorary D.Litt., City of London Polytechnic, UK, 1991
Honorary Doctorate, Athens University of Economics and Business, 1991
Honorary D.Litt., Williams College, USA, 1991
Honorary D.Litt., New School for Social Research, USA, 1992
Honorary D.Litt., Calcutta University, India, 1993
Honorary Professor, Delhi University
Honorary Fellow, Institute of Social Studies, The Hague
Honorary Fellow, London School of Economics
Honorary Fellow, Institute of Development Studies, Sussex University

Professor Amartya K. Sen
Bibliographical Data

Books

Choice of Techniques, Basil Blackwell, Oxford, 1960, 1962, 1968; Oxford University Press, Bombay, 1962, 1968. Spanish translation, Mexico City, 1969.

Collective Choice and Social Welfare, Holden Day, San Francisco, 1970; Oliver and Boyd, Edinburgh, 1971; North-Holland, Amsterdam, 1979. Swedish translation: Bokforlaget Thales, 1988.

Growth Economics (ed.), Penguin Books, Harmondsworth, 1970.

Guidelines for Project Evaluation, jointly with P. Dasgupta and S. A. Marglin, UNIDO, United Nations, New York, 1972.

On Economic Inequality, Clarendon Press, Oxford, 1973; W. W. Norton, New York, 1975. German translation: Campus, 1975; Japanese translation: Nihon-Keizai-Shinbun-sha, 1977; Spanish translation: Editorial Critica, 1979; Yugoslav translation: Cekade, 1984.

Employment, Technology, and Development, Clarendon Press, Oxford, 1975; Oxford University Press, New York, 1975; Oxford University Press, New Delhi, 1976.

Poverty and Famines: *An Essay on Entitlement and Deprivation*, Clarendon Press, Oxford, 1981; Oxford University Press, New York, 1981; Oxford University Press, New Delhi, 1982.

Utilitarianism and Beyond, jointly edited with Bernard Williams, Cambridge University Press, 1982; Cambridge University Press, New York, 1982. Italian translation: Il Saggiatore, 1984.

Choice, Welfare and Measurement, Basil Blackwell, Oxford, 1982; MIT Press, Cambridge, Mass., 1982; Oxford University Press, New Delhi, 1983. Italian translation: Il Mulino, 1986.

Resources, Values and Development, Basil Blackwell, Oxford, 1984; Harvard University Press, Cambridge, Mass., 1984; Oxford University Press, New Delhi, 1985.

Commodities and Capabilities, North-Holland, Amsterdam, 1985; Oxford University Press, New Delhi, 1987. Japanese translation: Iwanami Shoten, 1988; Italian translation: Giuffre Editore, 1988.

The Standard of Living, Tanner Lectures with discussions, edited by G. Hawthorne, Cambridge University Press, 1987.

On Ethics and Economics, Basil Blackwell, Oxford and New York, 1987; Oxford University Press, New Delhi, 1990. Italian translation: Editori Laterza, 1988; Spanish translation: Alianze Editorial, 1987.

Hunger and Public Action, with Jean Drèze, Clarendon Press, Oxford, 1989.

The Political Economy of Hunger, in 3 vol., jointly edited with Jean Drèze, Clarendon Press, Oxford, 1990 and 1991.

Inequality Re-examined, Clarendon Press, Oxford, 1992; Russell Sage Foundation, New York, 1992; Harvard University Press, Cambridge, Mass., 1992.

The Quality of Life, jointly edited with Martha Nussbaum, Clarendon Press, Oxford, 1993.

Articles

(i) Economic Methodology

'Behaviour and the Concept of Preference', *Economica*, 45 (1973): 241–59; reprinted in Jon Elster (ed.), *Rational Choice*, Basil Blackwell, Oxford, 1986.

'The Concept of Efficiency', in M. Parkin and A. R. Nobay (eds.), *Contemporary Issues in Economics*, Manchester University Press, 1975.

'Rational Fools: A Critique of the Behavioural Foundations of Economic Theory', *Philosophy and Public Affairs*, 6 (1977): 317–44; reprinted in H. Harris (ed.), *Scientific Models and Man: The Herbert Spencer Lectures 1976*, Clarendon Press, Oxford, 1979, and also in F. Hahn and M. Hollis (eds.), *Philosophy and Economic Theory*, Oxford University Press, 1979.

'On the Labour Theory of Value: Some Methodological Issues', *Cambridge Journal of Economics*, 2 (1978): 175–90.

'Interpersonal Comparisons of Welfare', in M. Boskin (ed.), *Economics and Human Welfare*, Academic Press, New York, 1979.

'Description as Choice', *Oxford Economic Papers*, 32 (1980): 353–69.

'Plural Utility', *Proceedings of the Aristotelian Society* (1981), 193–215.

'Accounts, Actions and Values: Objectivity of Social Science', in C. Lloyd (ed.), *Social Theory and Political Practice*, Clarendon Press, Oxford, 1983.

'Goals, Commitment and Identity', *Journal of Law, Economics and Organization*, 1 (1985): 341–55.

'Rationality, Interest and Identity', in A. Foxley, M. McPherson, and G. O'Donnell (eds.), *Development, Democracy, and the Art of Trespassing*, University of Notre Dame Press, Notre Dame, Ind., 1986.

'Adam Smith's Prudence', in S. Lall and F. Stewart (eds.), *Theory and Reality in Development*, Macmillan, London, 1986.

'Prediction and Economic Theory', *Philosophical Transactions of the Royal Society of London*, 407 (1986), 3–23.

'Freedom of Choice: Concept and Content', *European Economic Review*, 32 (1988): 269–94.

'Economic Methodology: Heterogeneity and Relevance', *Social Research*, 56 (1989): 299–329.

'Utility: Ideas and Terminology', *Economics and Philosophy*, 7 (1991): 277–83.

(ii) Social Choice Theory

'Preferences, Votes and Transitivity of Majority Decisions', *Review of Economic Studies*, 31 (1964): 163–5.

'A Possibility Theorem on Majority Decisions', *Econometrica*, 34 (1966): 491–9.

'Necessary and Sufficient Conditions for Rational Choice under Majority Decision', jointly with P. K. Pattanaik, *Journal of Economic Theory*, 1 (1969): 178–202.

'The Impossibility of a Paretian Liberal', *Journal of Political Economy*, 78 (1970): 152–7; reprinted in F. Hahn and M. Hollis (eds.), *Philosophy and Economic Theory*, Oxford University Press, 1979.

'Interpersonal Aggregation and Partial Comparability', *Econometrica*, 38 (1970): 393–409; 'A Correction', *Econometrica*, 40 (1972): 959.

'The Impossibility of a Paretian Liberal: A Reply', *Journal of Political Economy*, 79 (1971): 1406–7.

'Liberty, Unanimity and Rights', *Economica*, 43 (1976): 217–45.

'Social Choice Theory: A Re-examination', *Econometrica*, 45 (1977): 53–89.

'On Weights and Measures: Informational Constraints in Social Welfare Analysis', *Econometrica*, 45 (1977): 1539–72.

'Strategies and Revelation: Informational Constraints in Public Decisions', in J. J. Laffont (ed.), *Aggregation and Revelation of Preferences*, North-Holland, Amsterdam, 1979.

'Social Choice and Justice: A Review Article' (on K. J. Arrow's *Collected Papers: Social Choice and Justice*), *Journal of Economic Literature*, 23 (1985): 1764–76.

'Foundations of Social Choice Theory: An Epilogue', in J. Elster and A. Hylland (eds.), *Foundations of Social Choice Theory*, Cambridge University Press, 1986.

'Social Choice Theory', in K. J. Arrow and M. Intriligator (eds.), *Handbook of Mathematical Economics*, iii, North-Holland, Amsterdam, 1986.

'Social Choice', in *The New Palgrave Dictionary of Economics*, Macmillan, London, 1987.

'Welfare, Freedom and Social Choice: A Reply', *Recherches Economiques de Louvain*, 56 (1990), 451–85.

'Minimal Liberty', *Economica*, 59 (1992): 139–59.

'Internal Consistency of Choice', *Econometrica*, 61 (1993), 495–521.

(iii) Welfare Economics

'Distribution, Transitivity and Little's Welfare Criterion', *Economic Journal*, 73 (1963): 771–8.

'The Efficiency of Indirect Taxes', in *Problems of Economic Dynamics and Planning: Essays in Honour of M. Kalecki*, PWN—Polish Scientific Publishers, Warsaw, 1964: 365–72.

'Mishan, Little and Welfare: A Reply', *Economic Journal*, 75 (1965): 442.

'Labour Allocation in a Cooperative Enterprise', *Review of Economic Studies*, 33 (1966): 361–71.

'A Game-Theoretic Analysis of Theories of Collectivism in Allocation', in T. Majumdar (ed.), *Growth and Choice*, Oxford University Press, 1969.

'Planner's Preferences: Optimality, Distribution and Social Welfare', in J. Margolis and H. Guitton (eds.), *Public Economics*, Macmillan, London, 1969.

'On Ignorance and Equal Distribution', *American Economic Review*, 63 (1973): 1022–4.

'Informational Basis of Alternative Welfare Approaches: Aggregation and Income Distribution', *Journal of Public Economics*, 3 (1974): 387–403.

'Welfare Inequalities and Rawlsian Axiomatics', *Theory and Decision*, 7 (1976): 243–62.

'Non-linear Social Welfare Functions', in R. Butts and J. Hintikka (eds.), *Logic, Methodology and Philosophy of Science*, Reidel, Dordrecht, 1977.

'Poverty and Welfarism', *Intermountain Economic Review*, 8 (1977): 1–13.

'Welfare Theory', in M. J. Beckman, G. Menges, and R. Selten (eds.), *Encyclopedic Handbook of Mathematical Economic Sciences*, Gabler, Wienbaden 1978.

'Personal Utilities and Public Judgements: Or, What's Wrong with Welfare Economics?' *Economic Journal*, 89 (1979): 537–58.

'A Reply to "Welfarism": A Defence against Sen's Attack', *Economic Journal*, 91 (1981): 531–5.

'The Profit Motive', *Lloyds Bank Review*, no. 147 (1983): 1–20.

'Goods and People', *Structural Change, Economic Interdependence and World Development: Proceedings at Seventh World Congress of the International Economic Association*, Macmillan, London, 1987; also published in *Resources, Value and Development* Basil Blackwell, Oxford 1984.

'The Concept of Well-Being', in S. Guhan and M. Shroff (eds.), *Essays on Economic Progress and Welfare*, Oxford University Press, 1986.

'Welfare Economics and the Real World', acceptance paper for the Frank E. Seidman Distinguished Award in Political Economy, published by P. K. Seidman Foundation, Memphis, 1986.

'Justice', in *The New Palgrave Dictionary of Economics*, Macmillan, London, 1987.

'Social Välfard', ['Social Welfare'], in the *Annual Report* of the Swedish Economic Council, 1991.

'Money and Value: On the Ethics and Economics of Finance', the First Baffi Lecture, published by Bank of Italy, Rome, 1991.

'Welfare Economics and Population Ethics', presented at the Nobel Jubilee Symposium on 'Population, Development and Welfare', Lund University, 1991.

'Welfare, Preference and Freedom', *Journal of Econometrics*, 50 (1991): 15–29.

'The Economics of Life and Death', *Scientific American*, no. 266 (1993).

'Markets and Freedoms', *Oxford Economic Papers*, 45 (1993), 519–41.

(iv) Economic Measurement

'On the Development of Basic Economic Indicators to Supplement GNP Measures', *United Nations Economic Bulletin for Asia and the Far East*, 24 (1973): 1–11.

'Notes on the Measurement of Inequality', jointly with P. Dasgupta and D. Starrett, *Journal of Economic Theory*, 6 (1973): 180–7.

'Poverty, Inequality and Unemployment: Some Conceptual Issues in Measurement', *Sankhya: The Indian Journal of Statistics*, 36 (June and December 1974).

'Real National Income', *Review of Economic Studies*, 43 (1976): 19–39.

'Poverty: An Ordinal Approach to Measurement', *Econometrica*, 44 (1976): 219–31.

'Ethical Measurement of Inequality: Some Difficulties', in W. Krelle and A. F. Shorrocks, (eds.), *Personal Income Distribution*, North-Holland, Amsterdam, 1978.

'Issues in the Measurement of Poverty', *Scandinavian Journal of Economics*, 81 (1979): 285–307.

'The Welfare Basis of Real Income Comparisons: A Survey', *Journal of Economic Literature*, 17 (1979): 1–45.

'The Welfare Basis of Real Income Comparisons: A Reply', *Journal of Economic Literature*, 18 (1980): 1547–52.

'Poor, Relatively Speaking', *Oxford Economic Papers*, 36 (1983): 153–69.

'The Living Standard', *Oxford Economic Papers*, 36 (1984): 74–90.

'A Sociological Approach to the Measurement of Poverty: A Reply to Professor Peter Townsend', *Oxford Economic Papers*, 37 (1985): 669–76.

'The Standard of Living', in S. McMurrin (ed.), *Tanner Lectures on Human Values*, vii, Cambridge University Press, 1986.

'The Nature of Inequality', in K. J. Arrow (ed.), *Issues in Contemporary Economics: Markets and Welfare*, Macmillan, London, 1991.

'The Concept of Wealth', in R. Mayers (ed.), *The Wealth of Nations in the 20th Century*, forthcoming.

(v) Axiomatic Choice Theory

'Quasi-Transitivity, Rational Choice and Collective Decisions', *Review of Economic Studies*, 36 (1969): 381–98.

'Choice Functions and Revealed Preference', *Review of Economic Studies*, 38 (1971): 307–17.

'A Note on Representing Partial Orderings', jointly with M. Majumdar, *Review of Economic Studies*, 43 (1976): 543–5.

'Rationality and Uncertainty', *Theory and Decision*, 18 (1985): 109–27; also in L. Daboni, A. Montesano, and M. Lines (eds.), *Recent Developments in the Foundations of Utility and Risk Theory*, Reidel, Dordrecht, 1986.

'Information and Invariance in Normative Choice', in W. P. Heller, R. M. Starr, and D. A. Starrett. (eds.), *Social Choice and Public Decision Making: Essays in Honor of Kenneth J. Arrow*, i, Cambridge University Press, 1986.

'Rational Behaviour', in *The New Palgrave Dictionary of Economics*, iv, Macmillan, London, 1987.

(vi) Food, Famines, and Hunger

'Famines and Failures of Exchange Entitlements', *Economic and Political Weekly*, Special Number, 11 (1976): 1273–80.

'The Statistical Chickens', *Ceres: FAO Review on Agriculture and Development*, 58 (1977): 14–17.

'Starvation and Exchange Entitlements: A General Approach and Its Application to the Great Bengal Famine', *Cambridge Journal of Economics*, 1 (1977): 33–59.

'Famines', *World Development*, 8 (1980), 613–21.

'Famine Mortality: A Study of the Bengal Famine of 1943', in E. J. Hobsbawm *et al.*, *Peasants in History*, Oxford University Press, 1980.

'Ingredients of Famine Analysis: Availability and Entitlements', *Quarterly Journal of Economics*, 96 (1981): 433–64.

'Food Problem: Theory and Policy', *Third World Quarterly*, 4 (1982), 447–59.

'Food Battles: Conflicts in the Access to Food', *Food and Nutrition*, 10 (1984): 81–9.

'The Causes of Famine: A Reply', *Food Policy*, 11 (1986): 125–32.

'Food, Economics and Entitlements', *Lloyd Bank Review*, no. 160 (1986): 1–20.

'Reply: Famine and Mr Bowbrick', *Food Policy*, 12 (1987): 10–14.

'Africa and India: What Do We Have to Learn from Each Other?' in K. J. Arrow (ed.), *Proceedings of the Eighth World Congress of the International Economic Association*, i, Macmillan, London, 1988.

'Hunger and Entitlement', World Institute of Development Economics Research, Helsinki, 1987.

'Food and Freedom', text of Sir John Crawford Memorial Lecture, Washington, DC, 1987; reprinted in *World Development*, 17 (1989): 769–81.

'Entitlements and the Chinese Famine', *Food Policy*, 15 (1990), 261–3.

Public Action to Remedy Hunger, The Hunger Project, New York, 1990.

(vii) Family Economics and Sexual Divisions

'Indian Women: Well-Being and Survival', jointly with J. Kynch, *Cambridge Journal of Economics*, 7 (1983): 363–80.

'Economics and the Family', *Asian Development Review*, 1 (1983), 14–26.

'Malnutrition of Rural Children and the Sex Bias', jointly with S. Sengupta, *Economic and Political Weekly*, Annual Number, 18 (1983): 855–64.

'Women, Technology and Sexual Divisions', *Trade and Development*, no. 6, United Nations, New York, 1985.

'Family and Food: Sex-Bias in Poverty', in P. Bardhan and T. N. Srinivasan (eds.), *Rural Poverty in South Asia*, Columbia University Press, New York, 1988.

'Gender and Cooperative Conflicts', in Irene Tinker (ed.), *Persistent Inequalities*, Oxford University Press, New York, 1990.

'Women's Survival as a Development Problem', *Bulletin of the American Academy of Arts and Sciences* (November 1989); shortened version published in *New York Review of Books*, Christmas Number, 20 December 1990.

'Missing Women', *British Medical Journal*, no. 304 (1992).

(viii) Capital, Growth, and Distribution

'A Note on Tinbergen on the Optimum Rate of Saving', *Economic Journal*, 67 (1957): 745–8.

'On Optimising the Rate of Saving', *Economic Journal*, 71 (1961): 479–95.

'Alternative Patterns of Growth under Conditions of Stagnant Export Earnings', jointly with K. N. Raj, *Oxford Economic Papers*, 13 (1961): 43–52.

'Alternative Patterns of Growth: A Reply', jointly with K. N. Raj, *Oxford Economic Papers*, 14 (1962): 200–4.

'Neo-Classical and Neo-Keynesian Theories of Distribution', *Economic Record*, 39 (1963): 53–64.

'The Money Rate of Interest in the Pure Theory of Growth', in F. Hahn and F. Brechling (eds.), *Theories of the Rate of Interest*, Macmillan, London, 1963.

'Terminal Capital and Optimum Savings', in C. Feinstein (ed.), *Socialism, Capitalism and Economic Growth*, Cambridge University Press, 1967.

'On Some Debates in Capital Theory', *Economica*, 41 (1974): 328–35; also in A. Mitra (ed.), *Economic Theory and Planning*, Oxford University Press, 1974.

'Minimal Conditions for the Monotonicity of Capital Value', *Journal of Economic Theory*, 11 (1975): 340–55.

(ix) Economic Development

'Some Notes on the Choice of Capital-Intensity in Development Planning', *Quarterly Journal of Economics*, 71 (1957): 561–84.

'A Note on Foreign Exchange Requirements of Development Plans', *Economica Internazionale*, 10 (1957): 248–57.

'A Note on Mahalanobis Model of Sectoral Planning', *Arthaniti*, 1 (1958): 26–33.

'Choice of Capital-Intensity Further Considered', *Quarterly Journal of Economics*, 73 (1959): 466–84.

'The Choice of Agricultural Techniques in Underdeveloped Countries', *Economic Development and Cultural Change*, 7 (1959): 279–85.

'Peasants and Dualism with or without Surplus Labor', *Journal of Political Economy*, 74 (1966): 425–50.

'Interrelations between Project, Sectoral and Aggregate Planning', *Economic Bulletin for Asia and the Far East*, 21 (1970): 66–75.

'Strategies of Economic Development: Feasibility Constraints and Planning', in E. A. G. Robinson and M. Kidron (eds.), *Economic Development in South Asia*, Macmillan, London, 1970.

'The Philippines Economy: A Study', Economic Commission for Asia and the Far East; reprinted in *United Nations Economic Bulletin for Asia and the Far East*, 22 (1971), under 'Country Economic Surveys: Philippines'.

'Discord in Harmony: The So-Called New International Economic Order', presented at the Keio International Symposium, December 1979; published by Keio University, Tokyo; in Japanese translation, 1980.

'Economic Development: Objectives and Obstacles', in R. F. Dernberger, (ed.), *China's Development Experience in Comparative Perspective*, Harvard University Press, Cambridge, Mass., 1981.

'Public Action and the Quality of Life in Developing Countries', *Oxford Bulletin of Economics and Statistics*, 43 (1981): 287–319.

'Carrots, Sticks and Economics: Perception Problems in Economics', *Indian Economic Review*, 18 (1983): 1–16.

'Development: Which Way Now?' *Economic Journal*, 93 (1983): 745–62.

'Planning and the Judgment of Economic Progress', *Review of Indian Planning Process, Proceedings of the Golden Jubilee Celebrations of the Indian Statistical Institute*, ISI, Calcutta, 1986.

'Economic Distance and the Living Standard', in A. G. Drabek, A. Ewing, and K. A. Patel (eds.), *World Economy in Transition*, Pergamon Press, Oxford, 1986.

'Sri Lanka's Achievements: How and When?' in P. Bardhan and T. N. Srinivasan (eds.), *Rural Poverty in South Asia*, Oxford University Press, New Delhi, 1988, and Columbia University Press, New York, 1989.

'The Concept of Development', in H. Chenery and T. N. Srinivasan, (eds.), *Handbook of Development Economics*, North-Holland, Amsterdam, 1988.

'Public Action for Social Security', in E. Ahmed, *et al.*, *Social Security in Developing Countries*, Clarendon Press, Oxford, 1990.

'What Did You Learn in the World Today?' *American Behavioral Scientist*, 34 (1991): 530–48.

(x) Project Evaluation and Cost–Benefit Analysis

'On the Usefulness of Used Machines', *Review of Economics and Statistics*, 44 (1962): 346–8.

'Isolation, Assurance and the Social Rate of Discount', *Quarterly Journal of Economics*, 81 (1967): 112–24; reprinted in R. Layard (ed.), *Cost–Benefit Analysis*, Penguin, Harmondsworth, 1972.

'General Criteria of Industrial Project Evaluation', in UN Industrial Development Organization, *Evaluation of Industrial Projects*, United Nations, New York, 1968.

'Choice of Techniques: A Critical Survey of Class of Debates', in *Planning for Advanced Skills and Technologies*, Industrial Planning and Programming Series no. 3, United Nations, New York, 1969.

'The Role of Policy-Makers in Project Formulation and Evaluation', *Industrialization and Productivity*, Bulletin 13, United Nations, New York, 1969.

'Control Areas and Accounting Prices: An Approach to Economic Evaluation', *Economic Journal*, 82, Supplement (1972): 486–501; reprinted in R. Layard (ed.), *Cost–Benefit Analysis*, Penguin, Harmondsworth, 1972.

'Approaches to the Choice of Discount Rates for Social Cost Benefit Analysis', in R. Lind (ed.), *Discounting for Time and Risk in Energy Policy*, Resources for the Future, Washington, DC, 1982.

(xi) Education and Manpower Planning

'A Planning Model for the Educational Requirements of Economic Development: Comments', OECD, *Residual Factor and Economic Growth*, Paris, 1964; reprinted in M. Blaug (ed.), *Economics of Education*, ii, Penguin, Harmondsworth, 1969.

'Economic Approaches to Education and Manpower Planning', *Indian Economic Review*, n. s., 1 (1966): 1–21; reprinted in M. Blaug (ed.), *Economics of Education*, ii, Penguin, Harmondsworth, 1969.

'Education, Vintage and Learning by Doing', *Journal of Human Resources*, 1 (1966): 3–21.

'Models of Educational Planning and their Applications', *Journal of Development Planning*, 2 (1970): 1–30.

'A Quantitative Study of the Flow of Trained Personnel from the Developing Countries to the United States', *Journal of Development Planning*, 3 (1971): 105–39.

'Aspects of Indian Education', text of Lal Bahadur Shastri Memorial Lecture 1970; reprinted in P. Chaudhuri (ed.), *Aspects of Indian Economic Development*, Allen and Unwin, London, 1972; also reprinted in S. C. Malik (ed.), *Management and Organization of Indian Universities*, Indian Institute of Advanced Study, Simla, 1971.

'Brain Drain: Causes and Effects', in B. R. Williams (ed.), *Science and Technology in Economic Growth*, Macmillan, London, 1973.

(xii) Labour and Employment

'Unemployment, Relative Prices and the Savings Potential', *Indian Economic Review*, 3 (1957): 56–63.

'Surplus Labour and the Degree of Mechanization', in K. Berrill (ed.), *Economic Development with Special Reference to East Asia*, Macmillan, London, 1964.

Dimensions of Unemployment in India, Convocation Address, Indian Statistical Institute, Calcutta, 1973.

'Employment, Institutions and Technology', *International Labour Review*, 112 (1975): 45–73.

'Labour and Technology', in J. Cody, H. Hughes and D. Walls (eds.), *Policies for Industrial Progress in Development Countries*, Oxford University Press, New York, 1980: 121–58.

(xiii) The Indian Economy

'An Aspect of Indian Agriculture', *Economic Weekly*, Annual Number, 14 (1962): 243–6.

'Working Capital in the Indian Economy', in P. N. Rosenstein-Rodan (ed.), *Pricing and Fiscal Policies*, Allen and Unwin, London, 1964.

'Size of Holdings and Productivity', *Economic Weekly*, Annual Number, 16 (1964): 323–6.

'The Commodity Pattern of British Enterprise in Early Indian Industrialization 1854–1914', in *Proceedings of the Second International Conference of Economic History*, Mouton, Paris, 1965, 781–808.

'The Pattern of British Enterprise in India 1854–1914: A Causal Analysis', in B. Singh and V. B. Singe (eds.), *Social and Economic Change*, Alled Publishers, Bombay, 1967.

'Surplus Labour in India: A Critique of Schultz's Statistical Test', *Economic Journal*, 77 (1967): 154–61.

'Durgapur Fertilizer Project: An Economic Evaluation', jointly with M. Datta Chaudhuri, *Indian Economic Review*, 5 (1970): 43–70.

'Poverty and Economic Development', published text of Vikram Sarabhai Memorial Lecture, Vikram A. Sarabhai AMA Memorial Trust, Ahmedabad, 1976.

'How is India Doing?' *New York Review of Books*, 21, Christmas Number (1982); reprinted in D. K. Basu and R. Sisson (eds.), *Social and Economic Development in India: A Reassessment*, Sage, New Delhi, 1986).

'Indian Planning: Lessons and Non-Lessons', *Daedalus*, 118 (1989): 369–92.

(xiv) Social, Political, and Legal Philosophy

'Determinism and Historical Predictions', *Enquiry*, 2 (1959): 99–115.
'Games, Justice and the General Will', jointly with W. G. Runciman, *Mind*, 74 (1965): 554–62.
'Prisoner's Dilemma and Social Justice: A Reply', jointly with W. G. Runciman, *Mind*, 83 (1974): 582.
'Ethical Issues in Income Distribution: National and International', in S. Grassman and E. Lundberg (eds.), *The World Economic Order: Past and Prospects*, Macmillan, London, 1981.
'The Right Not To Be Hungry', in G. Floistad (ed.), *Contemporary Philosophy*, ii, Martinus Nijhoff, The Hague, 1982.
'Rights and Capabilities', in T. Honderich (ed.), *Morality and Objectivity*, Routledge, London, 1985.
'Rights as Goals', Austin Lecture to the UK Association for Legal and Social Philosophy, in S. Guest and A. Milne (eds.), *Equality and Discrimination: Essays in Freedom and Justice*, Franz Steiner, Stuttgart, 1985.
'The Moral Standing of the Market', *Social Philosophy and Policy*, 2 (1985): 1–19; reprinted in E. F. Paul, F. D. Miller, Jr, and J. Paul (eds.), *Ethics and Economics*, Basil Blackwell, Oxford, 1985).
'The Right to Take Personal Risks', in D. MacLean (ed.), *Values at Risk*, Rowman and Allanheld, Totowa, N J, 1986.
'Property and Hunger', *Economics and Philosophy*, 4 (1988): 57–68.
'Internal Criticism and Indian Rationalist Traditions', jointly with Martha Nussbaum, in M. Krausz (ed.), *Relativism: Interpretation and Confrontation*, University of Notre Dame Press, Notre Dame, Ind., 1988.
'Capability and Well-Being', in M. Nussbaum and A. Sen (eds.), *The Quality of Life*, Clarendon Press, Oxford, 1991.
'Objectivity and Position', Lindley Lecture, University of Kansas, Laurence, KS, 1992.
'Positional Objectivity', *Philosophy and Public Affairs*, 22 (1993): 126–45.

(xv) Ethics and Moral Philosophy

'Hume's Law and Hare's Rule', *Philosophy*, 41 (1966): 75–8.
'The Nature and Classes of Prescriptive Judgements', *Philosophical Quarterly*, 17 (1967): 46–62.
'Choice, Ordering and Morality', in S. Korner (ed.), *Practical Reason*, Basil Blackwell, Oxford, 1974.
'Rawls versus Bentham: An Axiomatic Examination of the Pure Distribution Problem', *Theory and Decision*, (1974): 301–9; reprinted in N. Daniels (ed.), *Reading Rawls*, Basil Blackwell, Oxford, 1975.
'Informational Analysis of Moral Principles', in Ross Harrison (ed.), *Rational Action*, Cambridge University Press, 1979.

'Utilitarianism and Welfarism', *Journal of Philosophy*, 76 (1979): 463–88.

'Equality of What?' in S. McMurrin (ed.), *Tanner Lectures on Human Values*, i, Cambridge University Press, 1980; reprinted in John Rawls *et al.*, *Liberty, Equality and Law*, Cambridge University Press, 1987.

'A Positive Concept of Negative Freedom', in E. Morscher and R. Stanzinger (eds.), *Ethics: Foundations, Problems, and Applications, Proceedings of the 5th International Wittgenstein Symposium*, Holder-Pichler-Tempsky, Vienna, 1981.

'Rights and Agency', *Philosophy and Public Affairs*, 11 (1982): 3–39; reprinted in S. Scheffler (ed.), *Consequentialism and Its Critics*, Oxford University Press, 1988.

'Liberty as Control: An Appraisal', *Midwest Studies in Philosophy*, 7 (1982): 207–21.

'Liberty and Social Choice', *Journal of Philosophy*, 80 (1983): 5–28.

'Evaluator Relativity and Consequential Evaluation', *Philosophy and Public Affairs*, 12 (1983): 113–32.

'Well-Being, Agency and Freedom: The Dewey Lectures 1984', *Journal of Philosophy*, 82 (1985): 169–221.

Individual Freedom as a Social Commitment, Giovanni Agnelli Foundation, Turin, 1990; a shortened version published in *New York Review of Books*, 16 June 1990.

'Justice: Means versus Freedoms', *Philosophy and Public Affairs*, 19 (1990): 111–21.

Index of Names

Index of Subjects